JOHN OLSON'S BOOK OF THE
RIFLE

JOHN OLSON'S BOOK OF THE RIFLE

RIFLE

by JOHN OLSON

J. PHILIP O'HARA, INC.
Chicago

Published by J. Philip O'Hara, Inc.
in cooperation with the John Olson Company

LC Number: 73–20849
ISBN: 0–87955–407–X Paper
ISBN: 0–87955–413–4 Casebound

Manufactured in the United States of America
Published simultaneously in Canada by Van Nostrand
Reinhold Ltd., Scarborough, Ontario.

First Printing H

Contents

Acknowledgments

The author gratefully acknowledges the cooperation of the following individuals and organizations who so kindly furnished technical advice, photographs and, or, art work:

Mr. Richard Dietz of Remington Arms Company, Mr. Ed Nolan of Sturm-Ruger Company, Mr. Val Forgett of Navy Arms Company, Mr. Frank Pachmayr of Pachmayr Gun Works, Mr. Fred Huntington of R.C.B.S., Director Breitenfeld of Steyr-Daimler-Puch AG, Winchester Repeating Arms Company, Weatherby Company, Leupold-Stevens Inc., Redfield Gunsight Co., Lyman Gun Sight Co., O. F. Mossberg & Sons, Savage Arms Corp., Marlin Firearms Company, Browning Arms Co., Harrington & Richardson Co., Ithaca Gun Company, Smith & Wesson Co., Colt Patent Firearms Co., and Garcia Corporation.

Special appreciation is directed to Earl Larson of Remington Arms Company for his valued advice and suggestions.

Finally, sincere thanks and appreciation to Mrs. Walter Glesias for her patience and fortitude in preparing the finished manuscript.

CHAPTER 1

The Development of the Rifle

THE DEVELOPMENT OF THE RIFLE

No book on the rifle would be complete if it did not include, however briefly, a capsule history.

While no one can come up with an exact date—much less the name of an inventor—it is generally believed that gunpowder was first developed in the early 13th century by the Chinese. An English philosopher and experimenter, Roger Bacon, provided us with the first Western record of its existence in a manuscript dated 1248. At any rate, man didn't waste any time finding ways to use this new-found source of energy.

Early experimenters quickly determined that gunpowder created tremendous pressure and that this could be used to propel a missile with considerable force if the powder were aligned behind the missile in a confined area and subsequently ignited. The problem was how to ignite the powder? While man found a rather obvious answer at the time, the method devised had some rather obvious shortcomings.

The first firearm was really a form of cannon. To ignite the powder charge, a hole was drilled through the top of the barrel adjacent to the powder reservoir. This hole was then filled with powder and a flame touched to it. The cannoneer later learned that he didn't have to fill that flash hole with powder, he could simply insert a heated wire through the hole and push this down into the powder charge. He still hadn't found a way, however, to eliminate the fire burning next to him.

In time, someone came up with a smaller and lighter firearm that worked on the same principle but which was hand held. With this, the shooter had to hold and aim the weapon with one hand while applying the flame with the other. Because this weapon weighed over fifty pounds, it appears that two-man teams were used to handle it.

Finally, someone found a way to make the gun mobile—he eliminated the need for the fire by developing a "match"—a cord saturated with an incendiary mixture that would burn for a considerable time. Then he moved the flash hole to the side of the barrel and mounted his "match" in a pivoting holder aligned with the flash hole. The result was called a "Matchlock"—the year, 1411.

This was the ultimate weapon for close to a century and then, in 1498, a Viennese gunsmith named Kollner developed the first rifled barrel. A year or two later someone came up with a spring-activated match holder and we had the first crude form of a trigger. This was called a "button lock" but, since the smouldering fuse system remained, stoic firearms historians continued to refer to it as a matchlock.

An improved stock, a forked muzzle rest and a further weight reduction and the "rifle" became a true one-man weapon—an "Arquebus" (or "Harquebus").

About 1517 a clever Austrian by the name of Kiefuss decided that something had to be done about that darn match that went out at the most inopportune times. He came up with a spring-powered wheel having a serrated perimeter and placed this in contact with a chunk of iron pyrites. Sparks from the spinning wheel were directed into a light powder charge contained in a flash pan abutting the flash hole.

Some years later, about the middle 1500s, another creative type decided that the wheel wasn't needed at all. One could get the same spark effect by simply slamming a piece of iron pyrites against a steel surface strategically placed over the priming charge. Called a "Snaphaunce," this was considerably easier to manufacture and use. The only problem with this design was that the cover of the flash pan had to be opened, manually, before firing.

A Frenchman by the name of Burgeoys improved on the Snaphaunce by combining the flash pan cover with the steel striker plate ("frizzen"). This was hinged to swing out of the way when struck by the pyrites.

Temporarily satisfied with their new ignition system, gunsmiths now turned to the task of simplifying and speeding up the slow and awkward loading procedure that required placement of the charge and shot through the muzzle. The first breechloading flintlocks were developed during the early 1700s but they weren't very successful. In 1776 George Washington's troops, and Howe's, were still loading the hard way.

Then, within the span of four or five years (1807–1811) an American by the name of Hall developed a practical flintlock breechloader and

a Scotsman, Reverend Forsyth, came up with a new priming mixture that would replace the often unpredictable light priming charge of black powder.

In rapid stages, Reverend Forsyth's priming compound evolved into a "pill lock," then "percussion cap" and to the pinfire breechloading cartridge system perfected by LeFaucheux of France. The year was now 1836.

An American by the name of Sharps took the next step with his disc primer in 1852 and this led, ultimately, to rimfire and center fire cartridges which first appeared in 1857.

From this point on, new developments came quickly: improved center fire cartridges in 1858 and 1861, the repeating rifle and the Boxer primer in 1860, the first machine gun (Gatling's) in 1862, smokeless powder in 1863 and a non-mercuric, non-corrosive priming compound in the 1920s.

America's first practical breechloader was invented by Sharps in 1848 and this employed a percussion firing system. (The French had the breechloading pinfire twelve years earlier.) Eventually the Sharps action was converted from percussion caps and paper cartridges to center fire metallic shells.

One rather significant point that is often overlooked in discussions on firearms history is that all rifle developments were primarily intended for military application. Anything the sportsman got by way of sporting rifle was simply an offshoot of a military creation. Gunmakers, it appeared, wouldn't seriously consider catering to the sporting market until the late 1800s.

What will the future bring? We don't have a crystal ball but we can make some calculated guesses!

The scarcity of copper is rapidily driving costs out of sight. It appears the brass cartridge case will have to give way to another alloy—perhaps a soft form of steel.

Shotgun shells have already undergone the transition to plastic; there's always the outside chance that someone will develop a reloadable plastic case to safely handle the higher pressures of rifle cartridges.

Caseless ammo is in use now and, while not revolutionizing the industry at this point, it has opened the door to further experimentation and development. An interesting possibility with caseless ammo is that it may give birth to the development of recoilless shoulder arms.

Why aren't rifles made with interchangeable barrels?

We've had interchangeable barrels on automatic and slide action shotguns for quite a number of years. They've also been employed, even in rifle calibers, on break-open, shotgun style receivers. In conventional rifle designs, they pose a number of problems. First, how would we benefit from interchangeable rifle barrels? In shotguns, they permit the shooter to change barrel length and choke; in rifles there would be no real benefit unless one could change the caliber, and appreciable differences in cartridge size would pose a considerable problem in the magazine area. Also, since the more desirable rifle sights are generally mounted on the receiver, it would be very difficult to align them properly for two markedly different cartridges. Accuracy would undoubtedly suffer when barrels are not rigidly fastened to the receiver and control of headspacing, too, would prove quite

troublesome. In short, shooters would undoubtedly prefer the conventional tactic of having two separate rifles designed specifically for their distinctly different functions.

The twenty-two rimfire rifle, the traditional beginner's tool, came under a black cloud when the Gun Control Act of 1968 restricted the sale of .22 R.F. ammo (because it could also be used in .22 caliber handguns). Some feel this restriction will be lifted in the near future. I can't help wondering, however, why manufacturers haven't come up with a new longer, and perhaps slightly bottlenecked .22 rimfire shell expressly for rifle use.

Advances in optical technology are giving us better scopes and future designs will surely continue the trend.

Metal finishes are also undergoing rapid development. We now have a painted and baked finish for steel that is far tougher and more durable than conventional bluing.

Teflon is another durable finish that is meeting with some success. Then, of course, there's always stainless steel which has captured considerable attention in the handgun field.

The cartridge, itself, represents the single most significant difference between our rifles and those of our fathers. We're using bullets that are smaller and lighter operating at substantially higher velocities: tomorrow's rifles are certain to be even faster!

CHAPTER 2
The Barrel

THE RIFLE BARREL

Every part of the rifle contributes, in some way, to overall performance but the barrel is undoubtedly the single most important component influencing accuracy. It is therefore important that the rifleman understands why a muzzle is crowned, why the twist of the rifling may vary from one caliber to another and, why we have such a variety of lengths, weights, contours, etc.

Barrels are made from a variety of steel alloys which may contain small percentages of nickel, vanadium or molybdenum. Generally, the raw stock is delivered to the manufacturer in the form of long, cylindrical rods which may measure two inches in diameter, or more, depending upon the weight of the barrels to be made. For certain calibers, like the .22 rimfire, the rod diameter may be considerably smaller.

After cutting the rods to a working length, the manufacturer drills them, from one end to the other, with a small pilot hole. Because this pilot hole measures approximately two feet in length, the manufacturer is working with a long drill of small diameter. The difficulty he has in keeping this drill running true to center is readily apparent; any long and slender drill bit will tend to flex in the shaft (if too much pressure is exerted) or "walk" while cutting. Obviously, it would be an impossible job for an ordinary drill press. For this reason barrel makers use a long-bedded lathe which enables them to use a number of steadying devices to guide the barrel blank and the drill.

Precision shaping of the drill bit and an oil bath help somewhat, but even with these aids it is virtually impossible to drill a perfectly straight hole.

Having accomplished the initial drilling, the barrel maker may drill again—to enlarge the hole —or he may go on to the rifling operation.

There are four commonly used methods for rifling barrels. The first (and oldest) is "cut rifling" which is accomplished by either pushing a cutter through the pilot hole (scrape cutting) or "hook rifling" in which a cutter is pulled through the barrel.

Often, only one groove is cut at a time, but multiple cutters are not unheard of.

Broach rifling employs a file-like cutting tool in which the teeth are stepped to result in progressively deeper penetration as the tool is pushed through the bore. Each tooth is a few ten-thousandths larger than the preceding one. Early broaching tools worked with a pulling action.

Broach rifling is practiced by some rifle makers

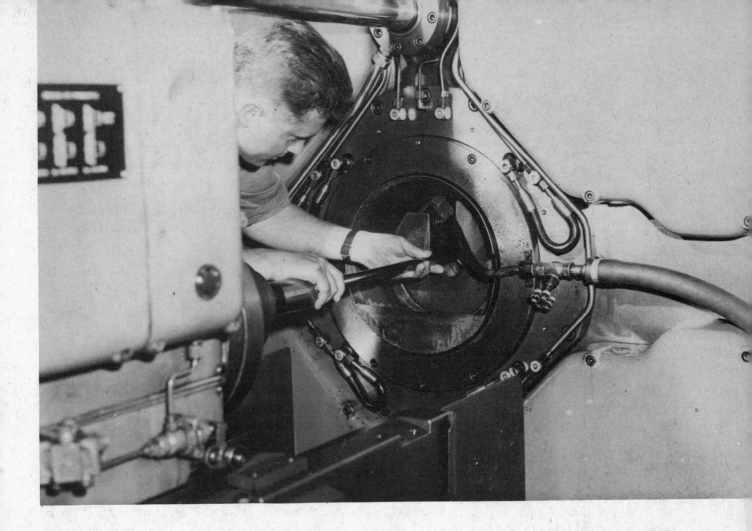

Steyr Technician setting up a barrel blank in a hammer-rifling machine. (Photo Courtesy of Steyr-Daimler-Puch AG)

but is apparently more popular with pistol and revolver manufacturers.

Button rifling is accomplished by forcing a hardened steel mandrel through an undersized pilot hole. The action is one of swaging (compression) rather than cutting, (the mandrel is made with the reverse configuration of the rifle bore).

Hammer rifling is the latest, and the most popular, of present-day rifling methods. Most of the larger makers are now using this system.

During WWII some submachine gun barrels were made by placing a full length mandrel (again, with a reverse bore configuration) inside an oversized pilot hole. The barrel blank and mandrel were then placed in a high pressure rolling machine which compressed the steel down to the size and shape of the mandrel. "Rolling" excited considerable interest because it was faster and resulted in a straighter bore.

Post-war refinements evolved into a right-angle, spiraling, hammering process.

The hammering machine that I had occasion to examine at the Steyr Works, in Austria, was designed with a total of four hammer segments arranged in two banks of two segments each. The Steyr engineer informed me that the machine de-

The Steyr people advertise the fact that their barrels are hammer-rifled by leaving the spiraled markings in the exterior finish, as a close look at the barrel in this photograph will attest. (Courtesy Steyr-Daimler-Puch AG)

livered something like 1000 blows per minute and that the total force expended was equivalent to 130 tons.

In comparing the four methods (comparison of the bores was made with a specially constructed rod-like, illuminated right-angle magnifier of 40 power), I found that cut and broach rifling often create minor flaws in the bore—slight scoring, chipping of sharp corners, etc. This is only to be expected from a cutting action where chips can interfere with the action of the cutter. Button rifling was somewhat smoother. In the hammer rifled barrel the finished bore was glass smooth. Furthermore, it appears logical to assume that the hammering action, itself, would tend to somewhat equalize wall thicknesses by flowing metal from the thicker areas into the thinner portions of the barrel.

Incidentally, the hammering process lengthens the barrel blank considerably, outside diameter is noticeably reduced.

BARREL WHIP

The newcomer to the field of firearms often feels, intuitively, that barrels must be made from a very hard and tough steel.

They're not . . . and they can't be!

While each manufacturer has his own standards for barrel steels, the one factor common to all is that barrel materials are relatively soft.

When a given cartridge—the 30/06 for example—is designed to develop a breech pressure of about 50,000 copper units of pressure, one quickly realizes that the slender barrel tube must have some malleability. When a cartridge is fired, the effect is not unlike the sudden introduction of a high pressure stream of water to a hose. Like the garden hose, barrels flex upon releasing internal pressure, and with a rifle, this occurs upon the release of the projectile. Bear in mind that the rifle is in the process of recoiling when this happens and that the whipping action of the muzzle is of very short duration. For these reasons, muzzle motion is not apparent to the naked eye. Ballisticians demonstrate the effect by means of high-speed cameras.

Realizing that we are dealing with a barrel that moves with every shot, it follows that accuracy is greatly dependent upon our ability to *return the muzzle to precisely the same at-rest position between shots.* While I am reluctant to put too much detail into an already complicated explanation, I must add here that featherweight or sharply tapered barrels tend to whip more than heavyweight barrels having shallow tapers. Also that high velocity cartridges—because of their higher operating pressures—will tend to cause more whip than lower velocity shells.

There are a number of methods commonly used to control muzzle whip. The simplest and probably most effective of these is to employ a heavier barrel without taper. This works well for benchrest guns and other forms of target rifles, but their excess weight would be burdensome to the hunter. When barrel size and weight must be limited, other methods must be adopted: these would have to do with the stabilizing effect of the stock and the depth to which the barrel is seated in the receiver. Long bearing surfaces between the barrel and receiver have a very positive minimizing effect on barrel motion. But, again, attempts in this direction can quickly lead to an overweight and cumbersome receiver.

In shooting, almost every decision is based on a compromise. The decision-making process should therefore start with a determination of what is expected of the new rifle. The shooter desiring less than minute-of-angle accuracy has to resign himself to the fact that he needs a heavy, target-type rifle that frequently exceeds twelve pounds in weight. As long as he intends to shoot this from a benchrest, excess weight is not a problem. If, on the other hand, he wants to do position target shooting, he'll have to compromise a bit and settle for a somewhat lighter rifle, one that he can comfortably handle in the sitting, kneeling and offhand positions.

(NOTE: In all forms of target competition—big-bore and small-bore—there are established rules limiting weights, trigger-pull weights, sighting instruments, etc. The shooter interested in pursuing one of these sports should write to the National Rifle Association, 1600 Rhode Island Avenue N.W., Washington, D.C. 20036 for a copy of the appropriate rule book.)

The hunter, on the other hand, has to give serious thought to field-application of the rifle. If he must carry it all day and, if he wants it to handle quickly and easily under hunting conditions, weight and size are very definite factors. He needs a light, carefully balanced rifle *in spite of the fact that he'll have to compromise accuracy!* The logical question here is, "How much accuracy can I afford to sacrifice?"

As a rule of thumb, the benchrest shooter strives for less than half minute-of-angle accuracy; the big-bore target shooter, minute-of-angle; the var-

This Remington Model 40XB-BR is a benchrest target rifle. Note the thickness of the barrel employed.

mint hunter can afford slightly more than minute-of-angle; and the big game hunter can do well with a rifle delivering three minutes-of-angle.

The foregoing, of course, is based on precision benchrest testing procedures where human error is all but eliminated. One can't expect to realize full accuracy potential in a hand-held rifle.

(The complete definition of "minute-of-angle" can be found in the "Sighting and Zeroing" chapter of this book. Also, a detailed explanation on the use of the stock to dampen barrel motion is provided in the chapter on "The Rifle Stock.")

Rifle makers and firearms dealers are often harassed by shooters who are either untrained marksmen (who wants to admit he's *not* another Daniel Boone?) or by shooters who fail to understand the compromises that were designed into their special-purpose rifles. How can a tradesman answer a letter that says, in effect, ". . . my new—— rifle can't hit a platter at fifty feet and it's darn embarrassing to me to have my shooting friends hitting poker chips at 100 yards"?

The reply to that one requires great restraint and diplomacy!

In fairness to all concerned, I have seen some rifles deliver sub-par performances, but rarely have I seen a rifle that could not easily be corrected! There is no way, however, to force target-accuracy from a lightweight hunting rifle!

The shooter who feels he has a legitimate complaint in this area should consult his local gunsmith or the manufacturer.

BARREL HEAT AND BARREL WALLS

Now that we understand barrel whip, we can discuss the importance of uniform barrel walls. Earlier, while describing the methods used to drill and rifle barrels, I touched on the problem manufacturers have in achieving a straight pilot hole. When the drill "walks" a bit—which it is bound to do—wall thicknesses will vary.

Their problem wouldn't be too perplexing if it ended right there, but up until now we've been discussing only the bore-hole and we have assumed that the outer configuration of the barrel-rod was straight when the raw stock arrived from the mill. Even if it were, we could draw little consolation from the fact! To make anything other than a rough finished heavyweight benchrest barrel, the manufacturer must remove some material from the external profile. Can you imagine the strains and stresses involved when a cutting tool starts to hog-out the profile of a lightweight hunting barrel? That long slim tube—which is getting slimmer with each turn of the lathe—wants to bow out, away from the cutting tool. True, the steady-rests are employed, again, to prevent flexing under the pressure of the cutter. Yet, some slight inequities are almost certain to result.

Even after cutting the external profile the problem continues to progress. The next step is to polish the exterior surface, on high speed polishing wheels, to prepare the barrel for finishing.

The reader should now realize that *the combination* of required manufacturing methods tends to lead him ever farther from the imaginary perfectly straight barrel.

While hammer-rifling methods by-pass some of these critical procedures, they, too, would be subject to minor variations in wall thickness—especially if made with a highly polished exterior surface.

"Okay," you ask, "so we've determined that variations in barrel-wall thicknesses are virtually inevitable. What do we do about it and what effect does it have on accuracy?"

First, it's not so important that you know to what extent the walls may vary in thickness. In fact, there's no way of determining this, short of destroying the barrel. It is important only that you realize the effect this may have on your shooting, particularly if you are using a lightweight (or featherweight) barreled rifle.

As I stated earlier, accuracy is greatly dependent

upon our ability to return the muzzle to precisely the same at-rest position between shots. As a barrel heats up through repeated firings, it will expand, and this expansion process will certainly tend to cause a slight bowing in an area where the wall thickness is most uneven.

For years I've listened to competitive riflemen argue the relative merits of a free-floating barrel over a pressure-bedded barrel, and vice-versa. Both groups had some very logical arguments and both, at times, have successfully demonstrated the validity of their opposing views.

I suspect that no one will ever irrevocably prove one method superior to the other, but I think I have stumbled upon a reasonable explanation for the apparent success of each system. One day, while shooting and adjusting a variety of different rifles from a benchrest, I noticed that a number of them were exceptionally accurate when their barrels were free floating. However, along came one that was horribly inaccurate. With each shot it seemed to get worse, in spite of anything I did to correct it! Finally, I wedged about .008's of shim-stock between the fore end and the barrel, an inch back from the tip of the fore end. Because this was a fairly light hunting rifle I would only fire three shots at a sitting. Then I would place the rifle in a gun rack and let it cool while I worked on another model. (All hunting rifles should be handled this way—they must be adjusted to shoot accurately from a cold start, as would be expected of them under hunting conditions. It makes no sense at all to shoot them into a "hot-barrel" zero.)

At this point, because pressure bedding of the light barrel immediately improved accuracy, I realized that the other rifles previously fired that day were all equipped with heavier barrels. Could it be that free-floating aids accuracy when barrel-wall thicknesses (and variations) are not critical and that, when they are highly critical, and proven erratic, that pressure bedding is the only way one can control muzzle position?

Since that day I've made it a practice to free-float barrels for test purposes by means of shimming under the action. If this test gave the desired result in accuracy I would then remove the stock (and shims) and relieve the wooden fore end to free-float the barrel. If accuracy was poor, however, I would remove the stock (and shims) and reseat the barreled action in the wood so that I achieved approximately a seven-pound pressure on the barrel from the fore end tip.

Since putting this theory into practice I've found it far easier to get satisfactory results with a minimum of time, effort and expended rounds.

In concluding this section on barrel wall thickness I feel I should emphasize the fact that my comments on pressure bedding are applicable only to rifles having full-length, one-piece stocks. These are, usually, bolt action models.

BARREL LENGTH

How long should a barrel be? Answer?—long enough to stabilize the desired bullet and short enough to provide the handling qualities expected for the specific purpose for which a particular rifle is intended, without unnecessary loss of velocity.

In general, this definition would seem to cover barrels as short as eighteen inches and as long as thirty inches. Actually, in practice it covers barrels from twenty inches to twenty-six inches.

Barrel length is determined by:

1. The intended purpose of a given model.
2. The overall balance and handling qualities of a given model.
3. Caliber (range of bullet weights and rate of twist).
4. Bullet velocity and stabilization requirements.

Many years ago, when our "nation of riflemen" was first establishing its reputation in international target competitions, shooters used long barrels of thirty or more inches. I always assumed that they did this primarily to gain extra sighting radius (they used aperture-type iron sights) and because longer barrels would tend to increase bullet velocity. They also shot from a "back position" with the muzzle end of their long barrels resting on their legs or feet. Today we can only guess as to their reasoning. Perhaps they liked muzzle heavy rifles, believing they would be steadier in match competitions. Or, could it be that the long-barrel style simply carried over from our famous Kentucky long rifles of flintlock days?

Unlike the shotgun which delivers peak velocity at one specific barrel length, the rifle delivers higher velocities as the barrel length is increased. Actually, the longer the barrel, the greater will be the muzzle velocity (to a point); the only problem is that it gets progressively more difficult to control whip and muzzle attitude as the barrel is lengthened.

In his "Handbook for Shooters and Reloaders" (1959 Edition), P. O. Ackley reported on an interesting experiment he conducted with various barrel lengths.

Using a constant control load for one caliber, Mr. Ackley started with a thirty-one inch barrel and, after measuring the velocity of the control load at that length, he proceeded to reduce barrel length one inch at a time while measuring the resultant velocity at each stage. He cut the barrels down from thirty-one inches to eighteen inches (minimum legal length) in thirteen steps.

This experiment was conducted twice; two different control loads were used. With one load he lost a total of 537 f.p.s. in going from a thirty-one to an eighteen-inch barrel—an average loss of 41 f.p.s. per inch. With the other barrel he lost 768 f.p.s. for an average of 59 f.p.s. per inch.

It appears that manufacturers have found barrel weight, velocity and accuracy are best balanced at the compromise length of twenty-four inches. Barrels longer than twenty-four inches would have to be uncommonly heavy if accuracy were to be maintained.

Barrels measuring less than twenty-four inches (such as those used on carbines) may lose a little in velocity, but could gain some stiffness that would tend to enhance accuracy.

At any rate, there are other methods that can be employed to increase velocity (lighter bullets, heavier loads) so there's no practical reason for anyone to tote an overly long barrel.

When Remington first introduced its Model 722 rifle in .222 Remington caliber, they equipped it with a twenty-six inch barrel. The rifle I picked up for testing was so equipped and it was this rifle that provided the only visual evidence I have ever realized from a barrel length variation. And this was due only to their subsequent change of this model to a twenty-four inch barrel.

Long barrels are inclined to whip more than shorter, stiffer barrels and I suspect that this had some bearing on their decision to make the change.

Nevertheless, to get back to the point, I was doing a considerable amount of experimenting with handloading in 1950. New reloading tools were just coming onto the market and in a field where only a handful of expert riflemen were experienced reloaders, I felt I had much to learn. I used the Remington 722 which I had modified extensively and which I had equipped with an elaborate scope for precision benchrest shooting. This rifle was exceptionally accurate with the 50 grain Sierra semi-pointed bullet and 20 grains of 4198 powder —it would drive thumb tacks at 100 yards. When I got a five shot group of 5/8 an inch, I was having a bad day!

Some time later, perhaps a year or two, Remington reduced the barrel length of this model to twenty-four inches and I sought out the shorter model for comparison testing. Again, I tuned the rifle, rebedded the barrel, and installed precision sighting equipment.

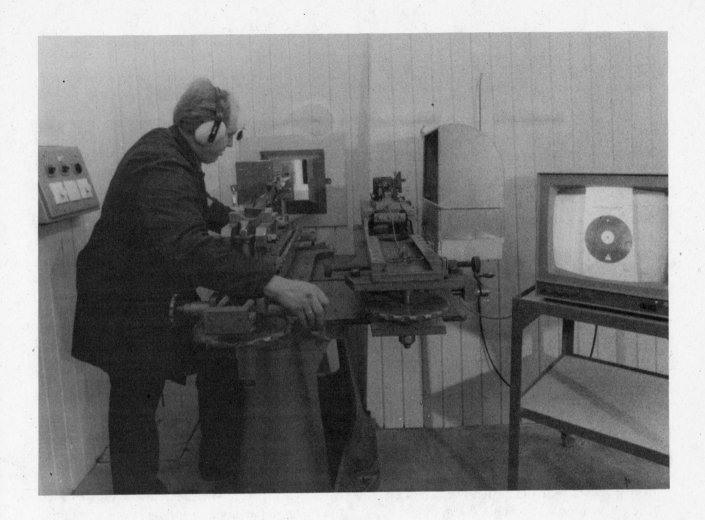

Precision machine rest used to test finished rifles at the Steyr Works. Note employment of closed-circuit TV which gives the inspector a close-up view of the target. (Courtesy Steyr-Daimler-Puch AG)

Back at the benchrest I discovered, much to my surprise, that this rifle simply couldn't match the performance of the earlier twenty-six-inch model. Yet, the difference was so slight, so subtle, that only precision benchrest testing with meticulously loaded custom cartridges revealed it. It is difficult to draw any hard and fast conclusions from this because other factors (barrel wall variations for example) may have contributed to the incident.

In summing up this dissertation on barrel length, I think I can safely say that most modern smokeless cartridges will perform well in any barrel measuring between twenty and twenty-six inches. If the rifle shooter is much concerned with precision accuracy, he should be highly suspicious of any rifle having a barrel shorter than twenty inches or longer than twenty-six inches.

Rifle (top) is a .308 caliber target model equipped with a heavy barrel for position target shooting. Note smaller diameter of barrel used in the standard hunting rifle (below). (Courtesy Steyr-Daimler-Puch AG)

MUZZLE CROWNING

That gracefully rounded section at the leading edge of the muzzle often appears to have only a decorative function. Actually, it is a highly important finishing step designed to protect the rifling.

Anyone who has hunted extensively knows how difficult it is to avoid bumping the muzzle on assorted hard objects. If the muzzle were simply cut with a flat face, the rifling at that point would inevitably suffer. Until one has seen the effect of a muzzle burr on accuracy, it is difficult to imagine how damaging it can be.

A dealer friend of mine once accepted a used lever action on a trade. He subsequently sold this piece only to get it back with the complaint that the rifle "couldn't hit a barn door at fifty feet!"

Dealers hear this comment so often that they become a bit indifferent to it. My friend exchanged the rifle for another and again, within a short time, sold the original lever action for the second time.

When it was returned a week later, for the same reason, it was decided that range testing was called for.

I happened to be at the rifle range when the dealer put the lever action through its paces. Twenty some odd rounds later we had established only that the rifle was shooting very erratically, though generally high and to the right. For over an hour we pored over that rifle with measuring instruments and assorted testing devices. Finally, while cleaning the bore for another visual examinaton we discovered an inexplicable resistance as the cleaning patch was being withdrawn from the muzzle. Close examination revealed a very slight and insignificant flattened area at the muzzle, embracing one land of the rifling and a portion of another.

Subsequent re-crowning, which took less than fifteen minutes in the shop, corrected the problem.

Whenever a rifle seems to go sour for no apparent reason, it's a good idea to examine it closely for this particular fault. Even if no damage is visible, try re-crowning before giving up on it.

RATE OF TWIST

Rate of twist is expressed in terms of the number

of inches required to make one complete revolution, i.e., one-in-ten, one-in-fourteen, etc., and applies to the revolutions made by the rifling in a barrel.

I doubt if one rifle buyer out of a hundred ever bothers to check this detail before making his purchase and, yet, it can have a very decided effect upon a rifle's performance.

Firearms designers and ballisticians must determine the rate of twist required to stabilize the flight of a given bullet when propelled at a given rate of speed. For example, if the twist is too fast for a light bullet being driven at a high velocity, it will over-stabilize it causing a wobbling erratic flight. The effect would resemble the flight of a football that is spun too energetically by the quarterback. So that the reader will understand the terminology of "too fast" as it applies to twist, permit me to insert here that one revolution in a comparatively short distance (say nine inches) is considered "fast." One revolution in fourteen inches is "slow."

Generally speaking, the slower and heavier the bullet, the faster will be the rate of twist. Light, high-speed bullets require a slower rate of twist.

Some years ago my experimental shooting brought me around to the Remington .257 Roberts cartridge, which I still think is one of the finest all-around shells ever designed. I became so interested in this cartridge that I continued experimenting with it in one of its popular variations by building a .257 Ackley Improved wildcat rifle which employs a blown-out, or fire-formed, version of the Roberts case. The barrel was made for me with a one-in-fourteen twist because I intended to employ primarily 87-grain bullets which I wanted to drive at about 3600 f.p.s.

To condense a very long story, I shot this gun until the barrel gave out—at least for precision benchrest purposes. Along the way I tried many different loads utilizing bullets ranging in weight from 60 grains to 117 grains. It was interesting to note the wide range of target groupings I would get when I'd try to drive the 60 grain bullet too fast or the 117 grain bullet too slow. In fact, that rifle never did handle anything heavier than a 100 grain bullet with any real degree of accuracy.

The point is that every rifle is made with a specific rate of twist which is really designed to handle *one weight of bullet* well. Of course, you can feed a wide range of bullet weights through it, but if you take the time and trouble to test them carefully you'll surely find that one given weight and load will do better than the rest.

Before you rush off to the local firearms emporium with your pet blunderbuss let me add that most rifles are designed with a barrel rifling twist that complements the bullet-load-cartridge commonly marketed for that particular caliber: i.e. the Winchester 94 lever action 30–30 is usually employed with a cartridge having a 170 grain bullet which is propelled at approximately 2220 f.p.s.

The Winchester people, of course, design the rifling to accommodate this load.

"Aha," you say, "but Winchester also makes a cartridge with a 150-grain bullet for the 30–30."

You're right. Nevertheless, the difference of 20 grains at a slight change in velocity (2220 to 2410 f.p.s.) is not going to alter performance to the extent that you would even see it.

Rate of twist gathers importance when the shooter wishes to introduce a broad range of bullet weights and when he seeks a wide spread in muzzle velocities.

The benchrest shooter, target shooter and varmint hunter have to be concerned with twist because they are looking for *precision accuracy*. Knowing their rate of twist they'll quickly determine what *not* to use, and limit their shells to the bullet weights and speeds ideally suited to their bores.

For the average shooter, difficulty is encountered with calibers like the 30–06—simply because there's such a wide range of shells made for this caliber. Commercially loaded shells may be had with bullets of 110, 125, 150, 180 and 220 grains. Handloaders can even buy custom bullets for this caliber in a number of lighter and intermediate weights.

While we have to stick with the premise that a given rate of twist is ideally suited to a given bullet weight and velocity, it is possible to slow down a lighter bullet to better accommodate a faster than desired twist. At the opposite end of the scale, it is far more difficult to speed up a heavier bullet for a slow twist, simply because breech pressures would quickly get out of hand.

The *direction* of the twist, incidentally, has some effect on the trajectory of the bullet, particularly in slow, heavy calibers. The shooter who zeros his 30–06 rifle using 150 grain bullets will often find that the gun shoots low and *to the left* when he employs 220 grain loads with the same sight setting. Low, because he has switched to a heavier, slower bullet which traces a more pronounced arc

Cut-away view of the chamber of a Weatherby Mark V rifle. Note unrifled portion of barrel in front of the bullet—this is the "throat" of the bore. Also, note slight tolerance in front of the neck of the casing. (This, as you can see, is a belted magnum cartridge.)

in its trajectory; left, because of the direction of his rifling!

Lateral deviation is particularly noticeable at long range and is often mistaken for wind drift.

The Germans cleverly compensated for lateral drift in their Navy Model Luger. With a military rear sight having the typical sliding elevator, the notched leaf shifts to the left as the elevator is raised for shooting at greater distances. This, supposedly, automatically adjusts for the left-to-right drift of the bullet.

Getting back to my football illustration, the rate of twist is designed to stabilize a bullet in flight so that it spins truly on its axis, like the perfect spiral forward pass. When this is accomplished, the bullet will fly predictably over a longer, straighter course.

THE CHAMBER

To understand the function of the barrel chamber we must first take a look at the internal ballistics of the fired cartridge.

The rifle cartridge consists of a primer, brass case, powder charge and bullet. When fully chambered, and when the breech is locked, there are some tolerances present between the casing and the chamber walls and breech face. This is necessary to facilitate feeding of the round and

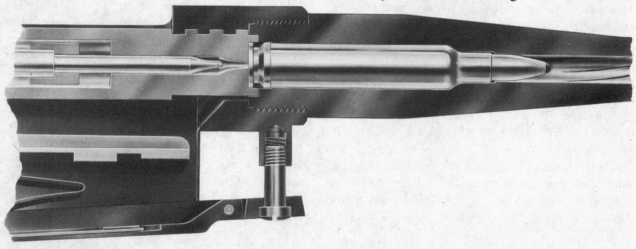

subsequent extraction and ejection. Also, because there are variations in cartridge dimensions—particularly from one brand to another—chambers must be made sufficiently large to accept all makes and variations, up to specific limits.

From this, we learn that a chamber must not be too small or it will impede the movement of the cartridge. But, what if it is too large?

When struck by the firing pin the chambered casing is driven forward by the impact. This creates a space between the case head (the flat primer-containing end) and the face of the breech. When sufficient resistance is met, the nose of the firing pin will crush the priming composition between the wall of the cup and the integral anvil, resulting in detonation of the primer and ignition of the pro-pellant powder charge. As the powder charge burns, it creates rapidly expanding gases that attain high pressure. In the 30-06 cartridge, for example, this approximates 50,000 copper units of pressure. Pressure reaches its peak just as the bullet overcomes inertia and commences its flight into the bore.

It is apparent that all design features are there-fore considered from the standpoint of containing and regulating *peak* pressure. It is at this point in time (a milli-second) when all components are under greatest stress: the walls of the brass cart-ridge casing are fully expanded to fill the chamber area and the head of the casing is pushed rearward to make contact with the face of the bolt.

On the surface it appears that all case dimensions are enlarged simultaneously but, in practice, it doesn't work quite that way! The side walls of the cartridge case generally have very little room to expand and they meet the chamber walls quickly—firmly affixing the position of the case within the chamber. The head of the case is retarded in its rearward motion by the resistance of the firing pin and, usually, has a bit more area to cover before it makes contact with the face of the bolt. Conse-quently, the side walls of the casing, in the area forward of the web, are *stretched* longitudinally. When called upon to stretch farther than their pre-determined design limits, they rupture, and that is when the shooter finds himself in serious trouble! Gases can escape through the rupture and are blown back through the breech mechanism.

While we have been discussing chamber dimensions, generally, we are specifically concerned with the longitudinal tolerance referred to as "headspace."

Having examined the danger of an oversized chamber, let's get back to the subject of peak pres-sure. As I implied earlier, each cartridge is de-signed to generate the specific pressure required to drive a bullet at a specific rate of speed. It is only when a new and foreign element is introduced that matters go awry.

Remembering that all considerations are based on containing peak pressure, it follows that the chamber must be designed and cut so as to avoid interference with the separation of the bullet from the casing at the instant of firing. For this reason, a "throat" is cut in the area of the bore between the rifling and the leading edge of the chamber. When a loaded cartridge is fed into the chamber, the throat area surrounds the bullet and prevents con-tact between the bullet and the start of the rifling. If the rifling were permitted to make contact with the bullet, the added resistance of that contact would greatly escalate pressures. For the same reason, the rifling, at the point where it meets the throat, is generally tapered into the throat dimen-sion.

Moving rearward into the chamber, we are next confronted with the neck area—that section where the bullet is encircled by the brass casing. Here, again, we must be concerned with a tolerance that will permit the case neck to expand easily, facili-tating release of the bullet. If the neck of a given cartridge casing is overly long, it can be inadvertently swaged to a smaller mouth diameter (by the locking force of the breech) to the point where it would be crimped to the outer walls of the bullet. This would add considerable resistance to the bullet's flight and, again, would result in an unanticipated increase in chamber pressure. (Handloaders often get into trouble here when they neglect to measure and trim case necks before each loading.)

The sloping forward area of the bottlenecked cartridge case—that point between the rearmost edge of the neck and the forwardmost edge of the main body—is called the shoulder. About halfway through this sloped area is an imaginary line of specific dimension that is referred to as the datum line. It is from this point—this line—that chamber length is measured and headspace ascertained for *rimless bottlenecked cartridges.*

When fully chambered, rimless shells like the 30-06, .270, .243 and .222 generally have a portion of their casings protruding, in an unsupported manner, from the mouth of the chamber. This is necessary to give the extractor adequate area in which to grip to the casing. The web—or heaviest portions of the brass casing—occupies the small space that protrudes into the extractor area and is ideally designed to handle the pressure that remains at this point *if headspacing is normal.*

Rimmed cartridges, rimfire shells and belted magnum cases are headspaced differently. With the conventional .22 rimfire cartridge, for example, the barrel maker is concerned with the distance between the face of the bolt and the flat surface of the chamber opening that abuts the forward edge of the rim of the cartridge. The same system applies to center-fire rimmed shells such as the .25–35 Winchester, .218 Bee., etc.

There are some cartridges that are popularly designated as "semi-rimmed" (such as the .225 Winchester). These are headspaced in the same manner as rimless shells but, because they provide a larger gripping area for the extractor (the semi-

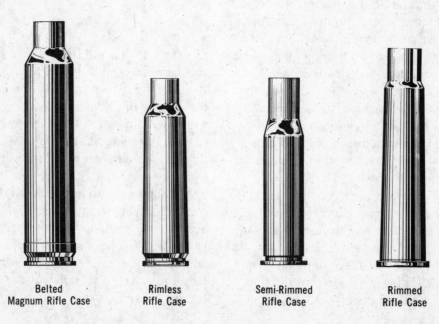

Belted
Magnum Rifle Case

Rimless
Rifle Case

Semi-Rimmed
Rifle Case

Rimmed
Rifle Case

rim), they can be made to function well with a chamber that supports more of the cartridge casing.

Belted magnum cartridges—like the 7mm Remington Magnum and .375 H & H Magnum—have the headspace dimension determined from the leading, or forwardmost, edge of the belt recess cut in the chamber to the face of the breech.

When a given rifle chamber yields only minimum headspace to a cartridge (say .001″ over minimum recommended length), the cartridge quickly resists the impact of the firing pin; primer detonation is faster, more positive, and the consistently rapid ignition of the powder charge tends to aid accuracy.

A rifle functioning with maximum headspace (.005″ over minimum recommended length), tends to cushion the blow of the firing pin and performs a bit more erratically at the expense of accuracy.

Headspace gauges, used by gunsmiths and barrel makers, are referred to as "go," "no-go" and "field" gauges. These, respectively, can be considered minimum headspace, maximum (but safe) headspace and dangerous headspace. Uninformed shooters often consider the "no-go" gauge as dangerous. Often it's not; it merely indicates that a given chamber has been cut to a maximum dimension and this, from a barrel maker's point of view, is not a desirable condition for a new barrel—hence the title "no-go." Gauge values are really dependent upon the recommendations of gauge and rifle manufacturers.

The field gauge, on the other hand, is most often made .002″ oversize and, if a given rifle accepts this, trouble is lurking just around the corner.

THE FEEDING CONE

There's an end to everything—even the rifle barrel—and now that you've suffered with me through the entire length of that simple-looking tube, we arrive at the end; the feeding cone or the edge that must accept the cartridge for chambering.

Cones vary according to the magazine system and action of the breech mechanism. Ideally, a cartridge should be positioned in a straight line with the chamber as it comes from the magazine lifter. Rarely is this possible! Most often, particularly in staggered box magazines, the shell must be fed into the chamber from a line that angles away from the axis of the bore. Considering the sloped shoulder of the average bottleneck cartridge, it is imperative that some provision be made to permit unimpeded feeding from such an angle. Coning of the barrel face is the only possible answer. However, the depth of the cone must be regulated carefully to avoid enlargement of the area where the rimless case is unsupported by the chamber walls.

In summing up this chapter on the rifle barrel, it should be pointed out that a barrel is threaded to the receiver portion with substantial force. Special barrel and receiver wrenches are used for this purpose so that the union is rigid.

CHAPTER 3

The Action

There are six basic forms of rifle action currently being produced. Other than to satisfy differences in taste, each is really designed to offer something unique by way of rapidity of fire, handling or performance. Each, too, has some limiting factors; the rifle selection process should therefore start with an examination of the uses for which the rifle is sought.

THE SINGLE SHOT RIFLE

There are four types of single shot rifles—the simple and inexpensive bolt type which is com-

The Marlin Model 101 is a good training rifle for beginners. It's a single shot with an independent cocking knob.

monly used as a beginner's rifle; the sophisticated and expensive bolt type which is used as a competition target rifle; the falling block type which runs the gamut (considering early forms that are now antiques) from cheap plinkers to very costly hunting and target versions; and, finally, the break-open (shotgun style) single shot rifle.

The bolt action single shot closely resembles a bolt action repeater except that it lacks a magazine. Also, to minimize costs and to render it safe for training purposes, this bolt action is, at times, not self cocking; a cocking knob at the rear of the bolt must be pulled back to cock the striker after the bolt is closed. Typical of such rifles is the Marlin Model 101.

Similar to the above, but equipped with self-cocking bolts, are the Remington Model 580, the Savage Models 63 and 73 and the Winchester Model 310.

The more sophisticated single shot bolt action rifle is usually designed with a special target trigger, heavy barrel, target stock, refined sighting equipment (or provisions for same) and a speed-lock action. Today, one can choose from the Winchester Model 52, the Savage/Anschutz 1400 series or the Remington Model 40–XB.

There are also a few less-expensive target versions available for the beginning target shooter. These are the Remington Model 540–X, Savage/ Anschutz Models 10–D and 64 and the Mossberg Model 144.

(Top to bottom) Remington Model 540X, Mossberg Model 144 and Savage-Anschutz Model 1411.

The Model 144 is easily converted into a repeater by substituting a magazine for the single-loading platform.

The only break-open type single shot rifle I could find listed in current factory catalogs is the H & R (Harrington & Richardson) Model 158C Topper Combination Rifle. This model is made with a .30/30 caliber rifle barrel designed to work interchangeably with a 20 gauge shotgun barrel.

Falling block rifles have made a dramatic comeback in recent years. In .22 rimfire caliber the shooter can choose from the Savage Models 72 or 74, or the Navy Arms Baby Carbine. Falling block

(Top) The Navy Arms Company's Model 1901 Remington rolling block rifle. (Bottom) Ruger's Number One Special Varminter falling block rifle.

single shot rifles are also currently being made in large center fire calibers. Ruger seems to have cornered the market on these with their Model No. 1. This model may be had in a wide assortment of modern calibers ranging from .22/250 to .458 Magnum. For the antique-minded gunner, they also produce a Model #3 in .45/70 caliber. Navy Arms Company, too, has a replica of a popular antique in a rolling block form—their Buffalo Rifle Creedmore Model in .45/70. In a falling block version, Navy has a Martini style rifle in .45/70 and .444 Marlin calibers. Browning has the Model 78 FB rifle.

While they look very much alike, there is a subtle difference between a rolling block and the falling block. The latter is operated by means of a lever extension of the trigger guard. When the lever is pushed forward the block drops down exposing the chamber for loading. These have an internal hammer. The rolling block rifle has an exposed hammer. To open the breech the hammer is first pulled back and then the block, operating in a similar fashion, is pulled back against the hammer.

There's a lot of romance connected with the old falling and rolling blocks. Most shooters have to succumb to it at least once during their shooting careers. When you do "fall" for one of these, you'll invariably find that original versions are slow and troublesome. Firing pins are especially fragile, extraction and ejection weak, and the fact that the stock is mounted in two separate pieces sometimes makes for questionable accuracy. The Ruger Company has done much to eliminate these faults in their Models 1 and 3. These modern versions have a significant number of improvements over the original form of falling block.

Browning 78 SINGLE SHOT RIFLE

SPECIFICATIONS

Approximate Weight—With octagon barrel, 7 lbs., 10 oz.; with round sporter barrel, 7 lbs., 14 oz.

Overall Length—42 inches.

Action—Classic falling block with automatic extraction and ejection. Lever operated.

Barrel—Individually machined from forged, heat treated, chrome-moly steel. Length 26″ on all models. Recessed muzzle. Right-hand rifling twist: .22/250—one turn in 14 inches; 6mm and .25/06—one turn in 10 inches; .30/06—one turn in 12 inches.

Trigger—Grooved. Clean, crisp pull adjustable between 3 and 4½ pounds.

Receiver—Forged and milled from single block of high strength steel. Famous High-Wall profile.

Sighting System—No iron sights. Furnished with specially designed 1″ scope mount system. Barrel and receiver drilled and tapped.

Safety—Exposed hammer with half-cock position.

Stock and Forearm—High grade, select walnut hand rubbed to gleaming finish. Hand checkered. Deluxe recoil pad installed on stock. Fitted with low profile studs for sling swivel attachment. Will accept special Browning 1″ or 1¼″ sling swivels #34201 or 35202, respectively (not included).

> Length of pull — 13⅝″
> Drop at comb — 1⅝″*
> Drop at heel — 2⅛″*

*Measured from a datum line 1.0″ above center-line of bore. This line corresponds to a theoretical line of sight for iron sights if they were installed.

THE DOUBLE RIFLE

Shotgun style break-open rifles were really created to satisfy the needs of the African dangerous-game hunter. British gunmakers came up with the idea that two separate rifles, in one, would be far more desirable than a repeater when the chips were down. The double rifle has two barrels, two sears and two triggers and the long and the short of it is that the shooter gets two very fast shots. (A gun bearer usually stands close by with a second loaded rifle to give the shooter four chances—sometimes six, if the bearer is a fast loader!)

Double rifles are made in some huge calibers; those intended for elephant and rhino, from .300 Magnum to .600 Nitro Express. Almost without exception they are equipped only with iron sights (shooting is rarely attempted beyond 75 yards) and a hinged forward trigger. Why a hinged trigger? Because recoil, as you can imagine, is a significant factor. If the forward trigger were not hinged to fold toward the muzzle on impact it would bruise the trigger finger when the rear trigger was pulled. For the same reason, trigger guards are usually made to generous dimensions.

A double rifle costs four to five times more than a high grade bolt action repeater. (Prices of $3,000.00 or more are common today.) One of the reasons for this is that alignment of the two barrels, to shoot to the same point of impact, is devilishly difficult and time-consuming.

Add this to the cost of an African safari and you'll understand why African outfitters will loan or rent guns to their hunting guests. The shooter interested in buying one will have to contact an English maker such as Holland & Holland or Purdey—or one of their American agents. (Delivery on a custom-made double rifle can rarely be accomplished in less than two years.)

COMBINATION GUNS

Just as the double rifle is typically British, combination guns are typically German. The European hunts on a game preserve where big game and bird seasons run simultaneously, thus he wants a hunting firearm that will permit him to take advantage of any given opportunity.

One will find combinations of one shotgun barrel over one rifle barrel—one rifle and two shot barrels or one shot and two rifle barrels. On occasion, you'll find two side-by-side shot barrels centered over a medium bore rifle barrel with a small bore rifle barrel nested in the center of the of the cluster—a four barrel gun!

It is the German custom to use 16 gauge shot barrels in combination with an 8x57R rifle barrel (or barrels). However, I've also seen shot barrels mixed with everything from .22 rimfire to 9mm.

Combination guns tend to be rather heavy and awkward. For this reason, barrels are made short (twenty inches or less).

This form of hunting weapon has never really caught on in the U.S., probably because our hunting seasons rarely overlap.

A good quality combination gun is quite costly. Today, if you can find one for less than $1,000.00, you're getting a bargain.

BOLT ACTION RIFLES

Peter Paul Mauser invented the bolt action rifle in the early 1860s and first patented it in the U.S. in 1868. Every bolt action rifle manufactured since then has made some use of Mauser's principles and few have found much room for improvement. This is a strong design that will handily accommodate almost any cartridge size. It has a powerful camming action that will chamber and extract even the most stubborn of cases. It is easy to clean and service, and it lends itself to a number of magazine systems.

Most significantly, the Mauser-type bolt is not overly heavy, contains a minimum of moving parts and is ideally suited to the one-piece stock.

Today the shooter will find an almost unlimited variety of bolt action rifles ranging in calibers from the lowly .22 rimfire to the largest elephant-gun sizes. A current list of bolt-rifle manufacturers reads like a "Who's Who in Guns": Remington, Winchester, Savage, Mossberg, Fabrique Nationale (F.N., Browning), Sako, Husqvarna, B.S.A., Weatherby and Steyr (Mannlicher-Schoenauer and Steyr-Mannlicher). We could also add to this list by including bolt rifle makers who are on the other side of the iron curtain but information from such sources is sketchy.

Center fire bolt action rifles are usually found with integral staggered-box magazines and, occasionally, with detachable clips. Except for the split-

This is a staggered-box magazine from a Savage bolt action rifle.

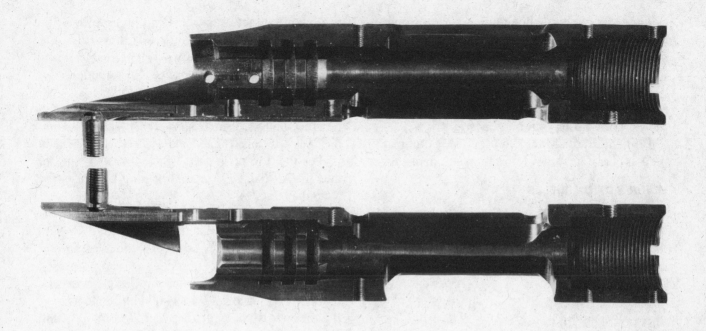

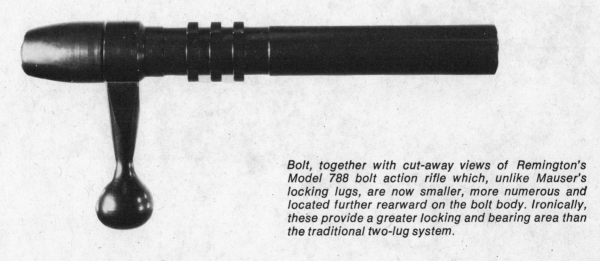

Bolt, together with cut-away views of Remington's Model 788 bolt action rifle which, unlike Mauser's locking lugs, are now smaller, more numerous and located further rearward on the bolt body. Ironically, these provide a greater locking and bearing area than the traditional two-lug system.

bridge Mannlicher-Schoenauer (now discontinued), all bolt actions will readily accept scope mounting. Military bolts, however, invariably require a bolt handle alteration.

Newly manufactered bolt action rifles, in center fire calibers, range in price from about $90.00 to the very bottom of your bank account.

Bolt rifles are slower than levers or pumps but their superior accuracy more than compensates.

LEVER ACTION RIFLES

Lever action rifles are typically American. The reason for this is that there is little need for this type of rifle in other parts of the world and few foreign manufacturers can afford to produce a rifle solely for the American market. If they lack a native market, or at least two or three interesting foreign markets, the economics of production cancels their possible participation in this field.

Even in the U.S. lever-rifle production is limited to a few makers. Winchester offers their 94, 88 and 64; Savage has their Model 99 series; Marlin makes the 336 series, the 1894, the .444 Sporter and the Model 1895 and Browning produces the Model BLR.

Twenty-two caliber lever actions include: the Browning BL-22, Ithaca 49, Marlin 39A and 39M, Navy Arms Model 66 and Winchester Models 150 and 250.

Traditionally, the center fire lever action is made in .30/30 or .32 Special calibers. However, it is now possible to get them in .243 Win., .284, .300 Savage, .308 Win., .35 Rem., .444 Marlin, .44 Magnum and .45–70.

With some top-ejecting levers such as Winchester's Models 94 and 64, scope mounting is a bit difficult, but the other models mentioned will pose no problem.

Top:
The Marlin Model 1895 lever action rifle in .45/70 caliber. Note straight grip and squared-off lever.

Bottom:
Browning's BL-22 lever action .22 Rimfire caliber rifle.

Remington Model 760 pump action rifle which, in author's opinion, is faster than the popular lever action.

PUMP ACTION RIFLES

This is another type of rifle common only to the U.S.; in fact, it's even rather rare here. Remington has one in production in center fire calibers! That's their 760 series in 6mm, .243 Win., .308 Win., and .30/06. The only other is Savage's Model 170 in .30/30.

In .22 rimfire, you'll find a few more, the High-Standard Sport-King, Remington's 572A and 572BDL and Winchester's Model 270.

Having outlined the basic types of rifles one has to choose from, let's get down to details of construction.

TRIGGERS

There are three basic types of trigger and, considering the many assorted designs we might encounter, it is best to discuss triggers in terms of "action" rather than make or design.

DOUBLE-STAGE TRIGGERS

This is a form of trigger that is common to military rifles—it is probably the safest form too, but far from the most satisfactory insofar as accuracy is concerned. As the double-stage trigger is pulled, there is considerable travel before any resistance is felt. Then, from the point where resistance is found, there is more travel until let-off is accomplished. Following let-off, there is usually some after-travel as well. This trigger gets its name from the two distinctly different stages of its action (after-travel is ignored).

Double-stage triggers are found on virtually all military rifles—they concern the sportsman only because considerable numbers of Springfields, Enfields and Mausers are found in sporterized form.

If we were to describe the various stages of this trigger action in shooter's terms we would say it "has slack, some creep, let-off and backlash."

"Slack" is travel without resistance.

"Creep" is travel with resistance.

"Let-off" is the firing point.

"Backlash" is after-travel.

Riflemen who have worked with target type triggers are unnerved by military triggers—there's simply too much unpredictable travel in them. These shooters, if seriously interested in the rifle, would quickly replace the military trigger with a custom-made sporter trigger such as made by Canjar, Jaeger or Timney.

SINGLE-STAGE TRIGGERS

These are triggers common to good sporting rifles. Resistance is felt immediately—there is little or no slack—and, with the best of sporter triggers, there's little detectable "creep" as well. I've often marveled at the trigger action found in some popularly priced, sporter rifles.

In a sophisticated target rifle you'll find an adjustable single-stage trigger that functions without creep and, often, with little or no backlash. American match rules generally stipulate a minimum

Factory triggers are surprisingly light and crisp. Because of their unique, enclosed construction it doesn't pay to tinker with them.
  This is the trigger of a Weatherby rifle.

trigger weight of three pounds; consequently these triggers are made to adjust from about two to five pounds.

Trigger weight, incidentally, is expressed in the number of ounces or pounds that can be lifted by a cocked trigger without let-off. For example, a three pound weight is placed on a table surface. To this is connected a long, stiff, wire extension. A hook in the wire is placed over the trigger of the vertically pointed rifle and the rifle is lifted, very gently, until the weight is lifted free of the table surface. Of course, the action is cocked (on an empty chamber) beforehand. If the rifle "snaps" during the weighing process, it is disqualified until the trigger weight is corrected. No one is much concerned with the total weight of pull, per se; they're only concerned that it is not less than the minimum three pounds.

SET TRIGGERS

These are triggers that can be "set" for an extremely light weight of pull—often as light as an ounce or two. It goes without saying that they can be tricky and dangerous—I certainly wouldn't recommend one to anyone other than an experienced rifleman *who shoots frequently*.

There are a number of different types of set triggers currently in production. The first is very conventional looking. Operated in the usual fashion, it functions like a normal single-stage trigger though the weight of pull may be a bit on the heavy side. To set this trigger, push it forward until it clicks. Subsiquent rearward motion will then cause a let-off. After setting, the weight of pull will be considerably lighter—the shooter has to make a special effort to engage the trigger very, very lightly.

Another form of single-set trigger is made with a small cocking lever or button inletted through the upper extremity of the trigger proper or mounted flush against the rear surface of the trigger. This trigger is cocked by pressing the setting button forward. Operation is similar to the single-set trigger previously described.

Suppose, after setting the single-set trigger, the shooter decides he doesn't want to take the shot, what does he do then? He certainly can't walk away with a rifle having a trigger set to go off at the slightest bump. Each trigger maker has his own unique method for "unsetting" the trigger and it is important that the shooter practice the described technique with an empty rifle.

DOUBLE-SET TRIGGERS

If I had to have a set trigger, this is the one I would prefer. Here, two triggers are mounted one behind the other. The forward trigger accomplishes the actual firing and can be operated with or without setting. When operated from an unset attitude it will have a weight of pull approaching

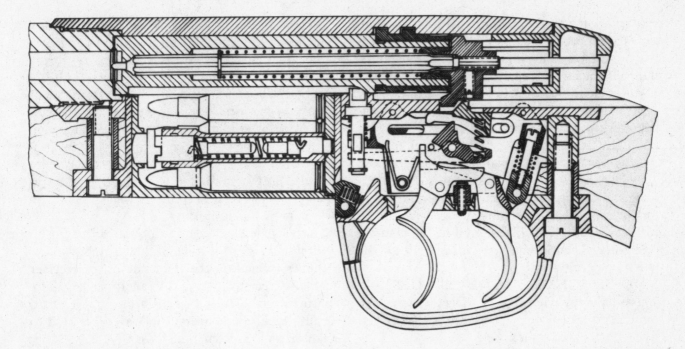

Schematic of Steyr's famous double-set trigger mechanism.

six pounds or more. It can, however, be adjusted to go with a pressure of an ounce or so through setting. The rear trigger in such a lash-up *never* fires the rifle—it's used simply as a setting device.

The double-set trigger made by Steyr (found in Mannlicher-Schoenauer and Steyr-Mannlicher rifles) can easily be unset by holding the rear trigger back, pulling the forward trigger, and easing the rear trigger forward. This is another tricky procedure that has to be practiced.

Also, the Steyr double trigger mechanism is made with an adjusting screw positioned midway between the two triggers. This permits the shooter to adjust the weight of pull on the firing trigger, *when set*. There is no adjustment for the unset trigger.

Another form of double-set trigger is typified by the one manufactured by Anschutz and used in

their international competition rifles. They place two triggers in line but turn the forward trigger around so that it faces rearward. With this mechanism, the forward trigger is the setting trigger while the rear one does the firing.

TRIGGERS FOR LEVER, PUMP AND SEMI-AUTOMATIC RIFLES

It is considerably more difficult to equip lever, pump and semi-automatic rifles with light and crisp triggers. The manufacturer has to work within the limitations imposed by the action and, at the same time, he must must create a foolproof safety device. One can't complain too loudly if he detects a little creep or slack; it's simply one of the prices he must pay for rapidity of fire.

TUNING TRIGGERS

Just as some of us couldn't resist the temptation to take our first wristwatch apart, there are shooters who are compelled to disassemble their new rifles with a view toward "improving" the trigger action.

It's a comparatively easy matter to stone the engaging surfaces of a military trigger, but it's something else again to pry into the trigger mechanism of a Remington Model 700. This is precisely why many gunmakers rivet their trigger mechanisms between two tinker-proof steel plates. Once you remove those rivets, you've blown your guarantee.

I'll never forget the shooting acquaintance who devoted the best part of a weekend to disassembling and stoning the engaging surfaces of his factory trigger. When he got it back together again, it worked beautifully—that is, until he got it to the rifle range. Then it fired every time he closed the bolt on a cartridge.

DON'T TINKER WITH TRIGGERS—if you're unhappy with a given trigger action, take the rifle to a competent gunsmith or, better yet, write to the manufacturer.

THE TRIGGER PULL

Competition shooters are very much concerned with trigger weight. I've always been more concerned with the action of the trigger—as long as it is crisp and without creep, I feel I can do well with it regardless of whether it pulls at two pounds or six. There are times, however, when a light trigger can be an asset, such as when trying to hit a bounding deer or when competing in an offhand target competition.

For this reason I try to equip all of my rifles with three pound triggers. Lighter triggers are simply not practical, particularly not on hunting rifles. Cold hands lessen the sensitivity of the trigger finger and you'll often find that with a light trigger you'll have a tendency to fire prematurely.

SAFETIES

The most desirable rifle safety a shooter could ask for is one that operates noiselessly and one which locks both the breech and the trigger. Rifles of modern manufacture are often so equipped.

The sensitive ears of a deer can detect the metallic click of a safety going off at a considerable distance. The noise factor is therefore especially significant to a hunter.

Rifle safeties will generally be found in one of four possible locations—on the tang, on the bolt extension protruding from the rear of the action, on the right side of the receiver or through the trigger guard. Manufacturers try to locate safeties close to the trigger so that safety and trigger operation can be accomplished by the trigger hand with a minimum loss of time.

Left-handed shooters are obliged to pay a bit more attention to this detail than a right-hander. Safeties located on the right side of the receiver can be especially awkward to a left-hander. Also, push button safeties located in the trigger guard really should be converted to travel from left to right in moving from "on" to "off."

Two other points to consider: Is the safety large enough to be operated easily by the gloved finger? Is there sufficient travel in the safety to avoid confusion between the two phases of attitude?

Finally, when converting military rifles such as Mausers and Springfields to sporter use it will often be found that a low mounted scope will interfere with the operation of the wing safety. When this occurs, a custom sporter safety (such as that made by Buehler) must be substituted for the military one. The only other alternative is to have a custom gunsmith install a tang extension with a push button or install a sliding side safety (these are expensive alternatives).

MAGAZINES

Rifles have been made with a great variety of magazine systems over the years but only three basic types have withstood the test of time. Today, virtually every magazine the shooter will encounter will be based on a form of the tube, box or rotary pattern.

Tubular magazines can be located under the

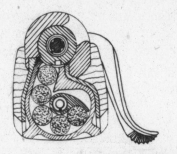

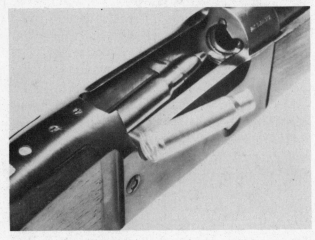

Diagram of Steyr rotary magazine (top) and photo of Savage 99 magazine (bottom). Note straight line feed. The Ruger 10/22 is the only other rifle equipped with a "spool" feeder.

barrel or through the buttstock. They are common to rimfire rifles in both forms, and to lever and slide action rifles in the under-barrel form. The tubular magazine is particularly popular in rimfire rifles because it provides a large magazine capacity without excessive bulk.

In center fire rifles the tube somewhat restricts ammunition choices, limiting them to flat-nose or round-nose bullet styles. This is due to the fact that the nose of one cartridge will bear against the primer of another when shells are placed end to end in the tube. I have, admittedly, seen shooters use pointed bullets in tubular magazines and I've never heard of an accidental firing but, with fire-

arms, I've learned not to tempt fate and I must strongly condemn this practice.

Box magazines are made in four versions: blind box—meaning that the magazine is built into the action in such a way that loading and unloading must be accomplished through the top; blind box with a removable floor plate—loads through the top and may be unloaded at the bottom; detachable box—a removable box magazine that is inserted through bottom of the action; and finally, a box magazine that is made with a rotary action follower which may or may not be detachable.

Blind box magazines are common to military rifles and are intended for use with a form of cartridge-holding clip—either the in-line stripper clip or the staggered clip. Generally, the clip remains in the magazine until the last shot is fired; then it is ejected with the last empty hull. The spring-activated follower in these magazines is designed so that the breech will not close on an empty chamber. When converting such a military action to sporter use, the tail surface of the follower is bevelled to facilitate closing without loading.

Another form of the blind box magazine is used in sporter rifles. This is intended for loading through the top; however, the floor plate is hinged so that unloading may be accomplished easily without having to run each shell through the chamber.

An important point that should be inserted here is that rifles equipped with box magazines of any kind should always be loaded *through the magazine*. When using a magazine rifle, never single load shells directly into the chamber. The reason for this is that extractors are designed to engage casings as they come from the magazine—the rim of the case slides *under* the extractor lip. If a shell is placed directly into the chamber, the lip of the extractor is forced to ride *over* the rim of the case and damage to the extractor is inevitable.

Detachable box magazines are easily removed from the action for loading and unloading. Some of these are made so that the shells are contained in line—one directly over the other—but most detachable boxes stagger the shells in a zig-zag fashion. Again, always load through the magazine, even when loading a single round.

One signficant advantage of the detachable box magazine is that the shooter can purchase additional magazines and carry them, loaded, for rapid reloading purposes.

The rotary magazine is not too common—I can only think of three rifles made today that are so equipped: the Savage 99A, F, E & DL; the Ruger 10/22 (.22 rimfire) and the Steyr-Mannlicher.

(Note: there are in existence, however, a number of military rifles which were based on the Mannlicher design and which made use of the rotary magazine.)

The rotary magazine (often referred to as a "spool" magazine) was invented by Ferdinand Ritter von Mannlicher in 1887 and has been employed in Steyr-produced rifles ever since. The primary advantage of the rotary magazine is that it positions cartridges directly in line with the chamber for loading—a feature that saves wear and tear on bullet noses.

Tubular magazines differ somewhat between rimfire and center fire rifles. In the latter, loading is accomplished through a loading gate located in the right wall of the receiver, directly below the ejection port. Such tubes are made with a self-contained spring and follower. Shells are simply fed, nose first, through the gate and into the tube. Shooters quickly learn to insert the first shell only halfway through the gate and to use another shell to push it in the rest of the way—in this manner the shooter only has to wrestle with the loading gate once—with the last shell.

Tubular magazines in rimfire rifles are made with a separate insert containing the spring and follower. To load these, the rod must be rotated (to unlock it) and removed far enough to clear the loading port in the outer magazine wall. Shells are inserted through the loading port nose-towards-muzzle and the rod slid back into place and rotated to lock it in position.

Be careful when emptying these; it's very easy for a shell to hang up, out of sight, inside the tube. Work the breech after re-installing the inner tube.

When handloading cartridges it is important to check the action of reloaded shells through the magazine. At times, if bullets are not seated deep enough, they'll jam in the magazine. Also, with some sporterized versions of military rifles, it will be found that cartridges slide forward in the magazine when the rifle recoils. Invariably this will result in damage to bullet noses. The conscientious custom rifle builder will usually add two thin vertical rails to the side walls of the integral magazine to engage cartridge shoulders and prevent such motion.

THE BOLT

In bolt action rifles, the sliding bolt is called just that—a bolt. With slide, lever or semi-automatic rifles the component that fulfills the same function is called a breech block or breech bolt.

Mauser, who invented the basic bolt system, used two large locking lugs and positioned these, one on each side of the bolt, close to the bolt face. As the bolt is operated to load or unload, these lugs slide in channels (sometimes called "raceways") cut into the inner side walls of the receiver shell.

Upon closing, the bolt handle is turned downward and this action turns the lugs into two recesses in the forward receiver ring, locking the breech for firing.

The distance that a bolt handle must arc (up and down) influences the speed with which the bolt may be manipulated. Some military versions have a 90° swing, which is considered excessive. Modern bolt action designers have come up with

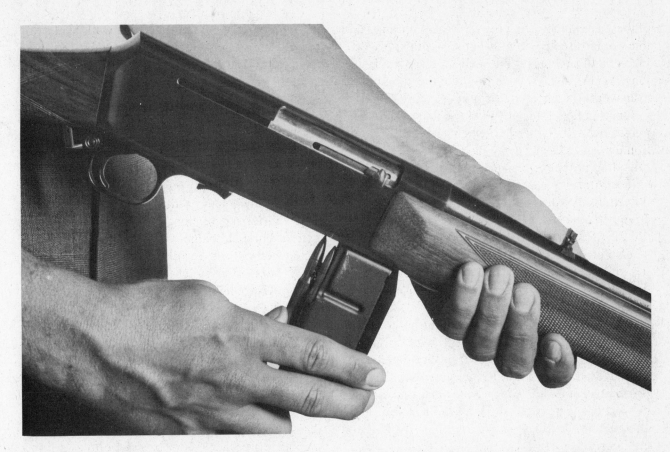

The Browning automatic rifle uses a detachable box magazine.

a series of smaller bolt lugs (sometimes located toward the rear of the bolt body) which, when grouped at 120° angles around the bolt body, reduce the swing arc to about 45°. Interestingly, the smaller lug system provides considerably more bearing surface than the older, and larger, Mauser double lug arrangement.

Fore and aft travel of the bolt likewise influences speed of operation. Ideally, this travel is only slightly greater than the overall length of the cartridge employed. However, because we have such a great variety of cartridge lengths, no manufacturer can afford to make the multitude of receiver and bolt lengths that would best suit them individ-

ually. Thus, with some smaller, or shorter cartridges, you'll often find a little extra bolt travel.

When the bolt handle is rotated up or down, at some point in that motion it must cock the action for subsequent firing. Most bolts cock on the closing stroke, and this is as it should be. For reasons that I cannot fathom, Steyr has always favored a bolt that cocks on the opening stroke of the handle. When coupled with a slightly stubborn casing, this feature can sometimes prove difficult. It's considerably easier to cam a bolt handle downward against cocking resistance.

Bolt faces were, for many years, simply flattened off to engage the base of the cartridge. Today, rifle designers strive to recess them and, in this manner, are able to enclose the head of the cartridge where

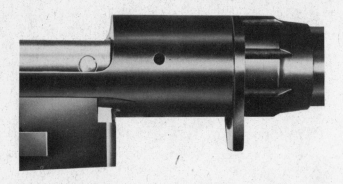

Gas ports (the small hole in the forward receiver ring, above) are designed to siphon off escaping gas when things go awry in the chamber.

it protrudes from the chamber. A much improved gas seal results and the rifle is infinitely safer.

While on the subject of gas seals let's discuss gas ports. These are those puzzling little holes that you'll sometimes spot in the forward receiver ring. (Some rifles are made with gas ports in the bolt body.) At any rate, they're intended only as a safety feature; if one should suffer a ruptured casing upon firing, gas ports should siphon off a portion of the escaping gas. Bear in mind that excessive breech pressure can, if directed entirely against the bolt face, shear the lugs on a bolt and drive it rearward out of the action. Before you get into a flap over this comment, let me add that it takes a rather horrendous pressure to do this. Also, most rifles are made with a bolt handle that will act as a third, reserve, safety lug.

Incidentally, when altering military bolts for scope mounting purposes, be careful to relieve the bolt handle where it abuts the receiver; you don't want this engagement substituting for that of the lugs.

When we speak of chamber pressures of 50,000 p.s.i., we don't mean to imply that the bolt face is subjected to this great pressure—it's not! For one thing, the bolt face is considerably smaller than one square inch and, secondly, the base area within

the cartridge case is smaller still. Pressure on the bolt face rarely exceeds three or four thousand pounds—all other factors being normal.

Pressure on the bolt face can be inadvertently increased by: one, overloading a cartridge; two, by suffering a case head separation upon firing (overload, excessive headspace, tired and brittle casing) or three, by forgetting to remove the sizing lubricant from the body of the cartridge case after handloading. It is very important that cartridge cases are clean and DRY—not oiled or lubricated in any fashion. (For the same reason, keep the chamber of your rifle clean and dry!)

EJECTORS AND EXTRACTORS

Some bolts and breech blocks are made with a simple groove in the left wall. The ejector is powered by a leaf spring and mounted inside the left wall of the receiver. As the bolt travels rearward, the ejector will slide in the groove until it meets the base of the cartridge. Upon contact, the cartridge is thrown out through the ejection port.

Other rifles are designed with ejectors built into the face of the bolt.

The plunger-type ejector (the button located next to the firing pin hole in this photo) actually aids accuracy! Bolt is from a Remington 700 rifle.

Of special interest here is the plunger type ejector now widely used on bolts having recessed faces. These provide a mild pinching action that ejects the spent case upon removal from the chamber— the extractor is pulling one side of the case toward the bolt face while the ejector, on the opposite side, is employing a pushing action. Not only do these work well, it appears to me that they are unusually durable.

Another little-known advantage of the plunger type ejector is that it AIDS ACCURACY! When a cartridge is chambered, the ejector plunger tends to push it forward so that it meets the stopping point of the shoulder or rim. This, then, eliminates the cushioning effect that would be given the firing pin if the case still had some forward travel remaining. The result, with the plunger type ejector, is a solid resistance to the firing pin blow and faster, surer ignition.

Extractors are simply designed to pull fired casings from the chamber. Don't confuse extraction with ejection. Ejectors throw extracted cases out of the action.

FIRING PINS, STRIKERS, SPEEDLOCK ACTIONS

It is a firearms industry custom to refer to any primer-striking device as a firing pin. However, since each of us is entitled to some eccentricities, I like to excercise one of mine by differentiating between pins that are hammer-powered and those that are spring-powered. To me, a pin that is struck by a hammer is a "firing pin"—one that is spring-powered is a "striker."

(No, . . . I'm not on the sauce!) Quite simply, I think separation of the two tells the buyer something about the action of a given weapon.

By way of explanation, let's discuss that vague term "speedlock." This is a description used for an action that was designed to minimize the delay between let-off and ignition. *There is no specific measured time for a "speedlock" action.* True, the time element can be critical, insofar as performance is concerned, but rarely will anyone other than a competition target shooter be aware of it. To him, a speedlock does have special significance.

If one anaylzes the motions of the various components comprising a firing mechanism, it will be seen that the trigger moves a sear, the sear disengages from a hammer (or striker), causing the hammer to fall against a firing pin. The firing pin then travels to the primer. With a striker mechanism the hammer is eliminated; the sequence is trigger, sear, striker. Obviously fewer moving parts would tend to speed the action. However, since this description is overly simplified for demonstration purposes, we must realize that other components are added to create light, crisp, no-creep trigger pulls. In fact, with set triggers, a spring-powered lever is often interjected between the trigger and the sear.

Finally, we come to the conclusion that lock time is the total time required for each component to fulfill its function. If a striker eliminates the need for a hammer, it follows that a striker mechanism would tend to be faster. That's why I prefer to differentiate between striker and firing pin.

Firearms designers who strive to shorten lock time do so by minimizing motion, by shortening the travel of the striker and by making lightweight strikers. Engaging surfaces, too, are kept to a minimum.

The nose contour of a striker or firing pin, and the depth to which it will indent a primer, are two very important factors that should not be treated lightly. When replacing a worn or broken firing pin, or when taking up handloading, the shooter should take pains to check these features. Replacement firing pins/strikers should really be fitted by a competent gunsmith rather than simply substituted for the worn or broken part. At times, if too sharply pointed, or too long, firing pins/strikers will tend to puncture primers and this is not a healthy condition.

Manufacturers have specific measurements for the desired depths of primer indentation; however the shooter can do a pretty fair job of gauging this for himself if he compares the shape, size and smoothness of the indentation with the configuration of his firing pin.

There should be no roughness or cratering surrounding the indent. Also, the diameter of the indent should approximate the diameter of the firing pin or striker body at the base of the nose. If the indent is considerably smaller, the firing pin is either too short (worn) or too weakly powered (tired spring). Above all, the indent should appear to be smoothly dimpled.

With rimfire rifles, the striker is generally made with a chisel-nose (oblong, square edge). This, too, should result in a smooth, though clearly defined, depression in the rim of the case.

Dry-firing—snapping a firing mechanism when the chamber is empty—is a bad practice that we're all taught to refrain from. When we must test the action of a trigger, an empty spent casing should be placed in the chamber to cushion the fall of the firing pin. With rimfire rifles, the practice of dry-firing is especially frowned upon because the nose of a firing pin will peen a portion of the chamber that abuts the rim of the chambered cartridge case.

LEVER ACTIONS

Winchester, who produced the first lever action rifle (or carbine, if you prefer) about 100 years ago, has been imminently successful with this form of action.

The Model 94, for example, is a slim, trim, flat-sided weapon that is fast, handy and ideally suited to scabbard travel.

Nevertheless, over the last few decades scope-sighting and handloading have gained considerable popularity and the Winchester Models 94 and 64 accept neither one gracefully. These actions lack the strength to chamber a slightly swollen casing and, if they should manage to close on a stubborn round, extraction and ejection could prove balky.

Ironically, it is a characteristic of these actions to enlarge casings. Also, their top ejection eliminates the possibility of mounting a scope in the usual manner; the scope must be offset to one side of the action or a special long eye-relief scope must be employed and this is positioned over the barrel, in front of the receiver.

Acknowledging these shortcomings the Winchester people went to work on a new form of lever rifle that would offer the most desirable traits of the 94 without the handicaps. The Model 88 resulted. The 88 has side ejection, a detachable clip magazine, a short-throw lever, is tapped and drilled for a top mount, and has a new form of breech block that locks up much like a bolt does. More importantly, the Model 88 is made in some modern high-velocity calibers and it is equipped with a one-piece stock for accuracy. Needless to say, the new breech block arrangement prevents swelling of the fired casings and they're highly reloadable.

Marlin's 336 series ejects from the side so scope mounting is not difficult. The principal problem with this action is that it does not lend itself to many of our more popular high-velocity calibers. Marlin's current selection includes only the 30/30, .32 Special, .35 Remington, .44 Magnum and .444 Marlin.

Apparently there are some brush hunters who like the old .45–70 cartridge because Marlin recently introduced a Model 1895 lever action rifle (somewhat similar to the Model 336) in this caliber.

With lever action rifles I can't help being partial to the Savage Model 99. This rifle has a massive breech block that locks well and a spool type mag-

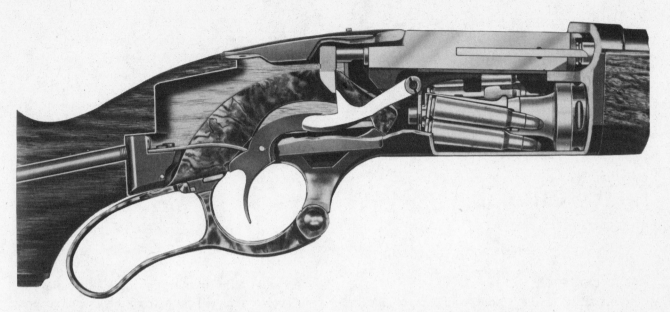

The Savage 99 has long been a favorite of lever action enthusiasts. This cut-away view shows details of lever, trigger, bolt, safety and magazine.

azine that feeds well. And, because it ejects to the side, it doesn't resist scope mounting. Most experienced riflemen will favor the one-piece stock of Winchester's Model 88 over the two-piece version employed by Savage. Normally, I would too! However, I've had sufficient opportunity to test a number of 99's on the range and I've never found accuracy lacking. Finally, the Model 99 may be had in .243, .284 and .308 as well as their traditional .300 Savage caliber.

SLIDE ACTIONS

Shooters who frown on semi-automatic rifles usually overlook the "pump" action and go to the lever when they want speed of fire. This is a mistake—the "pump" action is actually faster than the lever. Also, operation of a slide doesn't disturb the aim as much as a lever will.

With Remington's Model 760 and Savage's Model 170, there is no scope-mounting problem since both eject to the side. Reloaders, however, have to full-length size their cases to prevent feeding and extraction problems.

BREAK-OPEN TYPE RIFLES

Shotgun style rifles of the side-by-side, over and under or Drilling type can be made to accept a rifle scope but, as I stated earlier, scopes are rarely installed on heavy African-size double rifles. They are rather commonly employed on Drillings.

With this form of action, it's possible to get a fairly good trigger pull but the shooter will often find that there is a certain inconsistency between the pulls of two triggers mounted in one action or between the two separate pulls of a single trigger that operates two barrels.

Obviously, with break-open guns, loading of the chamber must be accomplished by hand so anyone reloading for guns of this type has to take pains with sizing operations. Ejection, too, can be problematical and, for that reason, makers generally try to tout buyers into calibers that are served by rimmed center fire cases.

In the following chapters we'll discuss the specifics of rifles for varmint, deer and dangerous game.

CHAPTER 4

The Stock

THE RIFLE STOCK

Read most anyone's advertising for a rifle or shotgun and you'll find terms like "Circassian Walnut," "European Walnut" or "American Walnut" used to describe wooden components.

Actually, there are two major species of walnut tree used in gunmaking—the American black walnut and the English walnut. The English walnut tree originated in China (should really be called "Chinese Walnut") and is grown throughout most of Europe. English walnut grown in Circassia is termed "Circassian Walnut;" in France, —"French Walnut" etc.

It is characteristic of the wood of any tree to reflect, in its grain, the conditions prevalent during its growth. When a walnut tree, for example, is grown in an arid region, in poor soil, and under difficult weather conditions, its wood will be densely grained and generally figured attractively because of the gnarls and curls of the trunk.

The same species, grown in good soil with adequate water and temperate weather conditions, will grow rapidly—tall and straight—and generally uninteresting for stock purposes. The wood will lack color and figure. Its grain will be rather porous, eliminating the possibility of fine-line checkering. Weight, too, will be considerably lighter after kiln-drying. The best stock blanks, from such a tree, will come from the lower extremity of the trunk where it joins the root system or from a crotch area where the trunk is divided or joined by a large limb.

An interesting little footnote on this walnut dissertation is that American walnut growers grafted black walnut trunks to English walnut root systems when the former were hit by a blight. (English walnut was apparently impervious to the blight.) Throughout northern California can be seen large orchards of these walnut grafts. The few stock blanks I've seen, taken from the grafted areas of these trees, were really exceptional.

Why walnut? Aren't there other woods suitable for stock-making?

There are, but fewer acceptable woods than one would tend to believe.

In gunstock making, we are looking for an unusual combination of many features. Walnut comes closest to filling the bill!

For instance, weight—we need a wood that is not too heavy, nor too light. After carving a suitable handle for that new rifle—and that is what a stock really is—we must arrive at a point where the finished product will complement the balance of the entire rifle unit. Balance is very important to the shooter and hunter. If the wood were too light, we'd have to design a large, cumbersome stock to get the desired balance. Too heavy, and the stock would be inadequate as a handle and barrel stabilizing device.

Weight factors, therefore, eliminate a lot of potential gunstock woods.

Durability—gunstocks are subject to a great deal of abuse. The wood must be hard enough to take it with only surface blemishes. Strong enough too, to resist checking, cracking and splitting. Grain should be very dense for two reasons—first, to resist absorption of moisture and, second, so that fine checkering and carving, employed for ornamental purposes, will hold up under use.

Stability—warping would ruin a stock. Can you imagine how a shooter would feel after spending a considerable sum to get a stock carved precisely to his dimensions, if the stock bowed one way or the other, or the comb should warp out of alignment, or the fore end twist to one side—pressuring one side of the barrel?

Appearance—the average shooter takes pride in the appearance of his firearms. When not actually in use, they are often displayed on a wall rack or in a glass-doored cabinet. Stocks then, must have figure and coloring for eye appeal.

Workability—while not for the shooter's benefit (unless one would want to consider the cost of time and labor), the gunstock blank must be easy to cut and shape. Rough inletting is accomplished by power tools but, with any fine gun, there's a highly skilled craftsman who must accomplish the final fit with chisels, files and sandpaper.

Why walnut? Because soft woods are too porous, soft and fragile. Beech and birch have some good physical properties, but they lack weight and color and often do not checker well. Mahogany is too heavy and doesn't cut as neatly as walnut in fine areas. Some maples have excellent properties but are very difficult to work, and are too light in color for some tastes.

It should be noted, however, that beech wood is often used for stocks on inexpensive weapons.

Mesquite, from the American West, is a surprisingly good substitute for walnut. The major difference is in color—Mesquite is a blond wood —but it can't be criticized for this because it does have some dark grain and gives a firearm a refreshingly different look, one that is attractive to many.

Some really beautiful exotic woods, while not suitable for whole-stock making, serve well for ornamental purposes. Ebony, jarrah, rosewood, cocobolo and zebrawood are representative of these and can often be found in pistol grips, grip caps and fore end tips.

DRYING & CUTTING OF STOCK BLANKS

When the logs are delivered to the mill a decision must be made on how they are to be cut—plain sawn or quarter sawn.

Plain sawn is the common cut for all woods; a log is fed into a large saw and simply slab cut so that it will yield the maximum number of boards of a given thickness.

Quarter sawing is considerably more complicated, and more expensive.

Here the mill operator is cutting toward the heart of the log, at an angle that will result in a grain that quarters through the blank. Hence the name "quarter-sawn." Yield is much reduced and the log must be manipulated frequently to achieve the desired angle for each cut. The waste factor, too, is high.

Why go to all this trouble and expense; wouldn't a plain sawn blank suffice?

The trouble with plain sawn blanks is that the length and direction of the grain tends to be too uniform—a condition that can result in warping. The first cuts of the log would yield blanks having an almost perfectly uniform vertical grain. As cutting progresses, the grain would tend toward the horizontal (in the center of the log) and back to vertical at the far side. Also, because characteristics vary from the heart to the bark, plain sawn blanks would consist of large portions of one type of grain. Figuring would be downright ugly, consisting of large areas of edge grain and comparable areas of flat grain.

With quarter sawing the grain runs diagonally through the blank. No two parallel lines are the same length. Wood characteristics vary greatly because we're cutting diagonally across the growth rings. Figuring is enhanced by the mix of edge and flat grain. In a nutshell, the quarter sawn blank is far more stable and attractive.

After cutting, blanks are either stacked in a crisscross pattern or laid on spacer strips to permit an air flow around each blank while in the kiln.

Drying techniques, kilns, and timing vary greatly, depending upon the wood, the kiln equipment and the fussiness of the kiln operator. Frank Pachmayr, a Los Angeles located master-gunsmith and manufacturer, deals extensively in fine California walnut. I'm told that some of his blanks spend two years undergoing the drying procedure that Frank insists upon.

Another kiln operator told me that with some of the latest kiln equipment it's possible to dry a stock blank in a matter of days. Other estimates of kiln time that I've tripped across range from weeks, to months, to years!

While this gets rather confusing, I think what all of these people are saying is that with fast-drying, the kiln operator expects to lose a percentage of his blanks. When dried too fast some blanks will develop extreme checks and cracks which will render them useless. The slower and gentler the drying procedure, the lower will be the percentage of loss, or waste. Certainly, if I had a kiln full of fancy high-grade walnut I'd be very reluctant to take any chances with it! Some of those blanks can bring upwards of $150.00 on the market.

It suffices to say that drying procedures tend to change the blank dimensionally. If accomplished too quickly there's a very good possibility the blank will be ruined. Slow drying minimizes the incidence of structural flaws.

How dry must a gunstock be? A stock cannot have a zero moisture content for one very good reason: because exposure to any normal atmosphere would eventually result in some moisture penetration and this would change the stock dimensionally.

Now that I've placed the cart in front of the horse, I'd better jump ahead to explain something about stock finishing. Many shooters labor under the notion that a proper stock finish eliminates the possibility of moisture absorption. Not so! It is virtually impossible to prevent the gradual interchange of atmosphere in wood with that of its environment. Wood *breathes,* and there's no way to prevent it. Even as one applies a lusty stock finish the wood can be absorbing moisture.

Gunstock makers simply strive to reduce moisture levels in the blanks to the average levels anticipated when in the hands of the ultimate user.

This runs anywhere from extremes of 6% to 12%. The average finished stock seems to have about an 8% moisture content.

Oftentimes a shooter will buy a new rifle or shotgun and will find the stock splitting (usually near the tang) after only a few months. Irate, because he believes the split was caused by faulty workmanship, he goes after the manufacturer hammer-and-tong. Actually, the manufacturer has no way of anticipating the unusal and extreme conditions to which the user may subject the stock. True, an occasional stock can have a flaw that escapes detection while undergoing manufacture, or a craftsman can have a bad day and overlook the cut that relieves the tang, but nine times out of ten, the fault is caused by atmospheric conditions after leaving the plant.

Homes heated via gas hot-air systems are primary culprits. This form of heating unit removes the little natural moisture that remains in the internal atmosphere. It drys out stocks and shrinks them to the point where splitting is almost inevitable.

My own home is so heated and, believe me, it raised hell with my gun collection until I added a humidifer to the system.

What can be done to prevent faults?

First, when a firearm has been stored for any length of time it should be examined carefully before subsequent use. Above all, retighten the stock fasteners. Look for swelling in the tang area and if some swelling is obvious, the wood at that point should be relieved. (The "tang" is that area where the wood abuts the rearmost surfaces of the receiver.)

Unless the shooter has the knowledge and skill to accomplish this task, he should seek the services of a good local gunsmith.

Gun owners who reside in unusually dry areas, like the desert country of Arizona, or wet and humid areas like portions of Louisiana or Florida, should be particularly careful with their gunstocks.

In summing up the stock blank, I am compelled to put down another erroneous notion common among laymen. Generally, the stock with the plainest and straightest grain is usually the strongest and the most apt to be flaw free. The fancier the grain the more likely it is to have some surface checks and imperfections. Because you've just laid out $150.00 for that stock blank with figuring like a briar pipe, you can't assume nor expect that you'll get a perfectlly flawless piece of wood! Before you have a chance to get all lathered up, let me hasten to add that surface blemishes are easily filled, repaired and covered during the finishing processes so that the completed work can be made to *appear* perfect. As long as the blank doesn't have any deep sub-surface checks and cracks it will make up into a handsome stock.

A friend of mine once set about refinishing the stock of a truly beautiful side-by-side shotgun of a well-known quality maker. When the old finish came off it was joined by a dime-sized piece of filler that had covered a flaw in the very center of one of the butt panels.

My friend was throwing a veritable fit in his workshop when I happened upon the scene. For over an hour I attempted to calm him down and along the way I used every argument I could think of to restore his faith in the gun and the maker. In the final analysis, my friend admitted that the fault could be refilled and covered but complained that his feeling toward the gun would change because he now knew the *fault was there!*

One can't expect perfection from nature—it's the many little imperfections that make it all so interesting!

PLOTTING THE STOCK

Blanks are usually cut to generous proportions so there's plenty of leeway for positioning a template to get the desired grain angles through the grip and forearm areas of the stock.

The most important decision influencing this phase has to do with the style and type of stock desired. One must determine whether it is to go on a featherweight, medium-weight, varmint, a target or benchrest rifle. Cheekpieces, grip angles, forearm styling etc., are other considerations. If the rifle is to be used with a scope, the comb of the stock should be high enough to position the face properly at scope height. When only open sights are expected, the comb should be considerably lower. Some rifle makers design sloping combs to accommodate either form of sighting equipment.

In plotting the stock on the rough blank, the craftsman wants to avoid short pieces of grain in certain critical areas. Also of primary importance is the direction of the grain through the pistol grip area: if the grain from the butt section tends to end at the pistol grip, the stock will be very weak in this area and highly susceptible to breaking. Grain should flow in a continuous line from the butt section, *through the grip,* and into the forearm for maximum strength.

When an ornate grip shape is desired, the direction of the grain at the lower—and often delicate—extremity of the grip must be planned carefully. Grip caps can help prevent trouble in this area.

In the chapter on the rifle barrel, we explained that a barrel vibrates in an up-and-down motion upon firing. The stock, therefore, is used to dampen this motion and stabilize the barrel in such a way that it returns to the same at-rest position between firings. Thus, the forearm is expected to resist this motion. To best accomplish this, the grain in the forearm should be angled slightly upwards—toward the barrel. If it angles in the opposite direction there's a chance that it will take a "set" *away* from the barrel. In a rifle designed with a free-floating barrel, this point isn't overly important. It does, however, have special significance when intended for a rifle having a pressure-bedded lightweight barrel.

INLETTING THE STOCK

Like everything else in gunmaking, there's an art to fitting a stock to a rifle. I've never ceased to be fascinated by the skill of a truly fine stockmaker at work. On one occasion I asked such a craftsman what he "looked for" in cutting the wood to the shape of the metal. He replied, "I want to make it look as though I stuck the metal in the ground and let the tree grow around it!"

The man who inlets a fine rifle really has to accomplish more than simply getting that hunk of wood fastened to the metal. He tries to minimize weaknesses. He keeps the caliber and anticipated recoil in mind and he strives to relieve the bearing surfaces in areas where the metal portions may conceivably cause splits or cracks when the rifle is fired. He strives to design the inletting in such a way that predetermined "strong" surfaces abut the metal snugly to absorb the shocks of recoil, thus sparing more fragile configurations. As you can imagine, the technique varies greatly from one type of rifle to another, as well as from one stock design to the next.

From the user's point of view, all of this leads up to the point that the quality of the fit must be preserved if the stock is to be maintained in good condition. So, when cleaning the rifle, separate the wood from the metal, clean the *stock* too! Look for hairline cracks, roughened inner surfaces and discolorations. Re-seal the inner stock surfaces with a *thin* coat of sealer, or at least, oil or wax the inner surfaces.

CHECKERING

The quality of checkering is measured by its fineness, the purity of configuration of the individual diamonds, the design of the overall pattern, the bordering method employed and, finally, the number of imperfections apparent to the eye.

The fineness of checkering is determined by the number of lines that is cut within one inch. This, unfortunately, is not always within the realm of the craftsman to decide. The density of the wood itself frequently provides the limitations. One can't carve a 24 or 26 line pattern in a coarse and porous piece of wood. The diamond structure simply shreds and crumbles. In such cases, a coarser pattern of 16 to 18 lines to the inch is executed.

The configuration of the individual diamond should be sharply defined with four distinct pyramiding flats capped by a sharp point.

In laying out the pattern a skilled artisan tries to complement the natural profile lines of the overall stock shape. Often it is necessary to modify existing patterns to suit the needs of the individual piece.

It is a general concept in the firearms trade that the best of checkering patterns are borderless.

Fine hand checkering is quite costly. You'll only find it, today, on custom rifles like these: (top) Remington 700 "custom" and (bottom) Pedersen Series 3000 Presentation Grade.

Most craftsman feel that borders are employed to cover errors. Certainly, it is far more difficult to cut a borderless pattern but, to my mind at least, the degree of execution difficulty is not always a valid measure for what is appealing ot the eye.

Checkering imperfections generally consists of irregular lines, run overs at the edges, shredded diamond peaks, distorted diamonds or lack of line depth near the borders.

Use a toothbrush to clean checkering and be careful to avoid filling patterns with finishing preparations such as oil, sealers or wax. Use such preparations carefully and sparingly in checkered areas and be sure to brush them in with the tooth-brush, removing all excess material immediately.

Truly fine hand checkering is very, very costly. Understandably so, because the work requires the painstaking services of a really skilled expert. Patterns are not easily cut. One stock, checkered with an ornate and extensive pattern, can take a number of days to complete. Consequently, a charge of $100.00, or more is not unusual. The point is, one can't condemn a rifle selling for $175.00 because the checkering is missing, machine cut or coarse. If you want fine hand checkering you'll have to pay for it. Don't expect to find it on any rifle selling for less than four to five hundred dollars.

American gunmakers have spent considerable sums of money to develop substitute methods for producing attractive and inexpensive simulated

While not hand checkered, attractive patterns like this basket weave on a Remington Model 742 have come from manufacturer's efforts to find a less-expensive substitute.

checkering. The results of their efforts can be found in countless popularly priced rifles and shot-guns.

THE IMPORTANCE OF STOCK FIT

I hate to see any rifle (or shotgun) sold with a factory-installed recoil pad. This seemingly bonus feature often robs the consumer of the ability to custom fit his firearm to his own physical require-ments. It is easy to shorten a stock—if that's what is required—but how does one add to the length of a stock that has already been shortened to ac-commodate a recoil pad?

When you've bought that sparkling new rifle—hopefully sans recoil pad—take it to a good local gunsmith. He'll measure you for stock length, check the pitch of the butt, determine eye-relief position (especially if you plan to mount a scope) and ascertain whether or not the stock should be shortened to compensate for the heavy clothing you might wear while hunting. For this last reason, it's a good idea to bring your heavy hunting jacket with you for the fitting.

If you've never had a stock so fitted you'll be amazed at how much better you'll perform with the customized rifle.

This may sound like an expensive procedure. It isn't, unless you have some special problem that

requires an unusual solution. Generally, the gun-smith simply has to cut the butt and reinstall the plate or fit a new recoil pad. Rarely will the cost for this work exceed twenty dollars. Often it can be accomplished for considerably less. It could be the best investment you'll make in that new rifle!

STOCK FINISHES

I've dreaded this particular portion of this book because, here, I have to delve into the proverbial "can of worms."

Shooters have their own ideas of what a stock finish should consist of and rarely will you find a man who will accept the objective solution of the knowledgeable firearms fraternity.

First, you must concede that a firearm—rifle or shotgun—is essentially a functional tool. As such, it is designed for use and is subject to a certain amount of wear. The stock is the one component that quickly shows the signs of having been used in the field. Scratches, nicks, gouges, etc., are in-evitable.

Now, if a man buys a rifle only for display purposes it will look great with a high-gloss-finished stock while hanging on his wall rack. But, take this fragile glossy finish into the field and it will look like the remnant from a bargain-base-ment sale in short order.

At one time gloss finishes were created with French polish (shellac, linseed oil and alcohol) or with assorted preparations consisting primarily of varnish. These were exceedingly fragile.

Today, most makers use a form of epoxy finish

which is considerably tougher. Nevertheless, even the toughest of epoxy finishes can be marred and they are extremely difficult to repair.

While most tradesmen will agree that a plain oil finish is the most practical, the public won't buy it! "It's too dull," "lacks sparkle," "doesn't show up well on the gun rack," "makes the rifle look cheap," are some of the objections most often encountered. So, when a gunmaker is obliged to consider the investment he has in his products, he can't afford to disagree with his potential customer.

There are some who think that an oil finish is created by simply applying numerous coats of boiled linseed oil to raw wood, rubbing each coat in, vigorously, by hand. Actually, the stock must first be whiskered (repeatedly moistened, dried, and sanded until the surface grain can no longer be raised). Then it is sealed and filled. Filling of the many tiny pores in the surface is necessary to attain the smoothness required for subsequent finishing. Finally, a carefully prepared mixture of oil and driers is applied. A true oil finish takes weeks to complete because the oil must be applied frequently with long drying periods between each coat.

Some gloss can be attained with an oil finish, although it tends to be more satin finish than bright gloss. The beauty of a true oil finish is that it is easily repaired. Nicks, scratches, etc., are sanded out with an extra fine sandpaper and the blemish simply re-oiled and rubbed down. Surface dents, too, can be raised by placing a wet cloth over the spot and heating it with an iron. When "up," simply sand and oil.

A genuine oil finish may not be as eye-catching as an epoxy gloss at the time of purchase but I'd like to see which firearm the average shooter would select after they've both seen a couple of season's use.

Whatever stock finish you select, or settle for, it pays to wax it thoroughly before taking it into the field. Use a paste wax and get it into every nook and cranny. When dry, buff it down with a soft cloth to restore the sheen. This will help the stock to shed moisture and will give it some protection against nicks and scratches.

WHAT STYLE STOCK?

There are many facets to a rifle stock. Each individual feature is selected for a specific purpose. Rather than examine the stock as a whole unit, it is easier, and more understandable to go over it feature by feature.

Weight and bulk If you're interested in a benchrest rifle, you can settle for a huge block of wood shaped only in the grip and comb area to facilitate shooting. Weight is limited only by the National Benchrest Association rules. At the other extreme, a rifle planned for mountain hunting should be as light as possible. Ultimate use, therefore, is the primary consideration. The accompanying illustrations will give you some idea of the sizes and shapes generally used for each purpose.

The forearm When pressure-bedding a lightweight barrel, a bit more body and stiffness is required of the forearm. A free-floated barrel can get by with a smaller forearm. When position shooting is anticipated with a sling, bear in mind that sling tension will put some pressure on the forearm so a little extra bulk is acceptable. In length, the forearm should support slightly less than half the length of the barrel. For example; if a barrel measures 22 inches in length, the forearm should be 9 to 10 inches long; with a 24-inch barrel the forearm should measure no more than 10½ inches.

The grip Sharp, right-angle grips that position the hand and trigger finger for a straight back trigger pull look rather classy but they're not practical on anything but a massive target stock. On a slender hunting stock they're an ugly protuberance. Grips are designed to blend into the overall shape and size of the stock. Wood grain, too, in-

Browning lever action rifle (top) is designed with a minimum of wood—no pistol grip, small fore end, and both are very narrow in cross section. This is a lightweight design.

Weatherby rifle (second from top) is a bit heavier. Here you'll note pistol grip and cheekpiece but, the narrow cross-section remains to cut down on overall weight—see slender forearm.

The Remington 700 BDL Varminter (second from bottom) is considerably heavier. Here, the pistol grip is fuller and the entire stock—especially the forearm—is heavier in cross-section.

The Anschutz Model 1407 (bottom) illustrates the bulky contours of the target stock. Now the pistol grip is at right angles to the bore (for a straight-back squeeze) and the weight of the forearm and butt is obvious. A benchrest rifle would be still heavier: that portion of the stock in front of the trigger guard would consist of a big, squared, block of wood.

A straight grip, like the one on this Marlin 336T, makes for a fast handling brush rifle, but positions the trigger finger awkwardly.

fluences grip pattern because it's not a good idea to have a grip with a self-contained portion of the grain. Rather, grip grain should be a continuation of butt grain.

When highly portable and fast-handling qualities are desired in the finished rifle, the stock is often made with a straight grip. This is one of the features that has contributed so much to the success of the Winchester 94 lever action c▓▓le.

The problem with a straight grip is that it positions the hand and trigger-finger rather awkwardly.

The cheekpiece These come in all sizes and shapes—some practical, some grotesque.

In a big bore-hunting rifle I look for a cheekpiece that has a fairly straight top line and one whose comb is well rounded and comfortable. I abhor the Whelen-type cheekpiece because it's too small and usually accompanied by a narrow and sharply dropping comb. Recoil is one thing, but a sharply pitched-down stock tends to magnify muzzle-jump and, to me, a blow under the cheekbone from a narrow comb is far more painful than any recoil I'll experience at the shoulder.

With a target rifle one can have a very generous dished cheekpiece. Here, I prefer one that tends to position the face in one particular spot.

With magnum rifles the shooter should be very fussy. Here I prefer a cheekpiece that slopes very slightly inward. Upon firing, this shape tends to pull away from the face. If you plan to mount a

scope on the magnum, be especially careful to avoid a cheekpiece that forces you to stretch your neck. If you have to move your head forward to obtain proper sight alignment, you could be dangerously reducing the eye-relief distance. Nothing smarts like the impact of a scope against the brow!

Butt section There are three important considerations here. Is the butt section long enough? What is the size and shape of the butt, itself, where it contacts the shoulder? How is the butt pitched?

While we must concede that the butt portion of the stock should be in tasteful balance with the rest of the rifle, there is a correlation between the size of the butt and recoil effects felt at the shoulder. Recoil can be concentrated by a small shoulder bearing surface and, conversely, will not feel as harsh when spread over a large surface.

Consider the caliber of the rifle you are contemplating and compare butt sizes with other rifles in the rack.

As I stated elsewhere, I hate to see a factory-fitted recoil pad on any firearm, primarily because it indicates that the stock has already been shortened to accommodate the pad. Many shooters really don't use a pad because they're recoil sensitive, but because they need the extra length the pad will provide. In my own case, I require a 15¼-inch length-of-pull. With a standard length stock my face is almost on top of the receiver. If a given rifle is already equipped with a pad, I'll wind up with a grotesque-looking stock by the time I get the butt extended.

"Pitch" is the term used to describe the angle of the butt as it relates to the line of sight. It's com-

Here, you can see the difference between the American and European scope-mounting preferences. Weatherby (top) positions scope so that it barely extends beyond the tail of the bolt. This is important—especially in a magnum rifle.

Bottom rifle is a Model 1972 Mannlicher-Schoenauer (a new model not yet released in the U.S.A.). Scope extends halfway to the start of the comb because Europeans shoot with their heads upright. Note, too, how much higher the European version is mounted.

Differences in butt angles can also be noted here.

monly employed in shotgunning and rarely mentioned when discussing rifles because the rifleman aims more deliberately while shooting from many different positions. For these reasons rifle butts are generally cut at about right angles to the line of sight. Nevertheless, there are times when a pitch change on a rifle can prove helpful and, on these occasions, I wouldn't hesitate to delve into the shotgunner's bag of tricks.

For example, if I were assembling a true brush gun—a rifle designed to take deer at close range in heavy cover—such a rifle would normally be "pointed" rather than aimed. Proper pitch would tend to make it point naturally. Also, shooters with unusually heavy or light builds will often find that

they can't comfortably shoulder the right angle butt. Here a slight change in pitch would eliminate the stabbing action of one point of the butt when the rifle recoils.

Certain rifles, especially those used only with iron sights, lend themselves handily to this brush gun concept (Winchester's 94 & 88, the Savage 99, Remington's 760 & 742 and Marlin's 336).

To determine pitch, don the clothing you intend to wear while hunting, pick out a small target about thirty feet away, assume an erect shooting stance, tuck the butt of the rifle under the appropriate armpit, close your eyes and shoulder the gun quickly. Hold it in that position while you open your eye and note where the rifle is pointing. Try this several times. If you keep coming up too low, or high, estimate how far your muzzle would have to be moved to put you on target. This correction should be small; if you come up with one that exceeds two inches you're either doing something wrong or you have a very unusual physique. Also, if each time you sight the rifle in this fashion, you find a different alignment, sometimes high, at other times low, leave the butt alone.

When you have decided that you'd like to change the butt angle (let's say to raise the muzzle one-half inch) stand the rifle on its butt close to a vertical wall. Slide it in towards the wall until the sight or top of the receiver makes contact while the butt is flat against the floor. With a ruler, measure the distance between the wall and the top of your front sight. You'll need an assistant at this stage (equip him with a block of 2″ x 4″ and a sharpened crayon.) Now, because your present measurement is three inches and you want to raise the muzzle a half-inch, hold the end of the ruler in contact with the wall and place the front sight at the 2½-inch setting. This will raise the toe of the butt slightly off the floor. Your helper then places the block of wood flat on the floor, abutting the side of the stock, and scribes a line on the stock parallel to the top of the wood block. This line will indicate the angle you want but, since it is obviously positioned in the wrong place you have to transfer the line rearward to get the right length of pull. (Refer to the "Home Gunsmithing" chapter for details on cutting the stock and refitting the plate or pad.)

As you can see, the stock contributes heavily to the performance of a rifle. Don't select one strictly on the basis of eye appeal.

CHAPTER 5

The Deer Rifle

On the surface, the selection of a rifle for deer hunting appears to be an easy task. One can simply buy the model recommended by the local dealer or follow the suggestion of good 'ol Joe, an experienced deer hunter and distinguished member of the local hot-stove league. I doubt if either party would steer the novice far wrong. On the other hand, it's not likely that these advisers would take the time or trouble to go into the question in sufficient detail. A little extra thought beforehand can spare the novice considerable disappointment and unnecessary expense. Buying a rifle is like buying a tool—the buyer won't realize its shortcomings until he tries to put it to use.

Many of the factors that influence the selection of a rifle are not readily apparent. Perhaps I could best serve the reader by listing the more important questions together with some of the appropriate qualifying considerations:

Caliber? This is by far the most important decision. Some calibers are found only in certain types of actions, which would tend to limit the assortment one would have to choose from.

Does the hunter plan to hunt anything other than deer? (Other targets would have an influence on caliber selection.)

Is the shooter recoil sensitive? Again, the question of caliber would have to be considered from this standpoint.

How good is the hunter's eyesight? Would he need a scope? If so, rifles that do not lend themselves to inexpensive scope mounting may have to be removed from the list of prospective models. Which eye is the master eye? Is the shooter right- or left-handed?

Where does the shooter plan to hunt? What are the characteristics of the terrain?

Does he own other rifles?

Does he load his own cartridges or does he rely on the availability of factory-produced shells?

Any physical handicaps?

I could go on but I'm more concerned with answering questions than asking them. Let's get down to specifics:

Choice of caliber—Members of the deer family are not difficult to kill; under ideal conditions even the lowly .22 rimfire will kill a deer. The problem crops up when the hunter realizes that conditions

A steep downhill angle influenced the author's shot which bagged this fine ten-point muley near Melrose, Montana. (Five-point, by western count.)
Rifle was a 30/06, fired from a sitting position at about 175 yards. (Photo by Tom McNally)

are rarely ideal. Hunters must be concerned with killing their game swiftly and cleanly, sparing the game unnecessary torment and preventing the escape of a wounded animal. All possible hunting conditions must therefore be considered.

Cartridges employing small, light or slow bullets are automatically eliminated from the range of shells we'll discuss because they simply do not deliver adequate killing energy at anything beyond point-blank range. At the other extreme, shells that are too big, too powerful, often damage a disproportionate amount of the meat the hunter hopes to place on his dinner table. They have a few other disadvantages, too, that will be revealed as we go along.

Generally, the cartridges we must examine fall between 24 and 35 caliber. Bullet weight, which is indicated in grains on all ammo charts (and on the individual boxes of shells) provides a good indication of the kind of performance one can expect. For example, the .257 Roberts cartridge may be had with bullets weighing 87, 100 or 117 grains. While all three will drop a deer, I wouldn't recommend any shell loaded with a bullet weighing less than 100 grains. Light bullets, no matter how fast they're driven, are easily deflected by brush and tend to come apart on impact without achieving real penetration. Also, since impact energy is computed on the basis of weight times velocity squared, impact energy drops off greatly as velocity falls off. Bear in mind that we're using the 100 grain bullet as the lightest bullet acceptable—this is not the ideal weight. With few exceptions, cartridges using bullets of 100 to 150 grains can be used successfully in open country shooting. These are not good brush-buckers. The shooter should be careful to avoid overly long shots as well (always a temptation in open country) because even mild wind conditions will effect trajectory. The best feature of lightly bulleted cartridges is that they generally offer little in the way of recoil. Young, small or feminine shooters will like them.

The ideal bullet range for all-around deer hunting runs from 150 to 220 grains. Mixed opportunities, of open country to brush shooting, are most advantageously met with cartridges containing bullets of about 180 grains. Cartridges like the 30/06, .308 and .300 Savage are typical of these.

When heavy brush conditions are the rule, the shooter must seriously consider only cartridges made with bullets of 200 grains or more. Recoil effects may be a bit harsher but selection of a heavy rifle will tend to minimize the punch felt at the shoulder.

I must admit that I hesitated to use the bullet-weight formula for this treatise because I felt it may be confusing to the new hunter. Yet, if one examines the ballistics tables elsewhere in this volume, the choices are easily discernible.

When a tentative list of shells has been compiled however, be sure to note factory-published muzzle velocities next to each shell. For all practical purposes the deer hunter is interested only in cartridges (and case sizes) that can propel the desired bullet at reasonable velocities. By my own rule of thumb, minimum velocities are 2500 f.p.s. for bullets of 100 to 150 grains, 2200 f.p.s. for bullets of 150 to 180 grains and 1750 f.p.s. for bullets of 200 grains or more.

BOLT, PUMP, LEVER OR AUTOMATIC

These days, too much emphasis is placed on rapidity of fire. I feel this leads to sloppy shooting and often results in wounded game that is eventually lost to the hunter. On a recent Montana trip, Tom McNally (Outdoor Editor of the *Chicago Tribune*) and I came across the remains of what must have been a prize black bear specimen. Having eluded the hunter who had wounded him, he expired in a thick little draw—much to the delight of the small carnivores. What a pity the hunter did not take the time to place his first shot more carefully—or miss cleanly.

It's the first shot that usually tells the tale.

I use a form of bolt action rifle for virtually all of my hunting and shooting. They're slower than an automatic, true, but only a bit slower than a lever or slide action. (Falling-block rifles are single shot weapons so anyone using them is certainly not interested in repetitive fire.) Why a bolt? Because they're consistently more accurate than any other type (most of the target rifles used in competition are bolt actions). Only a few falling-block, single shot rifles compete with them and then generally only in small bore .22 caliber events. Most bolt action rifles accept scope mounting handily; offer about a five-shot magazine capacity; have one piece stocks that aid accuracy; have few moving parts; are easy to clean and maintain; and are found in most any caliber a shooter desires. They're strong, reliable and generally well-balanced, when properly stocked. I'll gladly sacrifice a little speed of fire for this combination of features.

Lever-action enthusiasts will be quick to scoff, saying "More deer have been bagged with lever action rifles than any other kind!"

That's true, but I suspect the relative popularity of the lever was on the wane for a time simply because this form of rifle action could not accept the broad range of new and more efficient cartridges that excited the interest of the hunter. Anyone wanting a caliber more powerful than the .35 Remington or .300 Savage had no choice but to go to another form of action.

Today, the .308, .284 and .243 have given the lever new life. The popular Savage Model 99 may be had in any of these and so, too, may the one-piece stocked Winchester Model 88.

Nevertheless, with the way our population is spreading out, once rural areas are no longer quite so rural nor wilderness areas quite so wild. There's a good possibility that many of us will have to go back to the .30–30 and .32 Special for our big game hunting if the trend continues.

Some states have already banned the rifle and limit big game hunting to shotguns using buckshot and/or rifled slugs.

If the shooter has a strong hankering for a lever gun, I'd suggest he take a long look at the Savage Model 99 or the Winchester Model 88. These models are made in some fine, modern, deer calibers. The Marlin Model 336 in .35 Remington caliber is another good alternative for the brush hunter.

You won't find many to choose from today, but the slide action—disrespectfully called "pump gun"—is an excellent woods rifle when chambered for a good cartridge. I really believe they're faster than the lever action too—if rapidity of fire is an important consideration. If you think this may be your cup of tea, look for a Remington Model 760.

While on this topic, shooters who frequently hunt with a pump shotgun may find some advantage to having a rifle that functions in the same manner.

In view of my earlier remarks about rapidity of fire, readers who may lean toward automatic rifles may be expecting some scathing commentary about here; not so! If I lived and hunted in the heavy brush country of the Mississipppi lowlands or the swamp country of Louisiana or Florida, I would probably think the automatic rifle is tops! In brush so dense that deer are visible only for a fleeting instant, it's mighty frustrating to a hunter to get off only one poorly-timed shot at a trophy buck that springs in and out of the scenery in the wink of an eyelash.

Whatever you choose, remember the primary question above all other—caliber! If you select an adequate caliber, you'll have a rifle whose per-

Rifles arranged according to rapidity of fire: (top to bottom) Ruger Number One sporter—a single shot falling block rifle; Ruger Model 77 bolt action repeating rifle; Marlin 336C lever action repeater; Savage Model 170 pump gun; Remington Model 742 automatic repeater.

A Ruger Model 44 carbine—a true brush country rifle —equipped with a Williams scope and mount.
Brush guns should be fitted with scopes of low magnifications. When using a variable-power scope (like the one illustrated) set it for the lowest magnification while hunting. Increase magnification only when there is time to do so for a shot at a stationary target.

formance will be up to your shooting ability. And regardless of your choice of action type, bear in mind that it's the first shot that usually brings home the venison. No matter how much fire-power you have at your disposal, resist the tendency to rely on it.

On sighting instruments, a few important points must be repeated here. (Sights and scopes are discussed, at length, elsewhere in this volume.)

You can only shoot as well as you can see, and a scope will help you see better. Don't hesitate to put one on that new deer rifle, especially if your eyesight isn't what it used to be. Don't however, make the mistake some hunters make—don't buy a rifle scope with high magnification. Too much magnification is more of a curse than a blessing. Target shooters understand this and are reluctant to use any more magnification than is necessary to clearly define the target. Light gathering power, resolution and field of view are greatest at the lowest magnification; they tend to diminish rapidly as magnification increases. For the heavy brush country hunter I would strongly recommend either a 1X or 2½X scope. In mixed terrain the 4X is the best all-around magnification. Western, open-country hunters can go up to six or eight power.

Some scopes are made with variable power eye pieces. These are rated 1 to 4X, 2 to 7X, or 3 to 9X, for example, meaning that power can be adjusted from 1 power up to 4 power, etc.

When hunting with a variable power scope, always set the scope for the *lowest* possible magnifi-

Left-handed shooters can use pumps, levers, automatics or bolt rifles designed specifically for left-hand operation—like this Remington Model 700 BDL.

cation. This will assure you of the largest possible field of view and greatest visibility should a sudden opportunity present itself.

Manipulate magnification upward only when you have the time to do so for a deliberate shot at a stationary target.

If you've never hunted with a scope, you won't appreciate the significance of these remarks until you've tried to sight in on a target, at close range, in dense woods, with a high magnification scope. By the time you line up on that Pennsylvania deer he could be cutting out a harem in Michigan!

Finally, if you do choose to mount a scope, don't discard the iron sights. Leave them on the rifle and by all means, zero in the rifle for both the iron sights and scope. I've met a number of disgusted hunters who favored the uncluttered look of a sightless barrel but who ran into situations where the lack of auxiliary sighting equipment ruined ther hunts. Most hunters invest too much time, money and energy in their annual deer hunt to run such unnecessary risks.

Open sights and "peep" sights can be frustrating to the riflemen with a sight problem because they require the alignment of two sighting devices that are not in the same image plane. My own problem in this area is that I cannot clearly define the outline of the rear sight. I imagine near-sighted shooters have trouble defining the front sight. A good rifle scope puts everything into one plane and greatly aids sighting ability.

VERSATILITY IN A RIFLE

Frankly, there's no such thing! Versatility is attained only through a broad selection of *ammunition*. If you've been poring over cartridge tables, go back and take a second look. Note how limited the bullet selections are for some cartridges—only one or two different weights. Now take a look at the 30/06 with a selection of six or seven. Obviously, with a broad assortment to choose from, the hunter can find a suitable cartridge for most any purpose.

If a hunter feels that he needs one rifle for a number of purposes he should, by all means, select a caliber that offers a variety of loadings.

LEFT-HANDED

This is no longer the problem that it once was; some manufacturers are now making left-handed bolt action rifles. Some actions can be a problem if they eject the spent cartridge to the right rear where they would strike the shooter.

By far, the biggest problem to the southpaw is one that is often overlooked—is the stock cut straight, or does it have a cast-off or cast-on? A stock having a cheekpiece is obviously cut for shouldering from one side. How do you determine stock line when there is no cheekpiece? Easily! Simply lay a long straight edge on a line through the sights so that a piece of the straight edge extends over the buttstock. Sight down on the comb and see if the butt cants to one side. If the butt favors the right side of the gun (as you look from butt towards muzzle) the stock is made for a right-hander. Of course, it is often possible for a left-hander to get into a sight-alignment position with such a stock but, as soon as he starts to swing the gun from one side to the other, the sights will elude alignment. The southpaw who finds himself stuck with such a stock should see his local gunsmith. Sometimes the problem can be corrected cheaply and easily. Gun makers realize that many of their levers and pumps are bought by left-handers, so they often design them with straight stocks to accommodate either side. Nevertheless, it pays to check.

Today, left-handed shooters can choose from lever actions, slide actions, left-handed bolt actions or automatics. They should be careful, however, to note the direction of the ejected round and the attitude of the stock.

RECOIL

Three factors influence the recoil felt by the shooter. These are cartridge, rifle weight and stock design. The shooter who is highly sensitive to recoil should avoid ultra-high velocity cartridges, heavy bullets, featherweight rifles and rifles having stocks that are sharply pitched down or made with a sharp comb.

Recoil effects are best minimized when the rifle is fairly heavy and when the buttstock is draped with a large, rounded comb or a slope-away cheekpiece. Also the general alignment of the stock should trace a fairly straight line behind the receiver; if the topmost stock line drops off sharply towards the butt, the rifle will generate considerable muzzle jump and the comb of the stock will hammer the shooter's cheek.

The shooter who is interested in minimizing recoil should also be wary of any cartridge that offers a heavy bullet in a large casing, at a high velocity.

Compare cartridges in your local gun shop before making a decision.

Shooting form too has a lot to do with recoil effects. When the shooter has reason to expect a healthy kick, the worst thing he can do is brace himself with a spread-legged stance and bear down on the rifle with a white-knuckle grip. Even an elephant rifle can be fired with little discomfort, if the shooter learns to relax, stay loose and ride with the punch. Just be sure to position the butt of the rifle snugly into the shoulder!

AVAILABILITY OF AMMO

The shooter who buys an exotic rifle should realize that all sizes of cartridges are not always readily available! Backwoods gun shops in Maine, Michigan or Montana stock popular cartridges—they can't be expected to have a large stock of the exotics.

The hunter who plans to do a lot of traveling should be careful to select a popular caliber or be prepared to carry a considerable quantity of surplus ammo with him!

PHYSICAL HANDICAPS

Custom gunsmiths can do wondrous things with rifles to accommodate the handicapped hunter. If you've lost an arm, an eye or the fingers from your trigger hand, you need not abandon the sport of hunting. Stocks can be cut to facilitate left-eye sighting when the rifle is right shouldered. Auxiliary trigger devices can be designed for operation with almost any finger that remains. Special light and short rifles can be made for the one-armed shooter.

By all means, if you have a physical handicap, visit a local gunsmith or *write to one* (a lot of this custom work is accomplished by mail—though your local dealer will have to handle the actual purchase for you). Leg problems are something else again, yet I've heard of one handicapped shooter *who hunted from a golf cart!*

CHAPTER 6
The Varmint Rifle

The term "varmint" is really a dialectical derivative of the proper term "vermin." So, strictly speaking, any rifle that one can use to eradicate vermin could be classified a "varmint" rifle. However, since this would cover every firearm made, the term "varmint" should be defined as "a popular hunter's target—a pest or rodent that is not protected by game laws."

Crows, woodchucks (groundhogs) and prairie dogs generally fall into this category. Depending upon regional game laws you will also find, on occasion, the fox, coyote, bobcat, lynx, opossum and raccoon with a varmint classification.

Characteristic of all these creatures is that they're all rather small and most are inedible (I've only heard of the 'chuck and 'possum reaching the dinner plate). Varmint rifles therefore tend to be of small caliber.

Because most of these targets are difficult to approach, shooting is usually attempted at respectable distances; consequently, a flat-shooting high-velocity cartridge is usually employed. Also, because the target is small and hard to hit, the true varmint rifle often has some target rifle characteristics—a target-like trigger, a fairly heavy barrel, a high magnification scope, a heavy stock, etc.

Less than minute-of-angle accuracy is sought by all varmint hunters. The noise level, too, can be important to the eastern hunter operating in farm communities.

Every varmint hunter has his own unique ideas about the features that should go into his "varminter," so there's no way for anyone to describe a particular pattern. I've seen varmint rifles that weighed seven pounds, and others that were twice that weight.

Most varminters get their start with the .22 rimfire rifle. Later, after they've taken up big game hunting, they look for ways to use their big game rifles for long-range varmint shooting. With calibers like the 30/06—which can be used with factory-made lightweight, varmint-sized bullets—they're temporarily content with the result.

Then one day they'll run into a varmint hunter equipped with a slick precision rifle that gives pinpoint accuracy up to 300 yards. Contentment goes out the window and we now have a prime candidate for a new rifle.

Let's take a look at the varmint calibers, both factory-produced and wildcat.

FACTORY LOAD VARMINT CARTRIDGES

17 REMINGTON (.172″ dia.) This cartridge uses a light, 25-grain bullet which has a muzzle velocity of approximately 4000 f.p.s.

Where noise is a factor, this is a highly desirable shell. Currently produced commercially only by Remington.

218 BEE (.224″ dia.)   An old favorite that is now being phased out of the picture by the newer and better .222 class. Factory ammo is rather expensive. It is ballistically slower than the .222 (2860 f.p.s.). Otherwise this is a consistently good performer, rather quiet in comparison to some of the hotter shells around.

.22 HORNET (.224″ dia.)   Another old-timer that has seen its heyday. Uses 45 and 46 grain bullets, in factory versions, moves them, quietly, at about 2700 f.p.s.

.222 REMINGTON (.224″ dia.)   A very popular varmint and benchrest caliber. Very accurate. Good velocity—3200 f.p.s. Doesn't scare the farmers like some of the hotter shells. Used primarily with 50 grain bullets.

.222 REMINGTON MAGNUM (.224″ dia.) A later version of the standard .222. Employs a 55 grain bullet and pushes it about 100 f.p.s. faster than the 50 grain .222. Apparently doesn't offer enough in added benefits to warrant the step up. Most shooters are sticking with the standard.

.22–250 REMINGTON (.224″ dia.)   The same .22 caliber bullet in 55 grains, but loaded into a slightly larger case (.250–3000 Savage size). Gets a velocity of 3800 f.p.s. A bit noisier but still quite acceptable. This was a popular wildcatter's shell for many years before commercial loaders picked it up.

.223 REMINGTON (5.56mm) (.224″ dia.) Very similar to the .222 Remington Magnum but on a slightly modified case. Originally developed for military use in the AR-15 rifle but likewise ideal for varmints, 3300 f.p.s.

.224 WEATHERBY VARMINTMASTER This is a unique ultra high-velocity cartridge that was first introduced about ten years back. It is made on a belted magnum case and zips a 50-grain bullet along at close to 4000 f.p.s. Only Weatherby makes a rifle chambered for this shell.

.225 WINCHESTER (.224″ dia.)   Winchester's answer to Remington's .222. Uses the same 50 grain bullet, but drives it a bit faster (3675 f.p.s.). Also, a bit noiser but not objectionably so. Employs an interesting "semi-rimmed" case which (it appears to me) is more "rimmed" than "semi."

6mm REMINGTON (.243″ dia.)   Now we're moving up to the shells that start to frighten the natives. These tend to get loud. The advantage of these larger "varmint sizes" is that they can be used for smaller deer and antelope. Most cartridges in the .243″ class are more popular with Western hunters. This one pushes a 90 grain bullet at 3150 f.p.s.

.243″ WINCHESTER (.243″ dia.)   The Winchester version of a hot 6mm has been popular since 1955. Bullet weights are 80 and 100 grains with velocities of 3265 f.p.s. and 3100 f.p.s. respectively.

.25–06 REMINGTON (.257″ dia.)   Now we're at the upper limits of shells that are popularly employed for varmint hunting. The 25 caliber is really a combination varmint and deer shell. A bit too noisy for many Eastern chuck areas. The .25–06 is factory loaded with bullets of 87, 90 and 120 grains. Muzzle velocity with the 87 grain bullet is 3500 f.p.s.

.250 SAVAGE (.257″ dia.)   This is a cartridge that reigned long, and well, but which is now past its prime. Produced with 87 grain (3040 f.p.s.) and 100 grain (2865 f.p.s.) bullets.

.257 ROBERTS (.257″ dia.)   This is about as heavy as I care to go when discussing varmint cartridges. Handles the 87 grain bullet at 3310 f.p.s. Also available with heavier bullets of 100 and 117 grain.

WILDCAT VARMINT CARTRIDGES

"Wildcats" are shells that are not commercially

Cartridge at right is a standard, factory-produced .257 Roberts. Wildcat cartridge, at left, is a .257 Ackley Improved: made by firing the Roberts shell in an Ackley chamber. Note how the shoulder and taper have been altered. What is gained? . . . a little more room for a little more powder—thus, higher velocities.

produced but, rather, custom-made by the individual handloader.

Benchrest shooters and varmint hunters are very closely allied in their search for light cartridges offering precision performance. Thus, it is to be expected that there are large numbers of wildcats in the varmint size category.

Wildcat cartridges are made by a number of different methods—some by cutting down and re-shaping existing commercial cases in special forming dies, others by simple fire-forming, still others by a combination of these basic methods.

The term "fire-forming" stems from the practice of actually shooting a particular cartridge in the chamber of a wildcat rifle. Certain critical dimensions must be common to both the wildcat chamber and the case to be re-formed. Only the shoulder angle and forward, body taper of the case can be safely altered in this manner.

Because each wildcatter is really experimenting with his own unique version of a cartridge for his own use, he is not particularly concerned with maintaining or following any specified standard for uniformity. Variations are therefore as numerous as the blades of grass on a prairie. The only way one can begin to describe them is to lump them into categories according to bullet size and case capacities. Anyone interested in one specific type will have to get detailed information from the supplier of the barrel and/or loading dies.

.17 CALIBER WILDCATS   P.O. Ackley (Salt Lake City, Utah) was probably one of the first to develop a .17 caliber wildcat, back in 1944. His is called the ".17 Ackley Bee" and it's made by necking down a .218 Bee case and fire-forming it to reshape the shoulder. Using 20 or 25 grain bullets the .17 Ackley Bee achieves velocities of 3500 to 3600 f.p.s.

Other .17 caliber wildcats are made by shortening and reshaping the .222 case or by simply re-necking the .222 to .17 diameter. Some, too, are based on the .22 Hornet case. Velocities exceeding 4600 f.p.s. have been recorded by .17 calibers made on the unshortened .222 case. I suspect that these can be rather rough on a barrel.

The would-be wildcatter can choose from versions entitled ".17 Ackley Hornet," ".17 Javelina" or ".17/.222."

I've owned and used a number of Ackley-designed wildcats and I've never had occasion to be unhappy with any of them. If you're seriously interested in the .17 caliber I don't think you could go wrong with an Ackley version.

.22 CALIBER WILDCATS   Wildcats based on the .224″ diameter bullet are the most popular with both varmint hunters and benchrest shooters. Understandably, there exists a great variety of these. Following is a list of the better known versions:

.22 K-Hornet	.22/30/30 Ackley
.218 Mashburn Bee	Improved
.22 Varminter	.219 Donaldson Wasp
.22/4000	.22/250 Improved
2R Lovell	.219 Ackley Improved
.22 Super Jet	Zipper

Experimenters habitually refer to any bullet measuring .22″ as .22 caliber. However, with these wildcats, and others, you'll often find references to a variety of bullet diameters ranging from .223″ to .2247″. It is important, especially when working with near maximum loads, to know the *precise* diameter of the bullet employed by the compiler of the loading table.

While I'm on the subject, I sincerely wish that our ammunition industry would come up with a standardized system for labeling cartridges—a system that wildcatters, too, would follow. As it stands now, who would believe that the .218 Bee, the .219 Zipper and the .222 Remington all employ bullets of similar weight and diameter? But they do! The European system, which utilizes bullet diameter and case length, is far more practical and workable.

The above-mentioned list of wildcats includes shells made from the brass of the commercial .22 Hornet, .218 Bee, .219 Zipper, .222, .25/35, .30/30, 7mm Mauser and .250/3000.

In farm country where noise can be a factor, I'd choose a cartridge made on one of the smaller cases, like the .22 Hornet or .218 Bee. Barrel life

should also be considered when contemplating one of the super-hot wildcats made on a large case.

.23, .24 & .25 CALIBER WILDCATS   This includes the following current designations:

.228 Ackley Magnum	6mm–47
.228 Belted Express	6mm Belted Express
.230 Ackley	6mm–250
.230 Ackley (short)	6mm 30/30
.257 Ackley Improved	.240 Cobra
.228 Krag	.240 Nitro
.25 Krag	.240 Super
.25–06	.243 Rockchucker
.22 Newton	.244 Rem. Improved
.240 Page	

(Here you will note that I have included a few shells which are made with .228″ diameter bullets. These really belong in neither the .224″ nor .230″ class and the shooter living in an area where big game hunting is prohibited with less than .23 caliber should be careful not to use a .228″ for this purpose. Twenty-three caliber is .230″ minimum bullet diameter.)

One could write books on the variations of .23, .24 and .25 calibers that have come down the pike in the last thirty years. It's not possible to deal with them in detail here. Whenever one puts a small, light bullet in a case having large powder capacity, he's looking for high velocity. Whether the resultant performance justifies the effort (and expense) is something else again.

From my own experience I would say that 4000 f.p.s. is not worth the effort or the expense. I've had a number of wildcats that would push bullets along at 3800 f.p.s. or better, but, strangely, none ever impressed me with their accuracy until I loaded them down to about 3500 f.p.s. With one particular rifle I stubbornly insisted on getting performance at 4000 f.p.s. Twelve hundred rounds later the barrel was burned out. Accuracy was lousy from start to finish, and I had experi-

Two popular varmint rifles made by Ruger. The Model One (falling block) rifle (top) and the Model 77 bolt action (bottom).

mented with every weight and shape of bullet I could get my hands on. I should have thrown my money down a 'chuck hole and saved myself a lot of aggravation.

Of the aforementioned wildcats, I favor the .230 Ackley (short), the .243 Rockchucker and the .257 Ackley Improved. The last shell, particularly, is a fine performer—I've been shooting one for more than ten years and it's still going strong although the throat is rather badly eroded at this late date.

The best advice I can give the shooter who is contemplating a wildcat is to contact a specialist in this field (like P.O. Ackley or Fred Huntington of R.C.B.S.) for the appropriate barrel, dies and loading data.

The beauty of .24 (6mm) and .25 caliber cartridges, whether commerical or wildcat, is that they can be used successfully on game of deer size. I've had a number of one-shot whitetail kills with both the .243 and .257.

VARMINT SCOPES

Those who want a light varmint caliber of .17 to .22 caliber should mount an 8 or 10 power scope on the rifle, preferably of fixed power with a fine crosswire reticle.

With .24 or .25 caliber rifles a variable power 3x9X scope may prove more desirable—especially if there exists a possibility that the rifle will be used for deer hunting.

Westerners using heavy, benchrest style rifles for varmint hunting may prefer larger magnifications up to 20X, in target-type scopes.

When one buys a commericial sporter rifle in a varmint caliber, he'll generally get a medium-weight rifle having a slightly heavier barrel than ordinarily used, say for deer hunting. The Winchester 70 in varmint calibers, for example, is made with a

22-inch barrel and weighs about 7½ lbs. Remington makes their Model 788 with a 24-inch barrel in .222, .22–250 and 6mm calibers and these also weigh about 7½ lbs. Remington's Model 700 BDL "Varmint Special," however, weighs about 9 lbs. in all of the popular varmint calibers. The Ruger Number One falling block rifle may be had in two versions (8 or 9 lbs.) in .22–250 caliber. H & R, too, has a variety of bolt action varminters in the 7½ to 9½ lb. weight range.

When adding a scope, mount, sling, etc., to one of these rifles the shooter can expect to add about one to one and a half pounds to the overall weight.

Varmint hunters who make up custom rifles (often in wildcat calibers) frequently exceed eleven pounds. My own custom varminter tips the scales at fourteen pounds because I used a light, target barrel rather than a sporter version. Fourteen pounds can be a bit burdensome in hilly country but I've never found it too objectionable.

As a rule, commericial triggers are surprisingly good. They're of near-match quality with crisp three to four pound pulls.

My only objection to commercial varminters (and this is due entirely to my own rather outlandish requirements) is concerned with their size— they tend to be a bit too light and a shade too short.

Because scopes are the rule rather than the exception, the shooter will have to be careful to select a stock having a fairly high comb.

The sling can be important to the position shooting often employed by the varmint hunter, so here I would prefer a military type in a 1¼ inch width. Check the swivels on that commercial rifle—you may have to settle for a 1 inch sling.

"Zeroing" the varmint rifle can be tricky because the varmint hunter wants to take advantage of any given opportunity at any reasonable range. He says, "I want to have a chance at anything up to 400 yards, but I must be careful not to overshoot anything at half that distance." Remember, too, the varmint hunter is dealing with a small target. Basically, he wants to minimize the distance between the arc of his trajectory and his line of sight over the greatest possible distance. To do this he consults his ballistics tables: If shooting a .22–250, for example, he'll find that zeroing for 200 yards will place his bullet 1.1″ above the line of sight at 100 yards, 5.3″ below the line of sight at 300 yards and 16.3″ below at 400 yards. Realizing that the accuracy of range estimation is highly questionable beyond two hundred yards, he'll experiment with a greater deviation at short range to minimize the margin of error at 300-plus yards.

Three inches, for example, is about the depth of a chuck's head and would be rather easy to estimate when sighting through scope. Now he'll determine that zeroing three inches high at 100 yards will place his bullet 1⅞″ high at 200 yards and about 3 inches low at 300 yards. Thus, any shot from 1 to 300 yards would be within the pre-determined three-inch margin. The shooter simply has to remind himself to hold low at obviously short ranges up to 220 yards and slightly high as the distance increases to 300 yards.

Because a varmint hunter can pursue his sport on a year round basis, it's a great pastime for the ardent rifleman and it's sure to sharpen his shooting skills.

CHAPTER 7

Magnum Rifles

My copy of *Webster's New Collegiate Dictionary* defines the word "magnum" as "a two-quart bottle for wine or spirits." I'm all in favor of that, but it doesn't help me to explain what a magnum cartridge is. Left to my own devices I'd have to say that it is a term that originated with British gun or ammo makers who used it to describe a particularly large and powerful cartridge.

At one time it was possible to identify magnum-type rifle cartridges by their belted cases. This no longer holds true. Today we have a .22 rimfire magnum and a .222 Magnum (both of which are unbelted), together with a host of larger, belted shells. The term "magnum" has also carried over into handgun cartridges (.357, .41 and .44 magnums) and into shotgun shells (10 ga., 12 ga. and 20 ga. magnums).

As originally applied, the term magnum served to identify a shell using a large and heavy bullet. Even this has changed—today, the term is more often applied to ultra-high velocity cartridges and, in some cases, to shells that combine bullet size with high velocity.

Following is a list of the more popular rifle cartridges that bear the magnum label:

.22 Win. Magnum	.358 Norma Magnum
.222 Rem. Magnum	.375 H & H Magnum
.6.5 Rem. Magnum	.44 Rem.* Magnum
.256 Win.* Magnum	.458 Win. Magnum
.264 Win. Magnum	.224 Weatherby Magnum
.6.5x68 RWS Magnum	.257 Weatherby Magnum
7mm Rem. Magnum	.270 Weatherby Magnum
.308 Norma Magnum	7mm Weatherby Magnum
.300 H & H Magnum	.300 Weatherby Magnum
.300 Win. Magnum	.340 Weatherby Magnum
.338 Win. Magnum	.378 Weatherby Magnum
.8x68s RWS Magnum	.460 Weatherby Magnum
.350 Rem. Magnum	

* Designed, originally, as handgun cartridges.

We could add a considerable number of shells to this list if we were to include some models for which rifles are no longer manufactured, like the .240 and .375 Weatherby, or the host of wildcat magnums that enjoy a continuing popularity. There are also a considerable number of European shells that would qualify for a magnum designa-

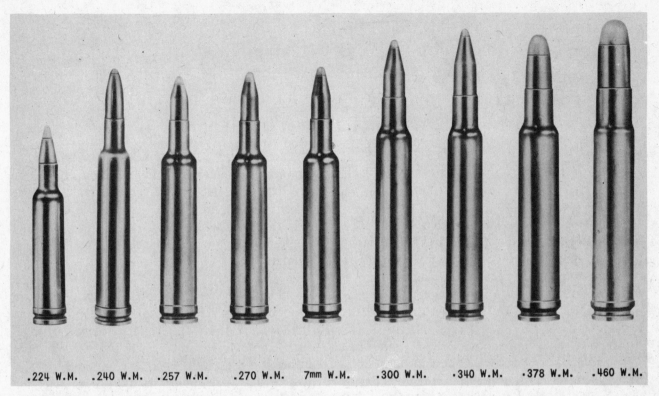

.224 W.M.   .240 W.M.   .257 W.M.   .270 W.M.   7mm W.M.   .300 W.M.   .340 W.M.   .378 W.M.   .460 W.M.

The complete line of current Weatherby Magnum cartridges, all *of which are made on belted cases.*

tion—some of these are marketed under the names Brenneke and Vom Hofe.

For one reason or another (perhaps too many imitators) British gunmakers are not consistent in their application of the term "magnum" to a powerful cartridge. It appears that the Holland & Holland firm favored the word *magnum* while others felt that the term "Express" better connoted rugged performance. There exists a great number of Express shells that could just as well have carried a magnum designation.

We list some of the more popular British magnum and express shells here:

.240 Belted Rimless Nitro-Express
.244 H & H Belted Rimless Magnum
.275 H & H Belted Rimless Magnum Nitro

7mm Rigby Magnum
.375 Flanged Magnum Nitro-Express
.404 Jeffrey Rimless Nitro-Express
.416 Rigby
.425 Westley Richards Magnum
.450 Nitro-Express
.470 Nitro-Express
.475 Nitro-Express
.505 Rimless Magnum

While we conclude the list with a .505 cartridge, this is not the largest shell recorded for a shoulder arm. There have been a number of bigger ones—up to .600 Nitro-Express. It appears that gun and ammo makers are limited only by the ability of man to endure the horrendous recoil of rifles that some would prefer to see mounted on wheels!

"Why a magnum?"

The man who is interested in a magnum caliber is looking for something unusual by way of per-

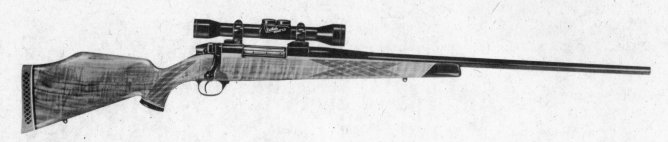

Weatherby Mark X Deluxe Rifle in .300 Weatherby Magnum caliber with 4X Imperial scope on a Buehler mount.

formance to fill a specific need. Either he wants devastating knockdown power, because he intends to hunt big, dangerous game or, he wants a flat-shooting, long-range shell because he plans to hunt in open or mountainous country where the odds against getting close to the target are decidedly against him.

There are also some shooters who are interested in a specific class of cartridge but who want something just a bit heftier than the standards. This is why we have a .22 rimfire magnum and the .222 magnum.

In discussing magnums it is necessary to make a special mention of the ultra-high velocity shells pioneered by Roy Weatherby. While most gunmakers were intent on providing shells having bigger and heavier bullets for knockdown power on dangerous game, Mr. Weatherby came up with the concept that a smaller and lighter bullet, driven at greatly increased speed, would not only accomplish the same result on dangerous game but it would also be much flatter shooting and, therefore, far more accurate at various ranges. The fact that many hunters have used Weatherby rifles successfully would tend to substantiate the validity of the theory.

If there is any disadvantage to the Weatherby formula, it would have to be that ultra-high velocity bullets of small size and light weight are easily deflected. These are not intended for brush country hunting. Conventional magnums, employing large and heavy bullets, on the other hand, would be better suited to hunting in wooded terrain.

Let's take a look at the various magnums that would normally have appeal for the American shooter.

.22 RIMFIRE MAGNUM While this shell would still only be used on traditional .22 rimfire targets, it is considerably more powerful than the standard .22 Long Rifle high-velocity cartridge. Both employ 40 grain bullets but the magnum pushes it out at 2000 f.p.s. as compared to 1335 f.p.s. Also, the magnum has more than twice the muzzle energy of the Long Rifle cartridge. Mid-range trajectory is 1.6″ at 100 yards as compared to 3.3″. Undoubtedly a good shell for small varmint hunting or squirrels.

.222 REMINGTON MAGNUM A slightly enlarged version of the long popular standard .222. The magnum pushes a 55 grain bullet at 3300 f.p.s. (MV) as compared to the standard's 50 grain bullet at 3200 f.p.s. Trajectories are very similar.

Perhaps there's something wrong with my thinking, but I just can't see that much advantage to the magnum over the standard. I think Remington should have saved the magnum label for their .22/250 which out performs both of these with the same .224″ diameter 55 grain bullet!

.224 WEATHERBY MAGNUM A good varmint cartridge built on a belted case which has certain advantages, particularly to a handloader.

Ballistically this shell is very close to the once popular .220 Swift, drives a 50 grain bullet at close to 4000 f.p.s. Good long range cartridge.

6.5 REMINGTON MAGNUM, .256 WINCHESTER MAGNUM, .264 WINCHESTER MAGNUM, .257 WEATHERBY and 6.5x68 RWS   All of these are in the ".25 caliber class" and really should be discussed as a group.

First, the .256 WINCHESTER MAGNUM is a bit out of its class here; this shell was designed primarily for handgun use but, I understand, a number of rifle makers are entertaining thoughts of adding it to their rifle lines. Unlike the other .25's, it uses only a 60 grain bullet, but pushes it along at a muzzle velocity of 2800 f.p.s. It has a surprisingly good (4″) mid range trajectory over 200 yards.

The .257 WEATHERBY MAGNUM was one of Weatherby's first super-velocity cartridges. It's a good combination varmint and deer caliber though generally available only in a Weatherby rifle. Employs a .257 dia. bullet on a necked down 300 H & H Magnum case. Bullet weights are 87, 100, 117 and 120 grains.

The REMINGTON 6.5mm MAGNUM is a comparative newcomer to the field of super-25's and while it's only available with a choice of 100 or 120 grain bullets at this writing, it's bound to have greater flexibility when handloaders and experimenters have had adequate time to put it through the wringer. A general-purpose, long-range varminter and deer cartridge, somewhat similar to the 25/06 but on a belted magnum case. Does a remarkable job with these heavy bullets and should be outstanding on antelope. Definitely an open-country shell. Note that the 6.5mm uses a .264″ diameter bullet (NOT a .257″ dia.), therefore it is a bit larger than conventional .25 calibers.

The .264 WINCHESTER MAGNUM also makes good use of a .264″ diameter bullet in weights of 100 and 140 grains. An excellent, long-range cartridge that may be used on medium-sized game such as deer and antelope as well as for western-style varmint hunting. Employs a very fast (for this shell) 1 in 9 twist, as does the Remington 6.5. There are some who claim that both the .264 and Remington's 6.5 can be used on game up to elk size, but I feel that's stretching them a bit. I wouldn't consider this one for woodsy hunting.

The RWS 6.5x68 MAGNUM   This one is rather scarce on the American scene. Only the now discontinued Mannlicher-Schoenauer was chambered for it and then only imported briefly during the mid 1960s. Actually RWS and European rifle builders have been playing with super-hot 6.5's since the late 1930s. This was simply a newer version but, since it was made only with a 93-grain bullet, it had very limited success here. I've been told that its 3937 f.p.s. muzzle velocity has made it a sensation in other parts of the world. Perhaps Americans can afford to be rather blase about it because we have a number of cartridges in that velocity range. A good varminter, could also be used on deer and antelope.

Now we'll step up into a class of slightly larger magnums which use bullets of .277″ and .284″ diameters. There are only three of these—the .270 WEATHERBY MAGNUM, 7mm REMINGTON MAGNUM and 7mm WEATHERBY MAGNUM. Perhaps a fourth should be added, in spite of the fact that it doesn't have a magnum label, and that's the 7x61 SHARPE & HART. It qualifies in all other respects. However, since it is available only in the Danish produced Schultz and Larson rifle it has had but limited success in the U.S. The new REMINGTON 7mm MAGNUM appears to have pushed this, and all the others, aside.

.270 WEATHERBY MAGNUM (.277″ dia.) This is a good open-country, big game caliber that can be used on anything found on the North American continent. In a pinch, it can also double as a

A Pedersen Custom rifle. Series 3000, Grade III in 7mm Remington Magnum caliber.

varminter through the employment of 100 grain bullets. Develops a muzzle velocity of 3400 f.p.s. with 130 grain bullets (which I prefer) and can also be used with 150 grain bullets when hunting the largest species of North American game. This one has lost considerable ground to the 7mm Magnums.

7mm WEATHERBY MAGNUM   Also on a belted magnum case, it uses a slightly larger bullet than the .270 version (.284″ diameter) in weights of 139, 154, 160 and 175 grains. Handloaders could add a 120 grain missile. Really too big for varminting, it is ideally suited to all North American big game as well as to thin-skinned African game. I'd try for a Kodiak brownie with this, using the 175 grain bullet, but really would prefer something a bit larger for that particular animal at close quarters. (I've hunted with enough guides to realize that you can't count on all of them to back you up in a pinch!)

The REMINGTON 7mm MAGNUM   (Caution: biased commentary follows!) This is one of my favorites. Whenever I head for the wide-open spaces of Montana, or thereabouts, my 7mm Remington is sure to be lugged along. It punches out less than minute-of-angle groups at 100 yards *with factory ammo* and has never failed to do the job. Every time I fire it I learn something new about its

capabilities and come away awed. Ballistically, there are a number of 7mm's that show up just as good as this one—the Weatherby, the 7x61, the Ackley and a host of wildcats. You'd be splitting hairs if you attempted to prove one superior to the others. My enthusiasm, I believe, is for the happy combination of cartridge AND rifle that gives such excellent performance. Factory loads are limited to bullets of 150 and 175 grains. Handloaders, however, can feed it 120, 139 and 154 grain bullets as well. Can be used for all North American game and African thin-skinned varieties.

Now we're up to the .30 caliber bore sizes and we have a host of them. Yes, even a number that would level that cantankerous Brown bear with ease.

This group covers the .308 NORMA, .300 WEATHERBY, .300 H&H, .300 WINCHESTER—all labelled "magnum" and made with belted cases.

.300 HOLLAND & HOLLAND MAGNUM The first of the "super-30's" (as it was once named) came into existence about the mid-1920s and rapidly made a name for itself on the largest thin-skinned game. While primarily a hunter's caliber, some durable individual cleaned the clocks of Wimbledon Cup (1000 yards) marksmen at Camp Perry with it one year and, thereafter, it dominated that competition for quite a number of years. This is an excellent cartridge with 150, 180 or 220 grain bullets but the new .30 caliber magnums

The Steyr-Mannlicher rifle in 8X68S caliber—a "magnum" by our standards!

have a slight edge over it. Handloaders can make up loads with 130 and 110 grain bullets for it as well, but they don't usually perform very well.

.308 NORMA MAGNUM This comparatively new shell is made on a case that is shorter than the H&H version—closer to 30/06 length, so a heavy durable '06 rifle can easily be adapted to handle it. Ironically, it is also more efficient than the H&H but it does kick up a bit more pressure. Factory ammo is available only with a 180 grain bullet, but handloaders can employ the full range, 110 to 220 grains. Will drop anything you can find in North America.

.300 WINCHESTER MAGNUM Uses a case that is slightly longer than that of the Norma which, consequently, provides a little more in powder capacity. Chief advantage is the availability of a larger assortment of factory-loaded ammo (bullets of 150, 180 and 220 grains). This is probably the most popular of the .30-caliber magnums —it will do anything that the others will do. Also because it is readily available in Winchester Model 70—rifle price is reasonable.

.300 WEATHERBY This is the largest of the .30-magnums employing a case that measures 2.820" (as compared to Winchester's 2.620"). It is, supposedly, the most popular of Weatherby's Magnums, but I suspect that the Winchester has made considerable inroads with potential Weatherby users because of the difference in rifle costs. While it enjoys an edge, performance-wise, differences are so slight the shooter would find it impossible to gauge them.

We now have to consider one lonely odd-sized magnum that mikes between the .30 and .33 classes. This is RWS's 8x68S which was first introduced in 1940 and re-introduced in the early 1960s. Employing a .323" diameter bullet (8mm) it is made on a conventional, though large, *unbelted* rimless case. Factory ammo, which tends to be scarce in the U.S., is made with 186 and 198 grain bullets. In performance it handily outdistances *all* of the .30 caliber magnums but probably never will catch on in the U.S. because rifles and ammo are hard to come by. Gaining popularity, rapidly, in Africa.

The next step up takes us into the newer magnums with a bore size of .338". There are, at present, only two of these.

.338 WINCHESTER MAGNUM First announced in 1958, this is a belted case cartridge designed to handle bullets over 200 grains in weight. Factory fare covers bullets of 200, 250, 275 and 300 grains. Has power to spare for all North American game and would be especially desirable for grizzly or brownie hunting. Unfortunately, some African governments have a "minimum" restriction which limits bore size to .375" on some species of game. (Actually, the .338 will do any-

The Ruger "Number One Tropical Rifle": the only single-shot (falling block) rifle made in .375 H & H and .458 Winchester Magnum calibers.

thing the .375 will do.) Has excellent trajectory and residual energy characteristics.

.340 WEATHERBY MAGNUM Also employs the full range of 200 to 300 grain bullets in the .338″ diameter. Slightly larger and faster than Winchester's .338. A fine long-range caliber for our largest game.

In the .358″ bore, we have the relatively new Remington .350 Magnum which is really not an African size cartridge in spite of its large bullet size. This one, rather, was designed for the American brush-country hunter who has long felt the need for something that could plow its way through heavy cover to reach the target. Before this one came along, brush hunters were turning to the .35 Whelen—a popular wildcat. The .350 Remington Magnum is made on a short (2.170″) belted case and is mated to Remington's Model 600 carbine. It uses bullets of 200, 250 and 275 grains. While it probably packs a healthy kick, in this combination, the Eastern woods hunter would be hard-pressed to find something better.

.358 NORMA MAGNUM If there is any similarity between this and Remington's .350, it is only that they use bullets of the same diameter. Otherwise, the Norma is a completely different shell that is really too big for most American game. I'd use it only on the Kodiak brown bear. Some compare the Norma .358 with the larger .375 H&H Magnum. Ballistically they are comparable. Achieves a muzzle velocity over 3000 f.p.s. with a 200 grain bullet and over 2600 f.p.s. with a pill weighing 300 grains. That's pretty darn hefty! (Still wouldn't qualify under some of Africa's .375″ restrictions.)

In the .375 class we have two shells to consider —the .375 H&H MAGNUM and WEATHERBY's .378.

.375 HOLLAND & HOLLAND MAGNUM This is considered the minimum size acceptable for certain species of game by some big-bore-minded African officials. (Apparently they've never thought to apply the velocity portion to the energy fomula $E=WV^2/32.174$.) At any rate the .375 H&H was one of the first belted magnum cartridges; it dates back to 1912. You won't find too much use for it in the U.S. (though some guides swear by it for dangerous bears). Probably the best choice for an African-bound hunter, because English cartridges are more readily found in that part of the world. Employs bullets of 270, 300 and 350 grains (the 350 grain projectile is not produced by American makers). With a 300 grain bullet the H&H gets about 300 f.p.s. less in velocity than the Weatherby. Muzzle energies, with all slugs, run from 4300 to 4500 ft. lbs.

.378 WEATHERBY MAGNUM This replaced Weatherby's .375 Magnum which is now discontinued. On a belted magnum case measuring 2.908″ (the H&H measures 2.850″) this is a real stopper. Flat shooting and hard hitting. Penetrates the heaviest hides including that of elephant, rhino and Cape buffalo. Definitely not a U.S. game weapon. Weatherby shells are made with .375″ diameter bullets in weights of 270 and 300 grains.

Top: Ruger's Model 44 Carbine in .44 Magnum caliber.
Below: Marlin's Model 444 Sporter in .444 Marlin caliber with a Marlin 800 scope.

If the 350 grain, .375″ bullet were readily available here, I imagine someone would quickly come up with loads for it. Boasting about his new .378 Weatherby, one friend remarked, "I plan to use it on Indian tiger . . . hit him in the whiskers and unscrew his head!"

Another lonely intruder into this upper limit, bore size is the REMINGTON .44 MAGNUM. This is really a shell designed for a super handgun but it's so big that some rifle makers cut it into lightweight carbines for the Eastern deer hunter. It uses a small (1.285″) case that pushes a 240 grain, semi-jacketed (.429″ dia.) bullet at speeds up to 1700 f.p.s. The .444 MARLIN (which doesn't carry a magnum handle) is really more of a deer caliber with its 2.162″ case and bullet velocity of 2200 f.p.s.

The upper limit of U.S.–produced magnums is occupied by cartridges of .458″ bore. There are two:

.458 WINCHESTER MAGNUM   The first of American-made "African" shells. Obviously Winchester wearied of British dominance of this field and decided that they would come up with something better that could even be employed in bolt-type magazine rifles. The .458 certainly fills the bill. It's been used very successfully on Africa's largest game and is now being offered in some European-made rifles. Bullets of 500 and 510 grains are provided by factory loadings but handloaders can go down to 250 grains, or *up to 600 grains!* Depending on bullet weight, velocities range from 1950 f.p.s. to 2730 f.p.s. Energies exceed *five thousand ft. lbs.* with the 500 grain, or larger, slugs. Belted magnum case measures 2.50″. Don't be fooled by the .458″ bore size—this one out performs most British "Express" shells—even those of larger bore sizes.

.460 WEATHERBY MAGNUM   This also uses a .458″ diameter bullet, but is billed as "the world's most powerful commercial cartridge!" (There are a couple of hellish wildcats that compete with it.) Recoil, as you can imagine, can separate the hunter from his shoes and, for that reason, Weatherby beefed up the rifle to twelve pounds and fitted it with a built-in recoil compensator. If you think you've got a flinching problem, shoot a few rounds from this one and you'll probably never flinch with a smaller caliber ever again! With a 500 grain bullet, the .460 Weatherby develops a muzzle energy of *8000 ft. lbs.* Velocity is some 500 f.p.s. faster than the .458 Winchester. There's no doubt about it, this is a great elephant shell—for those who can handle it!

One can't discuss magnum shells without including a few of the more popular British Express cartridges. Briefly, this is how currently-produced British loads stack up against our magnums.

.505 RIMLESS MAGNUM (Gibbs) Employs a 525 grain bullet with a muzzle velocity between 2100 and 2300 f.p.s. Muzzle energy runs between 5000 and 6200 ft. lbs. Has a slight edge over our .458 Winchester, but can't match the Weatherby.

.475 NITRO-EXPRESS There are two versions of this, both primarily intended for double-barrel rifles since they employ rimmed cases. Bullets are 480 or 500 grains. Ballistically comparable to the .458 Winchester.

.470 NITRO-EXPRESS Probably the most popular of African elephant calibers. Widely used in double rifles with 500 grain bullets. Again, comparable to the .458 Winchester.

.450 NITRO-EXPRESS A real oldie that still pops up in African hunting camps. Uses 485 and 500 grain bullets, but not quite as effectively as the .458 Winchester.

.500/.450 MAGNUM NITRO-EXPRESS Again, similar to our .458 Winchester, but employing bullets of 480 grains. A very long rimmed case for double rifles. Some "white hunters" swear by it.

.425 WESTLEY RICHARDS MAGNUM Another good elephant shell. Uses 410 grain bullets at 2400 f.p.s. MV—5300 ft. lbs. ME. Has a rebated rim for bolt rifles.

.416 RIGBY This is probably the most popular of English bolt-rifle cartridges. Ballistically on a par with the .458 Winchester in spite of the lighter (410 gr.) bullet.

.404 RIMLESS NITRO-EXPRESS I'd have to put this one next to the .375 H&H Magnum. It doesn't have that much more going for it and I suspect the .375 is flatter shooting. Bullets of 300 and 400 grains. Intended for bolt rifles.

.450/400 MAGNUMS Similar to .404 above.

.450/400 NITRO-EXPRESS (3") Similar to .404 above.

There are a considerable number of smaller express shells, but nothing that is not equaled or surpassed by American cartridges that are so numerous. It would serve no real purpose to go into them here, other than to bore our reader to death.

Anyone interested in British calibers, for whatever reason, should carefully consider the general availability and cost of ammo. Also, he should very carefully study the shell he's contemplating, comparing ballistics with American shells. Because of our long-range Western shooting, Americans have become specialists in the field of small and medium bores that drive bullets at high velocity. British dominance of African calibers is now also seriously contested by our .458 Winchester and .460 Weatherby, either one of which can handily replace a wide assortment of British cartridges.

CHAPTER 8

Tables of Cartridges & Ballistics

BALLISTICS FOR FEDERAL CENTERFIRE CARTRIDGES

Load No.	Cartridge	Bullet Wt. in Grains	Bullet Type	VELOCITY FEET PER SECOND				ENERGY FOOT POUNDS				MID-RANGE TRAJECTORY			Test Barrel Length
				Muz-zle	100 Yds.	200 Yds.	300 Yds.	Muz-zle	100 Yds.	200 Yds.	300 Yds.	100 Yds.	200 Yds.	300 Yds.	
222A	**222 Remington**	50	Soft Point	3200	2660	2170	1750	1140	785	520	340	0.5	2.5	7.0	26
22250A	**22-250 Remington**	55	Soft Point	3810	3270	2770	2320	1770	1300	935	655	0.3	1.6	4.4	26
223A	**223 Remington**	55	Soft Point	3300	2800	2340	1930	1330	955	670	455	0.5	2.3	6.1	26
243A	**243 Winchester**	80	Soft Point	3500	3080	2720	2410	2180	1690	1320	1030	0.4	1.8	4.7	26
243B		100	HI-SHOK S.P.	3070	2790	2540	2320	2090	1730	1430	1190	0.5	2.2	5.5	
2506A	**25-06 Remington**	90	Hollow Point	3500	3090	2730	2420	2450	1910	1490	1170	0.4	1.8	4.7	26
2506B		117	HI-SHOK S.P.	3130	2850	2590	2340	2500	2110	1740	1420	0.5	2.3	5.5	26
270A	**270 Winchester**	130	HI-SHOK S.P.	3140	2880	2630	2400	2840	2390	1990	1660	0.5	2.1	5.1	24
270B		150	HI-SHOK S.P.	2800	2440	2140	1870	2610	1980	1520	1160	0.6	2.9	7.6	
7A	**7 mm. Mauser**	175	HI-SHOK S.P.	2490	2170	1900	1680	2410	1830	1400	1100	0.8	3.7	9.5	24
7B		139	HI-SHOK S.P.	2710	2440	2190	1960	2280	1850	1490	1190	0.7	3.0	7.8	
7RA	**7 mm. Remington Magnum**	150	HI-SHOK S.P.	3260	2970	2700	2450	3540	2940	2430	1990	0.4	2.0	4.9	26
7RB		175	HI-SHOK S.P.	3070	2720	2400	2120	3650	2870	2240	1750	0.5	2.4	6.1	
*30CA	**30 Carbine**	110	Soft Point	1980	1540	1230	1040	955	575	370	260	1.4	7.5	21.7	18
3030A	**30-30 Winchester**	150	HI-SHOK S.P.	2410	2020	1700	1430	1930	1360	960	680	0.9	4.2	11.0	26
3030B		170	HI-SHOK S.P.	2220	1890	1630	1410	1860	1350	1000	750	1.2	4.6	12.5	
3006A	**30-06 Springfield**	150	HI-SHOK S.P.	2970	2670	2400	2130	2930	2370	1920	1510	0.6	2.4	6.1	24
3006B		180	HI-SHOK S.P.	2700	2430	2180	1940	2910	2360	1900	1500	0.7	3.1	7.6	
3006C		125	Soft Point	3200	2810	2480	2200	2840	2190	1710	1340	0.5	2.2	5.6	
300WA	**300 Winchester Magnum**	150	HI-SHOK S.P.	3400	3050	2730	2430	3850	3100	2480	1970	0.4	1.9	4.8	26
300WB		180	HI-SHOK S.P.	3070	2850	2640	2440	3770	3250	2790	2380	0.5	2.1	5.3	
300A	**300 Savage**	150	HI-SHOK S.P.	2670	2390	2130	1890	2370	1900	1510	1190	0.7	3.0	7.6	24
300B		180	HI-SHOK S.P.	2370	2160	1960	1770	2240	1860	1530	1250	0.9	3.7	9.2	
303A	**303 British**	180	HI-SHOK S.P.	2540	2300	2090	1900	2580	2120	1750	1440	0.7	3.3	8.2	26
308A	**308 Winchester**	150	HI-SHOK S.P.	2860	2570	2300	2050	2730	2200	1760	1400	0.6	2.6	6.5	24
308B		180	HI-SHOK S.P.	2610	2250	1940	1680	2720	2020	1500	1130	0.7	3.4	8.9	
**8A	**8 mm. Mauser**	170	HI-SHOK S.P.	2570	2140	1790	1520	2490	1730	1210	870	0.8	3.9	10.5	23½
32A	**32 Winchester Special**	170	HI-SHOK S.P.	2280	1920	1630	1410	1960	1390	1000	750	1.0	4.8	12.5	26
35A	**35 Remington**	200	HI-SHOK S.P.	2100	1710	1390	1160	1950	1300	855	605	1.2	6.0	16.5	22
*44A	**44 Remington Magnum**	240	Hollow S.P.	1750	1350	1090	950	1630	970	635	480	1.8	9.4	26.0	18½

Figures in this table are based on the barrel lengths shown in the last column. Mid-Range Trajectory shows the distance in inches that the projectile is above the line of sight at the mid-point of the yardage shown.

*Without Cartridge Carrier

**Only for use in barrels intended for .323-diameter bullets. Do not use in 8mm Commission Rifles (M1888) or sporting arms with similar rifling.

Cartridge	Bullet Wt. Grs.	Bullet Type	Muzzle	Velocity (fps) 100 yds.	200 yds.	300 yds.	Energy (ft. lbs.) Muzzle	100 yds.	200 yds.	300 yds.	Mid-Range Trajectory (inches) 100 yds.	200 yds.	300 yds.
218 Bee Super-X and Super-Speed	46	OPE(HP)	2860	2160	1610	1200	835	475	265	145	0.7	3.8	11.5
22 Hornet Super-X and Super-Speed	45	SP	2690	2030	1510	1150	720	410	230	130	0.8	4.3	13.0
22 Hornet Super-X and Super-Speed	46	OPE(HP)	2690	2030	1510	1150	740	420	235	135	0.8	4.3	13.0
22-250 Super-X and Super-Speed	55	PSP	3810	3270	2770	2320	1770	1300	935	655	0.3	1.6	4.4
222 Remington Super-X and Super-Speed	50	PSP	3200	2660	2170	1750	1140	785	520	340	0.5	2.5	7.0
225 Winchester Super-X and Super-Speed	55	PSP	3650	3140	2680	2270	1630	1200	875	630	0.4	1.8	4.8
243 Winchester (6mm) Super-X and Super-Speed	80	PSP	3500	3080	2720	2410	2180	1690	1320	1030	0.4	1.8	4.7
243 Winchester (6mm) Super-X and Super-Speed	100	PP(SP)	3070	2790	2540	2320	2090	1730	1430	1190	0.5	2.2	5.5
25-06 Super-X and Super-Speed	90	PEP	3500	3090	2730	2420	2450	1910	1490	1170	0.4	1.8	4.7
25-06 Super-X and Super-Speed	120	PEP	3120	2850	2600	2360	2590	2160	1800	1480	0.5	2.0	5.5
25-20 Winchester	86	L, Lead	1460	1180	1030	940	405	265	200	170	2.6	12.5	32.0
25-20 Winchester	86	SP	1460	1180	1030	940	405	265	200	170	2.6	12.5	32.0
25-35 Winchester Super-X and Super-Speed	117	SP	2300	1910	1600	1340	1370	945	665	465	1.0	4.6	12.5
250 Savage Super-X and Super-Speed	87	PSP	3030	2660	2330	2060	1770	1370	1050	820	0.6	2.5	6.4
250 Savage Super-X and Super-Speed	100	ST(Exp)	2820	2460	2140	1870	1760	1340	1020	775	0.6	2.9	7.4
*256 Winchester Magnum Super-X	60	OPE	2800	2070	1570	1220	1040	570	330	200	0.8	4.0	12.0
257 Roberts Super-X and Super-Speed	87	PSP	3200	2840	2510	2190	1980	1560	1210	925	0.5	2.2	5.7
257 Roberts Super-X and Super-Speed	100	ST(Exp)	2900	2540	2210	1920	1870	1430	1080	820	0.6	2.7	7.0
*257 Roberts Super-X	117	PP(SP)	2650	2280	1950	1690	1820	1350	985	740	0.7	3.4	8.8
264 Winchester Magnum Super-X and Super-Speed	100	PSP	3700	3260	2880	2550	3040	2360	1840	1440	0.4	1.6	4.2
264 Winchester Magnum Super-X and Super-Speed	140	PP(SP)	3200	2940	2700	2480	3180	2690	2270	1910	0.5	2.0	4.9
270 Winchester Super-X and Super-Speed	100	PSP	3480	3070	2690	2340	2690	2090	1600	1215	0.4	1.8	4.8
270 Winchester Super-X and Super-Speed	130	PP(SP)	3140	2880	2630	2400	2850	2390	2000	1660	0.5	2.1	5.3
270 Winchester Super-X and Super-Speed	130	ST(Exp)	3140	2850	2580	2320	2850	2340	1920	1550	0.5	2.1	5.3
270 Winchester Super-X and Super-Speed	150	PP(SP)	2900	2620	2380	2160	2800	2290	1890	1550	0.6	2.5	6.3
284 Winchester Super-X and Super-Speed	125	PP(SP)	3200	2880	2590	2310	2840	2300	1860	1480	0.5	2.1	5.3
284 Winchester Super-X and Super-Speed	150	PP(SP)	2900	2620	2380	2160	2800	2290	1890	1550	0.6	2.5	6.3
7mm Mauser (7x57) Super-X and Super-Speed	175	SP	2490	2170	1900	1680	2410	1830	1400	1100	0.8	3.7	9.5
*7mm Remington Magnum Super-X	150	PP(SP)	3260	2970	2700	2450	3540	2940	2430	1990	0.4	2.0	4.9
*7mm Remington Magnum Super-X	175	PP(SP)	3070	2720	2400	2120	3660	2870	2240	1750	0.5	2.4	6.1
†30 Carbine	110	HSP	1980	1540	1230	1040	955	575	370	260	1.4	7.5	21.7
†30 Carbine	110	FMC	1980	1540	1230	1040	955	575	370	260	1.4	7.5	21.5
30-30 Winchester Super-X and Super-Speed	150	OPE(HP)	2410	2020	1700	1430	1930	1360	960	680	0.9	4.2	11.0
30-30 Winchester Super-X and Super-Speed	150	PP(SP)	2410	2020	1700	1430	1930	1360	960	680	0.9	4.2	11.0
30-30 Winchester Super-X and Super-Speed	150	ST(Exp)	2410	2020	1700	1430	1930	1360	960	680	0.9	4.2	11.0
30-30 Winchester Super-X and Super-Speed	170	PP(SP)	2220	1890	1630	1410	1860	1350	1000	750	1.2	4.6	12.5
30-30 Winchester Super-X and Super-Speed	170	ST(Exp)	2220	1890	1630	1410	1860	1350	1000	750	1.2	4.6	12.5
30 Remington Super-X and Super-Speed	170	ST(Exp)	2120	1820	1560	1350	1700	1250	920	690	1.1	5.3	14.0
30-06 Springfield Super-X and Super-Speed	110	PSP	3370	2830	2350	1920	2770	1960	1350	900	0.5	2.2	6.0
30-06 Springfield Super-X and Super-Speed	125	PSP	3200	2810	2480	2200	2840	2190	1710	1340	0.5	2.2	5.6
30-06 Springfield Super-X and Super-Speed	150	PP(SP)	2970	2620	2300	2010	2930	2280	1760	1340	0.6	2.5	6.5
30-06 Springfield Super-X and Super-Speed	150	ST(Exp)	2970	2670	2400	2130	2930	2370	1920	1510	0.6	2.4	6.1
30-06 Springfield Super-X and Super-Speed	180	PP(SP)	2700	2330	2010	1740	2910	2170	1610	1210	0.7	3.1	8.3
30-06 Springfield Super-X and Super-Speed	180	ST(Exp)	2700	2470	2250	2040	2910	2440	2020	1660	0.7	2.9	7.0
30-06 Springfield Super-Match and Wimbledon Cup	180	FMCBT	2700	2520	2350	2190	2910	2540	2200	1900	0.6	2.8	6.7
*30-06 Springfield Super-X	220	PP(SP)	2410	2120	1870	1670	2830	2190	1710	1360	0.8	3.9	9.8
30-06 Springfield Super-X and Super-Speed	220	ST(Exp)	2410	2180	1980	1790	2830	2320	1910	1560	0.8	3.7	9.2
*30-40 Krag Super-X	180	PP(SP)	2470	2120	1830	1590	2440	1790	1340	1010	0.8	3.8	9.9

	Bullet		Velocity (fps)				Energy (ft. lbs.)				Mid-Range Trajectory (inches)		
Cartridge	Wt. Grs.	Type	Muzzle	100 yds.	200 yds.	300 yds.	Muzzle	100 yds.	200 yds.	300 yds.	100 yds.	200 yds.	300 yds.
*30-40 Krag Super-X	180	ST(Exp)	2470	2250	2040	1850	2440	2020	1660	1370	0.8	3.5	8.5
*30-40 Krag Super-X	220	ST(Exp)	2200	1990	1800	1630	2360	1930	1580	1300	1.0	4.4	11.0
300 Winchester Magnum Super-X and Super-Speed	150	PP(SP)	3400	3050	2730	2430	3850	3100	2480	1970	0.4	1.9	4.8
300 Winchester Magnum Super-X and Super-Speed	180	PP(SP)	3070	2850	2640	2440	3770	3250	2790	2380	0.5	2.1	5.3
300 Winchester Magnum Super-X and Super-Speed	220	ST(Exp)	2720	2490	2270	2060	3620	3030	2520	2070	0.6	2.9	6.9
300 H&H Magnum Super-X and Super-Speed	150	ST(Exp)	3190	2870	2580	2300	3390	2740	2220	1760	0.5	2.1	5.2
300 H&H Magnum Super-X and Super-Speed	180	ST(Exp)	2920	2670	2440	2220	3400	2850	2380	1970	0.6	2.4	5.8
300 H&H Magnum Super-X and Super-Speed	220	ST(Exp)	2620	2370	2150	1940	3350	2740	2260	1840	0.7	3.1	7.7
300 Savage Super-X and Super-Speed	150	PP(SP)	2670	2350	2060	1800	2370	1840	1410	1080	0.7	3.2	8.0
300 Savage Super-X and Super-Speed	150	ST(Exp)	2670	2390	2130	1890	2370	1900	1510	1190	0.7	3.0	7.6
300 Savage Super-X and Super-Speed	180	PP(SP)	2370	2040	1760	1520	2240	1660	1240	920	0.9	4.1	10.5
300 Savage Super-X and Super-Speed	180	ST(Exp)	2370	2160	1960	1770	2240	1860	1530	1250	0.9	3.7	9.2
303 Savage Super-X and Super-Speed	190	ST(Exp)	1980	1680	1440	1250	1650	1190	875	660	1.3	6.2	15.5
†303 British Super-Speed	180	PP(SP)	2540	2300	2090	1900	2580	2120	1750	1440	0.7	3.3	8.2
308 Winchester Super-X and Super-Speed	110	PSP	3340	2810	2340	1920	2730	1930	1340	900	0.5	2.2	6.0
308 Winchester Super-X and Super-Speed	125	PSP	3100	2740	2430	2160	2670	2080	1640	1300	0.5	2.3	5.9
308 Winchester Super-X and Super-Speed	150	PP(SP)	2860	2520	2210	1930	2730	2120	1630	1240	0.6	2.7	7.0
308 Winchester Super-X and Super-Speed	150	ST(Exp)	2860	2570	2300	2050	2730	2200	1760	1400	0.6	2.6	6.5
308 Winchester Super-X and Super-Speed	180	PP(SP)	2610	2250	1940	1680	2720	2020	1500	1130	0.7	3.4	8.9
308 Winchester Super-X and Super-Speed	180	ST(Exp)	2610	2390	2170	1970	2720	2280	1870	1540	0.8	3.1	7.4
308 Winchester Super-X and Super-Speed	200	ST(Exp)	2450	2210	1980	1770	2670	2170	1750	1400	0.8	3.6	9.0
32 Winchester Special Super-X and Super-Speed	170	PP(SP)	2280	1870	1560	1330	1960	1320	920	665	1.0	4.8	13.0
32 Winchester Special Super-X and Super-Speed	170	ST(Exp)	2280	1870	1560	1330	1960	1320	920	665	1.0	4.8	13.0
32 Remington Super-X and Super-Speed	170	ST(Exp)	2120	1760	1460	1220	1700	1170	805	560	1.1	5.3	14.5
32-20 Winchester (Oilproof)	100	L, Lead	1290	1060	940	840	370	250	195	155	3.3	15.5	38.0
32-20 Winchester (Oilproof)	100	SP	1290	1060	940	840	370	250	195	155	3.3	15.5	38.0
†8mm Mauser (8x57; 7.9) Super-Speed	170	PP(SP)	2570	2140	1790	1520	2490	1730	1210	870	0.8	3.9	10.5
338 Winchester Magnum Super-X and Super-Speed	200	PP(SP)	3000	2690	2410	2170	4000	3210	2580	2090	0.5	2.4	6.0
338 Winchester Magnum Super-X and Super-Speed	250	ST(Exp)	2700	2430	2180	1940	4050	3280	2640	2090	0.7	3.0	7.4
338 Winchester Magnum Super-X and Super-Speed	300	PP(SP)	2450	2160	1910	1690	4000	3110	2430	1900	0.8	3.7	9.5
†348 Winchester Super-Speed	200	ST(Exp)	2530	2220	1940	1680	2840	2190	1670	1250	0.7	3.6	9.0
35 Remington Super-X and Super-Speed	200	PP(SP)	2100	1710	1390	1160	1950	1300	860	605	1.2	6.0	16.5
35 Remington Super-X and Super-Speed	200	ST(Exp)	2100	1710	1390	1160	1950	1300	860	605	1.2	6.0	16.5
351 Winchester Self-Loading	180	SP	1850	1560	1310	1140	1370	975	685	520	1.5	7.8	21.5
358 Winchester (8.8mm) Super-X and Super-Speed	200	ST(Exp)	2530	2210	1910	1640	2840	2160	1610	1190	0.8	3.6	9.4
358 Winchester (8.8mm) Super-X and Super-Speed	250	ST(Exp)	2250	2010	1780	1570	2810	2230	1760	1370	1.0	4.4	11.0
375 H&H Magnum Super-X and Super-Speed	270	PP(SP)	2740	2460	2210	1990	4500	3620	2920	2370	0.7	2.9	7.1
375 H&H Magnum Super-X and Super-Speed	300	ST(Exp)	2550	2280	2040	1830	4330	3460	2770	2230	0.7	3.3	8.3
†375 H&H Magnum Super-Speed	300	FMC	2550	2180	1860	1590	4330	3160	2300	1680	0.7	3.6	9.3
38-40 Winchester (Oilproof)	180	SP	1330	1070	960	850	705	455	370	290	3.2	15.0	36.5
*44 Magnum Super-X	240	HSP	1750	1350	1090	950	1630	970	635	480	1.8	9.4	26.0
44-40 Winchester (Oilproof)	200	SP	1310	1050	940	830	760	490	390	305	3.3	15.0	36.5
†45-70 Government	405	SP	1320	1160	1050	990	1570	1210	990	880	2.9	13.0	32.5
†458 Winchester Magnum Super-Speed	500	FMC	2130	1910	1700	1520	5040	4050	3210	2570	1.1	4.8	12.0
†458 Winchester Magnum Super-Speed	510	SP	2130	1840	1600	1400	5140	3830	2900	2220	1.1	5.1	13.5

* — Western Brand Only   † — Winchester Brand Only   PSP — Pointed Soft Point   SP — Soft Point   OPE — Open Point Expanding
HSP — Hollow Soft Point   PP(SP) — Power-Point Soft Point   HP — Hollow Point   ST(Exp) — Silvertip Expanding
PEP — Positive Expanding Point   FMC — Full Metal Case   L — Lubaloy   FMCBT — Full Metal Case Boat Tail

Test barrels are used to determine ballistics figures. Individual firearms may differ from these test barrel statistics.

REMINGTON BALLISTICS CHARTS

All velocity and energy figures shown in the following charts have been derived using test barrels of established lengths.

The advantage of such established barrel lengths is obvious.

Since many rifles are available in a variety of barrel lengths, it would be difficult, if not impossible, to show performance figures for every barrel length available on today's market.

Reasonable approximations of velocity for bar-rels of any length can be made, however, using the table below.

CENTER FIRE RIFLE VELOCITY vs. BARREL LENGTH

Muzzle Velocity Range (fs)	Approximate Change in Velocity for Each 1" Change in Barrel Length (fs)
2000 — 2500	10
2500 — 3000	20
3000 — 3500	30
3500 — 4000	40

1. Determine how much shorter (or longer) your barrel is than the test barrel length.
2. In the left hand column (table left), select the muzzle velocity class in which your cartridge falls.
3. Reading to the right, determine the approximate change in velocity per inch of barrel length.
4. Multiply this figure by the difference in length from test barrel.
5. For shorter barrels, subtract this figure from the muzzle velocity shown for your cartridge.

Remington Center Fire

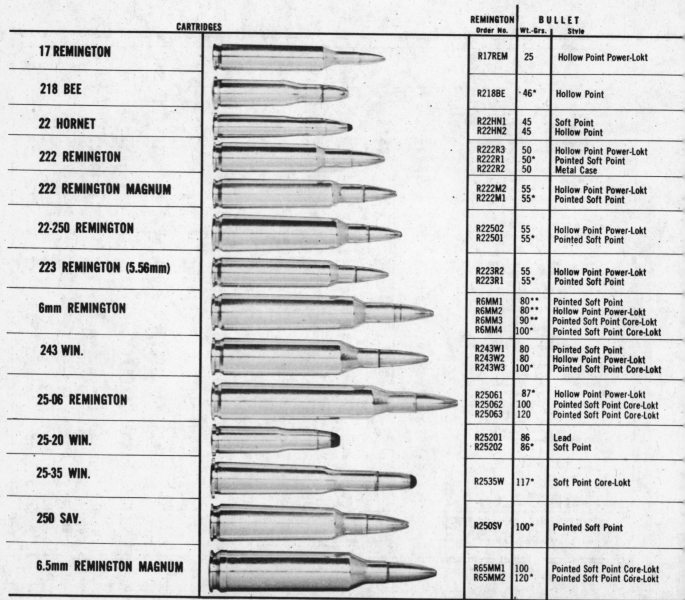

CARTRIDGES	REMINGTON Order No.	BULLET Wt.-Grs.	Style
17 REMINGTON	R17REM	25	Hollow Point Power-Lokt
218 BEE	R218BE	46*	Hollow Point
22 HORNET	R22HN1 R22HN2	45 45	Soft Point Hollow Point
222 REMINGTON	R222R3 R222R1 R222R2	50 50* 50	Hollow Point Power-Lokt Pointed Soft Point Metal Case
222 REMINGTON MAGNUM	R222M2 R222M1	55 55*	Hollow Point Power-Lokt Pointed Soft Point
22-250 REMINGTON	R22502 R22501	55 55*	Hollow Point Power-Lokt Pointed Soft Point
223 REMINGTON (5.56mm)	R223R2 R223R1	55 55*	Hollow Point Power-Lokt Pointed Soft Point
6mm REMINGTON	R6MM1 R6MM2 R6MM3 R6MM4	80** 80** 90** 100*	Pointed Soft Point Hollow Point Power-Lokt Pointed Soft Point Core-Lokt Pointed Soft Point Core-Lokt
243 WIN.	R243W1 R243W2 R243W3	80 80 100*	Pointed Soft Point Hollow Point Power-Lokt Pointed Soft Point Core-Lokt
25-06 REMINGTON	R25061 R25062 R25063	87* 100 120	Hollow Point Power-Lokt Pointed Soft Point Core-Lokt Pointed Soft Point Core-Lokt
25-20 WIN.	R25201 R25202	86 86*	Lead Soft Point
25-35 WIN.	R2535W	117*	Soft Point Core-Lokt
250 SAV.	R250SV	100*	Pointed Soft Point
6.5mm REMINGTON MAGNUM	R65MM1 R65MM2	100 120*	Pointed Soft Point Core-Lokt Pointed Soft Point Core-Lokt

Cartridge illustrations approximate size.

*Illustrated Above.

"Power-Lokt" and "Core-Lokt" are trademarks registered in the United States Patent Office by Remington Arms Company, Inc.

6. For longer barrels, add this figure to the muzzle velocity shown.

TRAJECTORY

The "Trajectory" figures shown in the following tables are actually the rise or drop in inches of the bullet from the line of sight at selected yardages, with sighting-in distances set at 100 or 200 yards. See drawing (left).

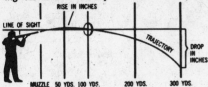

The line of sight used in the computations is .9" above the axis of the bore. This height is common to iron sights and low mounted scopes.

The tables may be used as well for high mounted scopes (1½" above axis of the bore). The difference in drops at the extreme 500 yard range is a mere .7". It is even less at intermediate ranges.

Since the rise or drop figures shown at the stated yardages are points of impact, it is necessary to hold low for (+) figures at these ranges. Conversely, hold high for (−) figures shown.

If you use the same cartridge a great deal of the time, you can commit the rise or drop figures for that cartridge to memory, and know instantly the right "hold," as soon as you estimate the range of your game or target.

Rifle Cartridge Calibers.

Primer No.	VELOCITY — FEET PER SECOND						ENERGY — FOOT POUNDS						TRAJECTORY† RIFLE SIGHTED IN AT 100 YDS.				RIFLE SIGHTED IN AT 200 YDS.					BARREL
	Muzzle	100 YDS.	200 YDS.	300 YDS.	400 YDS.	500 YDS.	Muzzle	100 YDS.	200 YDS.	300 YDS.	400 YDS.	500 YDS.	50 YDS.	100 YDS.	200 YDS.	300 YDS.	100 YDS.	200 YDS.	300 YDS.	400 YDS.	500 YDS.	
7½	4020	3290	2630	2060	1590	1240	900	600	380	230	140	90	−0.1	⊕	−2.4	−9.9	+1.2	⊕	−6.3	−21.2	−50.4	24"
6½	2860	2160	1610	1200			835	475	265	145			+0.2	⊕	−6.4	−15.9						24"
6½	2690	2030	1510	1150			720	410	230	130			+0.3	⊕	−7.8	−30.5						24"
6½	2690	2030	1510	1150			720	410	230	130			+0.3	⊕	−7.8	−30.5						
7½	3200	2690	2230	1830			1140	800	550	370			0.0	⊕	−4.0	−15.0						26"
7½	3200	2660	2170	1750			1140	785	520	340			0.0	⊕	−4.0	−15.7						
7½	3200	2660	2170	1750			1140	785	520	340			0.0	⊕	−4.0	−15.7						
7½	3300	2830	2400	2010			1330	975	700	490			0.0	⊕	−3.5	−13.1						26"
7½	3300	2800	2340	1930			1330	955	670	455			0.0	⊕	−3.6	−13.8						
9½	3810	3330	2890	2490	2120	1800	1770	1360	1020	760	550	390					+1.1	⊕	−5.3	−16.3	−35.1	26"
9½	3810	3270	2770	2320	1920	1580	1770	1300	935	655	450	305					+1.2	⊕	−5.8	−18.1	−40.1	
7½	3300	2830	2400	2010			1330	975	700	490			0.0	⊕	−3.5	−13.1						26"
7½	3300	2800	2340	1930			1330	955	670	455			0.0	⊕	−3.6	−13.8						
9½	3540	3130	2750	2400	2080	1790	2220	1740	1340	1018	770	570					+1.3	⊕	−6.0	−18.0	−38.3	26"
9½	3540	3130	2750	2400	2080	1790	2220	1740	1340	1018	770	570					+1.3	⊕	−6.0	−18.0	−38.3	
9½	3320	2980	2670	2380	2110	1860	2200	1770	1420	1130	890	690			−3.0	−10.9	1.5	⊕	−6.4	−19.0	−39.3	26"
9½	3190	2920	2660	2420	2190	1980	2260	1890	1570	1300	1060	870					+1.6	⊕	−6.5	−18.9	−38.7	
9½	3500	3080	2720	2410			2180	1690	1320	1030			−0.1	⊕	−2.8	−10.2						26"
9½	3450	3050	2675	2330	2020	1735	2115	1650	1270	965	725	535	−0.1	⊕	−2.9	−10.6	+1.4	⊕	−6.3	−19.1	−40.5	
9½	3070	2790	2540	2320			2090	1730	1430	1190			0.0	⊕	−3.5	−12.2						
9½	3500	3070	2680	2320	1990	1690	2370	1820	1390	1040	765	550					+1.4	⊕	−6.3	−19.2	−40.9	26"
9½	3300	2960	2640	2350	2080	1830	2420	1940	1550	1230	960	740			−3.1	−11.2	1.5	⊕	−6.6	−19.4	−40.4	26"
9½	3120	2850	2600	2360	2130	1910	2590	2160	1800	1480	1210	970	0.0	⊕	−3.4	−11.2	+1.7	⊕	−6.8	−19.9	−40.8	26"
6½	1460	1180	1030	940			405	265	200	170			+2.1	⊕	−23.9	−79.4						24"
6½	1460	1180	1030	940			405	265	200	170			+2.1	⊕	−23.9	−79.4						
9½	2300	1950	1680	1460			1370	985	730	555			+0.5	⊕	−8.2	−28.6						26"
9½	2820	2500	2210	1940			1760	1390	1080	835			+0.1	⊕	−4.8	−16.5						24"
9½M	3450	3070	2690	2320	1990	1700	2640	2090	1610	1190	880	640					+1.4	⊕	−6.3	−19.1	−41.0	26"
9½M	3220	2900	2630	2390	2160	1930	2780	2240	1840	1520	1240	990					+1.6	⊕	−6.6	−19.2	−39.2	26"

**Interchangeable in 244 Rem.   †Inches above (+) or below (−) line of sight.   Hold low for (+) figures, high for (−) figures.
"Specifications are nominal." Ballistics figures established in test barrels. Individual guns may vary from test barrel specifications.

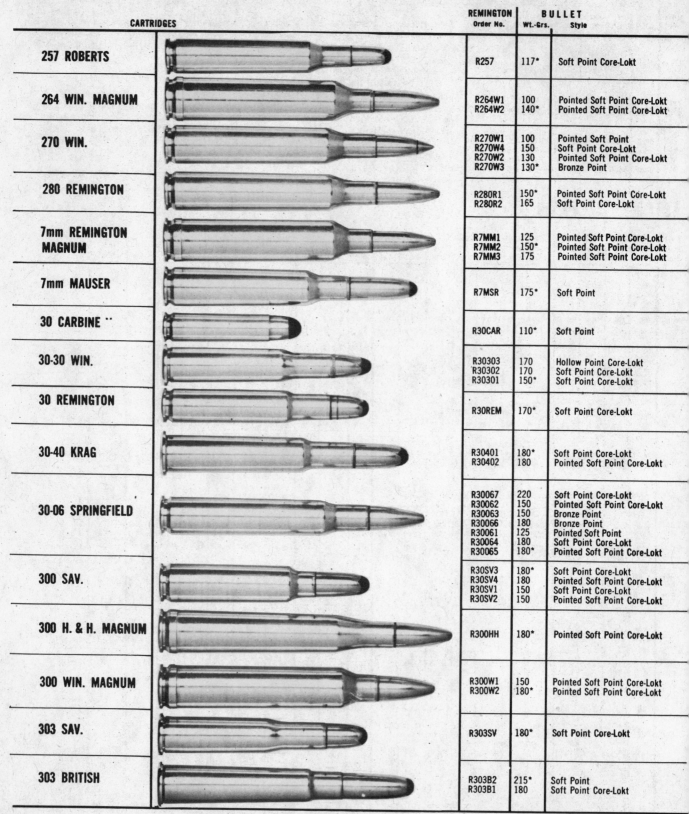

CARTRIDGES	REMINGTON Order No.	BULLET Wt.-Grs.	BULLET Style
257 ROBERTS	R257	117*	Soft Point Core-Lokt
264 WIN. MAGNUM	R264W1	100	Pointed Soft Point Core-Lokt
	R264W2	140*	Pointed Soft Point Core-Lokt
270 WIN.	R270W1	100	Pointed Soft Point
	R270W4	150	Soft Point Core-Lokt
	R270W2	130	Pointed Soft Point Core-Lokt
	R270W3	130*	Bronze Point
280 REMINGTON	R280R1	150*	Pointed Soft Point Core-Lokt
	R280R2	165	Soft Point Core-Lokt
7mm REMINGTON MAGNUM	R7MM1	125	Pointed Soft Point Core-Lokt
	R7MM2	150*	Pointed Soft Point Core-Lokt
	R7MM3	175	Pointed Soft Point Core-Lokt
7mm MAUSER	R7MSR	175*	Soft Point
30 CARBINE **	R30CAR	110*	Soft Point
30-30 WIN.	R30303	170	Hollow Point Core-Lokt
	R30302	170	Soft Point Core-Lokt
	R30301	150*	Soft Point Core-Lokt
30 REMINGTON	R30REM	170*	Soft Point Core-Lokt
30-40 KRAG	R30401	180*	Soft Point Core-Lokt
	R30402	180	Pointed Soft Point Core-Lokt
30-06 SPRINGFIELD	R30067	220	Soft Point Core-Lokt
	R30062	150	Pointed Soft Point Core-Lokt
	R30063	150	Bronze Point
	R30066	180	Bronze Point
	R30061	125	Pointed Soft Point
	R30064	180	Soft Point Core-Lokt
	R30065	180*	Pointed Soft Point Core-Lokt
300 SAV.	R30SV3	180*	Soft Point Core-Lokt
	R30SV4	180	Pointed Soft Point Core-Lokt
	R30SV1	150	Soft Point Core-Lokt
	R30SV2	150	Pointed Soft Point Core-Lokt
300 H. & H. MAGNUM	R300HH	180*	Pointed Soft Point Core-Lokt
300 WIN. MAGNUM	R300W1	150	Pointed Soft Point Core-Lokt
	R300W2	180*	Pointed Soft Point Core-Lokt
303 SAV.	R303SV	180*	Soft Point Core-Lokt
303 BRITISH	R303B2	215*	Soft Point
	R303B1	180	Soft Point Core-Lokt

Cartridge illustrations approximate size.

*Illustrated Above.
** 30 Carbine — Also for use in Ruger Revolver.
"Core-Lokt" is a trademark registered in the United States Patent Office by Remington Arms Company, Inc.

Primer No.	VELOCITY — FEET PER SECOND						ENERGY — FOOT POUNDS						TRAJECTORY† SIGHTED 100 YDS.				SIGHTED 200 YDS.					BARREL
	Muzzle	100 YDS.	200 YDS.	300 YDS.	400 YDS.	500 YDS.	Muzzle	100 YDS.	200 YDS.	300 YDS.	400 YDS.	500 YDS.	50 YDS.	100 YDS.	200 YDS.	300 YDS.	100 YDS.	200 YDS.	300 YDS.	400 YDS.	500 YDS.	
9½	2650	2280	1950	1690			1820	1350	985	740			+0.2	⊕	—5.7	—20.6						24"
9½M	3700	3260	2880	2550	2270	2030	3040	2360	1840	1440	1140	915					+1.1	⊕	—5.5	—15.6	—32.2	26"
9½M	3200	2940	2700	2480	2280	2100	3180	2690	2270	1910	1620	1370					+1.5	⊕	—6.1	—18.4	—36.7	
9½	3480	3070	2690	2340	2010	1700	2690	2090	1600	1215	890	640					+1.3	⊕	—6.3	—18.5	—38.7	24"
9½	2800	2440	2140	1870	1660	1470	2610	1980	1520	1160	915	720					+2.4	⊕	—9.5	—29.6	—61.7	
9½	3140	2850	2580	2320	2090	1860	2840	2340	1920	1550	1260	1000					+1.6	⊕	—7.0	—20.1	—40.7	
9½	3140	2880	2630	2400	2180	1980	2840	2390	1990	1660	1370	1130					+1.6	⊕	—6.5	—19.6	—39.7	
9½	2900	2670	2450	2250	2050	1870	2800	2370	2000	1680	1400	1160					+2.0	⊕	—7.8	—22.5	—45.5	24"
9½	2820	2510	2220	1970	1740	1530	2910	2310	1810	1420	1110	860					+2.3	⊕	—9.3	—27.6	—57.5	
9½M	3430	3080	2750	2450	2160	1900	3260	2630	2100	1660	1300	1010					+1.1	⊕	—5.7	—17.2	—36.2	26"
9½M	3260	2970	2700	2450	2210	1990	3540	2940	2430	1990	1620	1310					+1.5	⊕	—6.3	—18.4	—37.7	
9½M	3070	2850	2630	2430	2240	2060	3660	3150	2700	2290	1950	1640					+1.7	⊕	—6.7	—19.3	—39.0	
9½	2490	2170	1900	1680			2410	1830	1400	1100			+0.3	⊕	—6.4	—22.4						26"
6½	1980	1540	1230	1040			955	575	370	260			+1.0	⊕	—14.1	—51.8						18"
9½	2220	1890	1630	1410			1860	1350	1000	750			+0.7	⊕	—8.2	—29.6						26"
9½	2220	1890	1630	1410			1860	1350	1000	750			+0.7	⊕	—8.2	—29.6						
9½	2410	1960	1620	1360			1930	1280	875	615			+0.4	⊕	—8.3	—29.5						
9½	2120	1820	1560	1350			1700	1250	920	690			+0.6	⊕	—9.5	—33.8						24"
9½	2470	2120	1830	1590			2440	1790	1340	1010			+0.3	⊕	—6.4	—23.4						28"
9½	2470	2250	2040	1850			2440	2020	1660	1370			+0.3	⊕	—6.1	—20.2						
9½	2410	2120	1870	1670			2830	2190	1710	1360			+0.3	⊕	—6.7	—23.6	+1.9	⊕	—7.5	—22.6	—45.7	24"
9½	2970	2670	2400	2130	1890	1670	2930	2370	1920	1510	1190	930					+1.9	⊕	—7.5	—22.6	—45.7	
9½	2970	2710	2470	2240	2020	1820	2930	2440	2030	1670	1360	1100					+2.4	⊕	—8.5	—25.6	—52.7	
9½	2700	2480	2280	2080	1900	1730	2910	2460	2080	1730	1440	1190					+1.6	⊕	—7.4	—21.4	—44.9	
9½	3200	2810	2480	2200	1960	1740	2840	2190	1710	1340	1070	840	+0.2	⊕	—5.6	—19.2						
9½	2700	2330	2010	1740			2910	2170	1610	1210							+2.4	⊕	—9.0	—27.1	—55.7	
9½	2700	2470	2250	2040	1850	1670	2910	2440	2020	1660	1370	1110										
9½	2370	2040	1760	1520			2240	1660	1240	920			+0.4	⊕	—7.5	—25.3						26"
9½	2370	2160	1960	1770			2240	1860	1530	1250			+0.4	⊕	—6.5	—22.3						
9½	2670	2270	1930	1660			2370	1710	1240	915			+0.2	⊕	—5.9	—20.4						
9½	2670	2390	2130	1890			2370	1900	1510	1190			+0.2	⊕	—5.4	—17.9						
9½M	2920	2670	2440	2220	2020	1830	3400	2850	2380	1970	1630	1340					+1.9	⊕	—7.6	—22.5	—45.5	26"
9½M	3400	3050	2730	2430	2150	1890	3850	3100	2480	1970	1540	1190					+1.5	⊕	—6.1	—18.1	—37.7	26"
9½M	3070	2850	2640	2440	2250	2060	3770	3250	2790	2380	2020	1700					+1.7	⊕	—6.9	—19.4	—38.9	
9½	2140	1810	1550	1340			1830	1310	960	715			+0.6	⊕	—10.0	—33.8						26"
9½	2180	1900	1660	1460			2270	1720	1310	1020			+0.6	⊕	—9.1	—30.2						26"
9½	2540	2200	1890	1600			2580	1930	1430	1020			+0.3	⊕	—6.3	—22.5						

†Inches above (+) or below (—) line of sight.   Hold low for (+) figures, high for (—) figures.

"Specifications are nominal." Ballistics figures established in test barrels. Individual guns may vary from test barrel specifications.

REPRINTED COURTESY OF REMINGTON ARMS COMPANY

	Wt.-Grs.	Style
308 WIN.	150* 180 180	Pointed Soft Point Core-Lokt Pointed Soft Point Core-Lokt Soft Point Core-Lokt
8mm (7.9mm) MAUSER	170*	Soft Point Core-Lokt
32 REMINGTON	170*	Soft Point Core-Lokt
32 WIN. SPECIAL	170 170*	Hollow Point Core-Lokt Soft Point Core-Lokt
32-20 WIN.	100* 100	Lead Soft Point
348 WIN.	200*	Soft Point Core-Lokt
35 REMINGTON	150 200*	Pointed Soft Point Core-Lokt Soft Point Core-Lokt
350 REMINGTON MAGNUM	200 250*	Pointed Soft Point Core-Lokt Pointed Soft Point Core-Lokt
351 WIN. SELF-LOADING	180*	Soft Point
375 H.&H. MAGNUM	270* 300	Soft Point Metal Case
38-40 WIN.	180*	Soft Point
444 MAR.	240*	Soft Point
44-40 WIN.	200*	Soft Point
44 REMINGTON MAGNUM	240*	Soft Point
45-70 GOVERNMENT	405*	Soft Point
458 WIN. MAGNUM	510* 500	Soft Point Metal Case

Primer No.	Muzzle	100 YDS.	200 YDS.	300 YDS.	400 YDS.	500 YDS.	Muzzle	100 YDS.	200 YDS.	300 YDS.	400 YDS.	500 YDS.	50 YDS.	100 YDS.	200 YDS.	300 YDS.	100 YDS.	200 YDS.	300 YDS.	400 YDS.	500 YDS.	BARREL
	VELOCITY — FEET PER SECOND						ENERGY — FOOT POUNDS						100 YDS.				200 YDS.					
9½	2860	2570	2300	2050	1810	1590	2730	2200	1760	1400	1090	840	+0.3	⊕	−5.0	−17.8	+2.1	⊕	−8.5	−25.6	−53.7	24″
9½	2610	2390	2170	1970			2720	2280	1870	1540			+0.2	⊕	−6.0	−20.8						
9½	2610	2250	1940	1680			2720	2020	1500	1130												
9½	2570	2140	1790	1520			2490	1730	1210	870			+0.3	⊕	−6.6	−24.7						23½″
9½	2120	1800	1540	1340			1700	1220	895	680			+0.6	⊕	−9.5	−33.3						22″
9½	2280	1920	1630	1410			1960	1390	1000	750			+0.5	⊕	−8.5	−29.8						26″
9½	2280	1920	1630	1410			1960	1390	1000	750			+0.5	⊕	−8.5	−29.8						
6½	1290	1060	940	840			370	250	195	155			+2.8	⊕	−30.1	−97.2						24″
6½	1290	1060	940	840			370	250	195	155			+2.8	⊕	−30.1	−97.2						
9½	2530	2140	1820	1570			2840	2030	1470	1090			+0.3	⊕	−7.1	−23.7						24″
9½	2400	1960	1580	1280			1920	1280	835	545			+0.4	⊕	−8.1	−30.7						26″
9½	2100	1710	1390	1160			1950	1300	855	605			+0.7	⊕	−10.9	−39.4						
9½M	2710	2410	2130	1870	1640	1430	3260	2570	2000	1550	1190	910	+0.2	⊕	−5.1	−18.0						20″
9½M	2410	2190	1980	1790	1620	1460	3220	2660	2180	1780	1450	1180	+0.4	⊕	−6.4	−21.5						
6½	1850	1560	1310	1140			1370	975	685	520			+1.0	⊕	−14.5	−51.8						20″
9½M	2740	2460	2210	1990	1800	1620	4500	3620	2920	2370	1940	1570					+2.4	⊕	−9.8	−27.6	−56.0	25″
9½M	2550	2180	1860	1590	1380	1210	4330	3160	2300	1680	1200	975					+3.1	⊕	−12.5	−37.6	−79.2	
2½	1330	1070	960	850			705	455	370	290			+2.7	⊕	−29.1	−93.7						24″
9½	2400	1845	1410	1125			3070	1815	1060	675			+0.6	⊕	−9.6	−36.7						24″
2½	1310	1050	940	830			760	490	390	305			+2.8	⊕	−29.6	−95.2						24″
2½	1750	1360	1110	980			1630	985	655	510			+1.4	⊕	−17.5	−64.5						18½″
9½	1320	1160	1050	990			1570	1210	990	880			+2.4	⊕	−25.1	−81.2						22″
9½M	2130	1840	1600	1400			5140	3830	2900	2220			+0.6	⊕	−9.2	−32.1						25″
9½M	2130	1910	1700	1520			5040	4050	3210	2570			+0.6	⊕	−8.9	−29.4						

†Inches above (+) or below (—) line of sight. Held low for (+) figures, high for (—) figures.
"Specifications are nominal." Ballistics figures established in test barrels. Individual guns may vary from test barrel specifications.

STEYR BALLISTICS DATA

(Author's note: this is a rather unusual ballistics table in that it was not compiled by an ammunition maker but, rather, by a rifle-producing firm. Steyr offers their rifles in a broad range of U.S. and European calibers so they've produced tables based on performances in *their* rifles with a wide variety of ammo by Remington, Winchester, RWS, C.I.L. DWM and Norma.

Be careful of European measures for weights and distances: to convert bullet weights to grains multiply given figures by 15.45; to convert meters (m) to feet multiply given meters by 3.28; to convert meters to yards, multiply meters by 1.09.)

Caliber	Weight of bullet	Type of bullet	Muzzle velocity in m/sec	Impact force Eo in mkp	Optimum distance for sighting in	Location of hole punched into target in cm, if line of sight begins 5 cm above the axis of the barrel (telescopic sight)			
						100 m	150 m	200 m	300 m
.222 Rem.	3.24	Lead point	975	157	180	+3.8	+2.9	− 2.9	−32.8
.222 Rem. Mag.	3.56	Lead point	1006	184	185	+3.5	+2.9	− 1.9	−27.1
.223 Rem.	3.56	Lead point	1006	184	185	+3.5	+2.9	− 1.9	−27.1
5.6 x 57	4.8	Taper point	1040	265	215	+3.6	+3.9	+ 1.3	−15.7
.22-250 Rem.	3.56	Pointed lead point	1146	239	210	+3.3	+3.8	+ 1.0	−15.5
6 mm Rem.	6.48	Lead point, core-locked	972	312	195	+3.6	+3.2	− 0.5	−20.1
.243 Win.	6.8	Semi-jacket, round nose	912	288	190	+4.0	+3.3	− 1.2	−24.0
6.5 x 57	10.0	H-jacket, open hollow-point	800	326	175	+4.9	+2.6	− 4.5	−39.0
6.5 x 68 S	8.5	H-jacked, plastic point	985	430	220	+4.0	+4.3	+ 1.1	−17.6
.257 Weatherby Mag.	7.6	Hornady	1005	389.9	190	+3.4	+2.9	− 1.1	−22.1
.264 Win. Mag.	9.07	Pointed lead point, core-locked	975	440	195	+3.5	+3.2	− 0.4	−19.3
.270 Win.	10.0	H-jacket, hollow copper point	865	381	200	+4.9	+4.7	0	−29.7
7 x 57	11.2	H-jacket, hollow copper point	770	339	160	+3.7	+1.1	− 6.9	−42.0
7 x 64	11.2	H-jacket, hollow copper point	850	413	180	+4.0	+2.9	− 3.1	−28.5
7 mm Rem. Mag.	11.34	Lead point, core-locked	936	507	185	+3.9	+3.0	− 2.0	−26.9
.30-06 Spr.	11.7	H-jacket, hollow copper point	840	420	165	+3.9	+1.6	− 5.8	−36.2
.300 H. u. Mag.	14.26	Leadspoint, core-locked	799	464	160	+3.9	+1.2	− 7.4	−44.7
.308 Win.	11.7	H-jacket, hollow copper point	780	363	160	+4.2	+1.0	− 6.5	−41.5
8 x 57 JS	12.1	H-jacket, hollow copper point	820	415	170	+4.8	+2.2	− 4.8	−37.4
8 x 68 S	12.1	H-jacket, hollow copper point	970	580	200	+4.0	+3.7	0	−19.9
9.3 x 62	16.7	H-jacket, hollow copper point	780	518	170	+5.0	+2.5	− 4.8	−39.2
9.3 x 64	19.0	Brenneke-Torpedo-Universal	805	627	170	+4.0	+2.1	− 4.6	−33.3
.375 H. u. H. Mag.	19.44	Full jacket	777	598	150	+3.7	0	−10.5	−56.5
.458 Win. Mag.	33.05	Lead point	649	710	130	+3.3	−3.9	−20.5	−87.2

						Max. height of trajectory in cm			
						100 m	200 m	300 m	
.338 Win. Mag.	19.4	Silver tip	747	552		2.5 cm	11.6 cm	29 cm	
						Max. height of trajectory in cm			
						100 yd	200 yd	300 yd	
.308 Norma Mag.	11.66	Lead point	945	521		0	1.6	4.6	

CHAPTER 9

Fundamentals of Rifle Shooting

Whether you are right- or left-handed is not as important as the question of whether you are *right or left eyed!* Usually, the eye matching the dexterous hand will be found to be the "master eye," but, too often we'll find exceptions to the rule.

If you think I'm kidding you, let's conduct a little test to see which of your eyes dominates your vision.

With both eyes open, point a finger at a small, stationary object about twenty feet away. Now, while holding a steady point, close your left eye—does your finger still point true? Or does it appear to be pointing about two feet to the left of the target?

If your point remains true, you are right eyed and should be right-handed as well. On the other hand, if your point appears to shift, you are left eyed. Check again, sight with both eyes open, but now, close your right eye. If the point remains on target you have confirmed that your left eye dominates your vision.

The dominating eye is referred to as the "master eye" and this poses no problem as long as your master eye matches your dominant side. When learning to shoot with both eyes open, the master eye will automatically take control.

What happens if you are right-handed but left eyed?

This is a problem that gives the shooter only two alternatives—he must either train himself to shoot from the opposite shoulder or, he must learn to shoot with his master eye closed. One shooter I ran into simply couldn't keep his master eye shut; just as he was getting off the shot he'd find himself peeking. I don't have to tell you what this did to his scoring. He solved the problem by wearing an eye patch.

It is by far the better alternative to learn to shoot from the appropriate shoulder, however difficult this may prove to be.

Having determined which eye (and shoulder), let's discuss phase two of our preparations.

THE RIFLEMAN'S CLOTHING

A rifleman's clothing plays an important role in his overall performance.

Starting with the feet, I've always felt that only a form of semi-boot was really adequate. These should cover the ankles and be laced to fit the ankle area snugly, thereby lending support to the ankles when shooting from a sitting or kneeling position. Low quarter shoes or loosely-fitted boots

A target shooter's accessories! The only items missing from this scene are the shooting jacket and cap.

are more of a hindrance than a help. Shooters who have difficulty sitting on the side of their foot in the kneeling position can often use a thin piece of foam rubber under the shoe and wrapped around the ankle to relieve the discomfort.

A target shooter will generally find a leather boot, just covering the ankles, best for his purposes. The hunter, on the other hand, must often wear higher and heavier boots—sometimes of rubber—because weather conditions so dictate. In all

instances, however, it pays to have *laced* boots that fit snugly; they're easier to walk in and they lend support to the various shooting positions.

Target shooters usually wear only a thin pair of white cotton socks under their boots. Hunters, depending on the weather, are often obliged to wear more. The hunter should be careful to avoid overdoing it in cold weather. Three pairs of heavy woolen socks will not keep the feet any warmer than one pair of thin cottons and one pair of woolens. Too much foot covering tends to hamper circulation or cause foot sweat; either one of these results in very cold feet in very short order.

Clothing worn from the waist down should be loose and comfortable; tightly fitted trousers are to be avoided.

The upper torso is difficult to fit properly, because most conventional shirts and jackets are made with collars and lapels which interfere with the motion of shouldering the rifle. The ideal shirt would have little or no collar. (Some riflemen simply button the collared shirt up to the neck.)

Outer jackets, particularly so-called hunting jackets, are often designed to be loose and baggy. That's a mistake! A hunter's jacket should fit snugly across the chest and waist with little in the way of belts, pockets, flaps, etc. on the gun-mounting side. Rifle butts will snag on most anything protruding from the jacket—and usually when least expected.

In my opinion, the ideal hunter's jacket should be made with a few broad elastic bands extending across the back so that front panels are held smooth and flat. If these bands were independent of the back panel, the back of the jacket would remain loose and baggy.

The serious target shooter invariably uses a shooting jacket of the 10–X type that is well suited to position shooting. When selecting such a jacket, it is important only to pick one that fits properly— a bit tight, rather than loose. Under the shooting jacket most prefer to wear a sweat shirt. In very hot weather, a soft cotton shirt of the pullover type is substituted for the sweat shirt. Extremely cold weather poses more of a problem. I've used a sweat shirt or a tightly-fitted woolen pullover sweater together with a plasticized foul-weather pullover under the jacket.

TWO IMPORTANT ACCESSORIES
THE HAT AND THE GLOVE

Target shooters wear a special padded glove on their supporting hand to cushion the pinching effect on the sling. This glove makes position shooting considerably more comfortable and it would be rather foolish to compete without one.

Hunters who have learned to make use of their slings for shooting support would also do well to wear some form of glove on their forward hand.

Some form of head covering is generally desirable as well. This, depending again upon the weather, will range from a ventilated type golf cap to the hunter's woolen cap with ear muffs. Old army campaign hats seem to enjoy special popularity among target shooters.

With the head covering we are only concerned with two functions—shading the eyes and shielding the eyes from rain or snow. Consequently, we are really only concerned with a hat having a brim that will accomplish these two functions without interfering with our gun handling. A very long brim can be a nuisance but, at times, especially in inclement weather, a brim that encircles the head, covering the neck and ears, can be helpful.

FUNDAMENTALS OF MARKSMANSHIP

The first point I would like to make when discussing marksmanship in general is that *no one* can hold a rifle perfectly still in an aiming attitude. The harder one tries, the more the muzzle will dance and cavort around the target. In spite of the shooter's best efforts, that rifle is going to move, uninterruptedly, for as long as it is hand held. So, my first advice to a beginner is to expect this motion and understand that the game of marksmanship is dependent upon your ability to cope with the constant motion of the sights over the target area.

The detail that separates the master rifleman from the plinker is the former's ability to develop a position and a state of relaxed concentration that induces the rifle to move in a tight, *predictable* pattern usually in the form of a diagonal figure eight. This, coupled with the eye, mind and trigger coordination that comes with training and practice, leads the master rifleman to his enviable station in the shooting ranks.

Because the fundamentals of position target shooting apply to all forms of rifle shooting we'll examine them one by one.

THE SHOOTING POSITION

Regardless of the position you intend to use, it is of vital importance that you create, with your body, a shooting platform that *naturally wants to point the rifle directly at the target!* Consequently, the first step in assuming a shooting position is to position your body in such a way that the rifle will be pointing in the general direction of the target. Next, close your eyes and get comfortable in that position—you'll soon feel the rifle steadying and realize that this is the direction in which it will tend to shoot. While maintaining that position, open your eyes. You can expect the sights to be bearing right or left of the target. At this point, especially if you're fairly close to the mark, you'll have to overcome the impulse to move the left arm to bring the sights on target. Instead, move your entire body slightly in the desired direction. Close your eyes and test the position again. Don't worry about elevation; this is easily corrected by other means. At this point we are only concerned with lateral alignment. When the sights are bearing on a good lateral line, the shooter can make small adjustments in elevation through breath control: as he inhales he'll notice the muzzle dropping; upon exhaling the muzzle will climb. Thus, as the sights begin to bear on the center of the target he'll squeeze off the shot. If he maintains the position too long, sight movement will become erratic. Then it would be best to cancel the attempt—open the bolt—and rest a bit before trying again.

Major corrections in elevation can only be made by repositioning the butt of the rifle at the shoulder or by readjusting the sling. In the prone, sitting or kneeling positions, a loose sling will cause the rifle to point too low. An overly tight sling usually causes it to point too high. The one thing the target shooter must guard against is the temptation to make sight corrections by moving the supporting arm or hand. In target shooting, *the body points the rifle,* not the hands or arms! Hunters would do well to study the same technique—particularly for those occasions when timing is not critical and there is sufficient opportunity to assume a deliberate shooting position.

Very often, after a rifleman has perfectly zeroed his rifle, he'll find a series of shots favoring one side of the bull's eye. He'll quickly correct this by shifting this position. This, because he recognizes the fact that his natural body position is favoring that side of the target and that, by somewhat anticipating the shot, he's falling off to his natural aiming attitude at the last crucial instant.

Just as the novice tends to flinch with the shot, the master rifleman tends to anticipate it! They're *both* faults. When one anticipates the shot, he relaxes, dropping the rifle out of alignment at the instant of firing.

CALLING THE SHOT

Watch a master rifleman at work and you'll be amazed to discover that he can invariably recite the location of each shot before he examines the target! This is because he's *squeezing* the trigger, because he's *not* anticipating the shot, because his eye was open at the instant of firing, and because he made a mental picture of his sight alignment at the time the shot fell. When he misses a shot, he knows why he missed!

The new rifleman should make every effort to "call" every shot. He'll find that as he improves in this area, his scores will automatically improve as well.

SMALL BORE TARGET SHOOTING

There is a tendency on the part of many big bore

shooters to view, rather contemptuously, any form of shooting which employs the .22 rimfire cartridge. That's a mistake!

Small bore target shooting is probably the most demanding of all the target rifle sports. On the fifty-foot range, the small bore rifleman expects to hit a 10-ring that is actually smaller in diameter than the .22 long rifle bullet! When a perfect pinwheel bull's eye is scored, it completely removes the 10-ring of the target.

Because the .22 bullet is small, light and relatively slow, competition on the outdoor 100-yard range requires unusual skill. Wind conditions and mirage, to the iron-sighted small bore shooter, have special significance.

To get right to the point, any rifleman—whether a hunter or big bore target shooter—would do well to take up small bore target shooting, especially during the off-season when indoor gallery competition is popular. The fundamentals of four-position riflery, learned on the small bore range, carry over well into all areas of rifle shooting.

WIND AND MIRAGE

The printed page will not teach a rifleman how to cope with these obstacles of nature. The best we can do here is describe the problems and some of the steps that can be taken to overcome them. Real wind-doping and mirage-reading ability comes only through extensive practice, training and experimentation.

How great an effect can a cross wind (3 or 9 o'clock) have on a bullet?

This would depend on: one, the direction of the rifling and the *direction of the drift of the bullet;* two, the velocity and character of the wind (gusty? steady?); three, the shape and weight of the bullet; four, the distance from the firing line to the target and; finally, the speed of the bullet.

Assuming that the rifle has not been pre-zeroed to offset the effect of bullet drift at 1,000 yards and, assuming that earlier experimentation has shown that it will drift three feet to the left at this distance—with one particular cartridge, bullet and load—a right to left cross wind that would normally move the bullet ten feet to the left over the thousand yard range, would result in a bullet strike thirteen feet to the left of the aiming point. On the other hand, a left to right cross wind of the same velocity, under similar mechanical circumstances, would be partially negated by the drift effect and the bullet would strike only seven feet to the right of the target.

Notice that I used the 1,000 yard range in this example. That is because wind conditions generally have little effect on bullets over short ranges. It goes without saying, that the speed of the bullet in reaching the target determines how long the wind has to work on it! Light-fast bullets, driven at high velocities, get to short-range targets so quickly that wind deviation is virtually undetectable. However, because light projectiles react more readily to wind during an extended flight period, it is quite possible that heavier, though slower, projectiles may be more desirable in long-rang shooting. That old axiom about "compromises" pops up again! Bear in mind, too, that a bullet is decelerating from the time it leaves the muzzle.

The average shooter will often feel, intuitively, that a 3 o'clock or 9 o'clock wind is the most troublesome. T'ain't necessarily so! Not only can a twelve o'clock wind prove more disconcerting (because it can often range from ten to two o'clock *opposite* directions), but because it may also have a fickle vertical quality that will introduce a whole new set of variables to our wind-doping arithmetic. Gusts, too, are far more unpredictable than a constant, though high velocity, wind.

The best advice we can give the aspiring long-range marksman is, "get out there and shoot!" Experiment, make notes, test assorted loadings, seek the help of an experienced rifle coach. There's no substitute for practice and experimentation.

Mirage is something else again. The dictionary will define "mirage" as a distorted reflection of a distant image, at least insofar as the definition applies to our purposes.

There are three forms of mirage that apply to shooting. The first is caused by heat waves rising into the line of sight from the hot rifle barrel. The second is caused by heat waves rising from ground surfaces, between the shooter and the target, when under a blistering sun. The third is optical effect from the target itself.

Unlike wind factors, mirage effects can cause trouble even at short ranges.

Let's start with the target. Most targets are designed with a pitch-black circle surrounded by an almost-white field. On a slightly overcast day the shooter will find it comparatively easy to define that black circle sharply. Now, assuming he's using iron sights that require a six o'clock hold—such as those used on the service rifle—he'll try to develop a sight picture that balances that black bull's-eye perfectly on the front sighting post. Only the hint of a white line will be seen between the post sight and the bull.

If, at this point, the clouds should part and a bright sun should bear on the target, the bull's-eye will appear to *shrink* in size. The surrounding white field, under the bright glare of the sun, will encroach upon the black field, distorting the resolution between the two. The shooter with the six o'clock sight picture will now start shooting too high! Of course, the phenomenon works in reverse when conditions go from bright sun to overcast.

Range surface mirage, caused when a blistering sun is baking the entire range, results when heat waves climb into the line of sight. These greatly distort the definition of the target area and, simultaneously, cause it to appear *higher* than it really is. As soon as the experienced marksman starts to see those wavy heat lines he'll start to favor a lower hold on the target. Perhaps, depending upon the range, he'll simply click his sights down a bit. At any rate, he'll immediately take note of the heat waves and anticipate a high shot. When possible, he'll spot each shot with infinite care and as soon as one indicates a tendency to climb above the group he'll make a sight correction. The same applies when heat waves start to pour forth from an overheated barrel.

Many target marksmen employ a broad and fairly heavy webbed belt, stretched over the barrel from the receiver to the muzzle, to deploy heat waves to the sides, away from the line of sight.

Another important point—a slight wind will cause heat waves to move diagonally, rather than vertically. When this occurs it is necessary to make *diagonal* corrections which are considerably more difficult.

Again, the beginning rifleman should realize that experience is the best teacher.

PHYSICAL CONDITIONING

No matter what form of shooting or hunting one plans to do, physical condition is important. Would-be hunters should first get a thorough physical examination and then undertake to carry out a planned exercise program. Hunting, especially big-game hunting, can be exceptionally demanding.

Target shooters, too, will find an exercise program helpful, but it should be supplemented with positioning practice. In other words, they should actually sit in the "sitting" position for ten minutes at a time while holding the rifle in an aiming position. This will strengthen the muscles employed in maintaining their shooting attitude. The same applies to the kneeling position. In the offhand, or standing position, it even helps to suspend a five-pound weight from the muzzle of the rifle. Dry firing, with an empty hull or snap-cap in chamber, will add a trigger-squeeze and coordination exercise to the physical exercise progarm.

One factor that separates the expert rifleman

from the amateur is the former's ability to operate a trigger without discernible movements of the hand or forearm. Sounds ridiculous, doesn't it? Okay, extend your right arm and make a semi-fist as if holding a pistol. Now, activate your trigger finger and watch carefully to detect movement of the hand, fingers and forearm. One or two attempts will convince you that everything wants to move with the trigger finger. Suppose, now, you added a resistance of three or four pounds to the trigger finger? More movement!

To overcome this one needs a specialized form of exercise—one that strengthens the muscles controlling the trigger finger! If you can obtain a scrap gun containing a trigger mechanism, it's a comparatively simple matter to increase the trigger-pull weight to six or eight pounds, or more. Then, while relaxing in front of the television, simply operate the bogus trigger unit fifty or sixty times in an evening. This will help you develop the muscles that control the hand and forearm and you'll soon find that the trigger finger can be made to function rather independently.

As a marksmanship instructor I was often confronted with a student who simply refused to sit on the side of his foot when in the kneeling position. He'd claim it was too painful. It is—if one doesn't work at it! The only alternative is to place the toe of the sole down and curl the heel upward so one may sit on the heel of the foot. Frankly, I feel it's a lousy alternative. The result is like placing one marble on top of another—they both want to roll to the side! This causes undesirable body motion and the kneeling position is difficult enough without adding problems.

True, I've seen a number of Olympic riflemen shoot the kneeling positions while sitting on their heels, but they invaribaly place a small rounded pillow under their instep to relieve the pressure on their toes. It's still a poor compromise; I feel these riflemen score well *in spite* of the poor position because of their exceptional coordination.

Anyone can learn to sit on the side of his foot if he'll simply practice the position, perhaps holding the position for ten seconds today, fifteen seconds tomorrow, etc. In time, when he's toughened up his ankle, he'll find he can hold the position comfortably for long periods and that it will give him a much steadier platform for the difficult kneeling position. And that's what position shooting is all about—creating a steady platform for the rifle!

THE SLING

The accompanying photographs illustrate the various types and rigs for military and target slings. In position shooting with the military sling, a loop is formed in the long upper strap and through this loop is passed the left arm of the right-handed shooter. The loop is then drawn snugly around the upper arm and secured in place with the sling keeper. The lower strap serves only for the hasty sling position (offhand shooting) and for general carrying convenience. It is not employed as a support for the prone, sitting or kneeling positions. Accordingly, the frog of the lower strap is reinstalled at a point where it will give maximum slack to the lower end of the sling.

Target slings eliminate the lower strap completely and a cuff is generally secured around the upper arm. Adjustment of the one remaining strap is then simplified.

A trial-and-error method is employed by the shooter to determine the sling tension that puts him "on target" with the desired degree of sling stress. The sling should be adjusted so that it easily supports the rifle in the aiming attitude without conscious effort on the part of the left hand and arm. This can best be described as "comfortably snug."

An overly tight sling will pick up the pulsations of the heartbeat and these can be especially disconcerting. A sling that is too loosely fitted, on the other hand, is virtually useless, requiring considerable left hand support for the rifle. This can be very tiring and result, too, in dropped shots.

The conventional military sling setting for prone, sitting and kneeling. Some shooters would try to get the sling roll closer to the upper arm.

Most match rules stipulate that no point of the left arm or hand, below the elbow, can be in contact with the surface of the firing point. The shooter who tends to take a very low prone position has to guard against this.

When the shooter has found the frog position that gives him the desired sling tension for the prone position, it would save him time at future matches to scribe the letter "P" between the frog holes.

Because the left arm is bent to a greater degree in the sitting and kneeling positions, the sling must be shortened somewhat from the prone setting.

Start by moving the frog up one setting. If there is too little rifle support, take it up another notch. Generally, two positions above the prone setting will be about right. Settings are entirely dependent upon the individual's build and position preference, so it pays to experiment in an effort to find a comfortable sling tension that gives adequate rifle support.

In moving from sitting to kneeling most shooters will find it necessary to tighten the sling at least one more frog-setting.

For shooting from the standing (offhand) position, the hunter may use a hasty sling and now the short, lower strap of the military sling comes into use. There are a number of methods for doing this but the easiest is to simply set up the sling as you

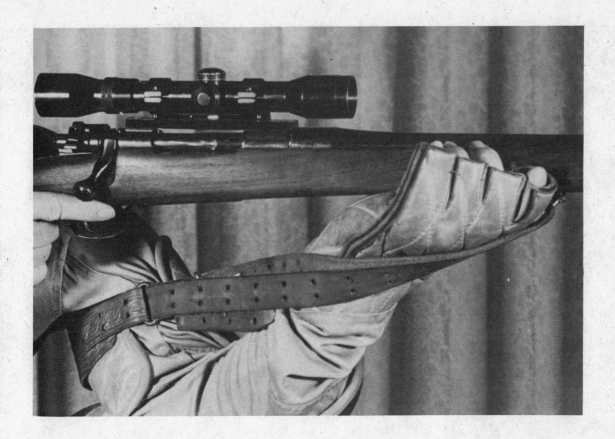

This target sling employs a broad cuff that encircles the upper arm. Note how sling is turned to fold naturally over the back of the leading hand.

normally would for display—tight from fore end to butt. Now reset the lower frog to create the slack needed for the hasty sling offhand position and slacken the upper sling.

It is important to rotate the sling about half a turn counterclockwise when getting into it. This turns the sling at the forward swivel so that the strap will fold gently, and naturally, over the back of the left hand.

Slings should be cleaned and oiled regularly.

SHOOTING POSITIONS

While the fundamentals of position shooting are fairly well standardized, it should be noted that most experienced marksmen employ unique minor form variations of a purely individual nature. Since no two shooters are of precisely the same physical build, it is natural for the shooter to modify the basics, in *small* ways, to exploit strengths and minimize weaknesses. The new shooter, however, must guard against the tendency to deviate from the fundamentals. To him, all positions are uncomfortable and unsteady. Only through continous practice will he loosen the joints and strengthen the muscles to the point where he can start to feel comfortable and confident.

The importance of a qualified rifle coach during the early training stages cannot be overemphasized. A good experienced coach will be able

to suggest changes in form without departing from the critical basics of the position.

IMPORTANCE OF PREPARATION

Before reaching the firing line, the shooter should be properly prepared. Here's my own check list when going into a timed-fire match:

1. Sights tight, properly adjusted
2. Sling set-up checked—adjusted for position
3. Clothing comfortable
4. Pockets emptied
5. Jacket snug across chest — buttoned to top
6. Hat and shooting glasses on
7. Glove on
8. Proper quantity and type of ammunition in hand.

Note number four—empty pockets! Nothing is more disconcerting than to find yourself in the prone position of a timed-fire match with your car keys digging a hole in your upper leg.

THE PRONE POSITION

The shooter is standing at the ready. He checks the number of his firing point, and looks for the corresponding target downrange. He turns his body 45° to the right (if he is right-handed). The rifle is held with the left hand on the forearm and the right hand cupped over the comb, near the butt. At the command, he drops to his knees, throws his right hand and the rifle butt straight out in front of him, and slides into the prone position by rolling to his left side when shouldering the rifle.

Throughout this entire maneuver, he's kept his eyes fastened on his target downrange. (It's much too easy to line up on the wrong target.)

Now he starts checking his position. First, direction—is the rifle bearing, generally, on the

The modern prone position with the right knee slightly raised. This takes some of the pressure off the chest and makes breathing easier.

proper target? Left elbow almost directly under the rifle. Right elbow comfortable and right hand in trigger position. Face comfortably positioned against the comb of the stock—sights in alignment with the eye. Left leg stretched out straight with left toe supporting the foot. Right knee drawn up slightly to relieve pressure on the chest. Sling adjustment appears to be correct.

At this point the shooter closes both eyes and relaxes into position, letting the rifle settle into the alignment where it feels motionless and where it is supported without strain. When that ideal condition is sensed the shooter opens his eyes, checks his target number and notes the bearing of the the sights with relation to the target. Now let's run through some position corrections to get the sights bearing precisely on the center of the target.

AIM IS TOO FAR LEFT: keep left elbow planted and wiggle body, snake-like fashion, in a slight arc to the left. Close eyes and recheck position. Continue correction, in small steps, until sights bear well laterally. Remember, a very slight change in body position can move the muzzle a considerable distance. Be careful not to rush it— move by degrees and take the time after each movement to recheck the position. Don't try to make elevation corrections at this point. Keep that target number in mind and make sure you're bringing the rifle to bear on the right target. Cross firing not only hurts you, it can compromise a shooter on an adjoining point.

AIM IS TOO FAR RIGHT: again, keep the left elbow stationary and wiggle body to the right. Same procedure but in reverse.

AIM IS TOO LOW: the question here is, "how much too low?" The shooter will notice that the muzzle will dip as he takes a deep breath. Upon exhaling, the muzzle will climb. Exhale slowly, as the sights come to bear on the target center, slow down exhalation and stop it altogether when alignment is right.

If the desired correction cannot be achieved

through breath control, the shooter will have to alter his body position and he must do this carefully to avoid destroying his lateral alignment. If sights are much too low, keep left elbow planted and inch the body straight back.

If sights are too high, inch forward—again, with the left elbow providing the point of focus.

If no amount of forth and back movement or breath control can correct the situation, the problem lies with the sling adjustment. A sling that is too loose will always bear low—a sling that is too tight will always cause the rifle to bear too high!

When in trouble you should, by all means, reposition the frog on the sling. At times, when the condition is not too critical, you can simply slide your forward hand rearward a bit to raise the sights into alignment. Or, if you have the room between your left hand and the forward swivel, slide your hand forward slightly to lower the sights.

While this procedure takes considerable time to describe, in actual practice it goes rather quickly. The important point is to take the time to follow the procedure—resist the temptation to rush. Even if you're competing in a timed match, the time allotted is usually generous. If you make your preparations carefully, the shooting will go quickly when you reach that stage. The more time you spend getting "set," the faster you will perform and your scores will reflect your patience.

The novice invariably identifies himself in a rifle match because he's the first one to get a shot off!

When you are provided with a sighting target, use it! Heat up the barrel before shooting for record.

One little trick I liked to employ in gallery shooting was to shoot at the various bulls in vertical sequence. For instance, if the ten-bull target consisted of a row of four on the left, three in the center, and four on the right, the middle target of the center row was considered the "sighter." After

sighting I would next shoot at the target directly below the sighter. Then the target above it. Having finished the center row, I would re-adjust my position to start with the top left target and work down in order. After each shot I would adjust elevation through breath control or squeeze my body forward slightly to lower the natural aim. When finished with the left row, I would remake the position for the extreme right row and start with the bottom bull, working upwards.

I found a number of advantages to this sequence of shooting! Though I've never encountered it, there is a possibility that some match rules will insist upon shooters following a predetermined pattern; check this before adopting my technique.

Another point shooters should take care to follow is that NRA rules require that no portion of the arms below the elbows can be bearing on the firing point, or on an artificial support. Those inclined to shoot from a very low, prone position should be particularly careful about this.

GETTING THE SHOT OFF

When the shooter is satisfied with his position—and only then—he loads the rifle and prepares for his first shot at the sighter.

Settling into the position he draws a breath (not too deeply) and slowly starts to exhale. Watching the progress of his sights carefully, the shooter starts to take up on the trigger as the sights near the center of the bull. Experience will teach a shooter how much pressure to exert and how fast to apply it. The expert will find that the shot falls just as the sight picture reaches the ideal state. Squeeze the trigger—slowly, carefully, so as not to disturb the sight picture. Don't anticipate the moment of firing and don't try to twitch the sights into alignment if they should stubbornly resist moving into the desired sight picture; rather, it is better to make a slight position correction.

Let's say the first shot is a bull's eye but favoring

three o'clock rather than dead center. No adjustment is called for—remember this is a cold barrel. (Some shooters fire two or three quick shots into the target butts to heat the barrel before seriously working on the sighter.)

If, after three shots, we're still favoring three o'clock in the ten ring, it is time to make a sight correction to bring the bullet strike into dead center. Two or three successive shots close to dead center and we're ready to shoot for record.

If given the means to spot shots during the course of the match, by all means do so. Practice calling each shot. If suddenly and inexplicably a shot should come in low when you've called it on center, you're relaxing before the shot has a chance to get away. You're anticipating the shot!

A series of nine o'clock nipper tens will tell you that your position is favoring the left side—move your right elbow back a fraction of an inch.

Work at the prone position until you can compete favorably with the experts. The fundamentals of trigger timing and positioning carry over into sitting, kneeling and offhand.

THE SITTING POSITION

Sitting is a bit more difficult than the prone position. The body doesn't provide as much support; the legs serve only as a platform upon which to rest the elbows. A good sling setting is of paramount importance. Increased muzzle motion is immediately apparent and trigger timing gains new significance.

To reach the sitting position the shooter faces his target, sling in position, rifle balanced in the left hand. He turns approximately 20° to the right, spreads his feet about twenty inches apart, squats, and drops into the sitting position, using his right hand to break his fall.

The procedure for position checkering, outlined for the prone position, also applies for sitting. Corrective measures, differ; to correct right or left,

it is necessary to use the buttocks as swiveling point, moving the heels right or left while maintaining the distance of their separation.

One should strive to achieve as much support as possible from the legs and sling. The left upper arm should be placed to engage the upper surface of the left shin. Keep the sling as high as possible on the upper arm to avoid interference in the bearing region.

The shooter is given considerable freedom in the sitting position. The rules state only that the arms must be kept above the ankles. Extra low positions, however, may hamper alignment of the shooting eye with the sights.

If a position check indicates that you're aiming too low, try sliding the left hand back slightly on the forearm. This will serve for small corrections. A larger correction will require either a new sling setting or a repositioning of the feet, drawing them rearward to raise the knees.

High sight pictures can be corrected by pushing the feet forward, sliding the left hand forward, or by loosening the sling.

Since the rules are not too stringent, it pays to experiment with this position. Test many variations, look for the one position most comfortable and steady for you.

If shooting from a rather soft surface, try stamping the heels into place—this often helps. Some shooters, more flexible than most, find it possible to sit with their feet flat on the surface. (Seems like a good idea for those who can manage it!)

When the knees tend to flare out sidewise, destroying the position, it indicates that the shooter is trying to set up against the inner surface of the shins. The left arm should be moved upward to embrace more of the top surface of the shin. Right arm, too, can be relocated to engage more of the top surface.

This position will vary depending upon the caliber of rifle used. The small bore shooter will find

A good sitting position: arms are positioned on top of shins or knees, feet are almost flat. Some shooters would try to position the rifle a bit more over the left elbow.

The properly executed kneeling position! Sling is high on left arm, muscle of upper left arm is on top of the knee while the bone is rolled over into the hollow in the face of the knee. Right elbow is purposely dropped. Rifle is almost directly above left elbow. Left foot is near flat. Note, too, that the right knee is angled slightly towards the left foot.

a high position to be comfortable and steady. The big bore shooter, however, will find that he has to get his body weight forward, into a lower position, to minimize recoil effects.

One common variation of the sitting position is the cross-legged style. Frankly, I feel that this form is next to useless. The knees are so greatly spread that they're almost flat. The shooter, forced to employ a high arm setting, uses the knees only as a table surface. Even the benefits of the sling are partially negated by the bend of the left arm. I'd venture to guess that shooters who do well with this style are simply good offhand shooters who are, in reality, shooting in an offhand manner from this awkward position.

THE KNEELING POSITION

It is easy to understand why so many shooters complain of problems with this position—few use all of the support that the position offers!

I'm probably letting myself in for some highly critical letters but I can see no purpose in defining this position as it is commonly practiced. The high stance with the left elbow delicately balanced on the left knee, and the shooter precariously perched on his right heel, simply doesn't conform with my interpretation of a good shooting position. Consequently, I feel I'll accomplish more by teaching this position as I practice it.

Tighten the sling by one frog setting over that used for the sitting position. Move the loop of the sling far up on the left arm. Get it as high on the arm as possible.

Face the target. Point the left toe about 20° to the right of the target. Step back with the right foot and lower yourself to your right knee. Lay your right foot on its side and sit on it. Don't attempt to have your right leg form a 90° angle with your left—the right knee should be angled slightly toward the left foot. Pull the left trouser cuff down so that the fabric is stretched tightly over the left knee. With your right hand, grasp the loose material of the left sleeve of the shooting jacket— halfway between the shoulder and elbow—and pull it towards you as you rest the center of the upper left arm directly on top of the left knee.

A diagonal hollow can be found on the left side of the face of the left knee. If you now roll your upper arm over the knee cap so that the flesh on the underpart of the arm tends to remain on top of the knee cap, you'll find that your upper arm naturally homes into this socket.

With a fairly snug sling you should find this to be a very solid and steady shooting position.

Try to keep your left foot as flat as possible on the ground surface. If necessary, point your left toe a bit more to the right.

Grasp the butt of the rifle with the right hand and press it firmly into the cup of the right shoulder. Check the position for alignment (as described in the prone position).

To make position corrections, use your right foot as a swiveling point. Maintain the same relative leg spread and angles, and move both the left foot and right knee either right or left to gain the desired lateral direction.

Elevation adjustments are accomplished by sliding the left hand forth or back. Move the left foot with reluctance because it tends to flatten the natural knee socket if it is moved in either direction.

Sling tension is very important to this position. If you have trouble maintaining a reasonably steady position, your sling is too loose. If you have difficulty achieving a proper sight alignment, there is a chance that your sling is too tight.

THE OFFHAND POSITION

The standing position—more commonly referred to as the "offhand" position—is subject to many interpretations. In military circles and service matches, the shooter is not permitted to have his upper left arm bear against his body. In NRA matches, he's not only permitted to rest his upper arm against his body, he's *expected* to position his left elbow on top of his protruding left hip.

Some matches permit use of hook butt plates, thumbhole stocks and palm rests. In other matches these are banned. Trigger pull weights, too, are often specifically regulated. Many NRA matches require a trigger pull of not less than three pounds —and each competitor's rifle is checked by a match official. In "free" rifle matches, which is the most popular form of international competition, restrictions are minimal; hooks, palm rests, thumbholes and ultra-light triggers are generally employed by all competitors.

In most matches, the use of a hasty sling is not permitted.

NRA OFFHAND: (Small-bore) The shooter removes his glove and sling. He stands facing the target and turns about 60° to the right. The feet should remain fairly close together, the right foot about eight to ten inches behind the left and about parallel to the firing line. The left toe points slightly towards the firing line. The right foot should also be slightly to the right of the left with the body weight evenly balanced on both feet.

When the feet are properly positioned, lock up the left leg and relax the right. This will cause the left hip to jut out toward the target. Now, with the upper arm lightly pressed against the upper torso,

NRA offhand position. This position varies quite a bit from one shooter to the next, depending upon physical limitations. Four points, however, are fairly consistent—left elbow is always directly under the rifle, and close to the body, right elbow is carried high, left hip juts toward target, and feet are fairly close together.

well, the shooter must relax, breathing slowly and deeply. Exhalation is slow and deliberate. When the sights approach the target center, the breath is held momentarily as the shooter prepares to release the shot.

It is most important, in this position, that no attempt be made to force the shot. If the sights simply won't bear after a short time, give up on the attempt! Open the breech and rest a bit before trying again.

In position shooting, the offhand performance often decides the winner of the match. Once a beginner has learned the fundamentals of position shooting, he should spend most of his practice time in developing his offhand shooting. It is also a good idea to spend fifteen or twenty minutes a day in dry firing at home.

MILITARY OFFHAND POSITION: Same general principles apply except that the upper left arm cannot be in contact with the body.

In shooting big bore offhand, it is necessary to distribute the body weight more evenly on both feet—otherwise recoil will disturb positioning.

Instead of balancing the rifle on the finger tips of the left hand, the forearm of the rifle is placed between the crook formed by the left thumb and forefinger.

Remember to keep the right elbow high and the left elbow directly under the rifle.

try to position the left elbow directly on top of the left hip. The forearm should be almost vertical, the left elbow directly under the rifle. If shooting without a palm rest, extend the fingers of the left hand so that the finger tips support the rifle. The thumb generally bears under the trigger guard.

Breathe slowly and deliberately. Keep the right elbow high. Relax, and watch the rifle settle down to a predictable pattern. Close your eyes and make yourself comfortable. Check your position and make all necessary corrections to get the sights bearing, naturally, in the target area. Slide your right foot forth or back to raise or lower the muzzle. You can also slide your left fingertips towards the thumb to raise the muzzle—stretch them farther apart to lower.

Good breath control and trigger timing are the primary keys to good offhand scores. To breathe

This is a difficult standing position. Considerable practice must be devoted to it before scores will show any real improvement.

SHOOTING POSITIONS FOR HUNTERS

The hunter would do well to study and practice the four positions outlined earlier for target shooters. The basics of target marksmanship apply to all forms of rifle shooting.

BE PREPARED

With the hunter we must discuss preparedness before anything else. Many opportunities are missed by big game hunters each season simply because the hunter is not ready for the shot when it presents itself!

When hunting, make it a point to carry the rifle in a ready position—not over the shoulder, slung across the back or in the crook of one arm. When the hunter happens upon that trophy buck, he's not going to have more than a few seconds to get off a shot. This is especially true in heavy brush country. Realizing that all of the precious time can be wasted in simply bringing the rifle to the shoulder, one quickly understands why the rifle should be carried in both hands at "port arms." It's tiring, true, particularly as a long day wears on, but if the

The Anschutz Model 1413 is considered a "Free" rifle of the type most often employed in International matches.

hunter stops frequently he can rest his arms on branches or rocks. It doesn't pay to hunt too quickly anyway!

Next, the hunter should watch his footwork, particularly if expecting an opportunity momentarily. Most hunters "freeze" to the spot, in whatever position they were caught, when game flushes. Get caught with the right foot way out in front of the left and there's no chance to shoulder the rifle properly for an aimed shot. Make it a point to move slowly, stepping out with the left foot and bringing the right foot up to—but not beyond the left. Take small steps, move quietly, pause frequently and scan the terrain. Listen carefully because the hunter will often hear a deer before it comes into view.

Another point; stay in the shadows. Move from one covered or shaded area to another. Never walk through the center of a field or down the middle of a broad game path. Game animals, no matter how sharp their vision, have just as much trouble as humans in defining objects that are in deep shadows.

The hunter must be concerned with a wide variety of shooting conditions. Unlike the target shooter, he can't predetermine the range and he doesn't know if he'll have a stationary or a moving target.

When presented with a stationary target, the hunter should make every effort to get into a good shooting position utilizing any available artificial

rest. A fence post, tree trunk, branch, rock, etc., can provide good support for the careful and deliberate shot.

In supporting the rifle by artificial means, it is important that the barrel itself is not rested on the support. Instead rest the forward hand or the forearm of the rifle. With a vertical support, such as a tree trunk, cup the palm of the forward hand

The hunter should not rest the gun itself on the support. Instead, he should rest his hand or forearm as shown here. It would help, too, if he had a bit more grip on the forearm.

Vertical supports such as trees, fence posts and the like, serve well as steadying devices. This is the way to position the left hand.

against the tree and form a crook with the thumb which will accept the forearm of the rifle. Try to keep the body weight balanced on both feet or bearing a bit more on the leading foot. Lean the body against any convenient support. Use the sling for added support if time permits.

When there is no available natural support, the hunter should prefer the prone position as it is described for the target shooter.

FUNDAMENTALS OF RIFLE SHOOTING   105

When ground cover is too high, the sitting position is the next best alternative. Use the offhand or standing position only when there are no other options.

The shot at a moving target denies the hunter his options. Here, he'll have to work with the position he's caught in, unless, of course, the target is out in a broad, open expanse allowing time for a bit more deliberation. Usually the hunter is caught in a standing position and, hopefully, with the rifle in both hands. Here it is important that the hunter have the ability to swivel in either direction to track the flight of the target. For this reason the hunter should, in one motion, shoulder the rifle and draw his feet closer together. I try to keep my left knee broken because this permits my torso to swing through an arc of close to 180°.

The novice often panics in this situation and rushes that first shot unnecessarily. The experienced hunter is more deliberate. He realizes that nothing can outrun his rifle bullet, so as long as he can keep the target in view, he'll try to pick his shot. This is especially true when in deep woods where a path through the trees must be determined.

Finally, it is vitally important that the hunter keeps his eyes focused on his target. Don't bring the face *down* to the rifle stock, instead bring the comb of the stock *up* to the face. Never take your eyes off the target!

CANTING THE RIFLE

This is one of the most common of rifle-shooting faults and one most difficult to guard against.

When zeroing in the rifle from a benchrest, or from a prone position, it is comparatively easy to keep the sights plumb on a vertical line. The crosswires of a scope, too, are easily maintained in a horizontal and vertical fashion. This is especially true when the shooter has a reference point like a flag pole, tree or horizon line. Take away the reference points, introduce a few angles to the target or the shooting site, and the fun begins.

Remember, the sighting equipment on a rifle lies some distance above the axis of the bore. By adjusting the elevation setting on your scope or sight, you can compensate for the difference so that your line-of-sight, and the path of your bullet, coincide or intersect at some given point downrange.

In effect, your sights are aligned to point *straight* at the target. The barrel of your rifle, however, is *angled slightly upward*. When a shot is fired—assuming the sights were maintained in a position directly over the bore—the path of the bullet will cross the line of sight a short distance in front of the muzzle. The bullet will then arc above the line of sight and return to it at the point of impact downrange.

Now, suppose you cant the rifle while aiming? The line-of-sight is no longer directly over the axis of the bore. The bore now lies somewhere to one side of your sight line and the predetermined convergence angle between bore and sight no longer bears a true relationship to the trajectory of the bullet. In short, cant the rifle to the left and you'll find the bullets hitting low and left. Cant it to the right and they'll strike low and to the right.

Why low, shouldn't it be shooting high? NO, because you're removing the upward angle of the bore and placing the bore on the same level with the sights. Since the bullet starts to drop immediately upon leaving the muzzle, the shots will fall low.

On occasion even the expert shooter will find himself canting the rifle to get the sights bearing directly down the middle of a crookedly-hung target. (One can drive an unsuspecting novice to the brink of the happy farm by hanging his targets at random angles.)

Canting often appears in the sitting and kneeling positions where a shooter is straining to maintain the position.

Hunters have to be particularly careful to avoid this fault. When hunting on the side of a mountain, for example, the shooting position, target and natural reference points often present the hunter with a mass of angles and it's too darned easy to settle on the wrong one for reference purposes.

Keep those sights directly over the bore!

As an afterthought, I have to add here that some highly skilled and experienced target marksmen purposely shoot with a canted rifle. They're the exception to the rule and they do this only because they've found it aids their positioning. Nevertheless, they know how to zero their rifles to compensate for the cant and, since they're shooting at one specific, known distance, they can get away with it. I certainly wouldn't recommend the practice to anyone else!

CHAPTER 10

Buying a Used Rifle

The only thing that makes gun trading less chancy than horse swapping is the integrity of the people manufacturing and dealing in firearms. Gunmakers design and build their products with large safety margins and firearms dealers—at least specialty gun dealers who regularly trade in used guns—are knowledgeable and responsible enough to test suspect weapons before offering them for sale.

Buyers of used guns, therefore, can be *reasonably* assured of getting secondhand weapons that are safe to shoot.

In spite of all this, it behooves the secondhand gun buyer to exercise some simple precautions before slapping his cheek to comb and "touching one off." After all, even the most knowledgeable of gun traders have been known to get caught with a lemon on occasion.

To illustrate the proper procedure for buying a used gun let's experience a hypothetical transaction:

On a trip to the local gun shop one Saturday morning, we spot a particularly interesting and attractive varmint rifle in the used gun rack. It's fully equipped with a scope and mount and it's sporting an attractive price tag.

We've long desired something "hotter" than that old .218 Bee as we pick it up for a closer examination. The first thing we look for is a caliber designation, and we're now on the brink of the first trap!

If we find this rifle to be in a currently popular varmint caliber, fine, all we need do is be sure that factory produced ammo is readily available for it. Suppose, however, it's chambered for one of those super-hot wildcat cartridges. Here, unless you're a very experienced handloader, you should immediately walk away from that model! There are wildcats and there are wildcats—rarely will you find two exactly the same—*even when they carry the same caliber designation.* (The chapter on "Handloading for the Rifle" will give you some insight into the many problems that can crop up with custom chambers and custom loads.)

Another point that would immediately arouse my suspicion: a finely equipped and decorated wildcat rifle with an attractive price tag could very well be sporting a burned-out barrel which would cost a minimum of fifty dollars to replace. It would probably be safe to shoot but I wouldn't wager a nickel on it's accuracy potential. Add at least fifty bucks to that price tag—is it still attractive?

Now suppose it's not a wildcat, but a rifle de-

108

signed to take one of those foreign high-velocity jobs. You can't escape it—the same rules apply as for wildcats. If anything, the foreign job could be twice as troublesome. Factory produced shells are most often imported and are *not* generally available. You might find yourself with a fancy conversation piece for which you cannot even obtain empty brass cases for handloading purposes.

Assuming that we recognize the caliber to be an old familiar U.S. standard, the next logical question is "how old?" Check to see if there are any popular U.S. rifles *currently* being made in this caliber. If there are, you're fairly safe. If not, cartridges for this soon-to-be-discontinued caliber could rapidly escalate in cost.

An acquaintance of mine recently complained that a box of shells for his .218 Bee rifle jumped from about six dollars to over eleven dollars *in one year!* This is because there is a very limited demand for this shell, production runs are small and costly, storage and distribution expenses, too, are likewise high.

Having resolved the questions concerning caliber and availability of ammo, we now quiz the dealer to see what he can tell us about this particular rifle.

Why was the rifle traded? Did the dealer put a test round or two through it? Would he happen to have any fired cases from this rifle? Has he checked the headspace?

Most specialty gun shops will be happy to run a headspace check for you *if* they have the required gauges for that specific caliber. Lacking the gauges but having a handy shooting facility, some shops will simply fire two or three rounds through it so you can examine the fired casings.

If you must work with only the fired casings, examine the primer first. Is it cratered, loose in the pocket or punctured? Any of these could indicate pressure or headspace problems. Also look for unusual swelling in the web area of the case. Com-

pare the fired casing with that of a factory new shell. Hold them up, side by side, and determine if the general taper of the body is the same for both. Look for a "step" in the taper of the fired round. Any unusual bulges, cracks or dimples in the fired casing?

If the case passes your visual inspection but you still have an uneasy feeling about the gun, you can always ask the dealer to measure the critical dimensions of the fired round and compare these to the dimensions of the factory new shell. The only measurement we're really interested in here is case diameter at the base of the web area. It should be larger than the unfired factory shell, but not more than .004″ larger—.005″ would put it in the "reject" category.

Let's say that everything checks out up to this point. What next?

If the dealer has a shooting facility, we buy a box of factory shells from him and retire to the range. Now, before loading the rifle we first examine the action carefully. Cock it, test the safety device, try the trigger by dry firing it (with that old fired case in the chamber). Test the smoothness of the action by opening and closing it several times. If it's a bolt action rifle, examine the locking lugs carefully, looking for unusual wear, burrs or hairline cracks.

Keep that empty fired casing in the chamber while testing the reliability of the safety. With the action cocked, put the safety in the "safe" position. Now, pull the trigger—obviously the firing pin shouldn't fall. Pull the trigger, energetically, three or four times to make sure the safety doesn't creep into the "off" position. Next, hold the trigger back with normal pressure and slide the safety slowly toward the "off" position. Note the point at which the gun fires. The safety should travel about halfway toward the "off" position before firing occurs. Why? Because we want some margin for error in putting the safety on. This would be especially important if we were considering a deer rifle, where we would often be operating the safety with a gloved finger.

How's the trigger pull—extra heavy . . . too light? While you're at it, check for travel or creep. Does the trigger action meet with your approval?

Function testing the magazine is the next step. Remove the empty casing from the chamber and load *one* new, factory-loaded cartridge into the magazine (keeping that muzzle pointed downrange). Why only one? Because we don't really know this rifle, *yet,* so why take chances with a magazine load? This is a particularly valid point in testing automatic rifles where the previous owner may have been tinkering with the action.

Run the one loaded round from the magazine to the chamber, slowly. Watch to see how it feeds—does the bullet enter the chamber smoothly or does the nose of the bullet "crab" in the cone. Next, empty the chamber and try feeding the shell through the magazine quickly. Any unusual action here? (Through all of this, keep that muzzle pointed in a safe direction!)

If the dealer has test fired this rifle to provide you with empty casings, you can go ahead and fire this one round—but *don't do it unless you're wearing a pair of shatterproof shooting glasses.* Upon firing, did you feel any hot powder particles strike you in the face. If so, this rifle is spitting through the breech and something is wrong with the chamber or the firing pin, or both!

The first round goes off O.K. Open the breech, slowly, and watch the extraction and ejection. Does it open easily? Does it throw the empty casing out of the breech with a positive action?

Examine the ejected casing to see how it compares with the first empty cases you looked at—no change?

If you're still satisfied at this point, load *two* rounds in the magazine. Work these through the action in the normal fashion—fire them—and

eject them quickly. No jams? No extractor drops in the breech? In the case of an automatic, no repeat fire with the second shell?

Again, check the empties!

Assuming that everything checks out up to this point, you can repeat the double loading and firing two or three times just for safety's sake.

Then go on to loading to full magazine capacity but, before firing any of these, work them all through the action to see if feeding difficulties arise when the magazine spring is fully compressed. Repeat this test two or three times and, if no trace of feeding difficulty is encountered, you can start testing the rifle for accuracy.

(Complete instructions for sighting and zeroing can be found elsewhere in this book.)

In range testing it will often be found that a heavily oiled rifle will spit some oil back through the breech and into the shooter's face. This is normal—the rifle was simply oiled heavily for storage purposes. Once it is cleaned up and lubricated properly the problem will disappear.

We have to do a little backtracking at this point for the benefit of those who may be contemplating a purchase from a dealer who lacks the tools for proper headspace checking and who cannot provide a shooting facility for function testing.

In this case we simply examine the rifle with a visual inspection and operate the action with an empty chamber. If impressed, we ask the dealer to sell us the rifle on a contingency basis by asking him to write on the bill of sale "merchandise may be returned within ten days for full refund!" Here, you'll have to negotiate the difference between a credit and a refund. A credit would force you to spend your investment on other merchandise with that dealer if you were subsequently dissatisfied with the rifle and wanted to return it.

All of the firearms dealers I've encountered are very reputable people and I don't think one of them would ever refuse a refund on a *used* rifle if you had a valid reason for turning the rifle back. Of course, you can't damage the rifle while it's in your care and expect the dealer to go along with you. At any rate, spell out the adjustment you would expect if you decide not to keep the rifle and have the dealer write it on the bill of sale over his signature and date. The bill of sale then becomes a legally-binding contract.

Having hammered out the terms of the sale, we carry the rifle home (together with a box of factory-loaded shells) and proceed to test it in the field.

Because we have no idea of what to expect we must use considerable caution. Remember, the dealer hasn't been able to run a headspace check on this model nor have we been able to run any test rounds through it. Before going into the test procedures outlined earlier, we must first get some assurance that this rifle is safe enough to shoot from the shoulder. This is best done by tying the gun down, securely, to an old rubber tire. Wrap it carefully in the areas to be encircled by the rope and lash it in such a way that recoil won't cause it to fly loose. Keep the breech accessible so you can load and fire it without untying it from the tire. Tie a string to the trigger so that actual firing can be accomplished from a safe distance and, preferably, from a protected point behind an improvised barricade. Make certain that the muzzle is pointed in a safe direction. Load one shell, carefully, and let fly! Examine the empty case and compare it with a factory new shell as outlined earlier.

If everything indicates "go," load two rounds and fire them both—again, with the rifle still tied to the tire.

If everything checks out, tape a piece of plain, preferably white, cardboard in an upright fashion in the area normally occupied by the face when aiming. (Careful with that tape near the stock finish!) Now fire another round and check that white cardboard to see if you can find evidence of powder particles coming back through the breech. If it's clean, you can untie the rifle and proceed with the normal firing tests outlined earlier.

One should *always* wear shooting glasses when firing a rifle—whether testing or not. Eye damage is very easily prevented—very difficult to repair!

So far we've ascertained that the rifle is safe to shoot and that it functions reasonably well. Two questions remain: how accurate is it, and is the stock sound?

Stock questions can usually be answered by simple examination. First, check the stock with the rifle assembled. Look for cracks, checks, discolored exterior surfaces, decaying finish, etc. Pay special attention to the tang. Hairline cracks will most often pop up here. Next, try to determine if it is an amateur or professional stocking job—especially if it's a custom rifle. Amateur stocking efforts are usually not inletted deep enough, or contrarily, are inletted too deeply. A barreled action should be set into the wood so that slightly *less* than half the barrel thickness is surrounded by wood.

Check, too, to determine if this is a pressure-bedded or free-floated barrel. A thin piece of paper looped under the barrel and slid into the space between the barrel and forearm will tell you this. If the paper can slide most of the way down the barrel—towards the receiver—it's free floating. If the paper can't be made to squeeze past the leading edge of the fore end the barrel is pressure bedded.

About the bore and rifling—most shooters believe that the rifling is blown away, or eroded, when a barrel is burned out.

Wrong! A barrel usually gives way first in the throat area where the hot flames from fired shells are concentrated. An eroded throat can't be seen by the unaided eye and this is where the accuracy is usually lost. Often, the barrel can be saved by cutting, setting it back in the receiver, and re-cutting the chamber, neck and throat. The problem

Clunker or cream puff? Look over that used-rifle bargain carefully! Availability of ammo is a prime consideration. Is it safe? Is it really suited to the type of shooting you want to do?

with this solution is that it compromises the inletting of the forearm which, if you like free-floated barrels, is not too hard to accept.

Examine the inletting of the barrel in the area of the forwardmost portion of the forearm. Is there a gap on one side of the barrel and a tight fit on the other? This would indicate the stock is warping and the inletting would have to be corrected before the rifle will perform accurately. If this is the only inletting fault, a gunsmith will probably charge about fifteen dollars to correct it. However, you'd also have to ask him to check out the rest of the bedding if this is a bolt-action rifle.

With rifles having two-piece stocks, inletting is

critical only in the area where the butt section meets the rear surface of the receiver.

How's the stock finish? Remember, an oil finish is comparatively easy to restore; a high-gloss, epoxy finish is darned difficult!

Does the stock fit *you*? Is it long enough or is it too short? If it is too short there's not much you can do with it except add a rather deep (one-inch) recoil pad. If it is already equipped with a recoil pad you've got a bigger problem. A stock that is too long, on the other hand, is easily corrected by your local gunsmith.

Read the chapter on the rifle stock and determine if this stock is made for a right-hander or left-hander. I'm ashamed to admit it, but I once bought a beautiful (and very expensive) trap gun that simply wouldn't perform for me. Too late, I discovered the gun was equipped with a southpaw's stock! Fortunately, all ended well when I found a left-hander who was completely smitten with the gun and who couldn't wait to buy it from me.

Finally, we check out the accessories on this rifle: what is the worth of the scope, mount, sling, etc.? It would be a good idea to look up current market values, subtract the expense of the accessories from the dealer's price for the rifle, and see what the stripped rifle is valued at. Generally, you'll find that you're getting the accessories almost as a gift. To avoid after-purchase expense however, it would be wise to check the scope for clarity, reticle definition, and reliability of focus and turret adjustments. The mount should be examined to determine if it is securely anchored. Try the screws—are they loose, or stripped? Stripped mounting screws could mean some added expense.

More importantly, is it the type of sighting equipment that you would want on this rifle or would you prefer something else—another magnification or another mount? Now, before the sale is finalized, is the time to negotiate with the dealer to arrange an exchange of accessories. Perhaps he has another scope and/or mount that he'd be willing to swap. The cost at this stage of the sale would be minimal. Don't wait until it is too late.

Guarantees: most firearms guarantees will cover the original purchaser and, even then, the limitations state quite specifically that the manufacturer's liability is limited to correcting defects in materials and/or workmanship. Don't expect guarantees to carry over for your protection—they don't! Also, you have no way of knowing what the original owner did with his tinkering on this rifle. So, if anyone tells you that the new-gun warranty is still in effect on this gun, you'd better take that statement with a grain of salt!

Another point I feel I should mention, in the event that you buy this used rifle, keep it six months, and then decide you'd like to trade it in on something else. What's this used rifle worth now?

To a great extent this would depend on what you'd like to trade it for! When taking a trade-in the dealer has to make *two* sales to show a profit—the gun you take and the sale of your trade-in. Consequently, you can expect any firearm to lose about 30% of its value the moment it leaves the shop. You fare best when you trade *up* to a better, more expensive model.

In conclusion, you'll find many fine rifles in used gun racks and many of these will be at real bargain prices. With some care and caution you can make an intelligent selection with minimum risk. If you care to reduce the matter of chance still further, do business with a dealer that you know—and one to whom you are known!

CHAPTER 11

The Youngster's First Rifle

There was a time when I would have labeled this chapter, "A Boy's First Rifle," but times have changed. So many young ladies are now showing up on shooting fields across the country we "Chauvinists" are hard-pressed to accommodate them. I recently didn't know whether to laugh or cry when I found a crew of rugged shooting types building a ladies' powder room on a club house that had, for decades, gotten by with a simple "one holer."

The most oft-asked question one hears relative to a youngster's first rifle is, "How old should my child be before I buy (him or her) a rifle?"

There is no prescribed age when a youth can be expected to have the sense of responsibility required for safe gun handling. Some youths are responsible at eight or nine. Others aren't responsible at age 21!

Parents will have to judge offspring carefully before coming to this decision. Ask these questions:

1. Does the child generally respect the property of others?
2. Is the child cruel to animals?
3. Does the child indulge in temper tantrums?
4. Is the child generally honest and trustworthy?
5. Does the child get along well with other children? With adults?
6. Does the child accept instruction easily?

If parents can unhestitatingly respond favorably to all of these questions a decision to start rifle instruction would not be unreasonable. However, favorable deportment on the part of the child *does not eliminate the need for continuous control and caution.*

There we have the first prerequisite influencing the selection of a rifle—a rifle that can be controlled, and by that I mean one that is quickly and easily rendered inoperable. It must be possible to remove some vital portion of the firing mechanism. To my mind only the bolt action really fills the bill. With most any bolt action, the bolt—which contains the firing pin—can be removed by simply opening the bolt, holding the trigger back, and sliding the bolt rearward, out of the receiver. (Some big bore rifles are equipped with an independent bolt latch which must be operated to accomplish bolt removal.)

Caliber? Under normal early training circumstances, the .22 caliber rifle is quite adequate. Ammunition is relatively inexpensive, the noise factor is negligible, there is no recoil worth mentioning and, while all powder-driven cartridges can be lethal, risks are somewhat reduced with a small, light and slow bullet such as the ".22."

Some older boys may scoff at the idea of a twenty-two but, in my opinion, parents would be foolish to heed their arguments for something bigger. Until a youngster has had some formal in-

Beginners should start with the .22 rimfire caliber. This inexpensive shell is still the best choice for instructional purposes.

struction in marksmanship and firearms safety, he can't understand how a bullet may ricochet off a rock, skip off the flat surface of water, or travel a mile and still prove dangerous at that extreme distance. One of the first steps in teaching safe gun handling is to demonstrate, vividly, just what a rifle bullet can do—even the lowly ".22!"

Set up a block of wood, a bar of soap and a small can containing a colored liquid (put the cap on) and shoot at them from a distance of about twenty-five feet. The strike of the bullet and subsequent examination of the damage will make more of an impression than anything you can say. A healthy respect for the rifle is the first vital trait required of the shooting student.

TYPE OF RIFLE

When I suggested a bolt action earlier, I probably gave the impression that I had a single-shot rifle in mind. While this is a good choice for very

young shooters, some form of magazine rifle may be more practical for the youth approaching teen years. If small-game hunting is an imminent possibility, this is an especially valid consideration.

There are two popular forms of magazines used in repeating .22 caliber rifles—the tube and the detachable clip. Tubular magazines have large capacities, often approaching a dozen or more shells. They are well suited to small game hunting when in the hands of an experienced shooter. On the other hand, they're a poor choice for a beginner's rifle because the novice will frequently leave one cartridge in the gun and go about his business believing it is empty. It's possible, of course, to leave a shell in the chamber of a bolt action rifle too, as it is with any firearm. For this reason the student is taught to lock the breech in the open position before he clears the magazine and then to check the breech carefully as it is being closed to be sure no stray cartridge is being chambered.

Getting back to magazines, every cartridge in the clip magazine is actually held by the clip. When the clip is withdrawn from the rifle all the shells are in it! (assuming the chamber is empty). With tubular magazines, shells are fed into the action by means of a spring-actuated follower. When the inner magazine tube is withdrawn, shells are emptied by simply tilting the rifle so that gravity will enable them to slide out of the tube. If the novice doesn't do this carefully, it's very possible that he will overlook one cartridge that remains hidden out of sight, somewhere inside the tube.

Tubular magazines will be found in a large variety of bolt action and slide action repeaters. Some semi-automatic rifles (frequently mislabeled "automatic" by the sporting fraternity) will likewise be found with tubular magazines.

Nix all of these if you're starting a youngster. Insist that the child limit his or her thinking to clips or simple single-shot rifles.

Another advantage that will be found with a

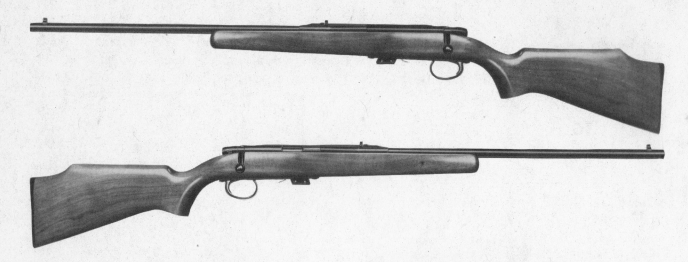

The Remington Model 581 .22 caliber rifle, in both right- and left-hand versions, is a clip-fed bolt action —a good choice for beginners.

clip-fed rifle is that removal of the clip very effectively transforms the rifle into a simple single shot. I started my son with a clip-fed, bolt action rifle and a clip-fed, bolt action shotgun. He didn't get to see the clips for either of these weapons until he had completed his initial training and had successfully demonstrated that he was competent enough to handle them as repeaters. I must admit there were times—especially when the crows were flying—when my offspring would complain bitterly about single loading his .410 gauge. On those occasions I was conveniently deaf.

FITTING THE FIREARM TO
THE YOUNG SHOOTER

It's almost impossible to teach a youngster anything about gun handling if the child must cope with a gun that is too big. I've seen some prime examples of this—children who would wrestle with awkward "man-sized" rifles until they gave up in frustration, not caring if they ever went shooting again!

You must cut down a buttstock when it is called for to fit a rifle to a shooter of small stature. True, the stock may have to be replaced if the child should grow too big for it but, replacement stocks for popularly priced .22 rifles are not expensive. Don't let them struggle with oversized equipment, this will take all the fun out of the sport.

TRAINING

There are many facilities available to the parent looking for qualified shooting instruction. To find

The Mossberg Model 340B is a seven-shot, clip fed .22 caliber repeater equipped with "peep" sights. A fine instructional tool. Excellent for the young target shooting enthusiast.

one locally, call your police department. Some shooting clubs are P.A.L. sponsored. The National Rifle Association at 1600 Rhode Island Avenue N.W., Washington, D.C. 20036, will also tell you if there are any NRA-affiliated shooting clubs in your area.

Often I've found shooting programs conducted by local school systems, colleges, Boy Scout organizations, YMCA's, churches and lodges.

One of the best training courses one can enter is the Hunter-Safety Program which is most often state-sponsored. Some states have now made successful completion of this course a mandatory prerequisite to issuance of a hunting license.

The National Shooting Sports Foundation (a firearms industry organization) and the National Rifle Association will often lend a helping hand to organizations interested in setting up a shooting club or firearms training program.

Write to the National Shooting Sports Foundation at 1075 Post Road, Riverside, Connecticut 06878.

Formal instruction in gun handling from a qualified, professional instructor is highly desirable and should be preferred over the traditional system of having Dad do the job in his spare time. Even though Dad is an experienced hunter and shooter, there are factors involved in the training of youths that may elude him.

SHOOTING ACCESSORIES FOR THE YOUNG SHOOTER

After acquiring his training rifle, the first thing a youngster will ask for is a telescopic sight.

I would suggest postponing this acquisition un-

til the initial training program has been satisfactorily completed. There are a number of reasons for this: first, some phases of marksmanship are best understood when demonstrated with the simplest forms of open sighting equipment—the traditional notched rear sight and blade front sight. With these sights the new shooter sees how and why sights are adjusted to align them with the impact of the bullet at a given distance.

He learns, too, how to align the rear sight with the front sight while aiming and how to maintain alignment during the shooting process. I feel that a natural progression through the three levels of sophistication in sighting devices is most beneficial: open sights to "peep" sights to telescopic sights.

To understand why I object to a scope in the hands of an untrained shooter, you would first have to familiarize yourself with the mechanics of scope shooting.

A scope is basically a metal tube containing a series of lens systems designed to enlarge a distant view. Into this system is superimposed a reticle which serves as an aiming tool. Because the scope will focus its gathered image at only one specific point behind the eyepiece, the position of the shooter's eye is unvarying. This point is called the "exit pupil" and its distance from the eyepiece lens is referred to as "eye relief."

Scopes for .22 caliber rifles have a relatively short eye relief—in other words, the shooter's eye is very close to the eyepiece. In fact, it is so close

The Stevens Model 73-Y is a cut down rifle in .22 caliber designed especially for small shooters.

that the shooter can see very little of anything surrounding that circle of light transmitted by the scope. Moreover, the shooter is usually concentrating his attention intently on that reflected image and is not using his peripheral vision as he would ordinarily.

If something, or someone, were to come between the scope and the distant image under observation, he or it, would of course be seen by the viewer. However, the field encompassed by the scope is so restricted that an intruder would be virtually in front of the rifle's muzzle before his presence would be detected.

Shooters are trained to shoot with both eyes open, even when aiming through a scope, and this minimizes the problem. Then, too, an experienced shooter will frequently sight over the body of the scope, preliminarily, before lowering his eye to the aiming position. Once in an aiming attitude, little time is wasted in getting the shot off.

Give a scoped rifle to a novice, however, and you'll generally find that he'll search for his target *through* the scope while clamping the opposite eye *tightly shut*.

Obviously, a scoped rifle can be hazardous in untrained hands. Teach them with simple iron sights!

One accessory that I would recommend highly, and possibly as a substitute for the sought-after rifle scope, is an inexpensive spotting scope. This is *not* mounted on the rifle, nor is it used for aiming. It is simply a high-magnification viewing instrument usually fastened to a tripod or bipod stand.

The spotting scope will make it possible for a target shooter to see the bullet holes in his target from his shooting point (at reasonable distances, of course) and it eliminates the need for running back and forth, from the firing line to the target.

A spotting scope will also enable a second party to take up a position close to the shooter, spotting shots and coaching the marksman. The same instrument can be used while varmint hunting to identify distant targets.

The rifle sling is unquestionably the most valuable accessory you can add to the basic rifleman's equipment. It is a shooting aid as well as a carrying strap, as described in the chapter on shooting fundamentals.

Other suitable accessories would consist of: a cleaning kit, wiping cloth, targets, assorted screwdrivers, a sight blackener, a peep sight, shooting glasses, a rifleman's jacket, a cartridge belt, a cartridge box, a gun case, ear protectors and a carrying case for accessories.

FIREARMS AND THE LAW

There is no way we can report on all of the thousands of ordinances covering the ownership and use of firearms because these are enacted by many different levels of government and they differ from one municipality to the next.

Federal law regulates the types of firearms and ammunitions that may be sold over the counter. It also establishes age limits and controls the interstate sale and shipping of guns.

Federal law has jurisdiction over migratory bird hunting practices; establishes seasons for the various flyways, bag limits, shooting hours, huntable species, etc. One important point we should interject here is that it is illegal to shoot at migratory waterfowl (such as a duck or goose) with a rifle.

Before venturing afield you must make it your business to check with your local firearms dealer for information on local ordinances. Questions that he can't answer should then be directed to your local police department.

Following is a list of important questions that you must have answered to avoid trouble with the law:

1. How old must a younster be before he is permitted to carry a firearm into the field?

2. Must I have a hunting license to go into the field with a firearm? Is a license required of a minor?
3. Can we hunt varmints without a license?
4. What can we hunt now, if licensed?
5. Bag limits?
6. Is Sunday hunting prohibited?
7. What are the legal shooting hours?
8. Is there a color requirement for hunter's clothing?
9. Where are the town limits? (Almost invariably, local municipalities will ban shooting within the populated borders of the town. Find out where those borders are!)
10. What are the distance requirements for shooting in the vicinity of roads, buildings, railroad right-of-ways, etc?

While this may sound like a complicated, time-consuming procedure, most states publish a little hunting manual that contains the bulk of this information. Ask your firearms dealer for one.

At one time it was possible for teenagers to hunt alone. Many states now require that a minor be accompanied by a responsible adult.

RESPECT THE PROPERTY OF OTHERS

Be sure the land you select for your hunting excursions is open to public hunting before stepping foot on it. If it is privately owned ask the permission of the landowner—*even though the land is not posted!*

Inconsiderate hunters frequently antagonize landowners to the point where property is posted and permission to hunt withheld.

Another thing, don't leave varmints where they fall. Remember, farmers must work their fields and it is no fun for the farmer to pick decaying carcasses out of his farm machinery. If you shoot a woodchuck in a farmer's alfalfa field, pick up the carcass and deposit it in a hedgerow or on the fence line.

Be careful of your skyline. Assuming that your shot misses its target, where will the bullet stop? If you can't predict a stopping point, don't shoot!

Identify your target carefully.

I'll never forget the time a hunting companion and I journeyed to a particularly fine woodchuck area where we were acquainted with a farmer who had always welcomed us.

After visiting with the farmer we went off to hunt his fields. We had enjoyed a fine morning hunt when we stopped to have our sandwiches in a cool grove of trees. Unknown to us, the farmer had discovered an unusually large woodchuck colony in a distant field and, as he was heading in for lunch, he took a route that would lead him through area where he knew we would be hunting. Coming through the field adjacent to ours, the farmer was walking in a narrow depression between two gently rolling hills. These knolls were at right angles to our vantage point and the more distant knoll was higher than the first. *We couldn't see the depression!* Now, to make matters worse, the farmer would sporadically take a few steps and then bend over to examine one of his plants.

My hunting companion spotted the sun glistening off the farmer's shock of light brown hair and immediately picked up his binoculars for a closer look.

Convinced that he had spotted another chuck he passed the binoculars to me. Just as I was about to confirm his observation, the farmer walked out of the depression. When his face filled the area under that crop of chuck-colored hair, the bristles on the back of my neck stood up! My hunting friend and I were both pretty badly shaken, and so was the farmer when we described the incident to him. He promised to make it a point thereafter to wear a brightly colored hat or cap when he had hunters in his fields.

HUNTING WITH THE NOVICE

When it is felt that the youngster has had adequate preliminary training, you can start thinking of a small game or varmint hunt.

Plan this carefully to make sure it is as pleasant and as enjoyable as possible. Pick a day when weather conditions are reasonable. Select an area where you *know* you'll find game, preferably a spot where you won't expect to run into other hunters. Bring adequate food and water and be prepared for a sudden change in weather conditions—how about rain-gear, a warmer (or lighter) jacket, a change of trousers, socks and shoes?

If Dad isn't too familiar with the small game that is to be hunted, it would be wise for him to do a little studying beforehand. It is always more interesting and enjoyable to a youngster when Dad can explain why game animals behave the way they do. Point out animals tracks, droppings, feeding areas, game trails, nesting sites, etc.

When you reach the hunting grounds, make it a point to get as far away from roads, houses, etc., as possible before letting junior load up. Restrict the loading to one shell and make sure he activates the safety as soon as the chamber is charged. Let him carry the balance of his ammo in his jacket pockets.

By now, the young shooter should know how to carry the rifle but don't take chances. Point out the direction you want him to travel and walk close

behind him! (Be careful of the direction of your own gun muzzle.)

Under no circumstances should you separate from the youngster during these initial hunts. Stay close to him constantly—always close enough to be able to reach out and grab his gun barrel if he should start to get careless with it.

Teach him to overcome the excitement of the hunt, to practice restraint—to pass up an opportunity if there's any potential danger in shooting. Show him the dangers. Watch him as he negotiates fences, streams or other obstacles. Correct him when he errs and have him repeat the action correctly. Don't let him shoot at non-game targets such as song birds, chipmunks or the like.

Since children naturally seek to emulate their teachers, you'll have to be careful, yourself, to follow the rules and obey the laws.

Some hunters disagree with me, but I don't believe in taking any game animal that I don't intend to eat. For this reason I don't usually shoot rabbits or squirrels. Only on those rare occasions, when a friend or neighbor asks me to bring back a pair of rabbits will I take advantage of such opportunities. I prefer to leave game that I don't enjoy eating for the hunter who does!

These early hunts with your son (or daughter) are golden periods in your mutual relationship, happy, memorable hours that will be engraved among your fondest recollections—enjoy them to the fullest!

CHAPTER 12

Sights, Scopes & Mounts

It was obvious, even before the advent of the firearm, that some form of sighting tool was needed if man was to direct his missiles with any degree of accuracy or consistency. Early attempts in this direction probably centered around the longbow and crossbow. When the firearm came upon the scene, circa 1300, man quickly came up with the notched rear sight and post front sight. To this day, the notch and post remains the sighting principal most frequently employed—it's as fundamental as the wheel! Except for the introduction of adjusting devices and the aperture disc, no significant progress was made in sight development until the telescopic sight was perfected in the mid-1800s.

If most sighting devices make use of the tandem-rigged notch and post, it follows that every budding rifleman should first learn to use this basic equipment.

Iron sights, such as these, are commonly fastened to the rifle by means of a male and female dovetail. The female dovetail is cut into the top surface of the barrel, near the muzzle, for the front sight. Another dovetail is cut into the top surface of the barrel near the receiver. Sights, then, are made with male dovetail bases which are slid into their female counterparts. Female dovetails are generally cut with a slight taper so that the mated portion will have to be hammered lightly into place. Tapers run from right to left (as you sight the rifle). Consequently, the rifleman must keep this taper in mind when he seeks to zero in the rifle by drifting the sights; one should avoid attempting to drift a sight from left to right simply because the sight may fall out. If the open-sighted rifle is shooting to the right of the target, drift the rear sight to the left (thereby tightening the base in the dovetail). If shooting to the left, drift the front sight to the left—again, tightening the base in the dovetail. It's sometimes possible to drift a sight *slightly* to the right, but you're always running the risk of loosening the union. The use of a brass drift pin between the hammer and the sight avoids marring of finished surfaces.

The simplest form of notch and post will be found on antique rifles where the notch was a simple V-groove filed in the top surface of the receiver or on the top surface of an attachment such as a barrel band. The mated front sight was usually a rigidly fastened protuberance shaped in the form of an inverted "V" or a simple blade. With stationary sights, such as these, it behooved the shooter to find a load that coincided with his sight setting if he wanted to avoid adjustments through filing.

121

From the simple V-notch gunmakers went to a U-notch and then to a simple square notch. The U-sight was used with a bead front sight and the square notch with a squared-off post. Sight makers, today, still use both the "U" and square notch versions.

On occasion you will find only a dovetailed rear sight with a bladed front sight. With this arrangement the front sight consists of a simple flat body that fits into a slot in a muzzle ramp. Both the ramp and blade are drilled to accept a tapered cross pin that locks the blade in place.

With a series of interchangeable blades of varying heights, it is possible to make elevation adjustments by simply changing blades. However, a simpler form of elevation adjustment is provided by the rear sight that utilizes a spring-steel arm between the male dovetail and the notched upright. Here, a sight step—shaped like an inverted saw blade—can be slid forth and back to raise or lower the notched body.

More expensive forms of adjustable rear sight use a notched insert that slides in a track. The insert can be locked at any desired setting by means of one or more lock screws.

European gunmakers favor a multiple-leaf rear sight. Here two or more notched uprights are hinged to a base plate; the lowest upright is closest to the front sight—by simply raising a higher leaf behind the first, one can block the lower notch from view and use the higher one for shooting over longer ranges. Generally these leafs are preset by the gunmaker for specific distances, i.e.—100 meters, 200 meters, 300 meters, etc. The only problem here is, "preset for what load?"

American sight makers borrowed the hinged-leaf idea for other reasons: if an aperture-type receiver sight is to be mounted behind the open rear sight, it is desirable to have the ability to move the "middle sight" out of the alignment—a hinged open sight can therefore be folded down and out

of the way. At other times, when a scope with a particularly large objective lens is mounted on the rifle, it is often found that an upright open sight interferes with the positioning of the scope. If this open sight is hinged, it can be folded out of the way without difficulty.

Open sights, whether "U" or square notched, are intended for a sight picture that buries the front sight completely in the notch. In other words, as the shooter aligns the front sight in the notch of the rear, he strives to have the top of the front sight level with the topmost edge of the rear uprights. In practice, however, many shooters adjust their sights differently—to their own viewing preferences—and often they will place the forward bead above the upper level of the rear uprights. Other shooters sometimes zero their rifles so that the front bead bottoms out in the rear notch. I've heard this referred to as a "fine-sight" picture.

Front sight posts and blades are made in a large variety of shapes and sizes. Many are fitted, too, with colored inserts, supposedly to aid definition. For example, one will often see a post sight topped by a white, gold or red bead. Sunlight will often reflect off a bright metallic blade or bead causing a glare that destroys definition. For that reason, some shooters prefer red beads or undercut blades. On the other hand, under poor light conditions, the white or gold bead is easier to see. The man who doesn't wish to be stuck with either compromise often elects to have a hood placed over his white front sight, but this, too, tends to make sighting difficult in poor light.

Military armorers have their own solution to the problem and I often wonder if theirs isn't really the best answer. Instead of a hood that completely encircles the front post, they build two ears—one on each side of the sight. These are usually curved up and out so as not to be confused with the sight itself. At first glance these appear to be rather useless appendages. Actually, they serve a number of purposes: they protect the front sight blade from bumps and the like (an important consideration for a combat weapon); they provide some shade; and, in a pinch, if the front sight is lost or damaged the shooter can simply center his target between the two ears and have some chance of hitting home.

Why ramps? With some of our modern lightweight barrels, the outside diameter of the barrel at the muzzle is so small, a sight would have to be unusually high to reach the operating level of the rear sight. High, and fragile! Sight designers circumvent the problem by building a sturdy ramp which raises the level of the front sight base to a point where only a normal post height is required.

Rear sight blades come in a variety of outside contours—flat-topped, shallow-V, buckhorn, semi-buckhorn, etc. Selection of one of these is simply a matter of personal preference. I prefer a flat-topped rear blade for two reasons: first, I feel that the wing of a buckhorn sight tends to obscure some of my view. Next, I have a problem finding the proper height for alignment of the front sight, if I don't have a perfectly flat reference surface in the rear blade.

THE SIGHT PICTURE

Many self-taught riflemen fail to realize that open sights are intended primarily for a six o'clock hold. In other words, when the front sight has been aligned with the rear, the target should be positioned *above* the front post or bead. The front sight should not cover the target area. Whenever a shooter blocks out his target he can't be sure where he's aiming—particularly if he has a small target.

If the big game hunter will use an NRA A-14 or A-15 target for zeroing at 100 yards, he'll find that these six-inch black bull's-eyes will have him shooting approximately three inches high when striking center with a six o'clock hold. For the average deer caliber this is about perfect. The rifle will shoot three inches high at one hundred yards and will be placing shots right on top of the front sight at two hundred yards.

The trick here is to remember to hold a wee bit low when close to the target.

This system will work with most popular deer calibers of from .28 to .32 caliber, but there are a few exceptions. If in doubt, test your rifle at both 100 and 200 yards.

APERTURE-TYPE RECEIVER SIGHTS

Except for some specialized forms of front sight inserts employed for target shooting, the "peep sight" (as it is commonly called) uses the same types of front sight that we've just finished describing—with one important difference. When a peep sight is employed it will generally be found to require a higher front sight to reach proper sight level.

I wish there were some quick and easy method for calculating the desired height of a front sight when installing a peep sight, but there isn't. This factor is influenced by a number of things, most especially the sight radius (distance between sights) of a given rifle.

Lyman makes front sights in many different heights, from .240″ to .560″. Incidentally, when measuring these, be sure to measure from the very bottom of the dovetail to the top of the bead, and use a micrometer.

A shooter will often crank his rear sight all the way down in an effort to lower his point of impact before he realizes that his front sight is too low and has to be replaced. Then, unthinkingly, he determines the front height he needs at this extreme setting. Result? He has no further room at the bottom of his adjustments for making sight corrections with the new front sight!

The shooter who bottoms out on his rear sight adjustment should first determine that he's shooting at a minimum range (100 yards for a center-

The Williams Guide Receiver sight is popular because it can often be mounted via the factory-drilled scope mount holes in the top of the receiver.

fire caliber) and then crank his rear sight *up* between one-fifth and one-fourth the length of its travel. At this point the desired height of a new front sight can be determined by consulting a sight chart or by improvising some extension to the existing sight and measuring (with a micrometer) the new height.

All the major sight manufacturers publish charts on sight specifications—drop into your local firearms dealer—he's certain to have a few of these handy. If you don't have a dealer near you, write to one of the companies—Redfield, Lyman or Williams—their addresses are given at the back of this book.

The simplest form of receiver sight is equipped with a sliding vertical bar that is locked in place by means of a lock screw. Elevation adjustments are therefore accomplished via the trial-and-error method. Adjustments for windage are usually provided by mounting the disc base on a threaded horizontal screw. One simply turns the screw in, or out, to move the disc right or left.

A bit more sophisticated is the inexpensive sight with ¼-minute click adjustments. With these, slotted knobs (accommodating either a coin or screwdriver) operate the machine screws that control the windage and elevation adjustments.

At one time there were a few such sights made with ½-minute click adjustments, but not any

longer. It costs about the same to produce ¼-minute adjustments and shooters prefer the finer calibration. It is interesting to note, today, that a few highly sophisticated target sights are being made with even finer, ⅛-minute, adjustments.

Receiver sights intended for hunting rifles are most often equipped with coin-slotted turret knobs while target sights are made with knurled knobs for finger operation.

The disc, or that portion of the sight containing the aperture, may be had in many different sizes. Discs with large outside diameters are target discs and these usually have very small-diameter apertures. Small discs with large viewing apertures are intended for hunting sights. Aside from hunting and target differences aperture size depends on a number of things—how well can the shooter define the front sight through the aperture? How far is the disc from the eye when being sighted?

It's not a good idea to buy a disc by mail unless you know, and have tried, an aperture of a given size. I'd much prefer to drop into my local gun shop with my rifle in hand and view a number of different discs before making a selection.

Williams' 5D Receiver sight is a popular hunter's "peep" sight.

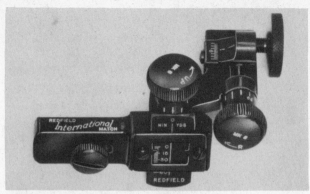

Redfield's International Match Mark 8 Receiver Sight is made with 1/8th minute click adjustments. Note knurled target knobs.

SIGHTING WITH THE PEEP SIGHT

When peering through a round hole, one naturally centers his target in the circle. Therefore the front sight—if it is a post—must be aligned so that it protrudes *less than halfway* into the sight picture. Sometimes a shooter will adjust his sights so that the rifle is zeroed with the front sight occupying exactly half of the aperture. The target then is forced out of its central alignment and occupies the upper third of the circle. Invariably, especially if hunting, this same shooter will take a quick shot while *centering his target in the sight picture.* You got it!—he misses!

There are shooters, of course, who understand these sighting quirks and who still prefer the halfway position for their front sight. There's nothing wrong with that *if* they remember to take the same sight picture consistently.

MOUNTING THE RECEIVER SIGHT

Most currently manufactured rifles are factory tapped and drilled to accept the mounting screws of a receiver sight. The factory simply puts dummy plug screws in these threaded holes before shipping the rifle to the dealer.

With a pre-tapped rifle it's a simple matter to remove the plug screws and attach the peep sight.

Appropriate mounting screws are supplied with the sight.

Very often though, the shooter will find that some wood has to be removed from the gunstock in the area of the sight. If he's not really skilled at woodworking with hand tools, he shouldn't try to do this himself. He could very easily ruin an expensive stock. Gunsmiths charge very little for this work and because they're so familiar with what has to be done, they can accomplish the task in less time than it takes to describe it. Give the job to the expert!

When a rifle is not factory drilled and tapped, the process of mounting a receiver sight is considerably more complicated. Now the hardened steel receiver must be drilled and threaded but, first, the sight has to be meticulously positioned on the receiver and clamped so that the locations for the screw holes can be ascertained. Obviously, this is no job for the average handyman. Receivers are sometimes so hard they require spot-annealing before drilling. At other times only a carbide-tipped drill will do the job. This is definitely a task for the professional gunsmith; he'll charge about ten dollars and save you a hundred dollars worth of grief!

CLICK ADJUSTMENTS

The elevation and windage adjustments for both receiver sights and scopes are colloquially referred to as "click adjustments" because a distinct click is heard for each step in their calibration as the turret is turned. Since one minute of angle subtends approximately one inch at 100 yards (actually it's 1.047″), each ½-minute click adjustment would move the strike of the bullet ½ inch at 100 yards, 1 inch at 200 yards, etc. It follows that ¼-minute adjustments would move the bullet ¼ inch at 100 yards and ½ inch at 200 yards, etc.

Some sighting instruments, usually foreign made, are equipped with adjustments that do not click. In such cases it is necessary to read the calibrated dial which is scored with one line for each increment of calibration. Also, with some imported equipment the shooter will find turret adjustments equipped with a lock screw. Adjustments with a device so equipped can only be accomplished after the lock screw is loosened.

At one time it was a European practice to equip a scope only with an elevation adjustment. Windage adjustments were provided in the mount. If you run into a scope with only one turret adjustment, you'll have to find a windage-adjustable mount to go with it.

With some scope turrets, the face of the dial is mounted in such a way that the shooter, after zeroing, can loosen two screws in the face of the dial and reset it so that the "O" on the face coincides with the indicator line on the body of the turret.

I like this feature because I can immediately return to the setting for my pet deer load after having experimented with other cartridges for other purposes.

THE RIFLE SCOPE

There is one very important point that I feel compelled to make at the very outset of this dissertation because I've seen too many shooters injured because of their ignorance of rifle scopes.

There are two distinctly different classes of riflescope—one for .22 caliber rimfire rifles and the other for larger caliber center-fire rifles. While it is possible to mount the scope intended for the center-fire on a .22 rifle you DARE NOT MOUNT A SCOPE INTENDED FOR A ".22" ON A CENTER-FIRE RIFLE!

And here's the reason why: a scope focuses its image at one given point some distance behind the eyepiece. The focus point, usually a circle about one third of an inch in diameter, is the precise spot where the pupil of your eye should be positioned to accept the total image transmitted by the scope. For this reason, this particular spot is referred to as the "exit pupil." The distance between the location of the exit pupil and the rearmost edge of the scope is referred to as "eye-relief" and this is the critical dimension that separates .22 rifle scopes from center-fire rifle scopes. The scope designed for a .22 rifle rarely has an eye-relief of more than two inches. Because a center-fire rifle recoils considerably, it is essential that eye-relief exceed *three inches*. With some magnum calibers I would even look for an eye-relief of four to five inches. From my own experience I would estimate that a scope for a 30/06 rifle should have a minimum eye-relief of 3¼ inches, preferably a bit more.

I'm sorry if I bore the experienced rifleman with these remarks but I must assume that some readers are newcomers to the sport and I would hate to see a sportsman's day of anticipated pleasure turn into a bloody disaster.

INTRODUCTORY GLOSSARY

Before getting involved in the technical descriptions of scope features, it is necessary to acquaint the reader with some scope jargon. Therefore I'll first define, briefly, some of the more commonly-used terms:

EYEPIECE LENS   The rearmost lens of an optical instrument, that which focuses and transmits the image to the viewer's eye.

FIELD OF VIEW   The extent of the area made visible through a scope at a specific distance. Rifle scopes are rated for field of view at 100 yards. Consequently, a 35-foot field of view would show the viewer a circle of image measuring 35 feet in diameter.

FIXED POWER   A rifle scope made to one specific magnification, i.e., 4-power (4X) will magnify the image four times.

FIXED RETICLE   A reticle that maintains its centrally located position in the transmited image in spite of any adjustments made, as opposed to a normal reticle which shifts its relative position in the image plane as adjustments are accomplished.

FOGGING   Condensation on lens surfaces of an optical instrument which partially or completely blocks image transmission.

GAS FILLED   An optical instrument that is filled with a gas, usually nitrogen, to prevent fogging.

LIGHT GATHERING POWER   The measured ability of an optical instrument to transmit the lighted image. (Some light is reflected and wasted by the various lens systems. Assuming that a scope gathers 100% at the objective lens, its efficiency is rated by the amount of light remaining at the exit pupil.)

MOUNT   The mechanical device that is used to fasten the scope to the rifle.

OBJECTIVE LENS   The forwardmost lens of an optical instrument, that which first accepts the image.

RESOLUTION   The quality and clarity of the transmitted image.

RETICLE   The crosshair, or post, or combination of these that forms the aiming point in the image transmitted by the scope.

TURRETS   The adjusting devices for windage and elevation.

VARIABLE POWER   A rifle scope made with an adjustable power device so that magnification can be increased or decreased within prescribed limits. i.e., 3–9X (3 to 9 power) can be adjusted to magnify an image from three to nine times its relative size or any step in between.

SCOPE OPTICS, GENERALLY

When one speaks of compromises in rifle building the subject is really paled by comparison with those compromises inherent to scope making. Every advantage one seeks to gain in designing a scope is paid for by one disadvantage or another farther down the line.

For example—increase the magnification and you reduce the field of view; design an adjustable-focus eyepiece and you lose some of the atmospheric seal; reduce the diameter of the scope body and you diminish the light gathering power; increase the size of the objective lens cell and you must mount the scope undesirably higher—farther from the axis of the bore.

Virtually everything a scope designer attempts to do is limited by the sacrifices he must make to achieve his goals! The question then, is, "how much is the *shooter* willing to sacrifice to get increased magnification, a larger field of view, or improved light-gathering power?"

Ideally, the rifle scope should transmit 90% of the light it takes in, provide a field of view of 100 feet at 100 yards, have power adjustment of from 1 to 30X, a fixed-center reticle and provide undistorted definition. Great! But the resultant scope would measure three feet in length, a foot in diameter and would weigh ten pounds!

Balance is the only answer to the whole complex problem. The scope designer attempts to create a superior rifle scope within the limits of size, weight and external profile deemed acceptable by the individual rifleman.

With an awareness for these considerations we can go on to discuss individual optical features.

MAGNIFICATION

The average American hunter reasons that the higher the magnification the better he'll see and the better he will be able to shoot!

Wrong! At high magnifications he'll see less area and what he does see may be somewhat distorted or grey. Also, he'll see things that *he doesn't want to see*—such as the pulsations which make his crosshairs do an unnerving little dance over the elusive target area.

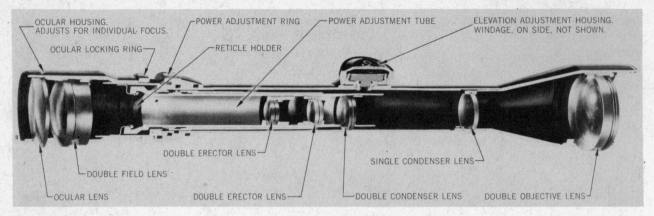

Labels on the image:

OCULAR HOUSING. ADJUSTS FOR INDIVIDUAL FOCUS.
POWER ADJUSTMENT RING
POWER ADJUSTMENT TUBE
ELEVATION ADJUSTMENT HOUSING. WINDAGE, ON SIDE, NOT SHOWN.
OCULAR LOCKING RING
RETICLE HOLDER
DOUBLE ERECTOR LENS
SINGLE CONDENSER LENS
DOUBLE FIELD LENS
OCULAR LENS
DOUBLE ERECTOR LENS
DOUBLE CONDENSER LENS
DOUBLE OBJECTIVE LENS

A cut-away view of a Williams variable power scope.

Before the brush hunter mounts that 6X scope on his deer rifle (because he wants to hunt varmints in the off-season) he should see what it's like to try to *find* a running deer in that scope at 100 yards. Better yet, try to keep that running deer in the image area long enough to get off a shot. It's quite a trick!

The first question a shooter should ask himself before buying a scope is, "what is the *minimum* magnification I can work with?" If he does insist upon hunting deer and varmints with the same rifle he should buy a variable-power scope.

The best light-gathering power, the best definition and the largest fields of view are provided by scopes of the lower magnifications.

These features are far more important than simple magnification.

Following is a table of my own recommendations for those powers best suited to various shooting pursuits:

VARMINT SHOOTING — 6X, 8X, 10X or 12X (Fixed) 2 to 7X or 3 to 9X (Variable)

BENCHREST SHOOTING — virtually unlimited— anything up to 36X is acceptable because the target is stationary.

BIG GAME HUNTING (Brush Country) — 1X, 2X, 2½X or 4X (Fixed) 1 to 4X, 2 to 7X (Variable)

BIG GAME HUNTING (Mixed Terrain) — 2½X, or 4X (Fixed) 1 to 4X, 2 to 7X, 3 to 9X (Variable)

BIG GAME HUNTING (Open Terrain) — 4X or 6X (Fixed) 2 to 7X, 3 to 9X, 4 to 12X (Variable)

DANGEROUS GAME — Strictly 1X to 2½X (Fixed) 1 to 4X or 2 to 7X (Variable)

TARGET SHOOTING   There are many forms of rifle competition so it is difficult to make any specific recommendations here. Much big bore shooting is done with iron sights only; gallery shooting is often done with both; and then there are restrictions depending upon whether the competition is being conducted under NRA rules, International rules or simply local range rules. Before buying a scope the target shooter should consult the NRA rule books covering the competitions that interest him. Also, it would pay to discuss the question with fellow club members.

RELATIVE BRIGHTNESS

While this is not the total measure of an optical instrument's efficiency, it does provide some indication of performance.

Very simply put, the *size* of the exit pupil (which we discussed earlier) is expressed in millimeters

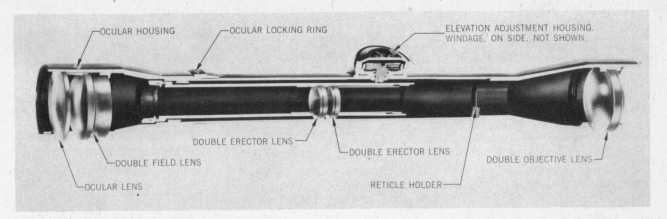

OCULAR HOUSING — OCULAR LOCKING RING — ELEVATION ADJUSTMENT HOUSING.
WINDAGE, ON SIDE, NOT SHOWN.

DOUBLE ERECTOR LENS — DOUBLE ERECTOR LENS — DOUBLE OBJECTIVE LENS

DOUBLE FIELD LENS

OCULAR LENS RETICLE HOLDER

A cut away of a Williams fixed power scope.

to yield a numerical factor—it is these numbers that manufacturers use in their charts and tables to indicate brightness.

Specifically, the square of the diameter of the exit pupil, in millimeters, is equal to relative brightness. To find EP diameter, simply divide the diameter of the objective aperture (in mm's) by the magnification. When you square the result you'll have the numerical factor referred to as "relative brightness."

This will tell you the *size* of the light beam, but it will not tell you anything about its intensity. The best advice I can give the reader on that point is to *compare* scopes before buying. Realizing that even the worst instrument will provide a good image under ideal light conditions, it follows that the real value of a scope's worth is determined by the amount of light it will transmit under poor light conditions.

Time your visit to the local gun shop so that you'll arrive toward dusk, and ask your dealer to let you sight selected models through an open doorway or an open window. (Never attempt this indoors, or through a glass pane.) Differences in light transmitting qualities, under these conditions, are readily discernible.

Before lens coating was developed (during WW II), a great deal of the light gathered by an optical device was reflected in the lens systems and wasted. Lens coating reduces reflection and generally increases optical effectiveness by as much as 50%. At first, only inner lens surfaces were coated because the coating material (magnesium fluoride) was soft and had very little rub-resistance. Today, though, manufacturers have developed a hard coating and it is possible to coat *all* lens surfaces. Make sure the instrument you buy is coated on the exterior surfaces of the objective and eyepiece lenses. The violet or purple colored coating can usually be seen if you view the lens from an oblique angle.

If you are so inclined you can make a few other simple tests at the same time. For example, it's easy to check for distortion—simply view some distant geometric pattern through the *edge* of the field. It will always look sharp coming right down the middle of the pike, but what a scope does to this image toward the edge of its field will give you a pretty good idea of the quality of the lenses employed.

Another simple test will confirm the figures you were given for the exit pupil and eye relief. Lay a piece of white paper flat on a counter and directly under an overhead light source. Hold the scope in a vertical fashion directly over the paper (eyepiece end down) and move it up and down to focus the small beam of light that it transmits to the paper.

SIGHTS, SCOPES & MOUNTS 129

Target scopes, like this Redfield Model 3200, can be used for varmint hunting as well as for benchrest and target shooting. The Model 3200 may be had in a choice of powers, i.e.—12X, 16X, 20X or 24X.

(Remember how you used to focus a magnifying glass to burn paper? This is done the same way.) When the circle of light on the paper is sharply defined, you can simply make two pencil lines on the paper to indicate the diameter of the circle, and measure the distance between the eyepiece and the paper to ascertain eye relief. With a caliber or micrometer you can now measure the distance between your two pencil lines and compare this dimension to the manufacturer's table of specifications.

PARALLAX

There are a number of definitions for this term but the one we are interested in is simple, "deviation."

With very few exceptions, rifle scopes are factory adjusted to be parallax-free *at one specific distance* —usually 100 yards. So, if you lay your rifle in a rest so that it remains motionless, and direct your scope at a target 200 yards distant, you'll see that the crosshair appears to shift its position on the target as you move your eye slowly from one side of the exit pupil to the other. This deviation is quite normal and you can expect it to have some effect on your long range shooting. If, on the other hand, you find parallax present when sighting at a 100 yard target, a correction will have to be made in the scope. This is done by *very carefully loosening the screws* that hold your adjusting turrets to the body of the scope. Whatever you do, don't loosen them too much! You simply want enough slack

to permit the turrets to move when lightly tapped. Now, by trial and error method, tap the turrets ever so gently toward the front of your scope— you don't want to move the turret more than 1/32 of an inch at a time. Stop—check for parallax again. If it appears to be diminishing, move the turret another 1/32″ in the same direction and continue this process, by degrees, until the parallax is gone.

If parallax appears to be increasing, you are moving the turret in the wrong direction, tap it rearward instead.

Be sure to retighten your mounting screws when you have reached the desired setting.

At times you may run into a scope that does not lend itself to this simple adjusting technique. In such cases, write to the manufacturer or see your local gunsmith.

High magnification scopes, and especially target scopes, are the exception to this rule. Very often you'll find 8 and 10X Varmint scopes equipped with an adjustable *objective* lens cell, calibrated for specific distances. When you set the cell for 300 yards, the instrument should be parallax-free at that distance.

Target scopes often have simple built-in parallax-adjusting devices. The manufacturer will be happy to send you his instruction sheet if you've lost the one that came with the scope.

One final word of caution—do not hammer on the adjusting turret. If it doesn't move easily when the screws are lightly loosened, take it to your local gunsmith.

FOCUSING THE EYEPIECE

The eyepiece cell of the rifle scope is generally threaded to the main body and equipped with a locking ring. Focusing, for your individual needs, is accomplished in the following manner.

1. Loosen the locking ring that abuts the eyepiece cell.
2. Hold the rifle in a ready position and look skyward to focus your eyes at infinity.
3. Maintaining your eye focus, slide the scope into view and look through the scope quickly. Don't refocus your eye to define the reticle.

    If the cross wires don't stand out, sharp and clear at first glance, a focusing adjustment must be made.
4. Screw the eyepiece in a bit (clockwise) and try it again.

If the cross wires are harder to define the second time, the eyepiece was moved in the wrong direction. Turn it out (counterclockwise) and repeat the procedure.

The difficult part of this procedure is that your eye will tend to compensate for poor focus if you linger too long behind the eyepiece. You must peek *through* the scope quickly with your eye focused at infinity. Only when the reticle stands out clearly under these circumstances can you be assured that the instrument is properly focused.

GAS FILLING & FOGGING

An optical engineer once told me that even the best gas-filled scope will lose its gas filling shortly after it is taken into the field. He explained that metal components expand and shrink with drastic changes in temperature and that the seals couldn't be expected to function effectively with these changes in the dimensions of the metal tube, However, in recent years I've noticed the development of many new forms of seal materials and adhesives. Today, I'm sure, manufacturers are much more successful in their quest to produce a leak-proof, gas-filled rifle scope.

In spite of all this (and now I'm going to stick my neck way out there) there's no reason for the rifleman to rely on gas filling to keep his scope fog-free! The average hunter abuses his scope so badly it's a wonder that manufacturers are not literally inundated with complaints at the close of the big game season.

The trick to preventing fogged lenses is simply to avoid rapid and drastic changes in temperatures. Don't carry your scoped rifle in the heated passenger compartment of your car and then pull it out into ten-degree weather when you reach the hunting grounds. Instead, transport the cased rifle in the trunk of the car. Let it adjust, *slowly*, to the differences in temperature.

When on a backwoods trip, don't bring your scoped rifle into a heated tent or cabin—find a safe place for it outside, under some form of shelter but exposed to the cold!

On my first Canadian hunt I drove four nails into the front wall of a backwoods cabin (under a porch). My companions and I hung our rifles on these at the end of each day's hunt. A few years later I returned to the same cabin and found that six to eight additional nails had been added beside my original four. The guide explained that since he'd learned this little trick he had passed it on to all of his "sports" and that he had not lost anymore opportunities because of fogged scopes.

If, per chance, you do slip up and find yourself with a badly fogged scope, here's how you clear the instrument:

Bring the scoped rifle into a heated room and place it near a stove (but not so close that you inadvertently scorch the stock.) Check it every fifteen minutes and, as soon as the lenses start to clear, start moving the rifle farther away from the heat source. Keep moving it, by degrees, to a cooler environment. If you do this very carefully, cooling it by degrees, you should be able to get the rifle back to outside temperatures, without fog-

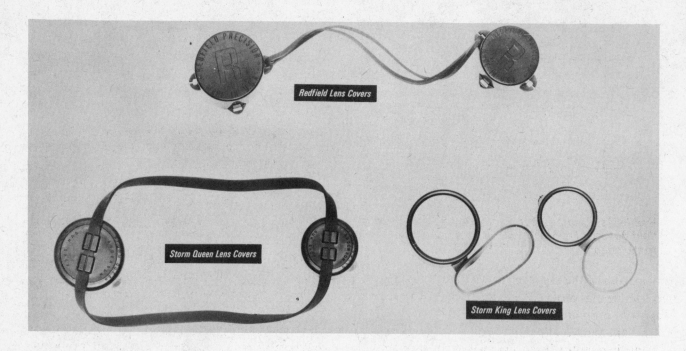

Three popular makes of lens caps.

LENS CAPS

The value of a pair of lens caps is not really appreciated until one runs into difficulty for lack of them. Of course, they protect lens surfaces from scratches and the like but, more importantly, if they're easily detachable they can protect lenses from rain and snow all the while one is hunting.

Lens caps come in a number of different forms —solid leather, plastic with clear-view inserts (that enable the shooter to sight through the caps), moulded rubber to snap off at a flick of the thumb and plastic with hinged end covers.

Leather caps are intended only for protection while storing or transporting the rifle.

Hinged, clear-view and snap-off caps can be kept on the rifle in the field. I prefer the rubber cap that flicks out of the way quickly.

If you've ever fought to keep the snow or rain from objective or eyepiece lens surfaces, you won't hesitate to invest in a good pair of lens caps.

RETICLES

Some day I'd like to collect drawings covering all of the many forms of reticles I've seen over the years. There's a limitless variety—every time I think the field is covered, some designer comes up with a new wrinkle and a new reticle.

The basic reticle is, of course, the common crosshair or cross wire. This is still the most popular form.

Because it is sometimes difficult, if not impossible, for a shooter to define a cross wire under poor lighting conditions, a heavy vertical post was added to replace the lower half of the vertical wire. Posts vary in size and shape and may be found thick, thin or tapered.

Some posts extend above the horizontal cross

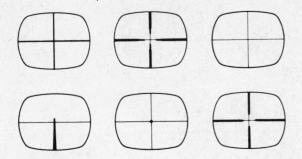

Redfield's current selection of reticles (for their Wide-field scopes) typifies the choices generally available to the shooter.

wire and, if the shooter knows how many minutes of angle this protrusion represents, he can use the post to estimate range.

Apparently, there are shooters who feel there is value in quantity because scope makers were quick to replace other segments of the cross wire with posts and now one can even buy a scope having *four* posts indicating the center point of the small section of cross wire remaining. Some European makers simply remove the cross wire entirely and market a combination of one, two, three or four posts.

A dot and cross wire is another popular combination. The dot, affixed at the junction of the vertical and horizontal wires, improves visibility somewhat in poor light. Since dots may be had in a variety of sizes, it is also possible to use them for range estimation purposes if one knows their min-ute-of-angle value.

Finally, we come to the range-finder reticle. Here the manufacturer employs either two or three parallel horizontal cross wires with one vertical wire.

To use this effectively, the shooter must know the approximate size of his target. Generally, when two horizontal cross wires are used, the distance between them subtends six minutes of angle. So,

A diagram of Weaver's Range-Finder® reticle. The distance between the two horizontal lines subtends six-minutes of angle.

if shooting at a six-inch target, and it is found that the target neatly fills the area between the two horizontal lines, the shooter knows the distance is 100 yards.

A deer measures approximately eighteen inches in depth through the body. At 100 yards the range finding cross wires would only cover one-third his body thickness. If the body of the deer, on the other hand, fills the space between the two range-finding lines, the distance to the target would be 300 yards.

After estimating the range, the shooter selects the cross wire that obviously centers through his field and uses this for aiming purposes, disregarding the second horizontal wire.

A three-wire range finder works the same way except that the aiming wire is clearly separated from the two that are used for range finding.

Frankly, I feel the range finding reticle is most useful to varmint or Western big game hunters and that it should only be used by a shooter who hunts frequently. It can be confusing to the casual or once-a-year hunter.

There are a number of special reticles on the market that are of interest too.

One of these is a cross wire but, unlike the common form, the special cross wire is tapered—very fine at the crossing point and much heavier towards the outer edge of the field. This appears to offer the advantages of both the post and the simple cross wire.

Another reticle, recently introduced by Red-

Redfield's Frontier (two piece) top mount.

field, substitutes a small circle for the common central crossing point.

A few years ago I tripped across a scope equipped with a reticle that developed a golden glow in poor light. Yet, in bright midday light the reticle was pitch black. I made some notes indicating make and model while in the field but somewhere during my travels I lost the notes. I'm still trying to unravel this mystery because I think that phosphorescent reticle really has potential.

With variable power scopes one will often find a reticle that is magnified, along with the image, as the power is adjusted upwards. This is a very poor feature because the shooter normally wants the highest magnifications for the finest shooting. If the cross wire magnifies, it can get so darn coarse at the upper powers no one could reasonably expect to do any precision shooting with it. If you

are in the market for a variable power scope, be sure to check the reticle for this undesirable quality.

SCOPE MOUNTS

Mounts are used to attach the scope to the rifle and they come in a large variety of sizes and shapes to accommodate the many different types and sizes of actions employed in rifle making.

Selection of a mount depends upon a number of factors. Unlike Europeans, American shooters strive to mount a scope as low as possible, as close as they can to the axis of the bore. By so minimizing the angle of convergence, the line of sight will bear a closer relationship to the path of the bullet and range estimation is subsequently rendered somewhat less critical. Stock height, too, is more easily determined if the levels of scope and iron sight are not too widely separated.

In attempting to achieve the lowest possible

The Williams Sight-Thru mount enables the shooter to use iron sights under the mounted scope!

mounting, the shooter will find that he is often limited by the size of the objective cell of the scope. With some bolt action rifles, particularly, one must be careful to give the bolt operating clearance *under* the mounted scope. Ejection, also, can be impeded by a scope that is set too low on some rifles.

Manufacturers make mount rings in a variety of heights to enable the gunsmith, or shooter, to overcome such built-in obstacles.

Top or side mount?

Most rifles are drilled and tapped for top mount and, usually, this is the easiest and least expensive form of mounting arrangement. There is also an almost unlimited assortment of mounts to choose from—two piece, one piece, some with built-in windage adjustments, quick detachable, and some

not-so-quickly detachable. Be careful, though, in selecting mounts for scopes over 6 power or for variable power scopes exceeding 7 power. Objective cells on high magnification scopes are uncommonly large and frequently require special high rings.

Side mounts can run into considerably more expense simply because they require the services of an expert gunsmith. Usually, the rifle must be drilled and tapped for the side mount and the stock cut away to accommodate the base. Proper alignment with the bore can be devilishly tricky too.

Some riflemen prefer side mounts because the scope is suspended above the barrel and it is possible to use the iron sights by simply peering under the scope. With Pachmayr, Williams, Griffin & Howe or Jaeger side mounts, it is possible to have one scope serve interchangeably on a number of rifles. Just buy extra bases for the added rifles and

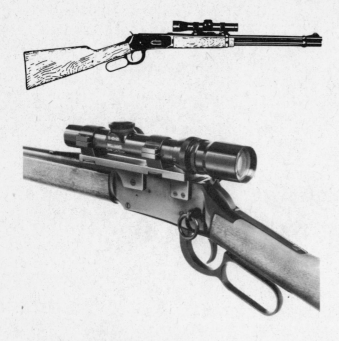

The two alternatives for mounting a scope on a top ejection rifle like the Winchester 94.

Top—Leupold's M8-2X long eye relief scope mounted forward of the receiver.

Below—Williams' Offset Mount placed to the left of the ejection path.

furnish the top half of the initial mount (rings with scope in place) to the gunsmith. When the gunsmith realizes that you plan to use the same scope on a number of rifles, he'll mount it on the new base without disturbing the existing relationship between the rings and the scope. Better yet, give the entire first rifle to the gunsmith along with the new rifle and base. If he's really a "pro," he'll be able to zero both rifles at 100 yards with the same scope setting. (You'll also have to furnish him with up to twenty rounds of your pet loads for each rifle.)

With some top mounts, such as Redfield's and Buehler's one-piece bridge mounts, you can often accomplish the same form of interchangeability. Two piece top mounts, on the other hand, are spaced according to the dimensions of the individ-

ual rifle and will often prevent interchanging of a scope.

How does one mount a scope on a top-ejection rifle like the Winchester Model 94?

There are two solutions to this problem—take your pick:

The first is to use an offset side mount, such as the William's QC offset Side Mount which retails for about $22.50, complete. This mount will place the rifle scope over the left side of the receiver (not over the bore) and out of the way of ejected cartridges. Because the scope is offset to the left of the bore, a small angle of left to right convergence is required to zero dead center. However, this angle is so slight it shouldn't cause any difficulty at reasonable ranges—especially not at the effective ranges of the 30–30 or .32 Special.

The second alternative is to mount a special long eye-relief scope on the rifle. These scopes would mount over the barrel, forward of the receiver, and consequently out of the path of ejected shells. There are a number of such scopes available. The only one I've tried, and which I wouldn't hesitate to recommend, is the Leupold M8-2X installed with a Leupold Special Detacho-Mount. This is a nice combination for top-ejection guns. Incidentally, the eye-relief on this scope is noncritical, meaning that it can be sighted properly at distances from 8 to 18 inches (according to Leupold's "spec" sheet).

For the shooter who desires to have access to his iron sights even when the scope is in place, there's one mount that deserves special mention—the Pachmayr Lo-Swing Mount.

Firearms authorities usually agree that any movement of the scope or the mount has to result in inaccuracies, and they're right! However, having used extensively not one, but two, Pachmayr Swing Mounts for more than ten years, I can truthfully say the Pachmayr Mount is the exception to the rule. Never have I found my point of zero change by so much as a quarter of an inch with

Pachmayr's Lo-Swing top mount is hinged so that the scope can be swung aside. A similar mount is made with a side-mounting base.

either of these Pachmayr mounts. No matter how many times I've swung them to the side—and back again—they've retained their alignment.

The value of this instant "swing-aside" feature really can't be appreciated unless you relate it to a bad moment with a dangerous game animal such as a grizzly. What do you do if your scope is smashed, or fogged and you find yourself with a grizzly bearing down on you? Frankly, I want more than a by-guess-or-by-gosh means for aiming the rifle because I can't run, nor climb half as fast as one of those awesome creatures. The Pachmayr Mount lets you get to those iron sights in an instant.

Another feature of Pachmayr's latest Swing Mount is that it is made with a center hinge that contains two eccentrically cut spherical cones. Adjusting screws—one at each end of the hinge pin—will often enable the shooter, or gunsmith, to compensate for any mis-alignment in the rifle's mounting holes without having to try the extremes of the scope's built-in adjustments. I even zeroed one of my rifles using only these mount adjustments!

MOUNTING RIGIDITY

One point that is too often overlooked in the mounting of a scope is the integrity of the union. Recoil that you feel at the shoulder is also jarring the scope and the mount. If mount rings are not securely fastened to the scope, and base screws securely fastened to the rifle, you can't expect that scope to retain its alignment for any length of time. Once the scope and mount are properly aligned, *every screw must be installed with some form of bonding agent such as "Lok-tite."* Some gunsmiths use shellac on the screw threads but I've never found this too effective. Another friend of mine used an epoxy adhesive, but then he couldn't get the screws out when he wanted to make a change of scopes.

However you decide to treat the threads BE SURE YOU CRANK THE SCREWS DOWN TIGHTLY! The trick to this is to use screwdrivers that fit the screw slots.

Finally, check all screws regularly—you'll be amazed by the frequency with which you'll find a loose screw or two.

SCOPES FOR .22 CALIBER RIFLES

There's an abundance of inexpensive short eye-relief scopes on the market intended for rimfire rifles. The reader will not have any difficult in finding two or three makes to choose from at his local gun shop.

If you've read this chapter from the beginning, please remember, now, that short-eye relief scopes for .22 caliber rifles can ONLY BE USED ON RIFLES OF .22 R.F. CALIBER. Never try to mount one of these on a center-fire rifle. You can, however, mount a big, quality scope intended for center fires on your little .22, but it really doesn't make much sense to do so.

Most .22 rimfire rifles are made with some provision to facilitate scope mounting, either they're drilled and tapped (on the left side of the receiver) for what is commonly referred to as the "N" mount, or, the top surface of the receiver is cut with two parallel V-grooves designed to accommodate a "Tip-Off" mount.

The scopes made by the W.R. Weaver Company (El Paso, Texas) probably best typify the broad assortment. Today, Weaver makes a D-4 model (4 power) and a D-6 (6 power). To these they've added a Model V22 which is a variable-power scope ranging from 3X to 6X. Any of these scopes can be had, at reasonable prices, with your choice of an "N" mount or a "Tip-Off" mount, at no extra cost.

Bear in mind that we're discussing *hunting* scopes for *hunting* rifles. While they can be used for plinking or informal target shooting, the scope one would select for serious target competition is something else again. Sophisticated target scopes are considerably more expensive; they range in price from about $80.00 to $150.00.

To conclude this rather lengthy chapter, I feel I should say a word or two about mis-matches. If you have a $300 rifle, don't fit it out with a bargain-basement scope and mount— you'll never realize the full potential from that fine rifle by employing cheap accessories. Not only that, but you'll be taking something away from the value of the rifle itself!

By the same token, don't spring for a $125.00 scope and mount combination if you're trying to outfit a $75.00 rifle.

A good rule of thumb is that scope and mount should never cost more than two-thirds the value of the rifle and, only when the rifle exceeds $200.00 in value is it reasonable to expect the scope and mount to be worth less than half.

CHAPTER 13

Sighting & Zeroing

In the chapter, "Sights, Scopes & Mounts" we discussed the three types of sighting instruments and the importance of fitting them properly. We also covered simple adjusting techniques and focusing for scopes. Here we are concerned only with the alignment of the gunsight ("zeroing") and answers to these two questions:

"How do we zero the iron sight or scope?"

"For what range should we zero them?"

SELECTING THE RANGE

This is where the average hunter makes his first mistake and too frequently it proves to be the one that costs him a trophy.

Unlike the target shooter who zeros his rifle precisely for one specific *known* distance, the hunter has to be concerned with minimizing the margin of error between his line of sight and the path of his bullet over the greatest possible distance.

If I've piqued your curiosity, bear with me because we're about to delve into a most complicated facet of the hunting rifle—an area that I feel is too often glossed over by other firearms writers. This has to do with range estimation: target shooters, dealing with known distances, are rarely ever concerned with the problem—to the hunter, however, it has special significance!

How well can you judge distances up to 100 yards, to within fifteen feet?

O.K. How about 200 yards; can you judge within thirty feet?

What about 300 or 400 yards?

It's not too difficult to estimate range at short distances but the margin of error gallops away from us as range is increased. If we now refer to simple ballistics, we're taught that a bullet starts to drop immediately upon leaving the muzzle. Theoretically, if the bore of the rifle is perfectly horizontal at the instant of firing, the bullet's velocity determines how far it will travel before it reaches the ground. If two rifles are mounted side by side, a specific distance above and parallel to ground level, and one of these is a 30/06 and the other a .22, fired simultaneously both bullets will strike the ground at precisely the same instant. The 30/06 bullet, however, will have traveled considerably farther than the .22 in spite of the fact that the 30/06 bullet is heavier. Obviously, the path of the faster 30/06 bullet is flatter than that of the .22.

Keep in mind that trajectory is not a uniform arc —bullets begin decelerating as soon as they leave the muzzle and the rate of drop increases as they lose velocity. Some idea of flight patterns can be gained from the accompanying diagram (A) which

BORE AXIS

A   B   C   D

This will give you a rough idea of the paths of four different bullets traveling at four different velocities if bores were placed horizontally. A—.22 Long Rifle bullet at 1335 f.p.s.; B—.35 Remington bullet at 2100 f.p.s.; C—30/06 bullet at 2970 f.p.s.; D—7mm Remington Magnum at 3260 f.p.s.

illustrates the trajectories of sample bullets from the 7mm Magnum, 30/06, the 35 Remington and the .22 Long Rifle.

Diagram (B) illustrates the path of a bullet when the muzzle is slightly elevated to place the bullet on the point of aim at a specific distance.

(Note: All of this, and the following, data is based on the use of a scope mounted approximately 1½ inches above the axis of the bore. Figures for iron-sighted rifles would differ.)

Using the 30/06 cartridge with a 150 grain bullet for this example, we find that a rifle zeroed at 200 yards will keep the path of the bullet within five inches of the line of sight from 0 to 250 yards! At 300 yards it's only 7.5 inches low and at 400 yards it is 22.6 inches low.

By way of comparison, if the hunter zeroed his rifle for 100 yards (which is the too common practice) the bullet would fall about 8 inches low at 200 yards, 23 inches low at 300, and 47 inches low at 400.

As you can see, any shot beyond the zero distance requires mental gymnastics. Another point: how does one plot the twenty-four inch difference between 300 and 400 yards? Suppose the target is located at 350 yards; where would the bullet be at that distance? (If you guessed between thirty-two and thirty-three inches low, you'd be right, but could you estimate a distance of 350 yards right on the nose?)

All of the foregoing ballistical data and commentary was designed to demonstrate one simple fact: "It's easier to hit a target at an unkown distance when the margin of deviation between line of sight and the path of the bullet is minimized over

Path of a 150 grain 30/06 bullet having a muzzle velocity of 2970 f.p.s. if zeroed at 200 yards: at 100 yards it would be 1.9 inches high, 7.5 inches low at 300 and 22.6 inches low at 400 yards.

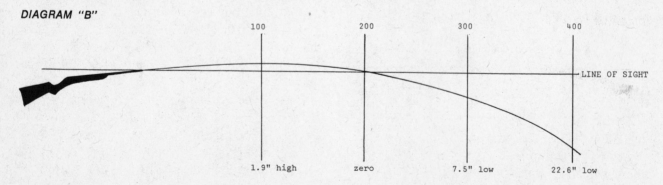

100   200   300   400

LINE OF SIGHT

1.9" high   zero   7.5" low   22.6" low

the greatest distance, and this is best accomplished by aligning the sights so that the path of the bullet is *above* the line of sight for as long as possible!"

Let's go back to the 30/06 using a 150 grain pointed bullet. Suppose we now zero this rifle so that it shoots three inches high at 100 yards, how would the bullet plot at 200, 300 and 400 yards?

Note how dramatically our numbers are reduced. We're no longer considering drops of 23 and 47 inches out at 300 and 400 yards. The trajectory with the new 266-yard zero is within twelve inches of the line of sight all the way out to 400 yards. In fact, up to 300 yards the bullet is never more than 3.4 inches away from the mark. Imagine how this will take the pressure off our range guesstimating! Instead of trying to come up with a precise range measurement—one that would try the best of calibrated eyeballs,—with big game animals we can now simply tell ourselves, "on targets obviously closer than 200 yards we'll hold for the lower ⅓ of the target area; at intermediate ranges approximating our 266-yard point of zero, we'll hold dead on. When the target appears to be about 400 yards off, we'll align our sights with the top-most edge of the body above the target area."

It's no longer necessary to use "daylight" elevation that would force us to hold off the target entirely.

Varmint hunters, who have considerably smaller targets, may find a four-inch mid-range

trajectory to be a bit awkward, but they can employ the same general technique with a slightly smaller MRT—say 2½ to 3 inches.

From the ballistics tables published elsewhere in this book, the reader can quickly determine a mid-range trajectory and zero point that he can work with to achieve the desired result. For example, those using the 30/30, 32 Special, 300 Savage or 35 Remington will soon discover that a 150-yard zero will give them the best possible trajectory over a distance of 200 yards. These calibers are really not effective at anything beyond that.

Cartridges of the .270 and 30/06 class can be sighted to shoot three inches high at 100 yards and this will give them a zero close to 266 yards. Bullet weight, however, has considerable influence on trajectories. It is important that the rifle be tested at the various distances with cartridges having the desired weight of bullet.

There's something to be said for the practice of using one given make and style of cartridge for all of one's big game hunting.

Finally, hitting a target at great range is one thing—dropping a big game animal at long range can be something else again. Take a look at energy figures at 300 yards; if your cartridge doesn't deliver at least 1000 foot pounds (minimum) at that distance, don't attempt such long shots. (On moose or bear, I'd feel much more comfortable with a minimum of 1500 to 1600 ft. lbs.)

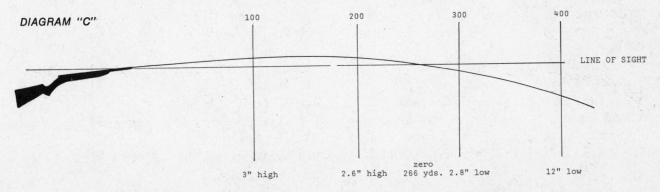

DIAGRAM "C"

100   200   300   400

LINE OF SIGHT

3" high   2.6" high   zero 266 yds. 2.8" low   12" low

All of the foregoing is based on the premise that the rifle is being used over a fairly level range. What happens when the shooter takes a shot having a steep uphill or downhill angle? Gravity is no longer working on the lower center of the bullet; now it's quartered toward the nose or tail. In *both* cases, uphill or down, the rifle will tend to shoot *higher!* There are mathematical formulas for determining the precise rate of drop in such instances, but the shooter would not have the means nor wherewithal to use them when faced with such a situation.

It's not likely, either, that one could memorize a complete table of angle and drop factors.

My own system has worked well for me and I, herewith, pass it on to you: when dealing with angles of 0° to 20°, I disregard the angle entirely. It's not going to have that great an effect on the shot. One inch, or less, is not going to cause one to miss a big game animal if he's zeroed in for an area as outlined earlier.

When angles appear to run between 25° to 40° I use a "twenty percent formula," i.e., if the distance to the target is 200 yards, I aim as if it were 160 yards away. At 400 yards, I'd pretend it was 320 yards off.

This formula was worked up some years ago for rifles in the .270 and 30/06 class. In practice, I've always found it accurate to within 2 to 3 inches at the outside limits of 25° and 40°.

"Fine, but what happens to the shot when one has to cope with an angle beyond 40°; suppose we're sighting on a mountain goat that is almost overhead?"

I hate those shots too!

About the only thing you can do is refer back to your mid-range trajectory. With a near vertical shot the bullet will have a drop factor that is virtually zero. Consequently, if you've zeroed about 4 inches high at 100 yards, a near vertical angle will cause the bullet to continue in a near-straight path —it will be about 8 inches above the line of sight at 200 yards, 12 inches above at 300 and 16 inches above at 400.

This is a very extreme example; I doubt if anyone ever finds himself shooting straight up or down; there's always some angle off the vertical. I cite it only to stimulate the shooter's thinking because 90% of the shots taken at severe up or down angles miss because they're *too high!* THINK LOW!

BORE SIGHTING

The first step in zeroing the rifle is to check, by visual means, the alignment of the sighting equipment with the bore of the rifle. This is called "bore sighting" and this is how it is accomplished.

1. Set up a target having about a six inch round, black bull's-eye at a distance of approximately 100 yards.

2. If you're working with a bolt action rifle, simply remove the bolt. If you have a slide, automatic, or lever action rifle, you'll need a right-angle viewing device like the prismatic "Boreskope" or a tool similar to a dentist's mirror—something that can be inserted into the breech to enable you to look through the bore from chamber to muzzle.

3. Set the rifle in a cradle or vise so that it can be rested to point directly at the target. Center the bull's-eye of the target in the center of the small circle of light seen through the bore. Prop or lock the rifle in this position so that it will keep the alignment without being held by hand. In other words, without holding or touching the rifle, you want to be able to see through the bore. Be careful with the alignment—the bull's-eye should appear dead center through the bore.

4. Again, without touching or disturbing the rifle, peek through the sights or scope to see where they're bearing in relation to the bull's-eye.

Bore sighting is accomplished by placing the rifle in a rest (like this rifle cradle) and sighting on a distant target through the bore. When bore is perfectly aligned, check the bearing of the sights, or scope, without disturbing the position of the rifle.

Gun cradles, like this one, are very useful—not only for bore sighting but for cleaning, stock inletting, etc.

5. If they're pointing high, low or off to one side, adjust the sights so that they're aligned with the center lower edge of the bull's-eye.

6. Check the bore and sights repeatedly until you're satisfied with the alignment.

Bore sighting saves a lot of time and effort, to say nothing of ammunition expense. Incidentally, while bore sighting, it pays to make sure that your sights and/or scope are securely fastened.

ZEROING

Once the rifle is properly bore sighted, we're ready to shoot it for a proper zero.

Set up a target at about fifty feet and, from a rest, slowly, carefully, squeeze off one shot. (Make sure you're not canting the rifle.)

Check the target to see where this shot fell. If it's on the paper, don't make any sight adjustments —yet! Instead, squeeze off a second shot—again, slowly and carefully. If you're doing this correctly, both shots should be fairly close together on the target. If they're not, you're either shooting improperly (jerking the trigger or flinching) or something is loose. Check the mounting screws of your sights or scope mount. Tighten the stock fastening screws of your rifle.

Try another shot. When you get two shots fairly close together, you can adjust the sights to bring subsequent shots into the center of the bull's-eye.

Many sighting instruments have ¼ minute click adjustments—each click would move the strike of the bullet one quarter of an inch at 100 yards. Since we're doing this preliminary shooting at 50 feet, it would take six clicks to move the bullet ¼ inch. Twenty-four clicks to move it one inch.

Some sights and scopes are found with half inch click adjustments, so be on guard here if you're not sure of your click values.

I'd like to be able to tell you "how" to turn the

adjusting knobs (which direction) but the plain truth of the matter is, no one has standarized these —instruments differ—you'll have to figure yours out for yourself! (It pays to keep the instruction sheet that comes with the sight or scope.)

If your two shots are grouped one inch to the right of center and two inches low, and you have ¼ minute adjustments, crank your vertical (top) knob to move the sight, down, 48 clicks. Turn your windage adjustment to move it to the right, 24 clicks.

Fire two more shots. Check to see that the two shot group is now centered where your sights are bearing. If it is slightly out, make a small sight adjustment to bring it in.

When the rifle is shooting close to point of aim at fifty feet, you can set up a target at 100 yards and proceed from there. However, to save time and trouble, sit down with a target and a ruler and mark the point of aim and the desired point of impact. If, from the material given at the beginning of this chapter, you've decided that you'd like to zero 3 inches high at 100 yards place a small "X" at your aiming point (the lower, 6 o'clock, edge of the black bull's-eye) and another "X" precisely 3 inches above the first. Don't use a "by-guess and by-gosh" method, because you'll only wind up fooling yourself on those 200 to 300 yard shots.

Use a ruler and plot your impact area carefully.

Fire each shot from a rest; if using a prone position, roll up a heavy jacket and place it over a log or box to give your forward hand all the support it needs to give you a steady "hold." Use sand bags or a gun cradle when shooting from a benchrest. SQUEEZE the shots off—let them catch you by surprise. Try to take a mental picture of your sight alignment at the instant of firing and CALL each shot before it's spotted.

Shooters who are accustomed to benchrest shooting will invariably rest the fore end of the rifle on a cradle or sand bag and curl their leading arm rearward to squeeze the bag that supports the butt of the rifle. This technique works well for benchrest shooters, but it is not a good practice for the hunter because the rifle will tend to shoot high when the forearm is not gripped by one hand. Even when using a benchrest cradle, place your leading hand on the cradle and grip the fore end of the rifle. This will give you a true zero.

Shooting at one hundred yards you must remember to convert the value of your click adjustments. When you want to move the strike of the bullet one inch, at this distance, it takes only four clicks to accomplish the change, if you have ¼ minute adjustments.

Slowly, carefully, squeeze off three shots at your 100-yard target. When finished, put the rifle aside (out of the sun) to let it cool. With a hunting rifle you must avoid heating the barrel.

As soon as you are able, replace your target with a new one. Take the first target (now containing three bullet holes) and retire to the bench or firing line to plot further corrections.

If you are shooting well, those first three shots should form a nice little triangle in the target. With your ruler, draw straight pencil lines through the centers of adjoining holes so that the target looks like this:

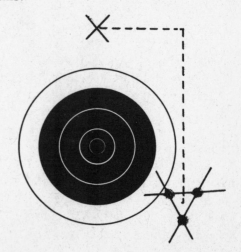

Find the center of this triangle, and measure the distance from that point to the center line of your target.

Now measure from the center line to the "X" mark that you had drawn earlier to indicate the desired impact point.

Let's say you want to move the strike of the bullet to the right one half inch and up, one inch.

Crank the windage adjustment on your sight to the right two clicks. Move the elevation adjustment (up) four clicks.

Fire three more shots in a very slow and deliberate fashion. Now you should find your group centered around the impact area "X" that you had drawn at the start.

If your scope or sight has locking screws, to lock the instrument at this setting, use them. Also, with some scope turrets it is possible to loosen two screws in the dial plate, and rotate it so that the zero on the dial corresponds with the white indicator arrow on the turret body. If your scope is so equipped, set the dials now, but be careful not to disturb the sight setting.

OPEN SIGHTS & PEEP SIGHTS

"Peep" sights are adjusted in the same fashion —their click adjustments are comparable to what you would find on a hunting scope. Follow the same methods.

Open sights, however, are adjusted in a slightly different fashion. If both front and rear sights are mounted in dovetails, draw a pencil line across the junction of the sight base and that portion of the barrel that it abuts. This will give you a starting reference point. Now, if your rifle is shooting to the left, tap the front sight to the *left, EVER SO SLIGHTLY.* A fractional movement of the sight will give you a dramatic movement in the impact point of the bullet at 100 yards. If your rifle is shooting to the right, tap the *rear* sight to the *left;* again—only slightly.

Since these adjustments must be accomplished by a trial-and-error method, don't attempt to make the entire correction in one step. Instead, move the sights by degrees, test shooting between adjustments so that you slowly work your impact point into the proper zero. With open sights you have to guard against moving the sights too far because you CAN'T COME BACK! Dovetails are tapered left to right, to provide a strong interlocking union between the sight base and the female slot in the barrel. If you go beyond your zero point, you'll inadvertently loosen this union when you attempt to move them in the opposite direction.

Elevation adjustments are most often accomplished by means of a stepped elevator—raise the rear sight to raise the strike of the bullet. Lower the rear sight whenever you find that you're shooting too high.

That's all there is to it!

Assuming that you've tuned everything up at home and, that you are now leaving for that long awaited Colorado hunt, make it a point to recheck the zero of your rifle when you arrive at the Colorado base camp. You'll be amazed how sights and scopes can be knocked out of adjustment while in transit. Differences in altitude can also change bullet flight patterns so a last-minute accuracy test is really a "must."

SIGHTING-IN CHARTS
(Reprinted Courtesy of Bausch & Lomb Co., Rochester, N.Y.)

The following tables indicate the most desirable zeroing range for each caliber. Mid-range trajectory and maximum point-blank range are also shown.

Cartridge	Bullet Weight in grains	Bullet Type	Maximum Point Blank Range	Height Above Center on Target at 100 Yds. in Inches	Recommended Zero Distance in Yards
.218 Bee	46	HP, OPE (HP)	226.2	2.8	199.3
.22 Hornet	45	SP, HP	216.1	2.9	190.2
.22 Hornet	46	OPE (HP)	216.1	2.9	190.2
.22 Jet CF Mag.	40		196.3	3.0	172.8
.22 Long Rifle	36	HP	127.6	1.2	109.7
.22 Long Rifle	36	LEAD	126.8	1.1	108.8
.22 W.R.F. (Rem. Spe.)	45	LEAD	135.0	1.7	115.9
.220 Swift	48	SP, PSP	333.2	1.9	294.5
.222 Remington	50	HPPL	273.3	2.5	238.6
.222 Remington	50	PSP, MC	269.3	2.5	235.6
.222 Remington Mag.	55	HPPL	286.7	2.4	249.9
.222 Remington Mag.	55	PSP	282.6	2.4	246.7
.22-250 Remington	55	HPPL	328.4	2.1	287.8
.22-250 Remington	55	PSP	319.9	2.1	280.6
.22-250 Weatherby	55	PT-EX	317.6	2.1	278.3
.223 Remington	55	HPPL	286.7	2.4	249.9
5.6mm Remington	55	PSP	282.6	2.4	246.7
6mm Remington	80	PSP, HPL	315.8	2.2	274.7
6mm Remington	100	PSP, SPCL	304.5	2.4	262.1
.224 Weatherby Varmint	50	PT-EX	308.0	2.2	271.2
.224 Weatherby Varmint	55	PT-EX	312.4	2.2	273.0
.225 Winchester	55	PSP	312.0	2.2	272.6
.240 Weatherby Mag.	70	PT-EX	334.4	2.1	293.5
.240 Weatherby Mag.	90	PT-EX	318.5	2.2	276.5
.240 Weatherby Mag.	100	PT-EX	321.3	2.3	277.7
.243 Winchester	75	HP	308.8	2.3	268.8
.243 Winchester	80	PSP	313.6	2.3	272.0
.243 Winchester	80	HPPL	314.9	2.3	273.5
.243 Winchester	100	PSP, CL, PP(SP)	292.8	2.5	251.7
.244 Remington	75	PSP, HP	308.8	2.3	268.8
.244 Remington	90	PSP	294.3	2.4	254.5
.25-20 Winchester	60	HP, OPE	186.7	3.0	163.4
.25-20 Winchester	86	LEAD, SP, L	139.1	1.9	119.5
.25-35 Winchester	117	SPCL	212.6	3.0	183.5
.25-35 Winchester	117	SP	208.3	3.0	180.4
.250 Savage	87	PSP	276.8	2.6	239.3
.250 Savage	100	PSP	263.0	2.7	227.0
.250 Savage	100	SPCL	247.0	2.7	214.6
.250 Savage	100	ST (EXP)	258.5	2.7	223.5
6.5mm Remington Mag.	120	PSPCL	287.4	2.5	247.6
.256 Winchester Mag.	60	OPE	221.0	2.8	194.4
.257 Roberts	87	PSP	292.3	2.4	253.0
.257 Roberts	100	ST (EXP)	265.3	2.6	229.5

Cartridge	Bullet Weight in grains	Bullet Type	Maximum Point Blank Range	Height Above Center on Target at 100 Yds. in Inches	Recommended Zero Distance in Yards
.257 Roberts	117	PP (SP), SPCL	241.5	2.8	209.0
.257 Weatherby Mag.	87	SP	325.3	2.1	284.8
.257 Weatherby Mag.	100	SP	320.6	2.2	278.4
.257 Weatherby Mag.	117	RN	297.9	2.4	258.0
.264 Winchester Mag.	100	PSPCL	327.3	2.1	285.4
.264 Winchester Mag.	140	PSPCL	307.4	2.4	264.3
.270 Weatherby Mag.	100	SP	323.6	2.1	283.1
.270 Weatherby Mag.	130	SP	314.0	2.3	271.3
.270 Weatherby Mag.	150	RN	299.7	2.4	259.0
.270 Weatherby Mag.	150	SP	306.5	2.4	264.2
.270 Winchester	100	PSP	310.6	2.3	270.0
.270 Winchester	110	SPP	307.6	2.4	265.2
.270 Winchester	130	PP, SP, PP (EXP), SP, BT, BP	301.5	2.5	259.3
.270 Winchester	130	ST (EXP), IBPSP, PSPCL, HPBT	296.9	2.5	255.8
.270 Winchester	130	FJBT	310.3	2.4	266.0
.270 Winchester	150	PP, SP	276.8	2.6	238.0
.270 Winchester	150	IBSP, SPCL	257.5	2.7	222.5
.270 Winchester	150	SPPBT, FJP	278.6	2.7	238.4
.280 Remington	125	PSPCL	298.7	2.4	257.7
.280 Remington	150	PSPCL	281.8	2.6	242.1
.280 Remington	165	SPCL	264.0	2.7	227.7
.284 Winchester	125	PP (SP)	298.7	2.4	257.8
.284 Winchester	150	PP (SP)	276.8	2.6	238.0
7mm Mauser	139		252.0	2.8	215.4
7mm Mauser	175	SP	232.5	2.9	200.6
7mm Remington Mag.	150	PSPCL, PP (SP)	308.4	2.4	265.7
7mm Remington Mag.	175	PSPCL	299.7	2.5	257.1
7mm Remington Mag.	175	PP (SP)	282.5	2.5	244.2
7mm Weatherby Mag.	139	PT-EX	310.3	2.4	267.6
7mm Weatherby Mag.	154	SP	302.0	2.4	259.7
7mm Weatherby Mag.	175	RN	290.4	2.5	250.2
.30 Carbine	110	SP, HSP	175.4	2.9	152.2
.30 Remington	170	ST (EXP)	202.1	3.0	173.4
.30 Remington	170	IBSP, MCL, SPCL	206.8	3.0	178.4
.30-06 Springfield	110	PSP (WIN)	284.3	2.4	248.6
.30-06 Springfield	110	PSP (REM)	287.9	2.4	251.4
.30-06 Springfield	125	PSP	290.9	2.5	251.6
.30-06 Springfield	130	SPPBT, FJBT	303.7	2.4	262.6
.30-06 Springfield	150	BP	285.1	2.6	245.1
.30-06 Springfield	150	PP (SP)	273.1	2.6	236.1
.30-06 Springfield	150	ST (EXP) PSPCL	279.8	2.6	241.2
.30-06 Springfield	180	BP	264.4	2.7	226.7
.30-06 Springfield	180	PP (SP)	249.9	2.7	216.8
.30-06 Springfield	180	SPCL	246.5	2.8	213.2
.30-06 Springfield	180	ST (EXP)	266.0	2.7	228.9
.30-06 Springfield	180	PSPCL	262.6	2.7	225.4
.30-06 Springfield	180	FMCBT, MCTH	269.6	2.7	230.5
.30-06 Springfield	180		257.7	2.7	221.8
.30-06 Springfield	220	PP (SP) SPCL	228.4	2.9	196.6
.30-06 Springfield	220	ST (EXP)	235.1	2.9	201.6
.30-30 Winchester	150	SPCL	212.9	3.0	184.9
.30-30 Winchester	150	OPE, PP, ST	218.1	2.9	188.9
.30-30 Winchester	160	MC	205.0	3.0	177.0
.30-30 Winchester	170	HPCL, SPCL	206.8	3.0	178.4
.30-40 Krag	180	SPCL, PP (SP)	227.9	2.9	196.8
.30-40 Krag	180	PSPCL, ST (EXP)	241.4	2.9	207.1
.30-40 Krag	220	ST (EXP)	212.3	3.0	181.3

Cartridge	Bullet Weight in grains	Bullet Type	Maximum Point Blank Range	Height Above Center on Target at 100 Yds. in Inches	Recommended Zero Distance in Yards
.300 Savage	150	PSPCL, ST (EXP)	253.6	2.8	218.4
.300 Savage	150	PP (SP)	249.0	2.8	214.9
.300 Savage	150	SPCL	240.5	2.8	208.4
.300 Savage	180	PSPCL, ST (EXP)	232.8	2.9	199.6
.300 Savage	180	SPCL, PP (SP)	220.3	2.9	190.2
.300 H. & H. Magnum	150	ST (EXP)	297.7	2.4	257.0
.300 H. & H. Magnum	180	ST (EXP)	281.8	2.6	242.1
.300 H. & H. Magnum	220	ST (EXP)	253.2	2.8	217.4
.300 Weatherby Mag.	110	SP	351.6	1.9	311.7
.300 Weatherby Mag.	150	SP	326.3	2.2	283.1
.300 Weatherby Mag.	180	SP	308.6	2.4	265.6
.300 Weatherby Mag.	220	RN	276.7	2.6	237.9
.300 Winchester Mag.	150	PP (SP) PSPCL	312.5	2.3	270.6
.300 Winchester Mag.	180	PP (SP) PSPCL	300.3	2.5	257.5
.300 Winchester Mag.	220	ST (EXP)	264.5	2.7	227.1
7.65 Argentine	150	SPP	275.9	2.6	237.7
.303 British	180	PP (SP) SPCL	246.7	2.8	211.6
.303 British	215	SP	220.6	2.8	192.2
.303 Savage	190	ST (EXP)	186.8	3.0	160.9
.303 Savage	180	SPCL	199.3	3.0	171.9
.308 Norma Magnum	180	NDC	303.0	2.5	260.0
.308 Winchester	110	PSP	283.1	2.4	247.4
.308 Winchester	125	PSP	285.2	2.5	246.3
.308 Winchester	150	PP (SP)	264.2	2.7	228.3
.308 Winchester	150	ST (EXP) PSPCL	270.4	2.7	233.0
.308 Winchester	180	PP (SP), SPCL	239.4	2.8	206.9
.308 Winchester	180	ST (EXP), PSPCL	254.7	2.8	218.5
.308 Winchester	200	ST (EXP)	237.0	2.9	203.6
8mm Mauser	170	SPCL, PP (SP)	228.7	2.9	198.4
.35 Remington	200	IBHP, IBSP, MCL, SPCL, HPCL	201.3	3.0	174.1
.350 Remington	200	PSPCL	254.8	2.8	219.7
.350 Remington	250	PSPCL	235.6	2.9	202.1
.351 Winchester	180	SP, FMC	175.0	2.9	150.7
.358 Norma Magnum	250	SPSP	263.7	2.7	227.0
.358 Winchester	200	ST (EXP)	235.3	2.9	203.3
.358 Winchester	250	ST (EXP)	217.6	3.0	187.0
.375 H. & H. Magnum	270	PP (SP)	260.9	2.7	224.4
.375 H. & H. Magnum	300	ST (EXP)	243.9	2.8	209.7
.375 H. & H. Magnum	300	FMC, MC	232.6	2.9	201.3
.375 Weatherby Mag.	270	RN	274.1	2.6	236.0
.375 Weatherby Mag.	300	RN	263.1	2.7	226.3
.378 Weatherby Mag.	270	RN	298.0	2.4	257.0
.378 Weatherby Mag.	300	RN	276.5	2.6	237.9
.38-40 Winchester	180	SP	127.8	1.2	109.7
.38-55 Winchester	255	SP	133.2	1.5	113.6
.44 Remington Mag.	240	HSP, SP	157.8	2.7	136.5
.444 Marlin	240	SP	201.6	3.0	176.4
.44-40 Winchester	200	SP	125.9	1.0	108.1
.45-70 Government	405	SP	133.2	1.5	113.6
.458 Winchester Mag.	500	FMC, SP	208.1	3.0	178.6
.458 Winchester Mag.	510	SP	201.9	3.0	173.8
.460 Weatherby Mag.	500	RN	246.3	2.8	213.1

CHAPTER 14

Handloading Rifle Ammunition

(The terms "reloading" and "handloading" are synonymous.)

The most expensive component of the factory-loaded cartridge is the brass casing and, since this portion of the round can be salvaged after firing, it makes sense to re-use it.

The reloader can make up his own shells (using salvaged cases) and realize a considerable saving over factory-loaded shells. Also, if he's willing to put forth some extra effort, he can handload shells that will prove more accurate. Finally, most reloaders will tell you that they enjoy handloading and that it's an interesting and pleasurable fringe benefit of their shooting hobby.

How much can one save through handloading?

To answer this question we must add some qualifying factors. Actual savings depends upon the quality and cost of components, and the number of shells one intends loading within a given time period. What many shooters fail to realize is that the initial investment in loading tools can quickly reach a figure exceeding one hundred dollars. If he's not going to need more than a hundred cartridges per year, it could take the shooter five or more years to recover his investment. One doesn't reload solely for the purpose of saving money unless one does a great deal of shooting.

Each fired casing requires a new primer, powder charge and bullet. While primer prices are the same for all rifle calibers, powder costs depend upon the amount of powder required by a given cartridge. Bullet prices, too, vary according to size and, to some extent, quality. In working up some sample costs for a few representative cartridges, I found the following average cost comparisons:

Cartridge Type	Factory Shells	Reloaded Shells
30/30 cal. 170gr.		
per box of 20	$5.15	$1.70
30/06 cal. 180gr.		
per box of 20	6.55	2.00
300 H&H Mag. cal. 180gr.		
per box of 20	8.40	2.20

(Note: To determine powder costs, one pound of smokeless powder consists of 7000 grains. Find the number of grains required for a given load and divide it into 7,000; i.e., if using a 50 grain powder charge, $7,000 \div 50 = 140$, consequently, one

149

could load 140 cartridges from one pound of powder.)

"Can I really expect better accuracy from a handload?"

Anyone who is willing to invest the time and effort required can load cartridges that will give better accuracy than could be expected from factory new ammo. This is not to imply that our commercial ammo plants produce inferior shells; it's just that the reloader is able to tailor shells to the liking of his particular rifle—factories are forced to produce shells that can be digested safely by many different makes and types of rifles. Even so, I feel they do a remarkable job because I've often managed minute-of-angle groups with factory shells, most recently with a 7mm Magnum rifle that was fresh out of the box. A rifle with a good chamber, cut to minimum dimensions, will invariably perform well with factory fare.

"Isn't handloading dangerous?"

No, not for anyone who is sensible and reasonably careful. If you're the type that has little patience, or who has to be doing more than one thing at a time or, who suffers from a compulsion to make things bigger, or faster, *handloading is not for you!*

On the other hand, if you have no trouble understanding what you read, and if you can follow directions, you just might enjoy loading your own cartridges—it certainly isn't difficult nor does it require a degree in engineering.

For one thing, modern smokeless gunpowders *do not explode*—they burn fiercely, true, but they're no more dangerous than a can of gasoline or charcoal lighter. I've always made it a point when teaching handloading to burn a little in an ashtray or saucer to allay unfounded fears. Accidents happen only through ignorance or carelessness. The step-by-step directions that follow contain information and advice for avoiding trouble.

"What tools will I need to handload shells for my 30/06 rifle?"

I would recommend the following minimum set-up for the beginner:

LOADING PRESS   A "C"-type or "O"-type loading press such as those made by C-H, R.C.B.S. or Lyman. ($20. to $60.)

LOADING DIES   One set, consisting of two dies for the caliber you wish to load. ($12. to $15.) If you should want to load for more than one caliber, you'll have to buy a separate set of dies for each new caliber.

POWDER MEASURE   These are adjustable and can be used to measure, volumetrically, all types of powders. Charges, however, must be checked by a grain scale. ($20. to $30.)

POWDER SCALE   These are calibrated to the tenth of a grain. ($20. to $60.)

POWDER FUNNEL   This facilitates the pouring of powder into the narrow case opening. A larger funnel is also useful, but this can be obtained at any variety store for about 50¢—look for one with an aperture of about ½ inch. ($1.50)

POWDER TRICKLER   Drops individual grains of powder. ($3. to $4.)

CASE LUBRICANT   Stamp-pad type applicator recommended with tube of lubricant. (about $6.00)

CASE LENGTH GAUGE   Brass cases tend to stretch through repeated loadings so a measuring tool is essential to determine if, and when, they should be trimmed back. A fixed gauge will run about $3.00—a sophisticated caliper having a micrometer dial will cost about $22.00.

CASE TRIMMER   These vary from a simple hardened steel die ($7.50) which requires filing of that portion of the case protruding, to a miniature, lathe-like tool, adjustable for all sizes of cases and equipped with a rotating cutter (about $14.00).

The RCBS Jr. #3 loading press is an "O" type—strong, practical!

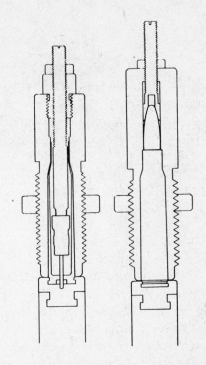

Diagram of RCBS two-die set for handloading rifle cartridges. Die on left decaps and sizes. Die on right is used to seat bullets.

The powder measure.

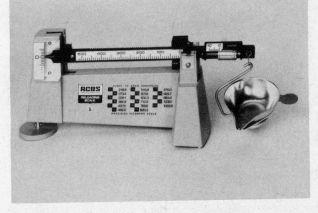

The powder scale is capable of weighing charges to the tenth of a grain.

Powder funnel.

Powder trickler.

Hardened steel die used for case trimming.

A micrometer-dial caliper, like this one, is very useful to the rifleman. It can be used for a number of handloading operations as well as for gunsmithing tasks.

While we'll endeavor to give our readers step-by-step directions for handloading, it's not possible to reproduce, here, all of the loading data one might need for a variety of calibers. Therefore, we suggest that the new handloader obtain a manual devoted exclusively to reloading—try the "Lyman Ideal Handbook" the "NRA Reloading Handbook" or Bob Steindler's "Reloader's Guide."

The aspiring reloader usually begins by saving empty brass cases (from factory rounds) long before acquiring his loading equipment. Right here, I'd like to recommend that he refrain from picking up empties that were fired in someone else's rifle. The hulls coming from his own rifle are perfectly mated to his chamber while someone else's hulls could give the beginner more trouble than he could handle. For one thing, there's no way of knowing how many times those strange hulls have been reloaded. Also, they could have been run through an oversized chamber, a factor that would cause jamming in a normal chamber. They could have other little flaws, too, that would escape the untrained eye.

For safety's sake, stick to your own cases.

While we're on the subject of "don'ts," let's discuss the others applying to cartridges cases.

Don't mix makes of cases—separate all cases, by brand, before loading the first one. Put the separated empty hulls back in their original boxes and mark each box to indicate how many times a given batch has been loaded and fired. This is important because with each successive firing you must examine EACH CASE carefully before attempting to use it again. The average handloader gets four loadings out of a case before he has to discard it. When conditions are ideal, and the handloader doesn't mind a little extra work, it's possible to get up to seven or eight firings from *some* cases.

Cases differ a bit dimensionally from brand to brand and often, from one lot to another in a given brand. Thus, you can expect to run into some eccentricities. For example, having started with a minimum load you've moved up, by stages, to a load about four grains short of maximum. Your Winchester cases take this load nicely and you're happy with its accuracy. Now, because you're forced to discard some fired Winchester cases, you replace them with Remington hulls. If the Remington cases, by chance, should be a bit smaller internally than the Winchester hulls you had been working with, you could unwittingly increase chamber pressures. When switching brands of cases, you should always reduce your pet loads by two or three grains and slowly work back up to the levels you had previously found desirable. I've found that this is best accomplished in half-grain increments. When working with big cartridges and heavy loads, stay about 10% below published maximum figures when checking out new brass.

Cut away of loaded Remington cartridge. Loaded shell consists of four components: primer, powder, case and bullet.

One very important point we have to make here is that published loading tables consist of figures obtained from one given test rifle with one specific combination of dimensions and components. The ballistician simply reports the results he obtained under controlled test conditions and this data is designed to serve only as a guide for other handloaders. The reloader may not obtain, nor should he expect, exactly the same performance from *his* rifle. Handloaders get into trouble when they insist upon duplicating some published maximum loads. If a given table, for example, states that 55 grains of XYZ powder will drive a 150 grain bullet at 3200 feet per second, some handloaders will insist upon using this load in spite of the pressure signals they'll get indicating trouble. Velocity will fall below the desired level, they feel, if they should cut back on the charge. The fact is they're already surpassing the breech pressure that was measured for the published load and, chances are, *they're exceeding the published velocity as well!*

When high pressure signs are spotted, *they must be heeded!*

The first indication of excessive pressure will usually come from the primer—instead of a smoothly dimpled firing pin indentation, edges will be roughly cratered. Sometimes, too, the reloader will notice that his primer is unusually flat (they're made slightly convex) and this condition, while not dangerous, indicates that the load used is about as hot as it can get.

If cratering is ignored, and the load further increased, cases may start to stick in the chamber, making extraction and ejection difficult or, the primer will be punctured. A punctured primer will invariably blow some hot debris back through the action.

Shallow-striking firing pins with well rounded noses often permit hot loads to go beyond the punctured primer stage. When this is the prevailing condition, excessive pressure will "pop" the primer (push it slightly out of the pocket or remove it from the pocket entirely).

An unusual amount of smoke upon extraction, and a heavily blackened neck area, could also indicate that pressures are getting out of hand.

The point is—use published data only as a guide for establishing starting loads and for determining dangerous levels that cannot be exceeded. Then, make up your loads to *suit your rifle*. If you're getting excellent performance from a 58 grain load while the manual claims the maximum load is 60 grains, forget the sixty grain load! Your barrel will last longer and you'll avoid trouble that could pop up from slight variations in components. For whatever it's worth, I've never gotten even passably good performance from a maximum load, and I've ruined a heck of a lot of barrels in my attempts!

SIZING THE CASE

Brass is an alloy comprised of copper and zinc. It's soft and tough—ideally suited to the function of a cartridge case. However, through repeated loadings and firings it tends to harden, especially in the neck area, and it will eventually become somewhat brittle. To prolong case life, the reloader can minimize sizing operations and he can also anneal case necks.

To anneal (soften) case necks to prolong case life, stand the cases in a pan of cold water so that only necks and shoulders protrude above water level. Heat the necks with a torch until they're cherry red and knock them over so that they're completely immersed. Heating and rapid cooling softens brass. The same method would tend to harden ferrous metals.

When firing a new factory round in your rifle, the case is fully expanded to fit the chamber. After firing, it excercises a spring-like quality and will shrink a bit from the walls permitting extraction and ejection. This case is then perfectly mated to your rifle's chamber.

In fact, with some lever, pump or automatic rifles, it may be too perfectly sized to the chamber, necessitating full-length re-sizing before subsequent chambering as a reload.

If, after conventional full-length sizing you should still experience difficulty in loading or extracting cases from your pump, lever or automatic rifle, you need a special full-length sizing die. Write to Fred Huntington at R.C.B.S. Inc., in Oroville, California.

To make a new cartridge from this used casing you must decide whether to neck size only or full length size. Then the sizing die must be installed in the press, adjusted, and the ram of the press equipped with the appropriate shell holder. The case is then lubricated and run through the die—decapping (removing the spent primer) is accomplished simultaneously. Most "C" and "O" presses can also be had with automatic priming feeds so that sizing, decapping and re-priming can be accomplished in one cycle of the operating lever.

I don't use this feature simply because I prefer to examine primer pockets before fitting them with a new primer. Therefore I suggest that only lubricating, sizing and decapping be performed initally. Make re-priming a separate operation following case examination.

Assuming you've firmly affixed your loading press to a good, heavy bench (preferably one that is anchored to the floor) you can now install the appropriate shell holder in the ram of the tool, following the manufacturer's directions. Next, take your sizing die, remove the inner stem and decapping pin, loosen the lock screw in the outer adjusting collar, and screw the collar towards the top of the die (away from the end that accepts the casing). Operate the lever of your press to position the empty shell holder at the top of its stroke—leave it there while screwing the sizing die into position through the top of the press.

Now, if you want to full length size, screw the die down so the bottom of the die *lightly* contacts the topmost edge of the shell holder. Be careful here, I've seen some handloaders install sizing dies with such a heavy contact that they sprung their "C" tools out of alignment—that lever exerts considerable force!

If you want to neck size only (which may be desirable for shells to be used in a bolt action rifle) install the sizing die so that it falls about 1/16 of an inch short of making contact with the shell holder. When you've gained some experience as a handloader, you may want to size only the lip of the neck—just enough to hold the bullet. This is done by increasing the distance between the mouth of the die and the top of the shell holder.

Once you've determined the proper position for the die, hold the body of the die in position with your left hand while screwing the locking ring down (with your right hand) to make contact with the topmost surface of the press. When the collar is in contact with the press, re-tighten the little lockscrew that runs through the collar. This die is now adjusted and locked into position for the desired sizing operation.

Move the shell holder out of the way by operating the lever. Take the decapping rod that you removed earlier and see that the slender decapping pin is firmly affixed to the end, under the expanding button. The expanding button can be tightened on the threads of the rod to lock the pin firmly into position. Make sure the decapping pin is not loose or swiveling because you'll break it in the first case you try to size. When firmly locked into position, the decapping pin should be a straight extension of the rod itself. Now slide the decapping rod, pin end down, through the top of the sizing die and screw it into position. Check to see that the decapping pin is extending about ⅜ of an inch *below* the mouth of the die and lock the rod into position with the locking collar provided.

Before you attempt to run any cases into the die, set up your lubricating outfit. Apply a light coating of lubricant to the stamp pad, being careful to spread it evenly over the entire surface of the pad. Scrape off excess lubricant. Let the lubricant soak in for a few minutes before attempting to use the pad. Remember, you must lubricate *lightly;* excess lubrication can cause trouble.

When you're ready, lay about five fired casings on the pad and roll them gently back and forth so that they pick up a light coating of lubricant. Now, with a small bore cleaning brush or a tightly folded cloth, apply a little lubricant inside the neck of the first case. This will lubricate the expanding button inside the die.

Place the case in the shell holder and, while operating the lever, guide it gently into the mouth of the die. Do this slowly and carefully. Once started, press it to the top of the stroke and slowly remove it. The spent primer should have fallen out below the tool. If you can't remove the case from the shell holder it's because the primer has not been removed and it's protruding from the bottom of the case. Leave the case in the shell holder and adjust the inner decapping rod of the die so that it protrudes farther beyond the mouth of the die (turn the inner stem clockwise). Run the same case through again until the primer drops.

Try to catch those spent primers in some kind of container; they're a nuisance under your feet and if you should subsequently drop a live primer you'll be confronted with a needle-and-haystack situation.

When operations are progressing smoothly, lubricate, size and decap all of your empty cases. Upon finishing, remove the sizing die from the tool and store it away. Do the same with your lubricating equipment.

CASE EXAMINATION

It pays to have a loading block that will hold cases both right side up or upside down. Upon completing the sizing operation, return the cases to the block so that they're primer end up. When all the cases have been sized, you can easily examine the primer pockets without further handl-

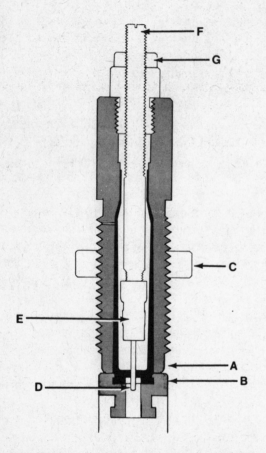

Diagram of an RCBS sizing die: A—mouth of die body; B—shell holder; C—locking ring; D—decapping pin; E—expander button; F—expander-decapping rod; G—rod lock-ring. (Solid black area represents cartridge casing. Gray area is die body. White areas are internal or external fittings.)

Loading blocks can be made from scrap blocks of 2" x 4"—like these! Holes can be made deep enough to hold shells upside down or right side up.

ing. In time you'll develop a practiced eye that will quickly spot flash holes that appear unreasonably large—discard such cases. If you find a heavy accumulation of debris in the primer pockets, clean them. There are some inexpensive gadgets on the market now that make this task easy. Before they came along I used a mashed and moistened toothpick.

When you're satisfied with the primer pockets and flash holes, set up your priming feed; the press manufacturer's instructions will tell you how to do this. Next, check your loading manual to see what kind of primer you should be using ("small rifle" or "large rifle"). Count your cases and set aside an equal number of new primers—you don't want

any strays laying around. If your press is equipped with a tube-like automatic priming feed, you can probably fit all the primers you will need into the tube.

Take one case at a time from the loading block and examine it carefully before installing a new primer. If this is the first reload for the batch of cases, you won't have to measure them for length, you can simply look for cracks, splits, pin-holes or any other irregularity in the case walls. The slightest structural defect requires that you discard the case.

Cases that have been reloaded more than once must be checked for length—any that are too long must be trimmed back to proper size. This is where careless handloaders get into trouble because they're too lazy to measure and trim cases and they can't understand why they have accidents.

As soon as you have okayed a case, fit it with a

A marked difference in flash hole diameter can affect performance when one is shooting for pin-point accuracy. Note the difference in flash hole sizes in the two shells at the bottom extreme right.

new primer. By employing this method of operation you'll never get confused between what has, or has not, been inspected.

Some further discussion of primers and the primer-seating operation is called for at this point.

Primers contain a hardened compound which is poured into the base cup while in a paste form. Over this is quickly fitted a metal anvil shaped something like a boat's three-bladed propeller. When the paste hardens, it is wedged between the cup and the anvil so that a concentrated blow on the cup will tend to break the hardened compound

against the resistance of the anvil. When so broken, the primer gives off an intensely hot flame, one that will easily penetrate the flash hole and ignite the propellant powder charge.

Primers are highly sensitive and they can be dangerous. When the Reverend Alexander J. Forsyth invented the first successful priming mixture in 1805, there were those who quickly referred to it as a "devil's mixture." It's still a fairly touchy component, even with all of the improvements that have been made over the years. Don't spill primers about carelessly; if you should drop one on the floor, pick it up immediately. Don't scatter them over your work surface. By all means, keep them out the reach of children. When seating primers, operate the press slowly and gently—at times you'll have to jiggle the primer arm a bit to get the primer started into the pocket. They will not detonate under the gentle, overall pressure of the primer arm, so don't be afraid to use slowly applied force to seat them properly. Make sure that each primer is fully seated below the level of the case head. Protruding primers are potentially dangerous.

Finally, and most important, NEVER ATTEMPT TO REMOVE A LIVE PRIMER FROM A CASING. (A friend of mine attempted to decap a live primer as he would a spent one—he's still walking around with metal fragments in his legs!) If you want to discard a primed case, put it in the chamber of your rifle, point it in a safe direction and fire it. Don't be surprised to see a cone of flame exit the muzzle.

LOADING POWDER

For this operation you'll need your table of charges, a powder measure, a powder scale, a powder funnel and a "Little Dripper" or "Little Trickler."

Set up your scale, first, on a solid flat surface. Adjust the beam to a "zero" setting. Check the balance beam to be sure it's operating smoothly by tapping it up and down. These grain scales are very sensitive and must be adjusted carefully. Adjustments are accomplished through a leveling device in the base. When the beam is at a zero setting, and the powder pan is in place, the pointer should be pointing at "zero" on the indicator. If it isn't, adjust the level of the base by turning the base screw in or out.

Now, consult your table of charges and select the load you'd like to start with; the table will tell you the brand name of the powder, the model number or name and the number of grains required for one cartridge. This will appear something like this, "Dupont 4064 46grs."

The number "4064" is a specific powder type and serves as a model number. Make sure that you

do not confuse one powder with another. The note "46grs." indicates the weight of the charge required so you go back to your scale and set the heavy beam weight for 45 grains (it's usually calibrated in five-grain increments) and the light beam weight at one grain. You'll notice that the fractional part of the beam is closest to the pan and that it is calibrated in tenths of a grain.

When the scale is ready, set the "Little Trickler" so that it will feed powder into the pan.

Next, set up the powder measure. This is usually equipped with some form of wing-nut anchoring device. I place a small block of wood in a bench vise and clamp the measure to a protruding end of the block. Adjust the feeding device to throw an obviously light charge.

Before opening the canister of powder, put out your cigarette or pipe and move your ashtray out of the work area.

Fill the reservoir of your powder measure and the hopper of the Little Dripper. This is where a large, inexpensive funnel will come in handy.

With all of the primed cartridges primer end up in the loading block, we're ready to start loading powder.

Throw the first charge from the measure and place it in the pan of the powder scale. It should be light, so bring it up to weight by trickling additional powder into the pan from the dripper. When you have some idea of how much additional powder is required to reach the desired weight, make an adjustment in the powder measure to throw charges as close as you can to the desired weight. Stay on the light side, however, because it's easier to add powder to the pan than it is to take it away.

At times, a powder scale will stick a bit—suddenly you'll find that the beam soars past the indicator from the dormant position, indicating an overly heavy charge. So, when first loading the pan, rap the table surface smartly; this will usually get the beam moving. Whenever you inadvertently throw an overweight charge, simply empty the pan back into the hopper of the measure. This will prove faster than attempts to correct it.

Some handloaders simply use the scale to check every fifth load once they've adjusted the measure to throw a desired charge. There's really no danger in this but I've never found a measure that would consistently throw exactly the same charge of powder. There are always a few light charges in the lot and these, I feel, will compromise the accuracy that I'm seeking. I weigh every charge and I firmly believe the new reloader should do the same. It takes a little time to develop a knowledge of the tools and the instinct to spot suspect loads.

The small powder funnel with the tapered feeding cone is used to pour the powder from the scale pan into the casing. Because the cases are stored primer end up turn them over, one at a time, just as you are about to funnel powder into them.

In this manner you'll always know which cases have been charged and which have not.

DOUBLE CHARGES AND LIGHT LOADS

The new reloader will inevitably hear a lot of talk about double charges. That's all it is—talk! With modern cartridges and powders it's highly unlikely that one could ever throw a double load into one case simply because the powder would spill out over the mouth of the case. Most normal powder charges come pretty close to filling the case. They barely leave room for seating the bullet.

There is an exception to this, however, and that would apply when loading *unusually light loads*. Some of the powders used for light loads could prove highly dangerous if accidentally doubled.

"Why would anyone want to make up light loads?"

There are many reasons for these, based primarily on noise factors or the economy of inexpensive lead bullets.

We'd better interject, here, a word of caution about light loads because they can, at times, prove just as dangerous as overloads. When using those loading tables make it a point to stay close to the minimum charge recommended. Don't reduce them unnecessarily. Some powders, when loaded too lightly, can be detonated by a hot primer.

The effects of detonation are comparable to the effects one could expect from a heavy overload.

When, and if, you reach a decision to make up some unjacketed bullet loads, be sure to follow the specific data recommended for these.

Having charged all of your primed cases, pick up the loading block and hold it under an overhead light source—one that enables you to see down into the cases. You'll accomplish two things by this examination: you'll be able to confirm that each case contains a powder charge and you'll quickly be able to recognize any charges that appear to be lower or higher than the rest. If you should suspect a few given loads, pull them out and re-check their charges on your powder scale.

POTENTIAL TROUBLE AREAS

When working with the powder scale it is at times possible to jar one of the beam weights into a different setting. Check the scale setting frequently to make sure it hasn't been altered. If you should ever find it misaligned you'll have to go back and re-weigh every load.

When you have finished the powder loading operation, empty your powder measure and your powder trickler. Be sure you put the powder back into the right canister—it could prove disastrous to mix this powder with another type. Also, MAKE SURE THAT BOTH THE MEASURE AND TRICKLER ARE REALLY EMPTY! Careless emptying could result in mixed powders the next time you set up a loading session.

To complete this segment let me add that the weight of the powder in the measure's hopper will influence the weight of the charges thrown. You'll save yourself some dripper time if you don't let the hopper load fall below the halfway mark.

BULLETS & BULLET SEATING

The easiest bullets to work with, and the best from a performance standpoint, are commercial varieties of jacketed bullets such as those turned out by Sierra, Hornady, Speer, Nosler, Remington and Winchester. These are made with copper-jacketed lead cores and are generally offered in a broad range of shapes, weights and sizes.

You'll find, too, that it is possible to select a particular style of bullet for a specific hunting or target shooting purpose.

At this stage of the game you're obliged to make four decisions:

1. diameter of bullet?
2. weight of bullet?
3. style of bullet?
4. seating depth?

Referring to your loading manual, you'll usually find bullet diameter identified next to the caliber designation; for example, the manual will read— "30/06 CALIBER (.308 dia)." It's the ".308" dia." that you're interested in, so you can tell your dealer that you want a box of "30 caliber .308 diameter bullets." Again, with the reloading table in front of you, go back to the load that you started with, i.e. "Dupont 4064, 46 grains." On the same line you'll find a reference to a *specific weight* of bullet. Under a column title saying "bullet weight," it will say, for example, "150 gr." This is very important from a safety standpoint—you cannot mix bullet weights any more than you can powder weights. The two go together in combination so you must use the bullet called for with a particular powder charge.

Style of bullet: The magazine of your rifle may be a determining factor here. You can feed virtually any style of bullet through a staggered-box or clip magazine. Tubular magazines, however, eliminate the possibility of using spire or semi-pointed bullets because cartridges are arranged end to end with the point of one bullet bearing against the primer of another. This is a potentially dangerous condition. Can you imagine the chain reaction that would result if, through careless loading or recoil, a bullet fired the primer bearing against it? For this reason use conventional flat-nosed or round-nosed bullets in tubular magazines.

Insofar as performance is concerned, you'll have to test an assortment of bullet styles in order to determine which one works best for the purpose you have in mind. Hollow-pointed bullets are basically intended for hunting purposes. Boat tails are primarily match bullets.

Most round-nosed bullets are hunting bullets though I've seen them used on occasion in large caliber rifles for long range target shooting purposes.

Pointed bullets of the semi, spire and spitzer types can be used for both hunting and precision target shooting. There are, however, some special designs available for big game hunting pursuits. One bullet maker, Nosler, produces a partitioned bullet in a semi-pointed nose style expressly for hunting.

In my light benchrest and varmint rifle I've never had much luck with the sharply tapered spire point bullet. This particular rifle likes spitzer or semi-pointed bullets. On the other hand, spire points do well in one of my 30/06 rifles.

Finally, we arrive at the fourth question concerning seating depth.

There are a number of methods you can employ to solve this problem. You can use the dimensions of a factory-made shell, the specific recommendations made in some loading manuals, or you can let your rifle determine the depth that is best for you. Whichever method you use, however, you must be sure that your rifle's magazine will handle cartridges of the length you select.

The range of acceptable bullet depths is easy to ascertain. Lay a bullet beside the neck of one of your cases and determine how deep it would have to be to position the base of the bullet at the lowest end of the neck. You don't want the bullet to extend, inside the case, into the shoulder area. Now, using a pencil, put a line on the bullet at the point reached by the mouth of the case neck. That portion of the bullet, between the pencil line and the base of the bullet, will indicate the greatest depth to which that bullet should be seated.

If you've rejected a couple of empty (though sized) cases, you can use them at this point to make up some dummy rounds. I drill a few holes through these to identify them as dummies. (Polish off any burrs that result from drilling.)

Assuming that you've left your shell holder in in the ram of the press and removed the sizing die, you can now take the remaining die from the two-die set and install it in the top of the press. Again, loosen the set screw and move the locking ring towards the top of the die. Also, remove the bullet-seating stem from the center of the die.

Place your dummy round in the shell holder, activate the lever, and place the case at the top of the stroke. Hold it there while you screw the body of your bullet seating die down and over the dummy casing. When the die is stopped, back it off a half turn and tighten the locking ring to make contact with the press. Re-set the lock screw.

Next, place your marked bullet over the mouth of the dummy case and simply hold it there (don't attempt to start it in the case because it won't go) while you again work the lever to slide the case and bullet into the die. The bullet will wiggle about as you're forced to release it with your fingers, but this is normal. The die will center it in the proper position.

Hold the position of the case at the top of the stroke while you screw the bullet seating stem back into the center of the die. When you meet resistance, you are close to the bullet starting position. Back the case out a bit from the die and give the bullet seating stem three full clockwise turns. Push the case (and bullet) back up into the die and you'll feel the pressure as the bullet is started into the neck.

Obviously, this bullet is protruding much too far from the mouth of the case—we'll correct that next. Take the dummy round and feed it into THE CHAMBER OF YOUR RIFLE. Close the breech fully, and slowly open it again to extract the round. The bullet should have engaged the rifling and the pressure of the breech should have forced the case forward to increase the engagement between case and bullet. (Look for slight rifling marks on the nose of the bullet.)

Go back to the press and, again, run the dummy round back up into your bullet seating die. When it reaches its topmost position, hold it there while you screw the bullet seating stem down into the center of the die. The stem will stop when it makes contact with the bullet. Back the case out of the die and give the stem one more full turn clockwise. (Some reloaders use half a turn.) Lock the stem into position with the locking ring provided. One more time, work the dummy round back into the die to seat the bullet at the new depth.

When you now extract the dummy round it will be adjusted for the maximum overall length acceptable to the *chamber* of your rifle. The pencil line on the bullet should still be visible.

Notice that I said "acceptable to the chamber" —this doesn't mean that a cartridge of this length will feed through your magazine. At this point we've only determined, with the one dummy, the safe minimum and maximum seating depths for that particular bullet.

Try loading the dummy round into the magazine and feeding it through the action of your rifle. Does it work? If not, you'll have to keep lowering the bullet seating stem, by degrees, to seat the bullet until the cartridge does function in your rifle. About that pencil mark indicating maximum depth—while you can easily get into trouble with a bullet that protrudes too far, *most of the time,* a bullet that is seated too deeply will not pose a problem. There are always exceptions, however, and that is the reason why I mark a bullet to show me when I've reached what I consider the maximum desirable depth. I'll go beyond this only when I'm forced too, and then only grudgingly.

Once you've got your dummy shell made up to suit your rifle's chamber and magazine, scribe the casing with the name, weight and style of bullet. Whenever you load for this particular bullet again, you'll be able to adjust your bullet seating die, quickly, just by feeding the dummy into the die and turning the pre-loosened stem down to meet it. On contact, simply lock the stem in position and you're ready to go.

We must point out, here, that one stem position WILL NOT apply for all types of bullets. Obviously sharply tapered bullets, such as spitzers and spire points, can be seated shallower to result in a long overall cartridge simply because their taper will keep them from bearing against the rifling. If you should change to a round or square nosed bullet, you'll have to repeat the entire process of making a dummy round in order to determine the proper seating depths for these bullet shapes.

Another minor point: on occasion you'll find that a particular bullet seating stem deforms the nose of a soft-nosed bullet. You can often write to the manufacturer to obtain a stem designed to accommodate a particular nose contour. Simply tell him the make, diameter, weight and style of bullet you are interested in loading. Enclose about five dollars with your letter to save time and a lot of unnecessary back and forth correspondence. He'll send you the stem together with any refund you have coming.

There are two other acceptable methods for determining bullet seating depth. Use a factory-loaded round as a dummy and simply set up your die to accommodate the factory shell. Just take care to determine that the bullet contours between the factory shell and your own are somewhat similar.

The other method is to use a specific dimension as recited by a particular loading manual. The NRA book, for one, offers an abundance of such information with its loading tables.

CRIMPING BULLETS

There are occasions when a casing must be crimped around a bullet to prevent subsequent motion of the bullet within the case. This is usually true of shells intended for feeding through tubular magazines or of cartridges that are to be loaded with unjacketed or semi-jacketed bullets. Some loading authorities also feel that crimping is desirable when working with heavy calibers where recoil may influence bullet seating depth.

Most modern bullet seating dies will crimp if adjusted to do so.

When first installing the body of the bullet seating die, place an empty dummy case in the shell holder and position the ram to the top of its stroke. Screw the body of the die down into the press so that it encompasses the casing. It will stop when it makes full contact with the case neck. Now, back the casing out of the die, just a bit, and give the die another half turn clockwise. Re-insert the casing to the top of the stroke and against the resistance that is clearly felt. Remove the case and examine the lip of the neck where it encircles the bullet. If the neck lip is bevelled slightly inward, the die is crimping properly and you can lock it in position. Be careful not to crimp too deeply—you want only the slightest trace of an inward bevel.

Some bullets are specifically designed for crimping. These are made with a cannelure—a scored ring that encircles the bullet about halfway between the base and nose. With such bullets, set the bullet seating adjustment so that the crimped lip of the case neck engages the cannelure.

I know this has been a rather lengthy description of a comparatively simple process, but with this particular phase of loading I feel a little knowledge is worse than none at all!

Having established the proper bullet seating depth, you can go ahead and seat bullets in all your charged cases. Take care to determine that each case contains powder before installing the bullet.

Having completed your first batch of reloads, there remains only the test to determine if they'll all function through your magazine and action. Take them out to the range, load the magazine, point the rifle in a safe direction and feed each one from the magazine to the chamber and eject. (Try to catch ejected rounds on something soft so as to avoid damage to bullet noses.) Chamber these rounds gently; if one starts to feel stubborn or sticky, don't force it into the chamber—it may jam up in there so that you can't get it out. There's nothing I dislike more than hammering a jammed shell out of a chamber. To do this you have to leave the breech open, pad the face of the bolt, and tap the case out by means of a cleaning rod inserted from the muzzle.

CAST BULLETS

Almost without exception, cast lead bullets must be fitted with gas checks if they're to be used in a rifle. (A gas check protects the base of the bullet from the intense heat of the ignited powder charge.)

To prevent separation from the bullet, particularly in the bore, gas checks are carefully fitted and firmly crimped to bullet bases. If a gas check should come loose, and should it fail to clear the bore upon firing, it would act as an obstruction for the following round and a bulged or burst barrel would result.

It's fun to cast bullets, and they are very inexpensive, but I wouldn't recommend this practice to the new handloader. Work with factory-made jacketed bullets until you develop a thorough understanding of handloading problems. Even experienced reloaders get into trouble with these on occasion. Phil Sharpe, in his book, COMPLETE GUIDE TO HANDLOADING, reported one incident where an experienced handloader blew up his rifle by simply seating his gas-checked bullets too deeply in their cases. The gas-checked portion of the bullet extended below the neck of the case and the check was sheared off by the shoulder of the case neck. One obviously lodged in the barrel, causing the accident.

KEEP RECORDS

To be a good handloader, one must be very methodical—label dummies, boxes of cases, loaded rounds, etc. Restore powders to their original containers as soon as you finish a particular loading session. Restore bullets and primers to their appropriate containers.

Keep a log indicating case lot numbers, describe the types of loads used, detail components and report results.

SWITCHING COMPONENTS

If you have been loading with one particular make of case, primer, powder and bullet, be careful when substituting a new make of component for one of the originals. The new component may not behave in the same manner and you could be asking for trouble. Back off, especially if you're close to a maximum load, and work your way up, again, wiith the new components.

PROBLEMS IN HANDLOADING

Differences of opinion: the new handloader will often run into conflicting advice—even from those he considers to be "experts." (The term "expert" was recently defined by one individual: "ex"—out of mode, "spurt"—a little drip expelled under pressure!)

Here are some very important "don'ts" that can save you a lot of grief:

1. Don't try to memorize loading information. If it's not printed in a manual, right in front of you —abandon the thought of using the load you *think* you remember.

2. Don't adopt someone else's loading suggestions without comparing their recommendations with your own published data.

3. Some shooters advocate the seating of bullets so that they engage the rifling when chambered. Some "experts" even recommend this practice saying it enhances accuracy. True, many shooters do this consistently and get away with it but, you'll *always be safer* seating your bullets short of the rifling. Then, too, if you've erred anywhere else in making up your handloads, this practice could provide the safety valve that keeps your breech pressures manageable.

4. Whenever you've been obliged to replace a firing pin or bolt in a given weapon, treat the rifle as you would a new and strange entity. Back off on your handloads and work up, slowly, to the loads that you used prior to the alteration.

5. Be sure to measure the length of your cases before each loading! Over length cases are the primary cause of shooting accidents.

6. Keep your brass in specific lots so that you can easily keep track of the number of loadings they've had. When you suddenly find that a number of cases have to be discarded because of cracks or the like in the case walls—DISCARD THE ENTIRE LOT! They're all weak and potentially dangerous.

7. Be darned careful when full length resizing. Don't assume that every resizing die can be adjusted to give you the proper overall length simply by placing the shell holder in contact with the base of the die. Some dies, especially among those made for wildcat cartridges, are made intentionally *short* so they can be adjusted to size properly. If in doubt, check with the manufacturer or compare the dimensions of a newly sized case with the dimensions of a case that has recently been fired in your chamber. (Because the datum line of a given bottlenecked case is difficult to determine, it would make sense to have a qualified gunsmith do this comparison measuring for you.)

(Definition of the term "WILDCAT": a wildcat cartridge is made by fire forming existing factory cases or by cutting and reshaping factory cases in special loading dies. Generally, wildcatters strive to increase velocities of conventional bullets by creating cases having greater powder capacities.)

LOADING ECCENTRICITIES

The hardest facet of handloading for the beginner to understand is that any change in tools, components, procedures or techniques will certainly cause changes in the final result. The less you take for granted, the safer you will be.

Ironically, a handloader can often get away with repeating the same error or fault over and over again. Then, one day he introduces some insignificant little change—like a new make of primer or a new bullet shape and he has an accident!

A good friend of mine once bragged about a certain load that was giving him fantastic groups at the benchrest. He said, "It's cratering my primers something awful, but just look at these groups!"

He used that load for almost two years until, one day, a fragmented primer blew back through the action. He thanked his patron saint that he was wearing shooting glasses at the time. Some particles were actually embedded in the lenses.

Another time I was called upon to testify as an "expert" in the trial of a rifle maker who was being sued by a wildcatting handloader. The plaintiff had misused his sizing die and had blown up his rifle causing relatively minor injuries to himself. He claimed the rifle maker built the gun with excessive headspace and he based this conclusion on the fact that the action accepted a "NO-GO" headspace gauge AFTER THE ACCIDENT!

First, acceptance of a "NO-GO" gauge does *not* indicate headspace condition at the time of the ments taken AFTER the fact will not accurately indicate headspace condition at the time of the accident—often the accident itself will be so violent that it will set back locking lugs, increasing tolerances in the area of headspace. Finally, I picked up a new set of dies for this man's wildcat caliber, from the same maker, and proved that a cartridge sized in them in the usual manner, would prove too short for the chamber of his rifle. These dies were intended to be adjustable simply because so many *different* versions of that particular wildcat were in use.

Wildcat cartridges can be exceedingly dangerous, even for the experienced handloader.

Those who can't resist the temptation should have their rifles made so that the barrel chamber and sizing die are cut by the same man with the same chambering reamers.

TIPS FOR ACCURACY

Benchrest shooters, in their constant quest to come up with a load that will place every shot through the same hole, have perfected handloading skills to the "Nth" degree. They're engaged in a never-ending experimentation program. So, if you want precision accuracy you'll have to adopt some benchrester's tricks:

Cases—measure and trim all cases to precisely the same length. Then, after separating cases by make, weigh each case and separate cases into groups of comparable weight. Discard odd cases that are unusually light or heavy.

Next, pick up a box of tapered, *round* toothpicks. Use one of these as a gauge for checking flash holes. To do this, start with a case having a flash hole that is obviously larger than the rest—gently insert the pick and twist it lightly to score a faint line at the stopping point. Use this as a gauge to measure the balance of the flash holes but be sure to use it without pressure so that you won't change the dimensions of the soft wood. Again, group cases according to flash hole size.

Bullets are made to surprisingly uniform specs; nevertheless the reloader will occasionally find variations of one or two tenths of a grain in some makes. It pays to check these on a scale and separate them according to weight.

Some benchrest shooters even weigh their primers!

One can carry these checks to extremes but when one is competing for the big prize, time spent in preparation is not wasted.

Here are a few other practices I've run across over the years: "miking" bullet diameters and cases. Measuring the depths of primer pockets and/or the depths of seated primers. Weighing finishing rounds. Checking concentricity of finished rounds. (To do this, make up a couple of V-supports and anchor them to a base board. Drill two holes through the base, midway between the supports. Lay a cartridge in the V's and insert a string through one of the base holes—make one turn of the string around the cartridge and run the end out through the other base hole.) Now, by working the string ends back and forth, you can spin the cartridge. Watch the bullet nose. It should spin true.

TROUBLES

BROKEN CASING IN THE SIZING DIE On occasion you'll tear the extractor rim off a sticky case when trying to remove it from the sizing die. As long as the balance of the head remains attached to the body of the casing you can remove it with a broken shell extractor. (This is a kit containing a drill bit, a tap and a special bolt. It's sold in most gun shops at modest cost.) Remove the die from the press, drill through the primer pocket to remove the wall of the flash hole, thread the hole with the tap provided, and re-install the die in the press. Now, place the special bolt in the shell holder, raise the ram and screw the bolt into the tapped primer pocket. Activate the lever and remove the case.

When attempting to load a tired old casing "just one more time" you'll sometimes tear the head off the case in the sizing die. This can be more of a problem: leave the die in the press but remove the locking collar from the inner stem. Drop the stem out of the die through the bottom. Find a piece of hard wood doweling, or a brass cleaning rod that you can insert through the top of the die to engage the lip of the case neck. Tap lightly to remove the broken case. Be careful when doing this to avoid damage to your sizing die. Above all, do not use a steel drift pin and don't employ excessive force.

Very often, when a handloader runs into trouble, it's caused by rust or dirt in his equipment. Keep your tools clean and lightly oiled. Check the fluid in your scale dampener to make sure it is clean and of light consistency. Use a fine grade of light machine oil to lubricate friction points in your scale and measure. Oil can contaminate powder and primers, so be careful; use only a drop or two in areas close to these components.

Never use a harsh abrasive in your loading dies. Clean them with a clean, dry cloth and wipe them with one that is lightly oiled and lint free.

Clean and oil your loading press after each loading session. When not in use, cover the press with a plastic bag—wrap the open end of the bag around the lower portion of the lever and secure it with a rubber band.

Finally, handloading requires some concentration. Try to set up your loading bench in a quiet, isolated corner of the cellar—a place where you can work without distractions.

Notice that I said "cellar"—not "attic"—gun powder should be stored in an area where it can be kept cool and dry. The ideal storage facility is a heavy wooden chest: equip it with a lock (and wheels if it is very heavy) and paint it bright red.

RIFLE

DU PONT POWDER	CHARGE (grains)	VELOCITY (ft/sec)	CHAMBER PRESS. (cup)

.22 HORNET
45 GR., .2233" DIA., .230" SEAT BARREL—24 IN.

DU PONT POWDER	CHARGE (grains)	VELOCITY (ft/sec)	CHAMBER PRESS. (cup)
IMR 4227	11.5 C	2575	41000
IMR 4198	12.0 C	2445	33700
IMR 3031	12.5 C	1980	20300
IMR 4064	12.5 C	1875	19900
IMR 4895	12.5 C	1695	18800
IMR 4320	13.5 C	1930	20800
IMR 4350	13.0 C	1375	14300

.220 SWIFT
50 GR., .2240" DIA., .140" SEAT BARREL—26 IN.

DU PONT POWDER	CHARGE (grains)	VELOCITY (ft/sec)	CHAMBER PRESS. (cup)
IMR 4227	25.0	3400	54000
IMR 4198	33.0	3825	54000
IMR 3031	38.0	4050	54000
IMR 4895	40.5	4010	53100
IMR 4064	41.0	4110	53600
IMR 4320	41.0	3995	53000
IMR 4350	45.0 C	3895	47900

.220 SWIFT
55 GR., .2240" DIA., .190" SEAT BARREL—26 IN.

DU PONT POWDER	CHARGE (grains)	VELOCITY (ft/sec)	CHAMBER PRESS. (cup)
IMR 4227	25.0	3240	52800
IMR 4198	33.0	3685	54300
IMR 3031	37.0	3850	54000
IMR 4895	39.0	3835	53300
IMR 4064	40.0	3950	54000
IMR 4320	40.5	3835	53600
IMR 4350	45.0 C	3800	51000

.222 REMINGTON MAG.
50 GR., .2240" DIA., .180" SEAT BARREL—26 IN.

DU PONT POWDER	CHARGE (grains)	VELOCITY (ft/sec)	CHAMBER PRESS. (cup)
IMR 4227	19.5	3200	50000
IMR 4198	24.0	3410	50000
IMR 3031	27.5 C	3575	50000
IMR 4064	28.5 C	3420	47000
IMR 4895	28.5 C	3465	49300
IMR 4320	29.5 C	3420	49000
IMR 4350	29.0 C	2920	32300

.222 REMINGTON MAG.
55 GR., .2240" DIA., .250" SEAT BARREL—26 IN.

DU PONT POWDER	CHARGE (grains)	VELOCITY (ft/sec)	CHAMBER PRESS. (cup)
IMR 4227	19.0	3000	49000
IMR 4198	24.0	3270	49000
IMR 3031	27.5 C	3400	49500
IMR 4895	28.0 C	3355	50500
IMR 4064	28.5 C	3350	49000
IMR 4320	29.5 C	3300	49000
IMR 4350	29.0 C	2845	33700

.22-250 REMINGTON
50 GR., .2242" DIA., .230" SEAT BARREL—24 IN.

DU PONT POWDER	CHARGE (grains)	VELOCITY (ft/sec)	CHAMBER PRESS. (cup)
IMR 4227	22.5	3285	52700
IMR 4198	30.5	3710	51500
IMR 3031	35.0	3825	51100
IMR 4895	37.0	3815	51300
IMR 4064	37.5	3835	51000
IMR 4320	38.0	3810	52000
IMR 4350	40.5 C	3530	41700

.225 WINCHESTER
55 GR., .2240" DIA., .130" SEAT BARREL—24 IN.

DU PONT POWDER	CHARGE (grains)	VELOCITY (ft/sec)	CHAMBER PRESS. (cup)
IMR 4227	17.5	2795	49100
IMR 4198	22.0	3095	49700
IMR 3031	26.0	3235	48700
IMR 4320	28.0	3255	48800
IMR 4895	28.0	3275	49300
IMR 4064	32.5	3515	48600
IMR 4350	37.0 C	3410	45100

.243 WINCHESTER
75 GR., .2428" DIA., .240" SEAT BARREL—26 IN.

DU PONT POWDER	CHARGE (grains)	VELOCITY (ft/sec)	CHAMBER PRESS. (cup)
IMR 4227	27.0	2990	51800
IMR 4198	34.0	3350	51000
IMR 3031	37.5	3385	50100
IMR 4064	41.5	3545	51500
IMR 4320	42.5	3535	51000
IMR 4895	43.5	3620	52100
IMR 4350	48.0 C	3575	51000

.243 WINCHESTER
100 GR., .2422" DIA., .400" SEAT BARREL—26 IN.

DU PONT POWDER	CHARGE (grains)	VELOCITY (ft/sec)	CHAMBER PRESS. (cup)
IMR 4227	26.0	2595	51300
IMR 4198	32.0	2825	51000
IMR 3031	36.0	2975	51500
IMR 4064	38.5	3030	52000
IMR 4320	40.0	3050	51500
IMR 4895	40.5	3125	52000
IMR 4350	44.5 C	3120	51500

6 MM REMINGTON
75 GR., .2428" DIA., .280" SEAT BARREL—20 IN.

DU PONT POWDER	CHARGE (grains)	VELOCITY (ft/sec)	CHAMBER PRESS. (cup)
IMR 4227	25.0	2755	50800
IMR 4198	30.0	2975	50900
IMR 3031	39.5	3305	51200
IMR 4895	41.5	3310	51700
IMR 4064	42.5	3350	51400
IMR 4320	41.5	3270	51500
IMR 4350	48.0 C	3325	49500

6 MM REMINGTON
100 GR., .2430" DIA., .420" SEAT BARREL—20 IN.

DU PONT POWDER	CHARGE (grains)	VELOCITY (ft/sec)	CHAMBER PRESS. (cup)
IMR 4227	23.5	2350	49700
IMR 4198	28.0	2580	49300
IMR 3031	37.0	2860	50300
IMR 4895	38.5	2865	50000
IMR 4064	40.0	2935	51800
IMR 4320	42.5	2895	50400
IMR 4350	44.5	2915	48800

.250 SAVAGE
87 GR., .2564" DIA., .280" SEAT BARREL—24 IN.

DU PONT POWDER	CHARGE (grains)	VELOCITY (ft/sec)	CHAMBER PRESS. (cup)
IMR 4227	23.0	2575	44000
IMR 4198	30.5	2930	44000
IMR 3031	35.5	3040	44000
IMR 4895	36.5	3055	44000
IMR 4064	37.0 C	3100	44000
IMR 4320	38.0	3030	44500
IMR 4350	43.0 C	3030	42000

DU PONT POWDER	CHARGE (grains)	VELOCITY (ft/sec)	CHAMBER PRESS. (cup)

.222 REMINGTON
45 GR., .2240" DIA., .150" SEAT BARREL—26 IN.

DU PONT POWDER	CHARGE (grains)	VELOCITY (ft/sec)	CHAMBER PRESS. (cup)
IMR 4227	17.5	3075	45500
IMR 4198	22.5 C	3340	45500
IMR 3031	24.0 C	3240	38400
IMR 4064	24.0 C	2995	34200
IMR 4895	25.5 C	3160	34800
IMR 4320	26.0 C	3125	40600
IMR 4350	25.0 C	2565	25000

.222 REMINGTON
50 GR., .2240" DIA., .180" SEAT BARREL—26 IN.

DU PONT POWDER	CHARGE (grains)	VELOCITY (ft/sec)	CHAMBER PRESS. (cup)
IMR 4227	17.0	3000	45600
IMR 4198	21.0	3230	45600
IMR 3031	24.0 C	3260	43000
IMR 4064	24.0 C	3050	37700
IMR 4895	25.5 C	3220	40500
IMR 4320	26.0 C	3160	44500
IMR 4350	25.0 C	2590	25700

.222 REMINGTON
55 GR., .2240" DIA., .250" SEAT BARREL—26 IN.

DU PONT POWDER	CHARGE (grains)	VELOCITY (ft/sec)	CHAMBER PRESS. (cup)
IMR 4227	17.0	2720	46000
IMR 4198	20.5	3055	45500
IMR 3031	24.0 C	3155	44000
IMR 4064	24.0 C	2950	38500
IMR 4895	25.5 C	3140	41000
IMR 4320	26.0 C	3050	46000
IMR 4350	25.0 C	2500	27500

.22-250 REMINGTON
55 GR., .2241" DIA., .245" SEAT BARREL—24 IN.

DU PONT POWDER	CHARGE (grains)	VELOCITY (ft/sec)	CHAMBER PRESS. (cup)
IMR 4227	21.0	3030	51300
IMR 4198	27.5	3410	51500
IMR 3031	34.0	3650	51700
IMR 4895	35.5	3630	51900
IMR 4064	36.0	3675	51200
IMR 4320	36.5	3635	51700
IMR 4350	40.0 C	3465	43900

.223 REMINGTON
50 GR., .2240" DIA., .180" SEAT BARREL—22 IN.

DU PONT POWDER	CHARGE (grains)	VELOCITY (ft/sec)	CHAMBER PRESS. (cup)
IMR 4227	18.5	3065	51500
IMR 4198	22.0	3250	51000
IMR 3031	26.0	3305	51600
IMR 4895	26.5 C	3100	42700
IMR 4895	27.5 C	3240	49500
IMR 4320	28.5 C	3250	50700
IMR 4350	27.0 C	2580	28400

.223 REMINGTON
55 GR., .2240" DIA., .250" SEAT BARREL—22 IN.

DU PONT POWDER	CHARGE (grains)	VELOCITY (ft/sec)	CHAMBER PRESS. (cup)
IMR 4227	18.0	2930	51900
IMR 4198	21.5	3105	48700
IMR 3031	25.5 C	3200	50900
IMR 4064	26.5 C	3065	44700
IMR 4895	27.0 C	3150	49500
IMR 4320	28.0 C	3165	50500
IMR 4350	27.0 C	2570	28400

.244 REMINGTON
75 GR., .2428" DIA., .240" SEAT BARREL—26 IN.

DU PONT POWDER	CHARGE (grains)	VELOCITY (ft/sec)	CHAMBER PRESS. (cup)
IMR 4227	28.5	2980	50500
IMR 4198	36.0	3315	49100
IMR 3031	41.0	3480	49800
IMR 4895	41.5	3535	51200
IMR 4064	43.0	3525	50000
IMR 4320	45.0	3520	49900
IMR 4350	51.5 C	3590	49900

.244 REMINGTON
100 GR., .2422" DIA., .500" SEAT BARREL—26 IN.

DU PONT POWDER	CHARGE (grains)	VELOCITY (ft/sec)	CHAMBER PRESS. (cup)
IMR 4227	26.5	2575	48900
IMR 4198	34.0	2880	49500
IMR 3031	37.0	2935	50000
IMR 4895	39.0	3085	50500
IMR 4064	40.5	3050	49800
IMR 4320	42.5	3100	49700
IMR 4350	47.0 C	3130	49400

.250 SAVAGE
100 GR., .2563" DIA., .430" SEAT BARREL—24 IN.

DU PONT POWDER	CHARGE (grains)	VELOCITY (ft/sec)	CHAMBER PRESS. (cup)
IMR 4227	22.5	2350	45000
IMR 4198	29.0	2670	44000
IMR 3031	33.0	2775	44000
IMR 4064	35.5 C	2830	44000
IMR 4895	35.5 C	2850	45000
IMR 4320	37.0 C	2810	45000
IMR 4350	42.5 C	2850	44500

.257 ROBERTS
100 GR., .2565" DIA., .435" SEAT BARREL—22 IN.

DU PONT POWDER	CHARGE (grains)	VELOCITY (ft/sec)	CHAMBER PRESS. (cup)
IMR 4227	24.0	2430	44100
IMR 4198	31.0	2735	44800
IMR 3031	37.5	2910	44900
IMR 4895	39.0	2920	45000
IMR 4064	40.0	2930	44000
IMR 4320	38.5	2865	44000
IMR 4350	46.5 C	3010	44500

KEY: C—COMPRESSED POWDER CHARGE

> Velocity and pressure readings represent average values obtained under controlled conditions. The values shown may vary substantially with the components and the reloading techniques employed. We suggest the charge weights shown be reduced initially by 10% to compensate for possible variations from the published data. The loads may then be increased as pressure indications permit.

Reprinted courtesy of E.I. DuPont de Nemours, Inc.

RIFLE

.257 ROBERTS
117 GR., .2570" DIA., .515" SEAT — BARREL—22 IN.

DU PONT POWDER	CHARGE (grains)	VELOCITY (ft/sec)	CHAMBER PRESS. (cup)
IMR 4227	23.0	2195	44000
IMR 4198	28.5	2435	44300
IMR 3031	35.0	2620	44300
IMR 4895	36.0	2630	44200
IMR 4064	37.0	2640	44000
IMR 4320	36.0	2600	45000
IMR 4350	43.5	2725	45000

6.5 MM REMINGTON MAG.
100 GR., .2640" DIA., .315" SEAT — BARREL—20 IN.

DU PONT POWDER	CHARGE (grains)	VELOCITY (ft/sec)	CHAMBER PRESS. (cup)
IMR 4227	33.0	2745	51400
IMR 4198	40.5	3025	51400
IMR 3031	48.0	3160	52000
IMR 4895	50.5	3180	52200
IMR 4064	51.5	3210	51800
IMR 4320	53.0	3215	52500
IMR 4350	59.5	3270	52500

6.5 MM REMINGTON MAG.
120 GR., .2640" DIA., .480" SEAT — BARREL—20 IN.

DU PONT POWDER	CHARGE (grains)	VELOCITY (ft/sec)	CHAMBER PRESS. (cup)
IMR 4227	31.5	2500	51500
IMR 4198	36.5	2660	52100
IMR 3031	43.5	2820	52700
IMR 4895	45.5	2850	51500
IMR 4064	47.0	2885	52000
IMR 4320	48.0	2900	52200
IMR 4350	54.5	2965	52700

.270 WINCHESTER
130 GR., .2770" DIA., .350" SEAT — BARREL—24 IN.

DU PONT POWDER	CHARGE (grains)	VELOCITY (ft/sec)	CHAMBER PRESS. (cup)
IMR 4227	31.0	2500	53000
IMR 4198	38.0	2690	53000
IMR 3031	45.0	3000	53000
IMR 4064	49.0	3100	53000
IMR 4895	49.0	3050	54100
IMR 4320	50.0	3100	54200
IMR 4350	56.5 C	3170	54000

.270 WINCHESTER
150 GR., .2770" DIA., .400" SEAT — BARREL—24 IN.

DU PONT POWDER	CHARGE (grains)	VELOCITY (ft/sec)	CHAMBER PRESS. (cup)
IMR 4227	29.0	2205	54100
IMR 4198	36.0	2470	53000
IMR 3031	43.0	2710	53100
IMR 4895	46.5	2785	53800
IMR 4064	47.0	2810	54200
IMR 4320	47.5	2815	54200
IMR 4350	53.5	2900	53100

.280 REMINGTON
125 GR., .2824" DIA., .330" SEAT — BARREL—24 IN.

DU PONT POWDER	CHARGE (grains)	VELOCITY (ft/sec)	CHAMBER PRESS. (cup)
IMR 4227	31.0	2520	49000
IMR 4198	39.0	2840	49000
IMR 3031	45.0	2920	49200
IMR 4895	47.0	3000	50000
IMR 4064	49.0	3050	49000
IMR 4320	49.0	2900	50000
IMR 4350	57.0	3020	49000

7 MM REMINGTON MAG.
175 GR., .2828" DIA., .500" SEAT — BARREL—24 IN.

DU PONT POWDER	CHARGE (grains)	VELOCITY (ft/sec)	CHAMBER PRESS. (cup)
IMR 4227	35.5	2300	52000
IMR 4198	42.5	2520	52000
IMR 3031	51.0	2680	52000
IMR 4895	54.0	2765	52000
IMR 4064	54.5	2760	51800
IMR 4320	56.0	2800	51500
IMR 4350	63.0	2875	52000

.284 WINCHESTER
125 GR., .2838" DIA., .420" SEAT — BARREL—22 IN.

DU PONT POWDER	CHARGE (grains)	VELOCITY (ft/sec)	CHAMBER PRESS. (cup)
IMR 4227	29.5	2480	52500
IMR 4198	37.0	2760	53900
IMR 3031	44.0	2925	52200
IMR 4895	49.0	3040	53000
IMR 4320	50.0	3040	53400
IMR 4064	51.5	3110	52900
IMR 4350	60.5 C	3170	52800

.284 WINCHESTER
150 GR., .2832" DIA., .550" SEAT — BARREL—22 IN.

DU PONT POWDER	CHARGE (grains)	VELOCITY (ft/sec)	CHAMBER PRESS. (cup)
IMR 4227	28.0	2245	53500
IMR 4198	34.5	2460	52700
IMR 3031	41.0	2645	53000
IMR 4895	45.5	2740	52800
IMR 4320	46.5	2745	52100
IMR 4064	49.5 C	2845	53200
IMR 4350	58.0 C	2955	53500

.300 H & H MAG.
150 GR., .3075" DIA., .260" SEAT — BARREL—26 IN.

DU PONT POWDER	CHARGE (grains)	VELOCITY (ft/sec)	CHAMBER PRESS. (cup)
IMR 4227	39.5	2615	53100
IMR 4198	52.0	2980	54000
IMR 3031	61.0	3195	53100
IMR 4064	65.0	3255	53000
IMR 4320	66.5	3230	53400
IMR 4895	66.5	3245	54100
IMR 4350	77.0 C	3380	54000

.300 H & H MAG.
180 GR., .3087" DIA., .520" SEAT — BARREL—26 IN.

DU PONT POWDER	CHARGE (grains)	VELOCITY (ft/sec)	CHAMBER PRESS. (cup)
IMR 4227	37.0	2350	53500
IMR 4198	48.0	2685	53800
IMR 3031	55.0	2850	53800
IMR 4895	59.5	2820	54400
IMR 4064	60.0	2950	54000
IMR 4320	61.0	2950	54000
IMR 4350	69.0 C	3080	54300

.300 H & H MAG.
220 GR., .3075" DIA., .550" SEAT — BARREL—26 IN.

DU PONT POWDER	CHARGE (grains)	VELOCITY (ft/sec)	CHAMBER PRESS. (cup)
IMR 4227	35.5	2075	53400
IMR 4198	46.5	2410	53200
IMR 3031	52.5	2520	53500
IMR 4064	56.5	2630	53500
IMR 4895	57.5	2615	53000
IMR 4320	58.5	2650	54000
IMR 4350	65.5	2735	54000

.264 WINCHESTER MAG.
100 GR., .2640" DIA., .250" SEAT — BARREL—26 IN.

DU PONT POWDER	CHARGE (grains)	VELOCITY (ft/sec)	CHAMBER PRESS. (cup)
IMR 4227	37.5	3000	54000
IMR 4198	46.5	3300	54000
IMR 3031	53.0	3445	53100
IMR 4064	56.0	3530	53100
IMR 4895	58.0	3510	53100
IMR 4320	58.5	3550	53000
IMR 4350	64.5	3600	54000

.264 WINCHESTER MAG.
140 GR., .2640" DIA., .400" SEAT — BARREL—26 IN.

DU PONT POWDER	CHARGE (grains)	VELOCITY (ft/sec)	CHAMBER PRESS. (cup)
IMR 4227	35.0	2450	54000
IMR 4198	43.5	2750	53500
IMR 3031	49.0	2865	53600
IMR 4064	51.0	2915	53300
IMR 4895	54.0	2925	54300
IMR 4320	54.5	3000	54000
IMR 4350	59.5	3050	54000

.270 WINCHESTER
100 GR., .2770" DIA., .280" SEAT — BARREL—24 IN.

DU PONT POWDER	CHARGE (grains)	VELOCITY (ft/sec)	CHAMBER PRESS. (cup)
IMR 4227	32.5	2870	53000
IMR 4198	37.5	3060	53000
IMR 3031	47.0	3390	53000
IMR 4895	51.5	3380	53800
IMR 4064	52.0	3420	54000
IMR 4320	52.0	3430	53000
IMR 4350	61.0 C	3450	53000

.280 REMINGTON
150 GR., .2824" DIA., .380" SEAT — BARREL—24 IN.

DU PONT POWDER	CHARGE (grains)	VELOCITY (ft/sec)	CHAMBER PRESS. (cup)
IMR 4227	29.5	2275	48800
IMR 4198	39.0	2520	50000
IMR 3031	43.0	2770	50000
IMR 4895	47.0	2820	50000
IMR 4064	48.0	2850	50000
IMR 4320	48.0	2800	50000
IMR 4350	55.5	2900	50000

.280 REMINGTON
165 GR., .2824" DIA., .420" SEAT — BARREL—24 IN.

DU PONT POWDER	CHARGE (grains)	VELOCITY (ft/sec)	CHAMBER PRESS. (cup)
IMR 4227	28.5	2150	50000
IMR 4198	36.5	2325	49400
IMR 3031	42.0	2580	50000
IMR 4895	45.5	2670	48900
IMR 4064	46.0	2680	50000
IMR 4320	46.5	2650	50000
IMR 4350	54.0	2780	50000

7 MM REMINGTON MAG.
150 GR., .2828" DIA., .400" SEAT — BARREL—24 IN.

DU PONT POWDER	CHARGE (grains)	VELOCITY (ft/sec)	CHAMBER PRESS. (cup)
IMR 4227	36.0	2490	52000
IMR 4198	45.0	2775	52000
IMR 3031	52.5	2925	52000
IMR 4895	56.0	3000	52000
IMR 4064	57.0	3025	52000
IMR 4320	58.0	3030	52000
IMR 4350	67.0	3155	51400

.30 CARBINE
110 GR., .3072" DIA., .250" SEAT — BARREL—18 IN.

DU PONT POWDER	CHARGE (grains)	VELOCITY (ft/sec)	CHAMBER PRESS. (cup)
IMR 4227	15.0 C	1880	39400
IMR 4198	15.0 C	1520	22900

.300 SAVAGE
150 GR., .3075" DIA., .275" SEAT — BARREL—24 IN.

DU PONT POWDER	CHARGE (grains)	VELOCITY (ft/sec)	CHAMBER PRESS. (cup)
IMR 4227	24.5	2220	45500
IMR 4198	33.5	2550	45700
IMR 3031	39.5	2655	44600
IMR 4895	41.5	2610	44500
IMR 4064	42.5 C	2680	46000
IMR 4320	43.5 C	2645	46000
IMR 4350	47.5 C	2515	39000

.300 SAVAGE
180 GR., .3085" DIA., .440" SEAT — BARREL—24 IN.

DU PONT POWDER	CHARGE (grains)	VELOCITY (ft/sec)	CHAMBER PRESS. (cup)
IMR 4227	22.0	1940	46000
IMR 4198	32.0	2300	45000
IMR 3031	37.5 C	2410	45100
IMR 4895	40.5 C	2445	45100
IMR 4064	41.5 C	2485	45900
IMR 4320	41.5 C	2435	45900
IMR 4350	47.5 C	2460	43600

.300 WINCHESTER MAG.
150 GR., .3085" DIA., .350" SEAT — BARREL—24 IN.

DU PONT POWDER	CHARGE (grains)	VELOCITY (ft/sec)	CHAMBER PRESS. (cup)
IMR 4227	39.5	2615	54200
IMR 4198	49.0	2875	53400
IMR 3031	60.0	3115	54500
IMR 4895	64.0	3175	54600
IMR 4064	65.0	3205	54400
IMR 4320	62.0	3115	52200
IMR 4350	76.0 C	3305	54200

.300 WINCHESTER MAG.
180 GR., .3075" DIA., .450" SEAT — BARREL—24 IN.

DU PONT POWDER	CHARGE (grains)	VELOCITY (ft/sec)	CHAMBER PRESS. (cup)
IMR 4227	38.5	2370	53800
IMR 4198	48.0	2655	54000
IMR 3031	56.0	2825	53500
IMR 4895	60.5	2895	52400
IMR 4064	62.5	2945	53200
IMR 4320	60.5	2885	54000
IMR 4350	72.0	3010	53900

.300 WINCHESTER MAG.
220 GR., .3075" DIA., .650" SEAT — BARREL—24 IN.

DU PONT POWDER	CHARGE (grains)	VELOCITY (ft/sec)	CHAMBER PRESS. (cup)
IMR 4227	36.0	2065	54400
IMR 4198	43.5	2285	53100
IMR 3031	52.5	2495	53200
IMR 4895	55.5	2550	53600
IMR 4064	56.5	2580	53500
IMR 4320	54.0	2520	53100
IMR 4350	67.5 C	2735	54500

KEY: C—COMPRESSED POWDER CHARGE

Reprinted courtesy of E.I. DuPont de Nemours, Inc.

.30-06 — 110 GR., .3080" DIA., .230" SEAT — BARREL—24 IN.

DU PONT POWDER	CHARGE (grains)	VELOCITY (ft/sec)	CHAMBER PRESS. (cup)
IMR 4227	34.0	2760	49500
IMR 4198	45.0	3155	50200
IMR 3031	52.0	3290	49400
IMR 4895	54.5	3270	49000
IMR 4064	55.5 C	3290	50000
IMR 4320	56.5	3210	50400
IMR 4350	62.5 C	3100	46000

.308 WINCHESTER — 110 GR., .3080" DIA., .220" SEAT — BARREL—24 IN.

DU PONT POWDER	CHARGE (grains)	VELOCITY (ft/sec)	CHAMBER PRESS. (cup)
IMR 4227	32.5	2860	51000
IMR 4198	41.5	3175	52000
IMR 3031	49.0 C	3320	51200
IMR 4895	51.5	3185	52900
IMR 4064	52.5	3200	52000
IMR 4320	54.0	3250	52000
IMR 4350	52.0 C	2750	35000

.35 REMINGTON — 200 GR., .3585" DIA., .320" SEAT — BARREL—22 IN.

DU PONT POWDER	CHARGE (grains)	VELOCITY (ft/sec)	CHAMBER PRESS. (cup)
IMR 4227	20.0	1720	34300
IMR 4198	28.0	1975	34600
IMR 3031	36.5	2100	35000
IMR 4895	38.5	2085	34800
IMR 4064	39.5 C	2060	35000
IMR 4320	39.5	2050	35000
IMR 4350	46.5 C	2030	34300

.375 H & H MAG. — 270 GR., .3750" DIA., .400" SEAT — BARREL—25 IN.

DU PONT POWDER	CHARGE (grains)	VELOCITY (ft/sec)	CHAMBER PRESS. (cup)
IMR 4227	41.0	2090	52900
IMR 4198	54.0	2375	53000
IMR 3031	66.5	2630	53000
IMR 4895	70.0	2675	54000
IMR 4064	71.0	2675	53000
IMR 4320	72.0	2650	53000
IMR 4350	86.0 C	2845	53300

.30-06 — 150 GR., .3075" DIA., .260" SEAT — BARREL—24 IN.

DU PONT POWDER	CHARGE (grains)	VELOCITY (ft/sec)	CHAMBER PRESS. (cup)
IMR 4227	30.0	2310	49200
IMR 4198	39.0	2600	50000
IMR 3031	47.0	2820	50000
IMR 4895	51.5	2965	51000
IMR 4064	52.0	2910	49700
IMR 4320	52.5	2850	50000
IMR 4350	61.0 C	3000	50000

.308 WINCHESTER — 150 GR., .3075" DIA., .330" SEAT — BARREL—24 IN.

DU PONT POWDER	CHARGE (grains)	VELOCITY (ft/sec)	CHAMBER PRESS. (cup)
IMR 4227	27.5	2305	51900
IMR 4198	38.0	2695	51800
IMR 3031	44.5 C	2850	51500
IMR 4895	45.0	2740	51600
IMR 4064	48.5 C	2905	51500
IMR 4320	48.5	2830	52000
IMR 4350	52.0 C	2660	40500

.350 REMINGTON MAG. — 200 GR., .3590" DIA., .420" SEAT — BARREL—18.5 IN.

DU PONT POWDER	CHARGE (grains)	VELOCITY (ft/sec)	CHAMBER PRESS. (cup)
IMR 4227	38.0	2400	52600
IMR 4198	48.5	2650	51300
IMR 3031	58.0 C	2775	51800
IMR 4895	61.0 C	2755	51200
IMR 4064	60.0 C	2680	44300
IMR 4320	63.0 C	2760	51800
IMR 4350	62.0 C	2150	31600

.375 H & H MAG. — 300 GR., .3746" DIA., .500" SEAT — BARREL—25 IN.

DU PONT POWDER	CHARGE (grains)	VELOCITY (ft/sec)	CHAMBER PRESS. (cup)
IMR 4227	40.0	1975	53000
IMR 4198	52.0	2260	53000
IMR 3031	63.0	2485	53000
IMR 4895	67.0	2500	53300
IMR 4064	68.5	2550	53300
IMR 4320	69.5	2520	52800
IMR 4350	82.0 C	2670	52000

.30-06 — 180 GR., .3075" DIA., .450" SEAT — BARREL—24 IN.

DU PONT POWDER	CHARGE (grains)	VELOCITY (ft/sec)	CHAMBER PRESS. (cup)
IMR 4227	28.5	2000	49000
IMR 4198	38.0	2320	49000
IMR 3031	44.5	2525	49500
IMR 4895	47.5	2575	50500
IMR 4064	48.0	2580	49300
IMR 4320	49.0	2600	50000
IMR 4350	57.0 C	2685	50000

.308 WINCHESTER — 180 GR., .3080" DIA., .420" SEAT — BARREL—24 IN.

DU PONT POWDER	CHARGE (grains)	VELOCITY (ft/sec)	CHAMBER PRESS. (cup)
IMR 4227	27.0	2105	52000
IMR 4198	34.5	2375	52000
IMR 3031	40.5	2555	51400
IMR 4895	42.5	2530	52000
IMR 4064	44.5 C	2630	52200
IMR 4320	44.5	2565	52000
IMR 4350	51.0 C	2625	52000

.350 REMINGTON MAG. — 250 GR., .3582" DIA., .650" SEAT — BARREL—18.5 IN.

DU PONT POWDER	CHARGE (grains)	VELOCITY (ft/sec)	CHAMBER PRESS. (cup)
IMR 4227	32.5	2000	51300
IMR 4198	45.5	2300	52100
IMR 3031	54.0 C	2430	52700
IMR 4895	55.0 C	2395	50000
IMR 4064	55.0 C	2350	44200
IMR 4320	55.0 C	2330	44100
IMR 4350	55.0 C	1840	26900

.44 REMINGTON MAG. — 240 GR., .4300" DIA., .385" SEAT — BARREL—20 IN.

DU PONT POWDER	CHARGE (grains)	VELOCITY (ft/sec)	CHAMBER PRESS. (cup)
IMR 4227	26.0 C	1765	40000

.30-06 — 220 GR., .3075" DIA., .520" SEAT — BARREL—24 IN.

DU PONT POWDER	CHARGE (grains)	VELOCITY (ft/sec)	CHAMBER PRESS. (cup)
IMR 4227	26.5	1875	50600
IMR 4198	34.0	2130	50700
IMR 3031	42.0	2355	49600
IMR 4895	44.5	2410	50800
IMR 4064	46.0	2455	50000
IMR 4320	46.5	2425	49400
IMR 4350	54.5 C	2590	50000

.338 WINCHESTER MAG. — 200 GR., .3380" DIA., .300" SEAT — BARREL—25 IN.

DU PONT POWDER	CHARGE (grains)	VELOCITY (ft/sec)	CHAMBER PRESS. (cup)
IMR 4227	40.0	2390	53500
IMR 4198	48.5	2615	54000
IMR 3031	60.5	2880	53800
IMR 4895	64.0	2920	53700
IMR 4064	65.0	2960	54000
IMR 4320	66.0	2940	53700
IMR 4350	76.5 C	3060	53500

.358 WINCHESTER — 200 GR., .3575" DIA., .260" SEAT — BARREL—24 IN.

DU PONT POWDER	CHARGE (grains)	VELOCITY (ft/sec)	CHAMBER PRESS. (cup)
IMR 4227	28.5	2145	52400
IMR 4198	40.0	2475	51300
IMR 3031	48.0 C	2625	52000
IMR 4064	51.5 C	2630	52000
IMR 4895	51.5 C	2605	51300
IMR 4320	52.5 C	2625	52000
IMR 4350	55.0 C	2390	44000

.444 MARLIN — 240 GR., .4300" DIA., .350" SEAT — BARREL—24.5 IN.

DU PONT POWDER	CHARGE (grains)	VELOCITY (ft/sec)	CHAMBER PRESS. (cup)
IMR 4227	28.0	1935	43800
IMR 4198	47.0	2355	43400
IMR 3031	57.0 C	2380	44000
IMR 4895	57.0 C	2255	41700
IMR 4064	57.0 C	2175	36100
IMR 4320	57.0 C	2160	37400

.30-30 WINCHESTER — 150 GR., .3080" DIA., .440" SEAT — BARREL—26 IN.

DU PONT POWDER	CHARGE (grains)	VELOCITY (ft/sec)	CHAMBER PRESS. (cup)
IMR 4227	20.0	1945	38500
IMR 4198	28.0	2255	37800
IMR 3031	33.5 C	2390	37900
IMR 4064	36.5	2380	37000
IMR 4320	36.5 C	2325	37300
IMR 4895	37.0	2485	38700
IMR 4350	42.5 C	2300	36000

.338 WINCHESTER MAG. — 250 GR., .3380" DIA., .500" SEAT — BARREL—25 IN.

DU PONT POWDER	CHARGE (grains)	VELOCITY (ft/sec)	CHAMBER PRESS. (cup)
IMR 4227	36.5	2060	53400
IMR 4198	44.0	2255	53700
IMR 3031	56.5	2555	53800
IMR 4895	61.5	2615	54100
IMR 4064	62.0	2660	54000
IMR 4320	62.0	2605	53900
IMR 4350	72.0 C	2765	54100

.358 WINCHESTER — 250 GR., .3575" DIA., .420" SEAT — BARREL—24 IN.

DU PONT POWDER	CHARGE (grains)	VELOCITY (ft/sec)	CHAMBER PRESS. (cup)
IMR 4227	25.0	1775	52000
IMR 4198	35.0	2100	52000
IMR 3031	41.5	2230	52000
IMR 4064	44.5 C	2240	51800
IMR 4895	44.5 C	2265	52200
IMR 4320	45.5 C	2250	51800
IMR 4350	52.5 C	2280	52000

.458 WINCHESTER MAG. — 500 GR., .4570" DIA., .570" SEAT — BARREL—25 IN.

DU PONT POWDER	CHARGE (grains)	VELOCITY (ft/sec)	CHAMBER PRESS. (cup)
IMR 4227	41.0	1585	52900
IMR 4198	56.0 C	1890	52400
IMR 3031	69.0 C	2075	52500
IMR 4064	73.0 C	2095	53100
IMR 4895	73.0 C	2090	50500
IMR 4320	75.0 C	2070	52300
IMR 4350	81.0 C	2050	53000

.30-30 WINCHESTER — 170 GR., .3075" DIA., .530" SEAT — BARREL—26 IN.

DU PONT POWDER	CHARGE (grains)	VELOCITY (ft/sec)	CHAMBER PRESS. (cup)
IMR 4227	18.5	1780	36800
IMR 4198	26.0	2040	37800
IMR 3031	31.0	2240	38300
IMR 4064	33.0 C	2150	38000
IMR 4320	33.0	2225	38000
IMR 4895	34.5 C	2280	38000
IMR 4350	37.5 C	2215	37300

.35 REMINGTON — 150 GR., .3585" DIA., .250" SEAT — BARREL—22 IN.

DU PONT POWDER	CHARGE (grains)	VELOCITY (ft/sec)	CHAMBER PRESS. (cup)
IMR 4227	22.0	2040	34000
IMR 4198	34.0	2360	34000
IMR 3031	43.0 C	2445	34800
IMR 4895	44.5 C	2350	35000
IMR 4064	44.5 C	2340	35000
IMR 4320	44.5 C	2330	34700
IMR 4350	48.0 C	2060	31000

KEY: C—COMPRESSED POWDER CHARGE

Velocity and pressure readings represent average values obtained under controlled conditions. The values shown may vary substantially with the components and the reloading techniques employed. We suggest the charge weights shown be reduced initially by 10% to compensate for possible variations from the published data. The loads may then be increased as pressure indications permit.

LOADING MANUALS

What loading manual should the new handloader buy? This is really dependent upon the interests of the particular handloader because each loading manual is somewhat unique. Following are some brief descriptions and personal comments on the manuals that are currently available.

P. O. Ackley's Handbook for Shooters and Reloaders

Volume I . . . .$ 9.00
Volume II . . . .$ 9.00
Two volume set $17.50

Volume I of this set is really a "must" for the varmint or benchrest shooter who is contemplating a wildcat caliber. This edition contains loading data for over 330 wildcat and standard cartridges, rifle and pistol. No shot shell data here.

Volume II contains data on the newer rifle and pistol shells and supplements Volume I. Also, in this edition shot shell loading information is included.

Handloader's Digest, edited by John T. Amber
. . . .$5.95

Describes rifle, pistol and shot shell loading. Offers a catalog section which illustrates tools and accessories. Contains information on production loading for clubs, etc. 320 pages 8½" x 11", soft cover.

Shooter's Bible Reloader's Guide by R. A. Steindler $4.95

A good basic manual for the beginner because it describes loading operations for rifle, pistol and shot shell in an easy-to-follow format. Also includes some loading tables. Discusses accessories, gadgets, etc., but does not offer a catalog section. Limited coverage on wildcats and cast bullets. 220 pages, 8" x 10", soft cover.

NRA Handloader's Guide $5.00

A professionally prepared manual that offers much in reading matter on powders, primers, bullets, etc., and which includes extensive pressure and chronograph data. I like this book because it gives specific measurements for cases, bullet diameters, loaded rounds, etc. Also covers, briefly, bullet casting and wax practice loads. Limited to popular calibers, though it contains some information on foreign cartridges. Has some shot shell data. 314 pages, 8½" x 11", soft cover.

Lyman Reloading Handbook $4.95

This was one of the first of the loading manuals. Today, in its 45th edition, it is still one of the best. Contains very complete technical descriptions on a broad range of rifle and pistol cartridges and combines data on jacketed and cast bullets. Covers many of the old favorites that have been dropped by other manuals. Also has some black powder data for muzzle loading enthusiasts. 300 pages, 8" x 9", soft cover.

(Note: Lyman publishes separate books on bullet casting, shot shell loading and muzzle loading.)

Complete Guide to Handloading by Phil Sharpe
. . . .$10.00

This one may prove difficult for the beginner but it is, in my opinion, the best of the handloading manuals. Probably the only really complete textbook on the subject. Covers all phases of rifle, pistol and shot shell loading. Detailed coverage on primers, powders, bullets and cases. Loading data on 6200 tested handloads. Over 500 pages, 8" x 10", hard cover.

CHAPTER 15

Transporting the Rifle

How I envy the hunter who can simply sling a rifle over his shoulder and walk out the back door to his hunting site! That's living!

Unfortunately, many of us are obliged to live close to the sources of our incomes and, for us, a hunting trip entails travel by car, train, bus, plane, boat, horse, trailer camper or motocycle. Today, perhaps, I should even add snowmobile. And that's where the rub comes in—how do we keep a rifle and scope intact while they're being moved from home to hunting ground?

Aside from the simple preservation of our equipment, what other problems can we expect to run into? What does the law have to say about the movement of firearms and ammunition? Can we leave the country with a firearm?

CROSSING INTERNATIONAL BORDERS

Canada and Mexico, as close and friendly neighbors, encourage the visits of American hunters and they go out of their way to make border crossings as painless as possible. Nevertheless, they do put some restrictions on the weapons, shells and personal gear that may be brought in.

To avoid complications and unnecessary expense the hunter must contact either a consulate of the country he hopes to visit or the official govern-

ment travel office of that country. One can't depend upon a guide or outfitter to furnish accurate, up-to-date information.

Once you get there—what problems will you have coming back? Here, since passage of the Gun Control Act of 1968, the hunter may find himself in real trouble if he's ignorant of the law.

Regulations are subject to change and that is why I am reluctant to cite them. Yet, to get the reader thinking along the proper lines, I will report on Canada's 1973 regulations. Mexican regulations are generally similar.

PERSONAL EFFECTS Toilet articles, clothing, camping, gear and hunting equipment are admitted duty free, with some limitations.

TOBACCO A traveler over the age of 16 may take in 50 cigars, 200 cigarettes and 2 pounds of tobacco.

ALCOHOLIC BEVERAGES A traveler over the age of 18 may take in 40 ounces of alcoholic beverages (includes wines) OR 24 twelve-ounce bottles of beer.

FIREARMS & SPORTING EQUIPMENT A sportsman can bring in fishing tackle, portable boats, outboard motors, canoes, tents, camping gear, golf clubs, radios, record players, cameras (with a reasonable amount of film), musical instruments and typewriters IF ALL SUCH ITEMS ARE THE PERSONAL PROPERTY OF THE TRAVELER.

He may also bring in rifles and shotguns IF they measure more than twenty-six inches in overall length. Ammunition is restricted to a total of two hundred rounds. If rifle and shot shell ammo should exceed two hundred rounds, the hunter will have to pay duty on the surplus.

AUTOMATIC WEAPONS, AS WELL AS PISTOLS AND REVOLVERS ARE EXPRESSLY FORBIDDEN. Any attempt to enter the country with one of these items will result in confiscation at the point of entry.

(NOTE: Rules covering handguns may be waived if the traveler is entering Canada for the purpose of competing in a target competition but, in this case, the shooter will have to present satisfactory proof of his intended participation in such an event. Obviously, under these circumstances, prior clearance through the Canadian Consulate is highly desirable.)

All firearms must be registered with a Canadian Customs Agent upon arrival. This would entail a written description of each weapon together with its serial number.

VEHICLES Providing his car is properly licensed in the U.S., the American sportsman can bring it to Canada, and use it for a period of up to twelve months, without duty or fee. Bikes and motorcycles fall under the same regulations. Trailers, however, require a special Canadian permit.

DOG The traveler may bring a dog into Canada if he presents a licensed veterinarian's certificate indicating that the animal has had a rabies vaccination within twelve months of the date of entry.

GIFTS The visitor to Canada may bring in gifts for Canadian friends, duty free, providing the value of each such gift does not exceed ten dollars. (Gifts of tobacco or alcoholic beverages are forbidden.)

RETURNING TO THE U.S.

(This is most important when traveling with firearms!)

Under the provisions of the Gun Control Act of 1968, an individual cannot import into the U.S. a foreign-made firearm. Now, because it's possible to buy assorted foreign firearms in the U.S., it is quite possible for a hunter to carry one, unwittingly, out of the country with the belief that he'll not have any trouble bringing it back. If he does not take steps to facilitate re-entry, *before leaving,* it is quite possible that his firearm(s) will be impounded when he attempts to return.

To avoid re-entry problems, write a description of each foreign made weapon and take special pains to record each serial number accurately. Be sure, too, to describe accessories such as scope and mount—especially if they are also foreign made.

DO NOT ASSUME that a given firearm is U.S. made simply because it bears the name of an American firearms firm. Read all of the engraved inscriptions that appear on each weapon while looking for a line that reads, "Made in Japan" (or Austria, Italy, England, Sweden, Germany, Belgium, etc., etc.) Any such weapon must be registered with U.S. Customs *before* leaving the country.

The best way to accomplish this is to bring the firearm, together with your written description, to a U.S. Customs office at a U.S. international airport or border crossing point. They'll provide you with the necessary documentation for re-entry.

If your own local airport is not an international one, check to see if your air travel will take you through a U.S. international airport. Then, if you can arrange a transfer of flights at that point and *if* you can arrange to regain possession of your luggage during the stopover, you can visit the customs office while you're waiting for your connecting flight.

On one occasion, and only because I had no other opportunity to register in advance, I asked the flight clerk at my take-off point to give me a note on his airline's stationary confirming the fact that I had, indeed, checked aboard the flight with the described firearm. Immediately upon my arrival at the Canadian International Airport I brought the rifle, note and written description to the U.S. Customs agent stationed there. He checked my air ticket, which showed that I had just arrived, and proceeded to give me the necessary clearance for re-entry. The only problem with this procedure is that you can't count on getting an accommodating agent! If you should be unfortunate enough to run across one of the newer "by-the-book" boys, you could wind up without your rifle or shotgun.

PASSPORTS?

We would be remiss if we did not include some information, here, on what it takes for the individual to cross international borders.

U.S. passport is *not* required of U.S. citizens visiting Canada or Mexico. However, each native-born American should carry some proof of his citizenship, such as a birth certificate, letters of identification, draft card, social security card, driver's license, etc. Except for the birth certificate, do not rely on any *one* of these to do the job. Carry as much identification as conveniently possible.

Naturalized citizens have to be a bit more careful—they should travel with their naturalization papers and, again, with as much identification as possible to establish the fact that they are currently residents of the U.S.

Aliens who are permanent U.S. residents MUST carry their Alien Registration cards.

Bear in mind that crossing *into* Canada or Mexico is only half the problem—you also have to prove your identity when coming *back* across the border!

So far, we've only been discussing trips into Canada and Mexico. To visit any other country U.S. citizens must have a passport and for certain countries an Immunization Certificate.

A passport takes some time to obtain, therefore application for one should be made well in advance of the planned departure date. First, get a certified copy of your birth certificate (if native born) or certified copies if your naturalization papers. Then visit your local county clerk for the passport applications. The clerk will tell you how to proceed from there. If it is inconvenient for you to visit your county clerk, inquire at your local court house or write to the Passport Office, Department of State, Washington, D.C. 20524.

You must also have a passport photograph taken. Ask the photographer for six prints; you'll only need two or three for passport purposes but you'll invariably find use for the extras, especially if you apply for an International Driver's License.

A passport is valid for five years unless expressly limited to a shorter period. Once you have acquired a passport you must present the expired passport with your application for a new one. If my memory serves me correctly a fee of about ten dollars is charged by the Passport Office.

Wait until you have your passport in hand before committing to a given departure date.

IMMUNIZATION CERTIFICATES   When applying for your passport you'll be asked to list the countries you plan to visit. Based on this information you'll be given an immunization booklet together with a list of shots or vaccinations required for travel to the listed countries. Take this to your local doctor and get the required immunizations. When the doctor has completed the necessary entries in your booklet you'll have to take it to your local Department of Health to have the doctor's entries authenticated.

VISAS   Just because you possess a U.S. passport, you can't assume that other countries are going to welcome you with open arms. Many countries, particularly in Europe, will let you move about freely, but some countries will require that you first obtain a visa. This is really a permit to enter the country for a specific purpose and for a specific period of time. Visas are not always easy to come by; many will take considerable time and effort.

Make up a list of the countries you plan to visit and turn the list over to your travel agent. He will tell you if any visas are required and will instruct you on the procedures for getting them. Here, an extra passport photo might be necessary. Again, start this operation long before your planned departure.

If you are planning to carry firearms with you, to Africa for example, make it a point to contact the U.S. Embassy of each African country, in writing, to determine what restrictions they may have on the types and numbers of arms and ammunition that you will be allowed to enter with. Make it a point to ask if there are any entry fees, licenses, etc., applicable to such entries and what these cost.

A few of my friends who recently returned from African safaris, complained bitterly about the treatment they received at the hands of an unscrupulous customs official who bilked them for sizeable amounts under the guise of licensing, etc. A letter from an Embassy may not completely prevent this, but it will at least give you some basis for "negotiation."

I've always found it best to make my travel arrangements through a local travel bureau because they take care of all the little incidentals, such as reservations, visas and the application for an International Driver's License, without charge. Tickets, etc., cost no more through such an agency than they would at an airline or railway ticket counter, so you're really getting a lot of free extra service.

TRANSPORTING GAME

Most foreign hunting licenses are issued for specific numbers of specific game animals. Costs vary greatly, however, and you should get all of this information, in hand, before leaving the U.S. If nothing else, this procedure can spare you some costly surprises later. Your travel agent's aid will be especially valuable to you in this area.

Armed with this information, your next problem will be in determining what the U.S. will let you bring back. For example, you may find it possible to obtain a license to hunt leopard. You may, in fact, bag one—you may even pay to have it skinned or mounted in the country of origin. Then, upon attempting to ship the trophy into the U.S. you'll find that our government has banned the importation of leopard hides and/or trophies. Before you spring for the expense of a license, hunt and mounting, be darned sure you will be permitted to bring the trophy home.

Finally, one word of caution about planning foreign hunts. Americans often believe that a bag limit will indicate the scarcity, or abundance, of a particular species of game. This is a good way to get fooled.

Our own Conservation Department is truly concerned with maintaining certain quantities of game and will adjust bag limits, up or down, to result in a harvest that will not endanger the species. Some foreign conservation(?) bureaus are more interested in attracting paying guests than they are in the maintenance of their wildlife. For this reason they purposely publish large bag limits, even though the animal you seek may be so scarce you'll never even find sign of one. Their attitude seems to be, "We don't have any of those anyway, so what the heck do we care if you take a dozen . . . take two!!"

Before you invest any of your hard earned cash in a foreign junket, make it your business to get some good, honest advice from an American hunter who has recently gone the route. If need be, you can even take out a classified ad in one of the popular hunting magazines, i.e. "Would like to

The hard gun case with a foam rubber lining is rapidly becoming an item of necessity for the traveling rifleman.

contact someone who has recently hunted snipe in Hooterville, write Box so 'n so . . ."

PROTECTING THE RIFLE

For all of you peripatetic types, like myself, we finally get around to the nitty gritties of transporting the firearm. Since methods vary according to mode of transportation, let's break this down in an easy reference fashion:

AIR TRAVEL   Before all those dim-witted characters started hijacking planes, it was possible to carry rifles and shotguns in soft gun cases. These, presented to the ticket agent at the airlines counter, were then hand carried aboard the plane and stored in the pilot's cockpit. This was a beautiful system —no losses, no damage, no trouble!

Today airlines will insist that your firearm(s) go through baggage and be stored, below deck, in the baggage area of the plane. Worse, yet, you'll have to arrive at the airport earlier to allow yourself time for the inspection that most airlines now insist upon. The ticket agent will take you into an anteroom and ask you to open the case and demonstrate that the firearm is actually unloaded. When satisfied, he'll ask you to lock it up again and will give you a baggage claim check.

This system presents two problems—damage to rifle (and/or scope) is now a real threat and, if some baggage handler is bent on a little larceny, the whole outfit could disappear between the conveyor belt and the plane.

To minimize problems, follow this procedure:

Do not use a soft gun case when air traveling with a firearm. Use one of those large, hard and bulky hinged cases having a foam rubber interior. These will serve not only to protect your firearm from handling damage, they're so big and awkward they will tend to thwart all but the most zealous pack-rat. Such cases are usually equipped with lockable hasps too. Anything else that you can add by way of straps or locks would also help to discourage a potential crook.

ABOVE ALL, DO NOT ATTEMPT TO CARRY AMMUNITION IN THE SAME CASE WITH THE FIREARM. Carry ammo in a bag containing your clothing or toilet articles. Preferably a case that is locked while in transit.

Try to keep your gun case in sight as much as possible. When boarding the plane I find a window overlooking the area where the baggage trucks are parked and I look for my distinctive gun case in the pile of baggage that is being loaded.

Be particularly careful when traveling through large cities such as Chicago, New York, Los Angeles or Philadelphia.

Airline clerks will tell you that all baggage is insured. They won't tell you that it's only insured for about one hundred dollars. (Read the back of your ticket.) If your scoped rifle is worth more than that (and most are worth upwards of $300.00 or more) you must ask the airlines clerk for an excess-value insurance policy covering the difference. They can make this out for you at the counter and it is well worth the small extra fee. In this way you will be covered against loss on the outward leg of the trip. You'll have to take out another policy at the take-off point for your trip home.

AIR TRAVEL WITH EXCESS BAGGAGE

There was a time when all baggage was weighed before each flight (it still is for international flights) but, today, domestic airline flights simply allow two pieces of normal luggage per passenger. Such luggage is checked at the ticket counter for transport in the baggage area of the appropriate plane. Airlines will also permit each passenger to carry some small hand luggage into the passenger compartment—this would be roughly equivalent to the contents of a small airline flight bag or attache case.

A reasonable amount of camera equipment is also exempted.

What happens when a passenger shows up with four or five large pieces of luggage?

They used to weigh these and bill them at a rate-per-pound for anything over the established maximum. Now they'll charge these at a *rate-per-piece* and the cost is scaled according to the one-way jet-coach passenger rates for the flight being taken. Regardless of what kind of a ticket you hold, the counter clerk will consult a manual which will indicate the coach price for your flight and, next to this, read the cost per piece for excess baggage.

These prices are subject to frequent change but, at this writing, the following scale is in effect and it will give you some idea of what to expect:

if one-way jet coach fare is	(over 2 pcs.) the excess baggage cost per piece is
up to $120.00	$ 6.00
$120.00 to $200.00	7.00
$200.00 to $280.00	8.00
$280.00 to $350.00	9.00
over $350.00	10.00

As you can see, for a short flight, three normal pieces of luggage will cost you an additional $6.00 —four, $12.00, etc.

O.K., suppose you show up with many pieces of additional luggage, then what?

The hunter, for example, who is traveling with several cartons of frozen game meat in addition to his normal luggage, may find that the surcharge is quite high, especially if he is taking a rather long flight. Here, after checking the per-piece cost with the ticket clerk, the traveler should ask what it would cost to ship the excess pieces on the same flight via *air freight!* The clerk would then check through, at no charge, the normal two free pieces of luggage, weigh the balance, and come up with a freight rate for the surplus. Oftentimes, when traveling with many pieces over long distances, the air-freight rate is the most beneficial.

Very large heavy cartons or crates, which cannot be considered luggage, should also be shipped via air freight.

TRAIN TRAVEL   If embarking on a short trip you can carry the rifle in any soft or hard case that will give it adequate protection. Usually, you will be able to store the cased rifle in the baggage rack over your head.

For an overnight journey, especially when I plan to sleep on the train, I prefer to check the rifle with the baggage people. From that point on I follow the same procedure as I would when traveling by air: I follow the movements of the case from the baggage office to the baggage car.

BUS TRAVEL   Bus companies will generally insist that the firearm be stored in the luggage compartment below the passenger deck. Again, that hard case is the one to use. Once I thought I could get away with the lighter, soft case on a bus trip. So, when turning the rifle over to the driver for storage in the baggage compartment, I stood by to see to it that the rifle was stored above the heavy suitcases and wedged between my duffel bags so that it wouldn't be thrown around. I hadn't figured on the fact that the bus makes many stops and that the driver is obliged to load off and on at each one. When I arrived at my destination I was amazed to find my rifle at the bottom of the heavy pile of suitcases.

BOAT TRAVEL   Here we have to take into consideration everything from canoes to ocean liners and, while conditions will vary greatly, we have to start with the premise that it is much more difficult to protect a rifle from bumps and knocks on water than it is on land. For this reason it appears that a hard gun case is desirable—especially when you have good reason to expect that strangers will be handling your luggage and equipment.

In rowboats, duckboats and canoes, hard cases can be a nuisance. There's just not enough room for them. Here I would prefer a heavily padded soft case with a vinyl (water-shedding) exterior covering.

Regardless of the case you decide to use, it's a good idea to equip it with a leather strap so that it can be lashed to the small vessel. A loose rifle would be lost if a canoe capsized.

AUTOMOTIVE TRAVEL   In the chapter on sights and scopes I mentioned the fogging problem that crops up when exposing a warm scope to cold air. Every effort should be made to transport the scoped rifle outside of the warm passenger compartment.

For the auto trunk either a hard or soft gun case will do the trick. If space permits, I'd lean toward the hard case.

When temperature changes are not a problem, a two-piece gun carrier can be mounted behind the seats or in the bed of a pickup truck.

The law may have something to say about the way you can transport your rifle in a vehicle. Most states prohibit the carrying of loaded firearms in a vehicle (even when the breech is left open) and many states will frown upon the practice of carrying an uncased, empty rifle so handily. Take a long, hard look at the brochure or pamphlet you received with your hunting license.

Scabbards serve nicely when traveling in an open vehicle such as a jeep or Land Rover. These are generally fastened to the sides or backs of such vehicles.

When traveling by motorcycle, trail bike or what have you, a scabbard is essential. It's highly dangerous practice to simply sling the rifle across the back.

HORSEBACK   Here, again, only the traditional scabbard is suitable.

In selecting a scabbard, look for one made from a heavy, fine grain cowhide, such as that produced by the George Lawrence Company of Portland, Oregon. The scabbard should have some rigidity and it should provide adequate protection against bumps, scrapes and the like.

The hunter who rarely makes a pack-horse trip will often find that his guide or outfitter can provide a scabbard. Check with him before investing in this accessory.

SHIPPING THE RIFLE The Gun Control Act of 1968 governs the movement of firearms by mail and common carrier. Insofar as the rifle is concerned, the following basic rules apply to *legal* rifles (those having barrels measuring no less than eighteen inches and actions that are *not* fully automatic).

"Licensees" are firms engaged in manufacturing or trading in firearms or ammunition and who possess valid Federal Firearms Licenses. The term "unlicensee" is used to refer to all others who are not so licensed and who are not under indictment and who have not been convicted of a crime punishable by more than a year's imprisonment; who are not marijuana, or narcotics, users or addicts; and who have not been adjudicated mental defectives or committed to a mental institution.

1. The unlicensee may purchase rifles or shotguns in his home state (in compliance with local laws) or in a contiguous state (which authorizes such sales) from licensed tradesmen. (A sworn statement, a seven-day waiting period and notification to the chief law-enforcement officer in the buyer's residential municipality are required in the latter instance.)

2. The unlicensee may purchase rifle or shotgun ammunition, over the counter, without restriction.

3. The unlicensee may purchase ammunition-loading *tools* from out-of-state sources without restriction.

4. The unlicensee may send his rifle or shotgun to a licensed manufacturer or a licensed gunsmith in another state for repair or alteration. In such instances the manufacturer or gunsmith may effect return shipment direct to the unlicensee.

5. The unlicensee may handload ammunition for his own use.

6. While the Gun Control Act of 1968 does not specifically prohibit the temporary loan or rental of a legal firearm to a nonresident unlicensee for lawful sporting pursuits, there are other factors to consider here—not the least of which is the legal responsibility of the owner in the event of a mishap.

The nonresident unlicensee whose firearm is rendered inoperative, or whose firearm is lost or stolen, may arrange for the purchase of a replacement; however, the procedure entails a sworn statement and clearance through the chief law-enforcement officer of the home municipality of the unlicensee.

7. The unlicensee may transport his legal firearms, and ammunition across state and international borders for lawful sporting purposes. He may also arrange to ship lawful equipment to a new or alternate residence in another state, though he must so inform the commercial carrier in writing.

8. Technically, the permanent transfer of a legal firearm should be registered in a "bound book of record" such as that maintained by a licensee. Yet, the Gun Control Act of 1968 does not specifically prohibit the sale and transfer of a legal firearm between two unlicensees who are residents of the same state. If one should rely on this exclusion to clear him of subsequent legal responsibility, he may find that *other* laws will render him vulnerable. For this reason, I strongly recommend that anyone contemplating the sale and transfer of a legal firearm to another resident of the same state, arrange for the transfer to be accomplished by a licensee so that a record of the disposition change is duly noted. Most firearms-dealer licensees will

handle the required entrees and record keeping for a nominal fee.

Finally, the Gun Control Act of 1968 restricts the sale of rifles, shotguns and their ammunition, to persons over the age of 18. Persons under 21 years of age may not be sold pistols and revolvers or ammunition for them.

For each firearm purchase the buyer must fill out Form 4473.

All firearms and ammunition sales must also comply with local and state laws.

TRAVELING WITH GAME MEAT

It is very important when traveling with game that the hunting license tag remains attached to the game. Even if the game is partially butchered, frozen and separately cartoned, number each carton (1 of 4, 2 of 4 etc.) and leave the license tag attached to that portion of the game contained in carton #1.

Often you'll hear complaints that game meat "tastes gamey" and that it's not pleasant to the palate. For the record, properly handled game meat is rarely "gamey." That objectionable odor and taste generally results from *tainted* meat! If prime beef were handled the way some hunters handle their game, it too would taste gamey.

To avoid such problems, clean game quickly in the field. Field dress it immediately after it is dropped. Remove the innards and wash the body cavity with clean fresh water and dry it carefully. Chill the meat quickly—don't leave it hanging, especially not when the temperature exceeds 35° during the day. Get the hide off it as soon as possible because this will help cool it. Quarter large carcasses and wrap them in a protective material (such as cheesecloth).

The surest way to destroy game meat is to transport an animal (in the hide) on a fender or car top, in warm weather or under a bright sun, over any distance.

Partially butchered game, stripped of its hide, can be transported by air with comparative ease. Wrap the meat in brown paper or freezer paper and pack it in heavy cardboard cartons. Wrap chunks of dry ice in newspaper and pack it with the meat. Use plenty of crumpled newspaper to surround the meat and the ice; it has an excellent insulating quality! If a long trip is contemplated, freeze the meat first—then wrap it and pack it with dry ice.

CHAPTER 16

Home Gunsmithing

For those who have some knowledge and skill with power and hand tools, there are a considerable number of gunsmithing jobs that can be accomplished satisfactorily in the home workshop. There are also some jobs that shouldn't be undertaken by anyone but a competent, trained gunsmith. In this chapter we'll discuss the simpler tasks that may be attempted by the skilled layman together with gun cleaning procedures that should be read by all.

CLEANING THE RIFLE

Steel rusts, as we all know, but with a rifle we frequently encourage rusting without realizing it.

For instance, perspiration from the hands is highly acid so, if one takes a rifle from a rack to show it to a visitor, the rifle must be wiped down with a clean oiled cloth before it is returned to the rack. I keep an oiled wiping cloth in a corner of my gun cabinet for this purpose.

Get in the habit of picking up the oiled cleaning rag first, and cup it in your hand to remove the rifle from the rack. Then, holding the rifle by the small of the stock, use the rag-covered hand to open the action. Aside from protecting steel surfaces, this procedure will let your guest know that you want the rifle handled with care.

The practice of opening the breech is not only a customary safety procedure, it also serves to discourage the visitor from pulling the trigger—the natural reaction of a non-shooter.

There are three distinctly different cleaning methods to be discussed, i.e.—cleaning for storage purposes (when considerable time may elapse before re-use)—general cleaning when subsequent re-use is imminent, and field cleaning when on an extended hunting trip.

Any form of cleaning is best accomplished by disassembling the rifle but, since a gunsmith's services would often be required to get it together again, the average shooter should attempt only field-stripping. Instructions for this partial disassembly are often included in the instruction booklet that is furnished with the new rifle.

Another point that we must bear in mind is that any form of disassembly will invariably change the zero of a rifle so, once the sights are properly aligned, it's not a good idea to field-strip the rifle if subsequent re-zeroing is not practical or possible before the rifle is to be re-used.

Finally, except for the simple bolt action, most lever, pump and semi-automatic actions are tricky to dismantle and reassemble. With these, cleaning should be accomplished with a minimum of takedown.

CLEANING EQUIPMENT   It pays to buy a

181

complete cleaning kit when buying the rifle because most of the equipment you'll need will be found in the kit and because you can be assured that you'll have brushes, slotted tips, patches and a rod that suits the caliber of your rifle.

The kit should also contain a liquid powder solvent, a light grade of oil and a container of light grease.

Additional materials that can be gathered from around the house are: an old toothbrush, paste wax, some lint-free rags (preferably flannel or cotton), alcohol, kerosene or carbon-tetrachloride. (Be careful with "carbon-tet"—its fumes are highly toxic—use only with plenty of ventilation.)

As for brushes, if you received a stiff bronze bristle brush with your kit, put it away somewhere. Wire brushes should only be used on badly neglected bores; the common bristle brush is adequate for most purposes.

Gather up some good screwdrivers that fit, tightly, the various screws you may have to remove to accomplish field-stripping. Undersized or worn-tipped screwdrivers will invariably burr screw heads.

How are you going to hold the rifle during cleaning operations?

Most shooters make a gun cradle from soft pine scraps. This is very helpful because it can also be used for some gunsmithing operations. If you have a large bench vise, you can also make up a set of heavily padded soft wood blocks that would permit clamping of the rifle in the vise.

Of course it is possible to clean a rifle by placing it on the kitchen table, or across your knees, but some form of cradle or vise-rig will help prevent scratches, nicks and the like.

CLEANING FOR STORAGE Field-strip the rifle and place the stock safely out of the way where it won't be splashed by solvents or cleaners.

If your action will permit it, insert the cleaning rod from the breech end to avoid damage to the rifling at the muzzle. If you must clean from the muzzle, be very careful when inserting or removing cleaning instruments. While operating the rod, use the muzzle guard—if you have one—or simply avoid ramming the handle of the cleaning rod into the muzzle.

Powder solvents can be highly corrosive if permitted to remain in contact with steel surfaces indefinitely. Use solvents only in the bore to remove heavy fouling, and be careful to remove all traces of it when cleaning is completed.

Try to position the rifle so that the muzzle is angled slightly downward. This should prevent any surplus solvent from dripping into the action area.

Set up the cleaning rod with a slotted tip and cloth patch. Moisten the patch with the solvent (avoid dripping) and insert it into the bore. Run it through, once, to its full length. Do not draw it back! Instead, remove the patch from the tip of the rod that should be protruding at the other end. Withdraw the rod and equip it with the bristle brush. Run the brush through the bore a few times stopping at intervals to apply more solvent. Three or four applications of solvent, followed by vigorous brushing, should suffice to loosen any sludge that has collected in the bore. Now, run a series of clean, dry, patches through until they no longer blacken.

Most shooters would stop right here and simply oil the bore. That's a mistake, especially if you've been shooting on a day that was very hot or wet. Instead, wrap a sizeable piece of your rag material around a soft wood dowel or plastic swizzle stick and insert it in the *chamber* of the barrel. The chamber cannot be cleaned by ordinary bore-cleaning methods because it is usually too large. In this fashion, you can dry the chamber, removing any solvent that has collected there. When dry, apply a light coating of oil with a clean patch. Never go into the chamber with a metal tool or harsh abrasive.

Having completed the inside of the barrel we can go to the action.

If you do not have the manufacturer's instructions, don't attempt field-stripping. Instead, simply open the breech.

Change the position of the rifle so that the muzzle is now canted slightly upward. Brush all accessible surfaces with your carbon-tet, alcohol or kerosene. Make sure you have adequate ventilation. *Do not use the powder solvent!*

With a brush and bits of rag, remove all the powder particles and sludge that has collected in the breech. Use only plastic or wooden instruments to poke the rag into corners and crevices. (A plastic swizzle-stick works well and an artist's bristle brush will also prove helpful.) If portions of the action are disassembled, immerse the loose parts in a pie pan full of kerosene.

Be sure to clean the magazine in the same manner.

Dry all components with a clean piece of rag and oil them thoroughly. Wipe down all exterior surfaces with a clean, oiled cloth.

Now, because you're preparing the rifle for storage, you must coat the bore, chamber, breech face and magazine followed with a light coating of grease. Use only cloth patches or rags for this. Make sure all exposed surfaces are treated.

Oil the trigger mechanism liberally before coating it with grease. Also, be sure to brush oil into the scope mount and wipe the scope down before greasing the metal tube. Remove the turret caps, wipe them with a lightly oiled cloth and pack grease into the threads before reinstalling the caps.

If the trigger guard and sling swivels are still attached to the stock, they must be removed, cleaned, oiled and greased in the same fashion.

Treat the stock to a liberal coating of paste wax, inside and out. Pack wax into the junction between the buttplate (or pad) and the butt. Brush accumulated debris from checkered areas with a toothbrush and then brush wax into the checkered patterns.

Finally, clean the take down screws and coat them with grease, if they screw into metal,—wax, if they go into wood.

Re-assemble the rifle.

Next hunting season, when you want to use this rifle, it is important that you remember to clean it, again, before using it. All grease should be removed, particularly from the bore and chamber. Failure to do this could result in a bulged barrel. Also, dry the chamber thoroughly—and *don't oil it!* Another thing: because this rifle has been disassembled and stored for a considerable length of time, it must be re-zeroed.

GENERAL CLEANING   After a particularly hot or wet shooting outing, it is very important that the rifle be cleaned within a matter of hours. Let it sit overnight and it can come up with an eye-catching display of rust.

The best way to clean it would be just as we've outlined earlier for storage purposes but omit the greasing operation.

Also, be careful to wipe the chamber dry after oiling.

Remember, any form of disassembly will require re-zeroing. Be sure you'll have an opportunity to target the rifle again before taking it into the field.

FIELD CLEANING   This is accomplished without field-stripping because there is little likelihood that the shooter will have an opportunity to retarget the rifle before resuming the hunt.

Leave the rifle intact and clean the bore and chamber as described earlier. Lightly oil a clean soft brush and work over the innards. Use clean rags and patches with a soft stick to get into crevices and corners. Be sure to dry and lightly oil the magazine.

Wax the stock and, if hunting in wet weather, pack wax into the crevices between metal and wood components. Don't overlook the area surrounding the trigger guard.

Wipe all exterior surfaces thoroughly with a clean, lightly oiled rag. Avoid using a powder solvent when the rifle cannot be disassembled.

Lever, pump and semi-automatic rifles are the most troublesome to equip with swivels because it's not always possible to mount them in the forearm. With some models, a special magazine tube or barrel band adapter (like the one at left, above) is required. Others may call for a device that fastens to the tip of the fore end or magazine tube (right, above).

When I'm planning an extended hunt, say a week in the Canadian backwoods, I'll wax the inner surfaces of the stock and lightly grease those portions of the metal that are buried in the wood. Then, after reassembling the rifle, I'll pack wax into all of the crevices between the wood and metal. This helps prevent the intrusion of rain, snow, etc., into areas I can't clean without field-stripping.

Of course, the last step in these preparations is to re-zero the rifle to shoot accurately with a cold barrel.

While in the woods my first chore, upon returning to camp at the end of each day's hunt, is to care for my rifle.

INSTALLING SWIVELS

When purchasing swivels it is important that you know the width of the sling that you intend using. Slings (and swivels) come in widths of ¾, ⅞, 1 and 1¼ inches. If you're not sure of sling or swivel dimensions, measure them!

The usual two-piece set of swivels consists of a wood-screw type butt swivel and a machine-screw fore end swivel with mated escutcheon. However, with some forms of pump, lever or automatic rifles, special fore end swivels must be employed. Check the model number of your rifle before visiting your local gun shop. Then ask the dealer if you can examine his swivel chart. If a special swivel combination is made for your rifle, use it. Anything

This is a 7/8ths-inch sling fastened to a swivel that was designed for a one-inch sling. Measure swivels and/or sling to avoid misfits.

Now measure the diameter of the butt swivel screw. Select a drill that is about the same diameter: if, towards the base, it mikes .125″ select a ⅛ inch drill. You'll need a second, smaller drill for the hole to accept the threaded body of the screw. This one should be about one half the average diameter of the wood screw.

Place the stock inside padded vise jaws so that the lower line of the butt is perfectly horizontal. This is important because you want the swivel head to lie flush against the stock. The swivel screw must be positioned at right angles to the sloping line—which would angle it slightly towards the butt. Tap the appropriate spot with a center punch and, with the larger drill bit, drill a very shallow hole, only 1/16 to 3/32 in depth. This is intended only to accept the base of the screw without chipping the stock at the topmost edge. Then substitute the smaller drill bit in your drilling apparatus, measure the length of your swivel screw, mark almost the same distance on your bit, and drill the deeper, narrower hole, through the center of the shallow one. Again, be careful to maintain the right angle. When the hole is completed, coat the swivel screw threads with paste wax and screw it into the hole. Be careful towards the end of its travel; don't seat it too deeply or you'll chip or split the stock. Seat it just flush with the stock line. If the swivel uses a cross-pin hole, make sure this is properly positioned as the swivel is seated.

If your rifle requires the employment of a special magazine-tube or barrel-mounting fore end swivel, follow the manufacturer's instructions for installing it. With most rifles having one-piece stocks, a common machine screw and escutcheon fore end swivel may be used. To install this, find a drill of the proper size, equal to or slightly larger than your machine screw. Again, with a straight edge and sharpened crayon, find the center line of your fore end. Next, measure back from the tip of the fore end about three to four inches and mark

else may prove impossible to install. By the same token, if you want an easily detachable sling, you'll have to obtain detachable two-piece swivel sets. The least expensive swivels are one piece and non-detachable.

To install the butt swivel, remove the stock from the rifle and find the center line of the lower butt section. Use a straight edge and a wax crayon—mark a thin line indicating center. Next, determine the location of the swivel on that line; don't place it less than 2½ inches from the buttplate. The danger of splitting the stock is too great when one works too close to the edge. Mark the exact location on the center line, preferably 2½ to 3 inches from the butt.

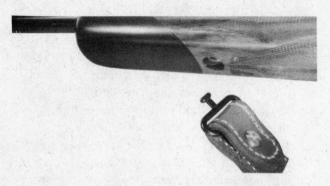

This is Pachmayr's new detachable swivel; when removed from the rifle there is very little protrusion of bases beyond the lines of the stock. Standard fore and aft set sells for about $5.50.

the precise spot on the center line with a nail set or punch.

Drill through the fore end at this point so that the drill emerges inside the center of the barrel channel. Measure the diameter and the *depth* of the escutcheon. Select a drill that matches the diameter, insert it into the barrel-channel end of the previously drilled hole and drill to a depth about 1/16 *less* than the depth of the escutcheon.

Fore ends are rather thin in this area, so you must be careful not to drill the escutcheon hole too deeply. I use 1/16 less than escutcheon depth because I've found that the squeezing action of the machine screw and escutcheon will compress the wood by at least 1/16 when the swivel is installed and tightened. If need be, use a small wood chisel to inlet the barrel channel for any flange material designed around the escutcheon. Again, work to shallow depths.

When installing the fore end swivel, make sure it is tightened to the point where the escutcheon cannot make contact with the lower surface of the barrel. Any contact between swivel screw and barrel could destroy accuracy. Check the length of the screw when installation is completed and shorten it if necessary.

Some high gloss stock fininshes are hard and chip easily. If you anticipate trouble in this area, wax the stock and then lay a piece of masking tape over the areas to be drilled. Mark your hole locations on the masking tape, punch and drill through the tape. This will often prevent damage to the stock finish.

INSTALLING A RECOIL PAD

What type of pad do you require—a thick shotgun style pad to absorb recoil, or a thin rifle pad that simply provides a soft, non-slipping butt? What is your length of pull? Do you want to change the pitch of the butt?

These are the first questions to be answered.

Since every stock differs in size and shape, it is not possible to buy a pad that will fit your stock perfectly. All butt pads and plates must be fitted and, for that reason, they're all made oversize.

Desired length of pull is the first question to be

Swivels are properly positioned on this Mossberg Model 810 SM 30/06 rifle.

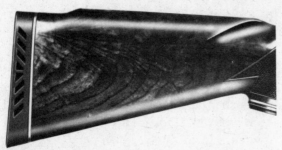

Shotgun-style pads are often used on rifles to in-crease the length of pull. Note how this pad was shaped to continue the lines of the stock.

Pachmayr's White Line Rifle Pad is slim and easy to install (when no increase in the length of pull is de-sired).

answered. Put on the shooting jacket or coat that you usually wear when shooting the subject rifle. Next, if right-handed, bend your right elbow so that you get a 90° degree angle between your fore-arm and upper arm. Lay the butt of the rifle on your forearm and engage the trigger with the first joint of your trigger finger. Holding the rifle in that position, gauge the distance between the butt of the rifle and your upper arm. If your neck is of aver-age length, the butt of the stock should fall about one half inch short of the junction between your forearm and upper arm. If you are of rather lean build with a long neck, forget the half inch toler-ance and fit the butt so that it meets the upper arm. Determine how much material you'd have to add, or remove, to get the desired length.

If you wish, you can also use a yardstick (instead of the rifle) to get the desired measurements. Simply lay the yardstick against your forearm and measure from the first joint of the extended trigger finger to the junction of the elbow. Then determine the length of pull of your rifle stock by measuring from the center of the trigger to the center of the butt.

Jot down the measurement you want and the thickness you will have to add, or cut away, to achieve it.

Next, refer to the chapter on the rifle stock (elsewhere in this volume) and read the instruc-tions for determining the proper pitch.

Plot the desired pitch on the side of the stock and see how this will affect the thickness of the ma-terial you want to add or remove. Bear in mind that a very slight change of butt angle will move the direction of the muzzle considerably. (NOTE: Rifles, unlike shotguns, usually require very little pitch because they're shot from many different po-sitions. If you come up with a rather severe angle you're doing something wrong. Rifle butts are al-most at right angles to the line of sight.)

Assuming you now have the proper angle traced on the stock, you must transfer it to the proper location to give you the desired length of pull.

At this point, simply remove the existing butt-plate from the stock and, with your measurements, ruler and buttplate, go off to the local gun shop and buy the new recoil pad. Make sure the pad you se-lect will fit the new length of your stock. Width can be fairly close but, if you're buying a rather thick pad it must be long enough to permit shaping so that it continues the flaring lines of the stock.

The process of selecting the pad, for size, can be rather tricky. If you think you will have to shorten the stock substantially, the pad should be shorter; if you have to add to stock length, it must be longer. Remember, the top and bottom lines of the stock are not parallel—they tend to converge slightly towards the pistol grip. The pad should be fitted so that its contour continues the natural stock lines.

This is a "750 Presentation Model" pad, by Pachmayr, which comes in a choice of three thicknesses: .600", .800" or 1.00." Also available in choice of colors (red, brown, black) and size (small, medium, large). Costs about $6.50.

Measure the thickness of the pad you're contemplating to see if it will enable you to get the desired length of pull.

Back at the bench, you'll need a few flat files, assorted grades of sandpaper, a fine (9 or 10 pt.) handsaw, a round-shanked screwdriver, a razor, paste wax, shellac, a brush, masking tape and a stationary electric disc sander (preferred) or belt sander.

Now we're ready to proceed with the installation.

First, determine *where* the stock has to be cut. That line you've drawn on the butt serves to indicate angle only—not desired length. Subtract the thickness of your pad from your desired length of pull. If your pad measures ⅞ of an inch, and your desired length is 13¾ inches, you'll have to measure from the center of your trigger along the side of the stock toward the center of the butt, 12⅞ inches. With your sharpened crayon place a dot in the center of the butt panel at that point. Next transfer the angle from your reference line to this point. A straight edge with parallel sides will serve to do this—simply place one edge on the dot and sight along the opposite edge to line it up parallel to your reference line.

With a sharpened pencil, draw a line on the side of the butt panel along the straight edge, and through the dot. This is the cut-off point. Now, with a flexible straight edge (a plastic ruler) ex-

tend this line all the way around the stock. (If the line doesn't return to its starting point, it's not straight.)

Closely fitted to the line, but on the side of the stock opposite the portion that is to be removed, run a strip of masking tape so that it completely encircles the stock. This should help prevent scratches in the stock finish near the work area. If you're much concerned with protecting your stock finish, wrap the entire stock in heavy paper or cloth, leaving only the work area exposed.

Sawing must be accomplished slowly and carefully—you cannot simply saw through the stock the way you would an ordinary piece of wood. In fact, you can't saw directly through at all—this would cause splintering of the lower wood surfaces.

Saw about 1/16 of an inch short of the line to leave yourself some material for final sanding. Draw the saw blade lightly and gently on a back stroke and cut a line, through the finish, completely around the stock. Extend the line in a rearward direction, never forward. Slowly deepen the cut, by degrees, and by systematically turning the

The easy way out! Pachmayr's Slip-On recoil pad simply slips over the butt of the rifle. No installation work required!

stock so that you're always cutting towards the middle, or core.

When cutting is finished, you must true up the base for the pad. Line it up very carefully against a disc or beltbed; use fine sandpaper and a light touch against the sanding surface. You want a perfectly flat, smooth surface.

Next, decide whether you want to glue the pad on or if you want it to be removable. Of course, if you have an anchoring bolt running through your stock, you haven't much choice—you have to keep it removable.

To assure a good tight fit of pad to wood, it's a good idea to hollow the center of the butt panel a bit so that only a quarter of an inch of wood, around the perimeter, is in heavy contact with the base of the pad. An electric grinding tool or small, half-round chisels can be used for this purpose.

After hollowing, scribe a vertical line through the center of the butt. This is to indicate the position of your mounting screws.

Take the screws (they come with the pad) and insert them the wrong way through the base plate of the pad. When the screw points protrude slightly through the rubber on the finished side, take your razor and make one simple cut, through the rubber, over each screw point. This will permit the screw heads to penetrate the pad without roughing up the finished surface.

Insert the screws from the right side so that their points protrude slightly through the base. Hold the pad against the butt and position it carefully so that there is plenty of surplus material extending below the toe of the butt where the sharply angled lower line of the stock is to be continued through the pad.

With a pencil, mark the positions of the screws on the vertical pencil line previously drawn on the butt. Check to see that neither of the two screws is located too close to the edge. Be especially careful with the toe screw because this is most often the culprit that splits a chunk of wood out of the stock. If the natural grain of the stock forms a small triangular block at the toe, you'll have to be very, very careful.

Now, if you have tapered speed bits of screw contour, use them; otherwise, select a drill bit of about half the diameter of your wood screws. Drill the upper, heel hole, first. Put some wax in the screw threads and try it in the hole. Stop the head about ⅜ of an inch short of seating. If it seems to be an overly tight and difficult fit, you may need a slightly larger drill for the lower hole.

Drill the toe hole, wax the screw threads, and try seating the screw to within ⅜ of the butt. If you think you're getting too much resistance, stop —remove the screw—and very carefully enlarge the hole. Try the screw again; when it moves smoothly, you're ready to continue.

Thin a small measure of shellac with a little alcohol, mix it, and paint this on the exposed grain of the butt. Seal the wood well, with two or three coats, and allow it to dry for at least an hour between coats.

If you plan to glue the pad in place, use the equivalent of Elmer's glue; treat both the base of the pad and the butt face to a light application, and screw the pad solidly in place. Wipe any surplus glue off exterior surfaces without delay.

The finishing steps of this operation will show the world what kind of a craftsman you are; get careless or impatient, and you'll blow the whole job.

Set up the disc sander with a medium grit paper on one side and a fine grit on the other. Do not use coarse papers—they'll tear the rubber so badly you'll never get a smooth professional finish. Another thing: you must use a very light touch while sanding the pad to size. Don't bear down on the work.

Before starting, study the stock carefully, sight the planes as you slowly revolve it between both hands. Notice how the flat sides flare outward towards the butt, how they narrow towards the grip? Do you see how the lines change around the toe and the heel as they move towards the sides? You must strive to maintain these contours so that the finished pad appears to be a natural extension of the wood.

Start with the most severe angle first, around the toe. Line up the bottom line of the stock so that it is parallel to the surface of the sanding disc. Sand a flat in the toe—work the base of the pad close to the edge of the disc so that there's no danger of the disc running through the masking tape that's protecting the stock finish. Don't try to get it down all the way—settle for "close" and leave a little bit of material for hand finishing. Follow the same procedure with the top of the pad—again, being careful to continue the natural line of the stock.

Next, do both sides by rolling the stock gently against the disc to pick up the gently sloping top to bottom curl.

When you've completed this step, you should have four fairly flat surfaces that trace the four basic lines of the stock. Go back and take the corners off, carefully; stock lines change rapidly in the corners so you'll have to do this by cutting a series of small flats—changing the feeding angle for each.

When you find the disc getting uncomfortably close to the masking tape, blend the flats together with a gentle rolling motion and go on to the next corner.

Final finishing is accomplished by placing the stock in a padded vise or gun cradle and by filing the base plate of the pad to size. Use a fine file and work slowly, with a pushing motion—don't draw the file rearward. Get the black base plate down to size and ignore the rubber portion of the pad for the time being. When it appears that you've arrived at a perfect fit, wrap some fine sandpaper around the flat file and polish the edge of the base plate and spacer.

If the rubber portion has a good shape, simply dress it with a sandpaper-covered file. Otherwise, go back to the disc sander—use the fine side—and lightly sand it without letting the disc touch the base plate.

Remove the masking tape and check your finished job by *feel!*

Work out any little ridges or bumps that remain.

Wax the stock and you're finished!

REPAIRING THE DOVETAILED SIGHT

Most open sights—both front and rear—are dovetail-mounted and when these are adjusted a little too often, unions will loosen.

Dovetails are tapered from right to left (as the rifle is sighted) and it is important that we keep this in mind, not only when adjusting the sights on the range, but also when repairing enlarged dovetails.

When only a minor correction is needed to tighten the union, remove the sight which contains the male half of the dovetail joint. Examine the upper lips of the female portion (in the barrel) and see if the sharp top surfaces are bent upwards. These can be peened down with a small, light brass hammer. Simply try to restore the shape of the dovetail—don't hammer too long or too hard. If the lips fail to respond to the light hammer, use a small diameter round brass drift pin and a heavier hammer. Make sure the work is tightly clamped in the padded jaws of a vise while doing this. If you lack a vise (and/or vise pads) have someone hold the barrel over a solid work surface, resting the lower wall of the barrel firmly on the work table.

Try the sight again.

If it still moves too far, or too easily, try peening the lower edges of the sight's male dovetail. Use slightly spread vise jaws, or a crack in your work surface to hold the sight so that resistance to your peening is offered only by the base of the sight.

If both of these methods fail to yield the desired result, get a thin piece of copper shim stock, about

Wiliams' two-piece front sight, designed for use in ramps, can often be fitted successfully to a worn dovetail because of its pinching action.

.002″ thick. Cut out a piece that is slightly smaller than the base of your sight. Re-install the sight so that the shim stock lies under the base of the sight. If the resulting fit appears to be a bit too tight, don't force it. Instead, remove the sight, place the shim stock on a flat surface and, with a steel hammer, flatten it some to reduce its thickness. Try it again.

If none of these methods do the job, you've got a problem. You have little choice but to buy another sight and this, too, can pose a problem because most sight manufacturers now use only the standardized ⅜ inch base. (Years ago, bases came in a variety of dovetail sizes.)

If the problem sight mounts in a ramp, you might try the two-piece front sight that Williams makes for their "Streamlined Ramp" series. With this, the head portion of the sight is separated from the base—the two units are screwed together. A pinching action results that should lock both pieces rather tightly to any worn dovetailed slot.

If you can't locate a sight with a larger base; you might try writing to Lyman, Redfield or Williams. Explain your problem and enclose your old sight.

TOUCH-UP BLUING

It would serve no useful purpose to discuss full scale bluing operations here because books can be written on this subject alone. Whenever the layman attempts to reblue an entire rifle, he's simply asking for trouble. Such work requires a considerable amount of equipment, a wealth of knowledge and a heck of a lot of skill. Even the so-called "cold blue" method is beyond the realm of the average hobbyist. Anyone contemplating such major work would be far wiser to ship the rifle off to a good gunsmith.

To those who have more than a hobbyist's interest in the subject, I recommend Roy Dunlap's book, GUNSMITHING. Mr. Dunlap covers the subject thoroughly.

Touch-up bluing should only be attempted on a small scale. Any effort to re-do the entire side of a receiver, for example, is invariably wasted. Two problems are universal—covering the worn area uniformly and matching the surrounding color of the original finish. Gun blues come in a wide variety of color ranges from deep blue to black. It may be necessary to experiment with more than one commercial touch-up blue to get a satisfactory result. All of the commercial preparations, however, will invariably call for the use of sterilized cotton, rubber gloves and a cleaning agent (alcohol or Oakite). To this list I usually add some Q-tips, an artist's brush (that has been cleaned thoroughly in Oakite) and a propane torch.

With small screws and bolts old German gunsmiths simply polish the heads and heat them with a high flame, quickly, before quenching them in oil. No commercial bluer is needed and the resulting color is pretty good. Be careful with this process; don't heat the screw or bolt too long nor make it too hot. The oil quench should be in a very small container, one that will just contain the part that you're bluing. Use a rather heavy machine oil. Don't attempt this process on anything other than screws or bolts.

With any form of bluing, it is important that the surface of the metal is polished carefully and cleaned in a degreasing agent. Once cleaned, the metal should not be handled with bare hands because natural oils, so transmitted, will cause resistance to the bluing action.

Read the directions that come with commercial bluers carefully. These vary greatly and each has to be handled in its own unique fashion. Use only thoroughly clean applicators and be sure to prepare the surface properly.

Often it will be found that a fairly good color match can be achieved by the application of several light coats of the bluing preparation. Also, when having difficulty, try heating the surface with a propane torch before applying the bluer. When doing this, especially on barrels or receivers, be careful to heat only the surface of the metal—apply a high flame, quickly, and immediately follow it with the bluer.

On some surfaces that had resisted my best efforts, I've sometimes managed a suitable result by heating the spot *after* applying the blue. As long as the work is about room temperature, use heat reluctantly. I'd experiment first with more liberal applications of the touch-up blue, or, by polishing less after bluing.

On one occasion, when all my best efforts had been in vain, I was amazed to discover that the blued spot blended in with its surroundings perfectly after I had given up and applied oil!

Touch-up bluing is, at best, a trial-and-error process for a number of reasons: first, one can't be sure of the composition of the steel and, secondly, there's no way of knowing what process the manufacturer used in applying his blue. With touch-up operations, we're trying to match an unknown finish on an unknown surface. Be prepared to experiment!

DRILLING & TAPPING FOR SIGHTS OR SCOPE

Is this trip necessary?

I've seen so many fine rifles torn up by amateur drilling and tapping attempts I can't help but feel some reluctance about discussing the process here. I'd hate to be the one to encourage a shooter into tackling something he can't handle.

The average gunsmith will charge between ten and twenty dollars to drill, tap and mount any sight or scope the shooter can come up with. Considering the fact that a great deal of sophisticated equipment is often required to do the job properly, would it be worth the effort to attempt it yourself?

For those machinists who haven't been dissuaded, we'll go on:

EQUIPMENT You'll need a drill press (preferred) or a good electric portable drill; carbon tipped drill bits of the appropriate size (preferred) or, high speed hardened steel drills or, machinist's carbon steel bits; drilling jig (preferred) or two machinist's squares and a shallow-cutting center drill. A machinist's level; a hardened center punch;

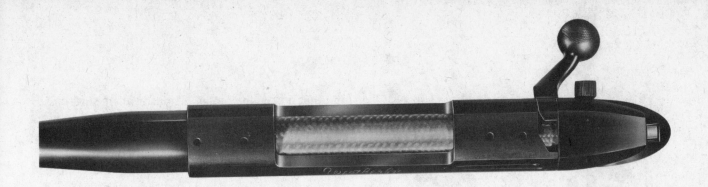

The Weatherby Mark X rifle is factory drilled and tapped but it illustrates what a good job should look like when completed. Pair of holes at left are "blind" holes, those at right go through the rear receiver ring. Be sure to remove bolt and rig drill with a "stop" to prevent internal damage.

drilling lubricant, a set of taps (usually #6–48, occasionally #8–40) and some small, hard, grinding heads; a micrometer or dial caliper and a tap wrench.

Lacking a drilling jig, the home gunsmith will have to employ one or two machinist's clamps.

By way of preparation, consider the material to be drilled and tapped. Barrels, on all rifles, are comparatively soft. If drilling is limited to barrel surfaces, it will not be difficult. However, because one cannot drill *through* a barrel (into the bore) holes must be blind-tapped and that, in itself, requires employment of a bottoming tap and a gentle touch.

Receivers are considerably harder, especially on some military surplus rifles like the Enfield and Springfield. (Mausers, for some reason, are seldom as hard.)

To drill a hardened receiver one must either anneal the surface, grind through the hardened skin and/or use carbide-tipped drills in a jig.

Test a hidden edge of the receiver with a hand file: this will tell you quickly whether or not it's going to be hard to drill. Hardness, in a receiver, is usually only a thin skin or "case" which varies somewhat in thickness; once through the skin, normal drilling is easy.

Determine where your sight or mount is to be positioned and determine which holes must be "blind" and which can go through the work. It's much easier to tap a hole if it's open at both ends.

When drilling into the barrel or forward receiver ring (over the chamber), the holes must be blind. Gauge the thickness of the material at the hole site and set up your equipment so that it will be impossible to penetrate more than half the thickness.

When drilling through the side or top of a receiver, behind the point at which the barrel ends, it is possible to drill all the way through.

With blind holes, use a plug tap to start threads and stop tapping operations at the first sign of resistance. Work the tap slowly and gently—half a turn clockwise and a quarter turn back, to clear the chips. Finish the blind hole with a bottoming tap. If the tap should squeak, you're close to its breaking point. Remove it from the hole entirely, clear the hole of chips and lubricate before continuing.

SETTING UP Remove the stock from the rifle and mount the barreled action in a drilling jig, if you have one, or in the padded jaws of a vise.

Check to see if you have a flat in the action that you can use as a reference point (with most military actions there's a flat underneath).

If you're mounting a scope, put the scope in the rings and fasten the rings to the base or bases. Be careful when disassembling split rings so that you don't inadvertently turn them around or switch the uppers on the lowers. Each half of the ring is mated

Redfield now makes engraved scope mount rings to go with a deluxe, engraved rifle.

to its counterpart and must be reassembled precisely the same way. When properly reassembled, on the scope, there should be a hairline of space between each joint in the rings.

Line the jaws of your machinist's clamps with some electrical tape to protect the rifle and mount surfaces; and clamp the scope and mount to the rifle to see how it will position. Here you must be careful to preserve the eye relief; the eyepiece end of the scope should not extend any farther rearward than the rearmost edge of the bolt body. If you don't have much room in the ring settings for sliding the scope back and forth you'll have to be particularly careful. For safety's sake you must have at least 3½ inches of tolerance between the eyepiece and your eye when sighting, if this is a medium to large bore rifle.

With scope and mount clamped into place, bore sight the combination on a target.

(The bore sighting procedure is described in the "Sighting and Zeroing" chapter of this book. I place the rifle in a gun cradle on my kitchen table and view a target through the open kitchen window.)

With a top-mounted scope, you must try to get the vertical cross wire centered perfectly over the axis of the bore. Invariably, you'll have to play with the clamps a bit, shifting the scope right or left to get the desired alignment. Make sure the mount base is properly positioned on the receiver

and that it is laying flat against its bearing surfaces. Lock everything into position by tightening the clamps.

Now, one final check of the alignment!

If you have access to the base screw holes in the mount, you can mark their location on the receiver by using a hardened center punch through the base holes; just make sure your punch has its point in the center and that the punch fits the base holes snugly. Lacking a proper punch, find a hardened drill bit that fits the base holes snugly and lightly drill the receiver through the mount base.

When you can't get through the mount base to mark the locations of the base screws, you'll have to mark the position of the base or bases on the receiver by other means (pencil, scribe, etc.).

Before going any further, a few pertinent points should be called to your attention: first, this same procedure should be followed when mounting a receiver sight without the aid of a jig. Next, a mounting jig will eliminate most of this clamp and alignment work—simply follow the jig manufacturer's instructions. Finally, I would strongly recommend that the novice drill and tap only one hole initially and that he re-install scope and mount and re-bore sight before going any farther. In short, make sure that first hole is properly aligned before cutting the rest.

Before removing the clamps, find a drill bit whose shank tightly fits the base screw holes in the mount and push the shank of the bit down into the first hole that you intend drilling. NOTE THE ANGLE OF THE BIT! This is most important; when drilling into a somewhat rounded surface it is much too easy to come up with the wrong angle. The angle of the hole must be right or you'll never get the screw to thread properly when it's inserted through the base! If you can rig up something to guide you, do it, even if it's only an assistant that will sight the angle for you as you drill. One trick I frequently employed (before I invested in a Forster jig) was to leave a short drill shank in one base hole while I drilled the parallel hole beside it. A helper took up a position where he could sight the drill against the guide. Needless to say, I left the mount base attached to the rifle while I drilled it. My clamps were attached only to the base so that the rings and scope could be removed without disturbing the position of the base. This works well with one-piece mounts; it's impossible with two-piece mounts.

If you must remove the base (because you're working with a hardened receiver, or using a two-piece mount) check the base position, again, before going any further. Clamp the base alone into the position you have scribed and check it against existing reference points. For example, if this is a military rifle, lay a machinist's square against the top surface of the base so that the right angle blade extension angles downward on one side of the receiver. Take a second square and position it against the bottom action flat so that its blade can be sighted against the upper one. If the two blades are not closely parallel, your base position is off.

Those who have access to a drill press will find it easier to use a machinist's level. Level the drill press table first. Mount the rifle in a padded drill press vise, and level the receiver using the lower action flat. Place the mount base in position, lightly clamped to the receiver, and level the top surface

Scope mount manufacturers often make rings in varying heights to accommodate a wide range of scope sizes. Scopes with large objective cells usually require high positioning. Leupold-Stevens ring choices are illustrated here.

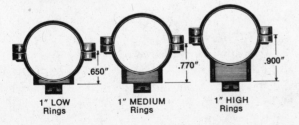

1" LOW Rings   .650"   1" MEDIUM Rings   .770"   1" HIGH Rings   .900"

of the base. When all three components are level (press table, rifle action and mount base) the base is in the proper position for drilling and can be clamped tightly into place. Check all levels once more before drilling and check, too, the forth and back position of the base.

If you are working on a really hard receiver you'll have to grind through the surface hardness before you can attempt drilling. Try to use a shallow pointed grinding head that is slightly larger than the hole to be drilled and be sure that you maintain precisely the same hole location. Grind only for the one, pilot, hole.

Drill the first hole, tap it carefully (as previously described) and try a base screw in it. Check the length of the base screw because they're often longer than they have to be and must be shortened to grip the base tightly.

Fasten the base with the one anchoring screw and remount the scope using one machinist's clamp to hold, lightly, the loose end.

Recheck the alignment by bore sighting and tighten the clamp when everything checks out.

With two holes completed, remount everything for the third time using only the two base screws to hold it in position. This time, bore sighting should confirm the alignment. If it does, simply mark the locations of the remaining base screws and grind, drill and tap, as you did earlier.

On occasion, you'll find some slight misalignment due to a poor contour in the receiver, a base that wasn't machined quite right, or a hole that is slightly off. All is not lost, as long as the error is small! Try correcting the position of the base by shimming it with copper .002" shim stock. If that doesn't do the trick, enlarge the offending base screw hole a bit until you can force the base into the proper position. Above all, don't drill and tap for the remaining base screws until everything sets up perfectly. Those last screws must be anchored perfectly!

Williams makes a "Guide Receiver Sight" to fit some rifles that are factory drilled and tapped for scope. The sight uses the scope-mount holes. This can often spare the shooter the effort or expense of drilling the side of the receiver.

When drilling blind holes it pays to have a drill with a shallow point—we might refer to this as a bottom-hole drill. Also, you must use a bottoming tap to thread the hole as deeply as possible. Be careful when tapping because, in soft steels, it's possible to pull the threads clean out of the hole if you should continue threading when the tap has reached bottom.

Before drilling open end holes, check the inside of the action to make sure you won't be drilling

into the innards of the action when you go through. Rig some kind of stop on the bit to avoid internal damage.

After installation is completed, examine the inside of the action to see if any screws protrude into the action well; shorten any that do and polish them flush with internal surfaces for a neat job.

Finally, remove one screw at a time and coat threads with **LOKTITE** or shellac to firmly anchor it. Tighten all screws carefully.

If you've been working on a side mount or receiver sight, you'll invariably find that the stock has to be inletted to accept it. Spot it into position carefully, mark the position of the wood that must be removed, cut out an undersized portion with a fine-toothed saw, and finish it off by spotting and hand filing with a fine file. Sandpaper lightly, treat

A one-piece bridge mount like Leupold's is easier than a two-piece mount for the amateur to install.

raw surfaces with a sealer (shellac or varnish) and wax when dry.

In conclusion, if the scope you intend mounting is one of the extra long varmint or target types that mount on the barrel, I would strongly recommend that you take it to a qualified gunsmith. Barrels vary greatly in size and shape, mounting blocks vary greatly too, and the positioning of bases is extremely critical. Spacing also determines the value of click adjustments.

This is no job for the average layman!

STOCK REPAIRS

The most perplexing problems with stock repairs are found with stocks that have high gloss epoxy finishes. The easiest stocks to work on are oil finished. While most repairs can be accomplished with little effort, restoration of finishes can prove very frustrating.

CRACKS AND SPLITS These should be caught and fixed as soon as possible. Neglect a hairline crack today and you can be faced with a major split tomorrow.

Almost any popular wood adhesive will do the job; however, a fast-drying type (like Elmer's) is probably easiest to work with.

Simply cushion a clamp in front of the split area so that the split will not enlarge when you spread it to apply the adhesive. With small tang splits and the like, I use round wooden toothpicks to open the fault. Then I carefully pack the crevice with the adhesive, making sure that the glue penetrates deeply. A flat toothpick—or the moistened and hammered end of a round pick—will help to push the glue down into the crack. Then, re-set the clamp over the work area to close the split tightly. Be sure you employ adequate cushioning material to avoid new damage to the stock or its finish. Also, wipe off any overflow immediately.

Let the repair dry overnight before removing the clamp. Buff off any resultant roughness with a fine grade of steel wool, restore the finish (if necessary) or wax.

With larger cracks or splits, an epoxy adhesive would probably prove more desirable. I use Micro-Bed or Bob Brownell's Acraglas Kit.

Before applying either of these, it pays to wax the stock carefully in the vicinity of the repair. Thus, if you get some overflow it will be easy to remove.

Open the crack, install the adhesive, apply a cushioned clamp and gently wipe off any overflow.

Major breaks can also be repaired with Bob Brownell's Glass and, if carefully done, the joint will be almost as strong as the stock was originally.

When repairing a butt section that has broken off completely through the small area of the pistol grip, a *hardwood* dowel (⅜" or ½") is required. Place both pieces together carefully—mark a pencil line across the break (along the side) to indicate the angle and position of the dowel. Scribe a line across the break from the top, or bottom, as well. Determine how long the dowel will have to be and put two pencil lines, indicating its length, across the earlier mark made for the angle.

Find a drill having the same outside diameter as the dowel.

Now, because you can't expect to drill into a ragged end grain and maintain proper drill position you must prepare the hole site with a hand grinder or chisel. Find the exact location for the start of the hole by crossing the two reference lines. Prepare the spot and, with an assistant to sight against one line (you'll guide against the other), drill into the end grain to the required depth. Do both halves in the same manner. Cut your dowel to length (perhaps ⅛" shorter than the length of the hole) and score it in a spiral pattern with a V-shaped coarse file. Round the ends slightly.

Assemble the stock, with the dowel, *dry*—to test the accuracy of your joint. Make any required corrections and, if you are forced to enlarge one hole to get the two halves aligned, you should employ some hardwood slivers as shims to strengthen the joint.

Test it again. Disassemble the unit, mix the glass in accordance with the manufacturer's instructions, and pack it into the holes carefully. Coat one end of the dowel and firmly seat it in one hole. Glue the bare end and force the remaining portion of the stock around it.

To keep everything in line until the glass hardens, you can tie some heavy cord through the trigger guard and around the center of the butt. Wrap the break with a single sheet of waxed paper and clamp it from the side.

Let it dry for at least forty-eight hours before removing the clamp and cord. Dress exterior surfaces with files and/or sandpaper and restore the finish.

When it is possible to drill through the break area from an internal plane, say through the action area (when the barreled action is removed), it is better to glass the two halves together first. Wait until the glass has hardened (24 to 48 hours) and drill after joining the two pieces. This eliminates alignment problems.

When the hole is completed to the proper depth,

score a ⅜ or ½ inch hardwood dowel, apply a liberal coating of glass to the hole and the dowel, and tap it into position. Again, let it harden before cutting the protruding end of the dowel.

For the strongest possible union, some would drill small diagonal holes through the break from the outer surfaces of the pistol grip. This practice would necessitate some rather professional finishing.

Repairs of this sort are suitable for light caliber rifles but I would hesitate to employ them on anything as large as a 30/06.

LIFTING DENTS   With oil-finished stocks, this repair is comparatively easy. Simply remove the finish from the dent area, apply a wet cloth over the spot and heat it with m'lady's iron. Let it dry and keep repeating the process until the fibers of the wood have raised to fill the depression.

If it is a stubborn dent, one that is rather deep, mask the area around it and repeat the steaming process until the fibers refuse to come up any further. Then, heat some thinned linseed oil, to just below boiling, steam the dent and drop the heated linseed oil into it.

You'll rarely be able to get it up to the point where the surface is fully restored, but you should be able to raise it enough so that a light sanding will even it with surrounding surfaces.

REPAIRING STOCK FINISHES

OIL FINISHES   The biggest problem here is matching the color of the original finish. Tubes of artist's oil paints in burnt umber and yellow ochre colors often prove useful, if used sparingly.

When the repair has been made, it should be sanded with a very fine grit of paper. Thin some shellac or varnish and seal any raw wood that remains in the repaired area. Buff it down with the fine paper, or steel wool, again.

If confronted with an abundance of open pores in the wood surface you'll have to fill them before applying the oil. Commercial fillers are best for this purpose.

Sand, again, and try a light coating of boiled linseed oil. Rub it in thoroughly and check it for color. Realizing that it will darken under successive coats, stick to applications of unadulterated linseed oil if you feel it will eventually bring the desired result.

When it appears that you'll have difficulty matching the color of the original finish, you'll have to experiment with the oil color additives. Thin a *small amount* with a little turpentine and mix it with the linseed oil. You'll soon discover that a little color goes a long way. Add it very, very sparingly to a much larger measure of oil. I usually start with only enough color to coat the tip of an artist's brush and paint it on the bottom of a mixing cup. Oil is added slowly, while stirring, until the desired tone is reached. Test it on a hidden stock surface before applying it to the exterior of the stock.

When the color match meets with your approval, use only plain boiled linseed oil over it to bring up the finish. Apply several coats, slowly, over a period of a week or ten days and permit each coat to dry between applications.

EPOXY FINISHES Most polyurethane resins are two-part liquids—resin and activator (catalyst). Such preparations are better suited to complete stock refinishing jobs. For small repairs I prefer a product called Flecto Varathane.

Since all of these products are sold with complete instructions for application, simply select what you prefer, or what is readily available, and follow the manufacurer's directions. Be sure, however, that you pick up a can of the thinner that is recommended for each. You'll need this to prepare your work surface.

All wax, dirt, etc., must be removed from the surface to be repaired. Clean, with the thinner, a large area surrounding the site.

If attempting to patch a deep scratch, wrap some fine sandpaper around a narrow round rod (the thin shank of a screwdriver) and sand the scratch lightly to remove sharp ridges or discolorations.

Working temperatures are important with resin finishes so it's a good idea to store both the stock and the finish in a heated room before attempting application.

When ready, mask a rather large area around the fault. Don't shake or stir your resin too vigorously because this will create an abundance of air bubbles in the finished surface. You can't brush heavily either. Use only a soft camel's hair brush (not nylon) and flow a thin coat of resin over the surface.

When working on a deep scratch, pour a little resin into a bottle cap after coating the damaged area. The material in the bottle cap will harden quickly so you'll have to watch it closely to determine when it has formed into a heavy, but workable, putty-like substance. With the softened tip of a toothpick, lay a ridge of this putty mix down the center of the scratch. Upon drying, this should help restore the level. Buff it down with a fine wet sandpaper.

Let the work dry overnight and apply two coats of finish the following day, with about six hours between coats.

Complete curing will now take at least 24 hours.

For final polishing, to blend the new surface with the old, use rottenstone and water. Rub it down vigorously, especially around the outer edges of the patch.

COMPLETE STOCK FINISHING

Regardless of the type of finish you wish to employ, the quality of the finished job is largely dependent upon your willingness to prepare the stock properly.

When inletting and shaping is completed, sand all surfaces thoroughly with successively finer grits of paper. Use fine files, flat and round, to smooth rough areas before sanding. Pay special attention to edge grain areas—under the lip of the cheek piece, around the pistol grip, the leading edge of the fore end.

Upon achieving a glass-smooth surface, wet a sponge in a mixture of water and alcohol, lightly wet all external surfaces and immediately expose them to heat (from a stove or propane torch) to force rapid drying. Take care to avoid scorching the surface of the wood.

This will raise "whiskers" in the wood grain. Rub them off with fine steel wool followed by extra fine sandpaper. Repeat the whiskering process as often as need be until the grain refuses to raise any further.

Now we can get on with the finishing.

OIL FINISH   Talk to ten gunsmiths and you'll get ten different formulas for a "genuine oil finish." I've never seen one that I could call bad, though I've seen some that I liked better than others, so you needn't view my own, eleventh, formula with apprehension. Before proceeding, however, I should comment that I much prefer tung oil over boiled linseed oil. Tung oil is the basis for many of those famous old English formulas; it's cleaner, thinner and has better drying characteristics. However, it is so costly and hard to come by now that I've had little choice but to revert to linseed oil.

First, thin some shellac with about an equal volume of alcohol. This really has to be thin and mixed well. With a soft brush, paint it over *all* stock surfaces—don't forget the butt and inletted areas. When dry, sand lightly.

Use a good commercial wood filler next. Pack it into the pores of the wood with your finger tips by rubbing across the grain. Wait until it sets up and wipe it off, lightly, with a coarse rag. Let dry and, again, buff it cross-grain fashion.

Mix some good, clear, marine varnish with tur-pentine to make a thin solution. Paint this on with a soft brush to bind the filler and prepare a base for the oil. Be sure to cover the butt and inletted areas too. After it has had adequate time to dry, sand lightly and repeat.

When the second coat has dried fully, sand the entire stock vigorously with very fine paper.

Now you're ready for the boiled linseed oil (such as G.B. Linseed Oil) but, first, find a rather warm work area. Store the stock and oil in that area overnight before commencing oiling operations.

Apply a liberal coating of oil to the stock and rub it in with your fingertips and the palms of your hands until the wood feels hot. Wait about an hour and wipe the surface down with a clean, heavy rag. Let it stand until dry. This, unfortunately, seems to take forever. Linseed oil dries so doggone slowly it takes ten days to two weeks to get any semblance of a real stock finish. All you can do is wait, rub it down with oil when it is dry, wipe off the surplus, and wait some more. The more coats you apply and the harder you rub, the better the finish. Quit when you've had enough.

EPOXY FINISHES   These require the same preparatory steps as an oil finish, up to the completion of the whiskering process. Then instead of an alcohol and shellac sealer, use the sealer and filler recommended by the epoxy manufacturer.

If there is no specific recommendation for a sealer, buy the suggested epoxy thinner and mix up a very thin coat of the epoxy for the base. When this has dried, follow it with the wood filler, wipe off the surplus, and apply another thin coat of your homemade sealer when the filler has dried. Remember, too, to sand lightly between each coat.

Follow the manufacturer's directions for applying the epoxy. Avoid creating air bubbles by stirring or shaking it too vigorously. Also, use a fine soft brush, or a spray, to apply it. Don't brush too energetically either; instead flow the liquid on the

surface. Runs, sags, bubbles, etc. can be removed between coats by light sandings with #400 wet or dry paper and water.

When completed, buff down exterior surfaces with rottenstone and water to get a smooth satin-gloss finish.

One word of caution: individual coats of epoxy have surprising thickness. Be careful around inletted areas where only a thinned solution should be employed. Two very thin coats will suffice in these areas. Checkered patterns should be handled in the same manner.

INLETTING THE SEMI-FINISHED STOCK

The first stock I ever fitted required some forty hours of tedious hand labor and the result was far from perfect. The last stock I fitted took something under five hours and was a heck of a lot better!

I relate these details only for the purpose of conveying the idea that a little know-how goes a long way. If you have a good assortment of hand tools, and are willing to invest in a few more, to fit a rifle stock you'll need only some basic woodworking ability that I can't pass on here.

Two-piece stock units are rarely fitted by the novice. Fortunately, it appears that there is more interest in bolt action rifle stocks. However, for whatever it's worth, two piece stocks are easier to attach but harder to fit properly. They must be spotted into position with meticulous care; I call it, "Worrying the wood away; spot a little, fit a little, cut a little"—an almost endless, repetitous process.

For the average bolt rifle job you'll need the following tools:

> Large barrel-channel rasp (⅝"O.D.)
> Small barrel-channel rasp (½" O.D.)
> Small, knife-edge diagonal chisel
> Two small, half-round gouging chisels (½" & ¼")
> Two small, square edge chisels (½" & ¾")
> Half-round coarse rasp
> Round coarse rasp
> Medium cut round file
> Assorted grits of sandpaper

Finally, and most important, you'll need a set of stockmaker's headless inletting screws, a spotting agent, and a flat Arkansas oil stone for chisel sharpening.

The inletting screws can be purchased from most gun shops or by mail order.

For a spotting agent, some use an alcohol lamp and simply smoke the metal components. Others use lampblack or artist's Prussian blue mixed with linseed oil. Almost anything that is easily applied, easily removed and non-injurious to wood or metal, will serve for this purpose.

The semi-finished stock, as it is produced by Bishop or Fajen, is 90% shaped and inletted. It's a bit on the heavy side to provide sufficient material for shaping to individual taste. Action areas are cut very close to finished size—very little work is required here. The barrel channel, on the other hand, has to be made quite narrow to accommodate a wide range of barrel contours and sizes.

Start work with the trigger guard; this must be fitted first to provide a guide for the barrel and receiver portions. Study the trigger guard carefully before proceeding. Compare it to the stock recess and note those points where it will tend to bind.

When ready, wrap a piece of medium grit sandpaper around a large, flat file, secure the stock in the padded jaws of your vise or cradle, and sand the bottom surface surrounding the trigger guard recess.

Try the trigger guard once, without spotting, and see if there is some simple cut that can be made that will appreciably lower the guard.

Next, spot the sides and bottom surfaces of the trigger guard, lower it carefully into the recess and press down firmly. If you have a soft rubber mallet you can tap it, lightly. Remove the guard, find the contact points, and carefully remove material from these areas. Gauge the amount of material that must be removed by the distance the guard has yet to travel to reach the desired depth. Respot metal surfaces and repeat this procedure until the base plate of the guard is lying flat against the base of the stock. Then, with a sharpened pencil, carefully scribe the outline of the guard on the stock. Cut away wood up to the line but be careful to avoid removing the pencil line. You must work slowly and carefully. Make sure your chisels are sharp and shave the wood. Use files whenever possible.

Most beginners make the mistake of removing too much wood around the edge of the recess where the guard first enters. This is because these surfaces always show up with the spotting color. If concerned about the fit here, measure the guard and the recess with a caliper before cutting any further.

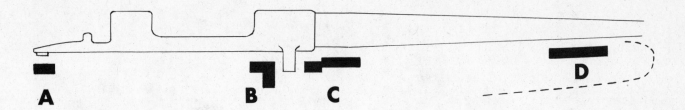

I prefer to file the walls around the magazine channel. Be careful in the corners because these are generally rounded—use round files. When filing, lay the file against the wood carefully and *push*—don't draw back.

The guard should now start to settle in the wood; continue spotting, trying and cutting until it is mounted flush with the bottom surface of the stock. Do not recess it; it will tend to draw in further when the action screws are employed and any recessing now could result in setting it too deeply.

Now we're ready for the tricky part of the job. Remove the bolt and the trigger mechanism from the receiver. Install your long inletting screws. Clamp the stock firmly in your padded vise and, again, with sandpaper wrapped around the flat file, carefully sand the top surfaces surrounding the barrel channel. Don't remove too much wood—just enough to create a smooth flat surface.

Carefully lower the barrel and receiver into position by guiding the inletting screws through the appropriate holes in the trigger guard. (The trigger guard must remain in the stock for this purpose.)

You'll usually find that the barrel, where it flares to join the receiver, is the first point of contact. With a sharp pencil angled slightly inward, trace this shape in the wood and start cutting.

For those with little woodworking experience—examine the direction of the wood grain on both sides of the barrel channel. You must angle chisels and cut in the same direction. When doing this

These are the pressure points for properly inletting a stock or, for applying glass bedding:
  A. just a little glass under the rear tang screw surface.
  B. under the forward receiver ring . . . (don't forget the rear surface of the recoil lug!)
  C. glass a two-to-three inch portion under the barrel at this point (measuring from the recoil lug forward).
  D. assuming this point is two inches from the tip of the fore end, glass a two-inch section. Glass should start four inches from the fore end tip and end two inches from it.
If barrel is to be free-floated, omit glass (or other pressure) at point D.

properly, the grain will tend to push the chisel out of the wood toward the channel. Whenever you sense that the chisel is biting deeper than you intended, you're cutting in the wrong direction. You'll generally find that you have to cut from the receiver towards the muzzle on one side of the channel and, in the opposite direction on the other side.

Most of the early cutting is accomplished entirely with half-round chisels. Flat chisels are employed more often in the action recess and then more for scraping than actual cutting. Sharpen your chisels frequently or the job will become increasingly more difficult.

As inletting progresses, pay special attention to certain critical areas around the recoil lug, forward receiver ring and action flat, tang, and the base of the barrel where it joins the receiver.

If this is to be a pressure-bedded job, you'll also have to be very careful with the last two to three

inches of the barrel channel over the tip of the fore end.

When a stock is properly fitted, the top surface of the magazine wall should fall about 1/16 of an inch short of making contact with the receiver. Contact of wood and metal should be solid around the rear tang screw, forward receiver ring, rear sur-

face of the recoil lug and the base of the barrel. There should be no contact under the recoil lug nor midway through the underside of the barrel. Another point: the barrel should be recessed only to slightly less than half its diameter.

Keep these details in mind.

Continue inletting by spotting, trying and cutting repeatedly. With a soft rubber mallet you can tap the metal lightly to set it into the wood. Be careful with top surfaces because the spotting agent will always show up there and it is too easy to cut away too much wood.

When nearing finished depth you can remove the inletting screws and use the normal action screws to draw the action down tightly.

After the initial gouging of the barrel channel,

barrel rasps can be used to smooth the channel. Chisels are used only to deepen the channel.

The constant spotting and testing phase of this work can get rather tiring. Resist any temptation to rush it. Work slowly, carefully and, suddenly, the pieces will fall into place.

The average beginner will find templates helpful. These can be cut from shim stock. Simply measure two or three cross sections of the barrel—and the forward receiver ring—trace patterns of equal size on the template material and cut them out. (See illustration.)

Receivers that are equipped with external bolt stops will usually start to bind about halfway into the wood. Check the pin that runs through the bolt stop; if it protrudes below the stop it will indent the stock. Take a small drill and inlet for the pin.

If this stock is to be glass bedded, you'll have to make room for the glass by removing some wood from the critical areas previously mentioned.

A free-floating barrel doesn't have to *look* free-floating. Bed the forward receiver ring and the base of the barrel tightly. Then relieve the balance of the barrel channel so that only a thin slip of paper, folded around the barrel, can be slid between barrel and stock down to the chamber area.

Assuming that the trigger guard, receiver and barrel are now firmly joined to the stock, you can install the bolt and inlet the stock to accept the closed bolt handle. Use a small half-round chisel and a round file for this. Watch the angle.

You'll also have to cut a little channel, to the rear of the tang, to accept the squared lug at the bottom rear of the bolt.

Now install the trigger mechanism and inlet the stock to accept it.

When all inletting work is completed, assemble the rifle and start shaping and finishing of exterior surfaces. Generally, you'll find that you'll have to remove considerable material from the fore end, from around the pistol grip and, on occasion, from

butt sections. Some like to flute the comb and undercut the cheek piece.

Wood finishing operations are described elsewhere in this chapter.

GLASS BEDDING

"MICRO-BED" and Bob Brownell's "ACRA-GLAS" are the glass bedding compounds designed specifically for gunstock work.

Complete instructions come with both of these products so it makes little sense for me to repeat them here.

I can be of better service by telling you *where* to put the glass, how to prepare the job and how to avoid trouble.

First, glass bedding compounds consist of an epoxy resin and a catalytic agent. When properly mixed, they set *fast!* Consequently, all work areas must be prepared to accept the glass without delay; allow yourself one half hour for application, no more! Another thing: these epoxys are non-discriminatory—they'll stick, tenaciously, to anything you smear them on—makes no difference if it's wood, steel or glass! Areas close to those being glassed will have to be treated with a release agent to facilitate subsequent removal of accidental deposits.

Finally, in order to glass bed a barrel and action, you must *make room* for the glass, in certain places.

When accurizing a bolt action rifle, glass should be applied to the stock at four points: under the top tang surface where the rear trigger guard screw is anchored, under the action flat of the forward receiver ring (and behind the recoil lug—but not under it!), under the balance of the forward receiver ring and extending forward from there to embrace about two to three inches of the barrel and, finally, under the barrel near the tip of the fore end.

Don't remove any wood from the tang area because it could only lead to trouble—a thin layer of glass will suffice here.

I don't like to relieve the recoil lug area either. (A heavy block of wood is needed here.) Instead I simply cut two shallow parallel channels in the face of the vertical plane that abuts the rear of the recoil lug.

Wood should be removed from under the receiver ring and barrel, but do this in such a way that you won't distort the top lines of the inletting.

Glassing shouldn't be visible when the rifle is assembled.

When the stock has been relieved at the points indicated, wax all exterior surfaces with a heavy paste wax and buff it down, lightly, to a dull sheen. Be sure to cover, adequately, all top surfaces near glassed areas.

Next, remove the bolt, trigger mechanism, magazine spring and follower and the floor plate from the rifle.

With a clean, dry cloth, wipe down the barrel, receiver, trigger guard and inner magazine well.

Use the release agent recommended by the manufacturer and treat all metal surfaces rather liberally. This is important. Also coat the action screws and their threaded recesses in the receiver. When the release agent has dried, put some paste wax into the threaded openings. Be sure that the trigger guard is fully covered, and don't miss the inner walls of the magazine well.

Install the trigger guard in the stock.

Mix your glass compound and apply it as directed. Lower the barreled action gently into position. Install the forward action screw and crank it down as tight as you can get it with a large screwdriver. Then install the rear action screw, but not quite as tightly as the first.

Because excess compound will flow out of various crevices onto surfaces that must be kept clean, you'll have to remove it. However, if you remove it too quickly, or if you should disturb the release agent under it, any further overflow could glue the metal to the wood in such a way that you'll be hard-pressed to separate them. I prefer to wait a bit—until the glass starts to develop a heavy putty-like consistency. (Check it frequently during that first half hour.) Then, with wood slivers and toothpicks, I very carefully remove the excess while diligently trying to leave the release agent undisturbed.

The only problem with this procedure is that you have to give yourself enough time to accomplish the cleaning before the compound hardens. Don't wait too long!

Store the rifle in a warm room overnight, in a horizontal (sights up) position. Twenty-four hours later you can take it apart, check the quality of your work and finish the cleaning operations.

After taking out the action screws, you may find that the barrel and receiver resist your best efforts to remove them. Smart taps on the lower barrel wall, with the palm of your hand, will help. Or use a brass pin or wooden dowel inserted through the magazine well, to engage the lower action flats; tap it lightly with hammer or mallet.

With a light hammer, tap a small wooden block against unwanted residue to remove it.

Now all you have to do is wipe the rifle down and oil it before reassembling.

Glass bedding, if done properly, does help most rifles to shoot more accurately.

CHAPTER 17

Muzzle-Loading Rifles

It may seem rather incongruous to have a chapter on muzzle-loaders in a book on modern rifles but, I assure you, it's an appropriate addition: the shooting customs and weapons of our forefathers are coming back. Muzzle-loading rifles, shotguns and handguns have found a new appeal for countless thousands of shooters across the country.

Not too long ago, "pioneer" black powder fans had to scrounge through attics, antique gun shows, or collector's musty assortments to find shootable front enders. Now, they can drop into their local gun shops and select a newly manufactured muzzle-loader at a reasonable price. The only problem is that muzzle-loaders are selling faster than they can be made—the new muzzle-loading industry is hard-pressed to meet the demand. Some shooters are even building their own and at least one commercial maker is offering "build-it-yourself" kits.

Why? What caused this sudden and inexplicable resurgence of interest in black powder guns?

I really don't know the answer to that, but I suspect that some filmed versions of historical 19th century adventures may have kindled some of the spark.

BLACK POWDER

"Gunpowder," as it was first known, is really a brown substance made from charcoal, sulphur and saltpeter. The black (slate-grey) color results when graphite is added to the granulated mix as a glazing agent.

Charcoal and sulphur, mixed in roughly equal parts, form the highly incendiary base of the powder. To this is added about six to eight parts of saltpeter (potassium nitrate) to provide the required oxygen for rapid burning.

The charcoal and sulphur are first ground into a fine powder, blended, and mixed with a moistening agent consisting of water and alcohol before the powdered saltpeter is added. It is important thoroughout the manufacturing process that the mix be kept well moistened because a violent explosion can occur if a portion of the mix is permitted to dry prematurely. For obvious reasons, flames, sparks and static electricity are the scourge of powder makers who, to prevent accidents, shape their tools from non-sparking materials such as copper, brass or wood.

When properly blended the putty-like mix is pressed into a cake, dried and subsequently broken down into granules of varying sizes. These, then, are sifted and sorted, according to size, to result in an assortment of granulations labeled, FFFFG, FFFG, FFG and FG (small arms sizes). Powders for military mortars, grenades, cannons, etc., are considerably larger. Incidentally, the more "F's" you find in the label, the finer the powder. Burn-

Navy Arms' Zouave 1864 Rifle. A popular percussion rifle in .58 caliber.

ing rates are retarded by larger granulations and, since the various bore sizes require varying degrees of propulsion, the black powder shooter uses the finest granulation for the smallest calibers and the larger granulations for big bores.

Black powder, while easily ignited, is considerably more indulgent than smokeless powder; therefore considerable latitude exists in the loads the shooter may elect to try. In fact, almost every manual published for black powder enthusiasts recommends differing and often conflicting advice on powder granulations and recommended charges. Theoretically, it is possible to stuff a rifle barrel full of black powder, place a bullet (ball) over the charge near the muzzle, and set it off without damage or injury to the rifle, the shooter or foolish onlookers. Mind you, I said "theoretically"—I wouldn't be inclined to test the theory with one of my valued muzzle-loaders—or with my own skin, for that matter!

The gist of all this is that the practice of black powder shooting is regulated by the "Rule of Thumb."

Frankly, I'm a conservative type—you won't hurt yourself if you follow my formula. First, concerning selection of granulation: in rifles bored for less than .56 caliber, use FFFG powder. Rifles of .56 to .69 caliber should be loaded with FFG powder. When using rifles of .70 caliber or over, use FG powder.

Incidentally, if using a flintlock type rifle, it is not uncommon to employ FFFFG or FFFG powder in the flashpan regardless of the powder used for the propelling charge. Rapid ignition has its advantages.

Now, as to the question of "how much powder?" One school advocates use of the volume of powder required to cover a bullet when held in the cupped palm of your hand. Ye gads, that's precision! Another school recommends specific powder charges for each given calibration. This isn't quite right either, because it fails to take into consideration variations in ball sizes and barrel lengths. Resurrected old English loading tables are also consulted by some for loading data. There must be some validity to these—after all, the British survived them.

If, along about here, you're getting the impres-

The #1778 Brown Bess flintlock musket by Navy Arms Company in .75 caliber.

sion that you're going to be forced to think for yourself, you're pretty close to the mark. My own theory may start to make some sense to you.

First, determine the mechanical quality of the rifle you intend using. If it is an old, resurrected antique, caution should be uppermost in your mind. On the other hand, if it is a newly manufactured powder burner, it has already been tested with some substantial loads and you are on far safer ground.

Determine also if you have a rifle or a *musket*. Muskets have thin-walled barrels which may, or may not, be rifled. They're usually of rather large size too—.58 caliber or larger. One has to be a bit more careful with these than he'd have to be with a heavy barreled rifle. Use FFG powder instead of FFFG where called for in a given table of loads and use a minie ball when possible, rather than a patched round ball.

Select, as I described earlier, the proper powder granulation for the caliber you are using. Then, if it is a .50 caliber rifle, start with 50 grains of the recommended powder. With a newly made rifle, test subsequently larger charges in one grain increments (i.e. 51, 52, 53, 54 etc.) until recoil and/or muzzle blast starts to become objectionable. It's also a good idea to conduct accuracy tests simultaneously because you'll often find that it is too easy to pass up the load that gives you the best in performance. With the larger calibers, .58 and over, you'll invariably find that you must settle for a charge within a grain or two of 58. Contrarily, some of the smaller calibers can take some rather heavy loads—up to 30% heavier. To provide some idea of upper limits, we are reproducing a table of recommended charges. Keep an eye on these when working up your loads.

The relationship between your ball size (or minie size) and bore size also may influence your powder charge. When loading a bullet that fits the bore very tightly, the shooter must realize that his pressure will be higher than it would be with a smaller ball or bullet. By the same token, patching material (we'll get into that shortly) can influence pressures.

With antique guns, be careful! I would hesitate to fire any of these from the shoulder the first time out. Tie 'em down to a tire and run off a few test shots first, just to get some assurance that they're safe to shoot.

Another point: when working with a border-line caliber, say one for which I have suggested FFG powder; the combination of ball size to bore size and barrel length may be such that the finer granulation (FFFG) powder may prove more desirable. With shorter barrels, under these circumstances, don't hesitate to test a few FFFG loads, but start light.

Because, with an overly heavy load, the unburned powder will be simply blown out of the barrel; it is possible to determine the efficiency of your charge by shooting from the prone position and placing an old sheet on the ground in front of the muzzle. With a good load you should see a few unburned powder particles but, if there is an abundance of them you're simply wasting powder.

A good sharp report upon firing is another indication of load efficiency.

Finally, on the subject of black powder, a few words of caution:

1. NEVER ATTEMPT TO USE SMOKELESS POWDER IN A MUZZLE-LOADING GUN. THESE ARE DESIGNED ONLY FOR BLACK POWDER.

2. BLACK POWDER IS EASILY IGNITED. DON'T SMOKE NEAR IT. DON'T STORE YOUR POWDER CANISTERS NEAR THE FIRING LINE. DON'T SUBJECT YOUR POWDER TO EXCESSIVE HEAT, PRESSURE, SPARKS OR STATIC ELECTRICITY.

3. DON'T STORE BLACK POWDER IN LARGE QUANTITIES. STORE POWDER IN

A COOL DRY PLACE. USE ONLY SEALED SPARK-PROOF CONTAINERS.

4. DON'T SHAKE POWDER CANISTERS TO DETERMINE IF THEY'RE EMPTY. HANDLE STORED CANISTERS GENTLY AND OPEN THEM TO DETERMINE CONTENTS.

To check the condition of stored black powder, first check its color—is it still slate gray? If not, destroy it! Also, place a granule in the palm of your hand and break it with your fingernail. If it breaks into a few pieces it's still rather stable. If it turns to dust it is decomposing.

TABLE OF RECOMMENDED CHARGES
(For Newly Made Replica Rifles & Muskets)

Caliber	Ball Size	Powder	Weight of Powder Charge
.36	.350″ Rd.	FFFG	45 grs.
.40	.395″ Rd.	FFFG	60 grs.
.44	.433″ Rd.	FFFG	60 grs.
.45	.445″ Rd.	FFFG	70 grs.
.45	.440″ Rd.	FFFG	70 grs.
.50	.515″ Rd.	FFFG	50 grs.
.52	.535″ Rd.	FFFG	60 grs.
.54	.560″ Rd.	FFFG	58 grs.
.54	.565″ Rd.	FFFG	68 grs.
.54	.535″ Rd.	FFFG	75 grs.
.56	.562″ Rd.	FFG	68 grs.
.577	.570″–.575″ Rd.	FFG	60 grs.
.58	.570″–.575″ Rd.	FFG	60 grs.
.69	.680″ Rd.	FFG	70 grs.
.70	.680″ Rd.	FG	75 grs.
.75	.740″ Rd.	FG	75 grs.

NOTE: With original antique rifles and muskets, have condition checked carefully by a competent gunsmith and then start with loads at least 10% lighter than those shown above. Minie balls can be fired with comparable powder charges, however, since these are used without patching, the shooter will have to consult a mould maker (Lyman or Shiloh) to obtain a mould for the specific diameter of his bore.

BALLS, MINIES AND PATCHES

Half the fun of black powder shooting is in casting the round balls or minie bullets. It's not difficult, nor does it require a great deal of expensive equipment. In fact, you'll soon discover that the most costly part of the process is the lead itself and this is largely dependent upon the amount of shooting you care to do! Then again, if you have a good plumber friend, you may be able to come up with some scrap lead fixtures that can be melted down for ball-making purposes.

The first question we must deal with here is that of ball or minie bullet size. If the firearm is a newly-made replica the manufacturer will often provide bore specifications and recommendations for ball sizes. If not, you'll have to slug the bore as you would when contemplating use of an old original.

To slug the barrel simply remove the breech plug and force a soft, oversized piece of lead through the length of the barrel. Be careful when doing this—especially near the muzzle where damage to the rifling could destroy accuracy. The slug shaped in this manner will provide you with an exact facsimile of your bore dimensions. Now, with a micrometer-dial caliper, measure both the land and groove diameters and make a note of these.

If we continue with the directions from here, they will no doubt prove confusing to the reader so for the sake of comprehension we should digress by explaining some of the idiosyncracies of the muzzle-loader.

If you've ever tried to fit the jacketed bullet of

This shooter is preparing to "let one go" with a percussion muzzle loader. (Photo Courtesy of R.A. Steindler)

a modern breechloading cartridge into the muzzle of the appropriate rifle, you'll remember that it was impossible. The bullet appeared to be greatly oversize. With a muzzle-loader you have to be able to feed the ball through the muzzle and it has to be loose enough to permit you to push it the entire length of the barrel so that it will seat against the powder charge. Thus, the ball is very much undersize.

If that's the case, how does it pick up the rotation imparted by the rifling?

This is accomplished by wrapping the ball in a piece of durable cloth which, hereafter, we will refer to as a "patch" or "patching." The patch is lubricated and compressed between the ball and the rifling in such a way that it transmits the spin of the rifling to the ball. Upon exiting the muzzle, the patch will drop away. As you can see, some allowance has to be made for the thickness of the patch.

The best in accuracy and performance is obtained when there is a rather tight fit between the patched ball and the bore. However, it is not easy to load a ball so fitted and, too, the process is time consuming. For this reason, the man who is hunting with a muzzle-loader will look for an easier loading combination, one that facilitates rapid reloading. (It is not uncommon, however, for the hunter to load his first ball in a target shooter's fashion, carrying a different combination of balls and/or patches for rapid reloading in the field.)

Minie bullets, which are generally used without patching, are designed with a hollow base cavity which, supposedly, results in expansion of the side walls to engage the rifling. Because they are cast slightly oversize they must be "sized" (to less than

Black powder fans enjoy dressing the part—fringed buckskin outfits seem to be especially popular. (Photo Courtesy of R.A. Steindler)

bore diameter) in a separate operation. Grooves in the outer walls of the minie are designed to hold a rather heavy lubricant. These are faster and easier to load than patched balls but are rarely as accurate.

For patching materials, one must select a variety of samples from durable scrap materials—linen, denim, muslin, etc. Thin materials that burn or melt easily are rejected. Modern synthetic fibers are often found to be unsatisfactory for this reason.

Having gathered some samples, test them with a match to determine which are the most heat resistant. Then "mike" them with a micrometer. Make sure the micrometer is compressing the cloth (so that you can't pull it free). Look for patch material that mikes between .010″ and .020″. These heavier materials will give you the greatest flexibility in loading. It's also a good idea to select only materials that will be available to you in quantity.

Suppose, now, you've come up with five specimens—take the dimension of the *thinnest* of these and subtract it from the *land diameter* of your bore. (This is the smaller of the two diameters of your sample slug.) The figure you arrive at is the recommended diameter for your round ball. If you can't get a round ball mould in this specific size, select the nearest available size (preferably smaller; don't buy a mould that gives you less than .008″ tolerance between ball size and bore size). Your patching materials will help you compensate for any minor differences.

For a patched ball to perform satisfactorily, it is necessary that the bore is well sealed to prevent the by-pass of gases around the projectile. Up to this point we've been concerned only with fitting the ball and the patch to the land diameter. Is the patch heavy enough to fill the *groove diameter* as well? Patch compression is also required here; that's why we were looking for a variety of patch thicknesses. By trial and error you'll have to determine which material provides the best combination for accuracy and loadability.

With some understanding of the "whys" and "hows," we now suddenly realize that deep cut rifling will give us the most trouble because we'll have difficulty filling the grooves while heavily compressing the patch at the lands. Again, the flexibility of the patch will come to the rescue. As it is compressed at the lands, surplus material is forced into the grooves. Still, we can see some advantage to rather shallow rifling.

Manufacturers of modern muzzle-loading replicas take all of this into consideration when establishing bore dimensions. If you should run into a rather unwieldly original you'll have to consult a specialist, like the Lyman Company, Box 147, Middlefield, Conn. 06455.

BULLET CASTING METALS

Unlike the metals employed in casting bullets for smokeless powder firearms, the metal required for muzzle-loading balls and bullets must be quite close to pure lead; in other words—as soft as possible. Lead alloyed with significant quantities of tin or antimony is unsuitable. For our purposes "pure" can be defined as 98% lead. Quantities of lead, of this purity, are not always easy to come by and for that reason you must be prepared to practice a little metallurgy.

The first and most obvious step in this direction is to get hold of some good quality lead projectiles, perhaps some swaged round balls which are usually of high quality.

The oxidized dull gray color of these, if a few are kept as samples, is indicative of the purity of the lead alloy. You'll soon learn that cast balls or bullets that retain a long-lasting bright and shiny exterior actually contain too much tin. Bullets that take on a heavy powdered white coat contain too much antimony. Other tests (not too accurate but helpful) are: score the soft lead sample

with your thumbnail and check the degree of penetration. (When you try to score a harder alloy you'll quickly see the difference.) Also, the melting point of your pot metal will give you a clue— if it melts below 315°C, it contains an excess of tin or antimony. In fact, if it melts at close to 183°C it is roughly ⅓ tin. The presence of antimony is not easily detected via the melting point method because a surplus of antimony will start to raise melting temperatures when content exceeds 20 to 25%.

If you are obliged to work with salvaged lead, you'll have to take steps to reduce the content of hardening alloys. We'll discuss appropriate methods as we get to those stages of casting but, first, you can do some preliminary weeding by sorting and sifting your raw scrap. Test scrap samples with your thumbnail, compare color to your samples, cut off and discard all shiny joints, unions, etc., because they indicate the presence of solder which is close to ⅓ tin. If your scrap is extensively oxidized or discolored, brush it with a stiff wire brush to get into the real colors below the surface. Pieces that have a heavy white-powder coating usually contain too much antimony and this is the most difficult substance to remove—you'd do better to discard such scraps. Don't attempt to remove solder from joints and the like; it's not worth the effort because such pieces rarely prove acceptable to the later mix.

Having assembled a substantial quantity of raw material, you can set up your pot. If you don't have a modern electric melting furnace (with a valve type bottom draw), you can use an old frying pan over a stove that will give you adequate heat. The beginner would probably appreciate,

The past and the present! Grandpappy placed his powder and ball in the barrel; we're doing similar work today but we put the charge in a brass case. (Photo Courtesy of Fred Huntington)

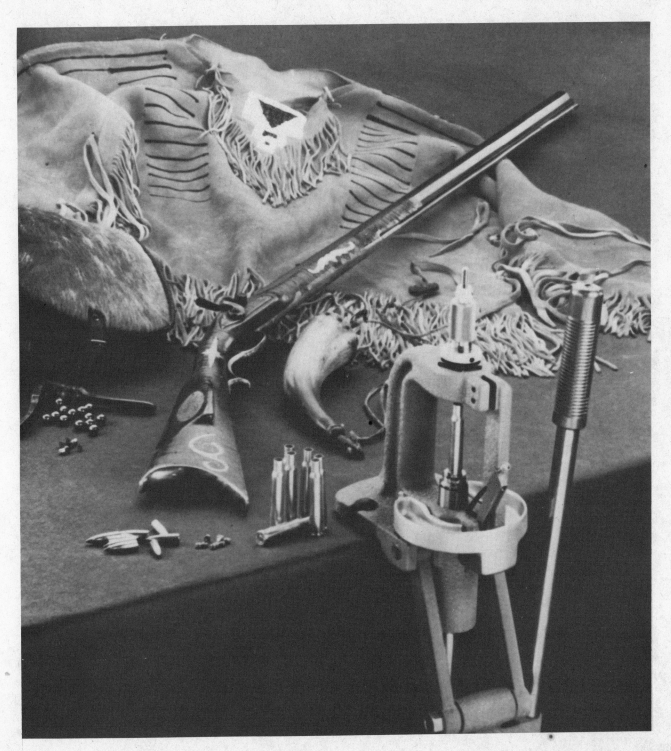

however, the qualities of the inexpensive lead melting pot that Lyman markets.

You'll also need your ball or bullet mould, a lead dipper, an old hammer handle (sans head) and a supply of beeswax or grease. You may also find use for an old toothbrush, an old meat thermometer and a bucketful of warm water.

Before you start melting operations, put on some protective clothing. Glasses or some form of face shield are a "must." Heavy gloves, a long-sleeved heavy shirt, heavy denim trousers and shoes that are easily covered by your cuffs are also advisable.

The only reason why I recommend all of this protective clothing is that experience has taught me that every novice will suffer his fair share of lead spatterings before he develops sufficient know-how to avoid them.

Next, you'll have to find a good safe place to set up your foundry operations. My first attempt took place in the kitchen and I came within a gnat's eyelash of the divorce court. The smells emanating from some reclaimed plumber's lead are beyond belief. The most polite adjective I can use is "ripe." I was also unaware at the time that some lead alloys give off highly toxic fumes when melted and that plenty of natural ventilation is required for safety's sake. Now I do my casting just inside the garage door with the door wide open—and I don't do any casting on rainy days. You'll discover the reason for the rainy-day prohibition the first time you unwittingly splash a single droplet of water into your molten lead mix. A loud bang will ensue and, when the smoke clears, you'll find your clothing well decorated with thin bits and pieces of now hardened lead. Aside from some mild and fleeting burns to unprotected areas of your epidermis you can't really be hurt, *providing you're wearing protective glasses!*

For a heat source I use a Coleman stove that burns lead-free gasoline. I've found this portable unit works very well. It's also easy to adjust the flame (by means of a valve) so that a stable working temperature is maintained.

Now that you've dressed properly and have set up your equipment, load your melting pot and place it on the heat.

While you're waiting for the lead to liquefy, clean up your bullet mould and dipper. Remove all traces of oil and grease, etc., scrub them in a solvent and then in hot soapy water, if need be. Be sure to dry them carefully and then place them near your melting pot to pre-heat them. Remember what was said earlier about a drop of water and your molten lead. Don't attempt to use these tools until they're absolutely dry!

Get an empty tin can or box for your waste lead and make a cushioned dropping area for your newly cast bullets.

If you were casting for smokeless powder bullets, you'd start cleaning and mixing your lead as it liquefies. However, you want soft lead projectiles so you're careful not to stir or flux at this stage. Instead, you wait until the dirty gray slag (called "dross") forms on top of your mix and, with a large spoon, you gently skim it off the surface and discard it. Dross is comprised primarily of dirt, unknown foreign substances and tin. The tin, lighter than lead, will tend to float to the surface when the lead is properly molten. Stirring or fluxing would tend to redistribute the tin thoroughout the lead—a condition you want most to avoid. Wait a bit and repeat the procedure. As the mix clears you'll often see a distinctly shiny slick on the surface—this slick is almost pure tin. When you have removed most traces of it, drop a teaspoonful of beeswax or grease in the pot (stand back, it may throw up a large flame). This is called "fluxing." It will temporarily reduce the temperature of your alloy but, at the same time it will bring new impurities to the surface. Wait a bit longer to skim them off.

Watch the temperature of your molten alloy—try to hold it close to 350°C.

Check your dipper again to make sure it's dry and then slowly immerse it in the mix. Close your mould, swing the gate closed, and slowly, gently, fill the mould by holding the mould sidewise against the pouring tube of the dipper and rotating both a ½ turn counterclockwise. Permit the sprue hole to overflow slightly and then place the dipper back into the pot. As soon as the overflow hardens (it's obvious to the eye) take the old hammer handle and smack the sprue-cutting gate open. This will cut off the surplus metal and simultaneously unlock the two halves of the mould. Open the mould and remove the cast bullet. If it won't fall out, tap the back of the mould with your hammer handle. NEVER try to pick the bullet out with a sharp metal tool because you'll damage the mould. Catch the bullet on your cushion. It shouldn't look like much of a bullet because the mould is too new and too cold. Discard the bullet in your scrap can—don't throw it back into the mix. Run off another six to ten bullets in the same fashion until they start to look well filled out.

Working with pure lead, it is difficult to achieve perfectly proportioned bullets. Lead casts better when it contains a little tin. If you're getting slightly malformed projectiles, you can assume that you are working with a good soft alloy. You'll simply have to play with the mix and mould temperatures until you obtain the desired result. If nothing seems to help, you'll have no choice but to add about 2% tin to the mix. Take a small portion of the shiny tin waste you discarded earlier and restore it to the pot. When it has liquefied, stir it into the mix carefully and make it a point to stir the mix periodically throughout the casting operation.

In time, your mould will overheat and bullets will take on a frosted appearance. .

Wait a bit before resuming and then slow down your operations. If this fails to do the trick, you'll have to fill the mould and, with contents and sprue in place, dip the mould blocks into a pail full of warm water. This will cool the mould sufficiently to permit continued use, however it will probably be necessary to repeat the dunking procedure periodically. Be sure that the mould is absolutely dry after immersion, before attempting to refill it with molten lead.

An electric melting pot does much to simplify bullet casting because it has a self-contained heating element, a bottom-drawing fill valve (eliminates dipping), permits better control of temperatures, and since impurities and hardening agents tend to float to the surface, lead drawn from the bottom will prove to be softer and cleaner.

MINIE BULLETS

These are shaped more like the conventional bullet, but you'll notice that they are made with an unusual number of exterior grooves which are intended to hold a lubricant.

Minies are generally not as accurate as a patched round ball because they are most often employed without patching. Instead, they're cast with a slightly hollowed base which, under pressure, expands the base walls of the bullet to engage the rifling. The advantage of this system, obviously, is faster and easier loading. However, since effectiveness is predicated on the theory that the base will expand sufficiently to spin the projectile in the rifling, there is some doubt that engagement will be great enough to result in a non-yawing rotation. Performance seems to indicate that it's not.

Minie bullets are a bit more troublesome to make because they require employment of a bottom punch (to form the base cavity) and because, after cooling, the bullet must be sized and lubricated. For these reasons, the minie is usually cast slightly oversize—subsequent sizing brings it down below bore diameter. Lubricating can be accomplished simultaneously with sizing if one invests in a combination "lubricator-sizer." Otherwise it can be done separately by simply packing grease or bullet lubricant into the grooves by hand.

IMPORTANT DO'S AND DON'TS

It is important that you keep your mould clean and free of rust. There are a number of products available that can be applied to inner cavity surfaces for this purpose. Check with your local dealer. Be sure, too, that you remove all protective coatings before resuming casting operations.

Any damage to interior mould surfaces will result in fins (because the blocks don't close properly) or imperfections to the cast product. Take care to avoid scratches, burrs, etc., on inner surfaces.

Keep all casting operations far away from flammable materials such as solvents, cleaners, gasoline, etc. Needless to say, you should never attempt casting in the vicinity of your stored black powder.

When fluxing molten lead, particularly with beeswax, a flash of flame can result when the wax makes contact with the molten lead. Be sure there is nothing overhead or nearby that can be ignited. Fluxing also produces a considerable amount of smoke.

When casting work is completed, take care to cool and clean all of your equipment. Don't walk away from your white-hot melting pot if there are children in the area.

CHECKS FOR ACCURACY

When you have finished a run of bullet making, you can weigh each projectile on a powder scale. Balls that are unusually light contain pockets of trapped air and are not worth using. Throw them into your scrap bucket. If trapped air seems to be a continuing problem, you may have to have your mould vented. However, most modern moulds are self-venting. You can also spare yourself some loading headaches if you inspect each ball or minie, discarding any that are deformed.

PATCH LUBRICANTS

We described patch selecting methods earlier. Assuming that you've come up with a variety of suitable materials for this purpose, you now require a patch lubricant to simplify loading. This isn't hard to come by: our forefathers simply used saliva! (I always thought that lump in their cheeks was a plug of chawin' tobacco. Now I've learned that it was only a supply of patches!)

Each muzzle-loading enthusiast has his own unique formula for a lubricant. Some use Crisco, others plain grease. Some mix grease with wax and there are some who simply resort to one of the newly marketed commercial lubricants.

Why such a fuss over a lubricant? Because, in addition to making loading easier, it is felt that a good lubricant will help reduce bore fouling which, as you'll discover, gets to be a problem after four or five shots.

At any rate, take your pick and we'll go on to the long awaited loading and shooting.

LOADING THE MUZZLE-LOADER

Step one   It is vitally important that you clean the rifle carefully, especially if it is a newly manufacturered one that is loaded with grease, oil and preservatives. Hot soapy water, solvents, etc., will accomplish this if accompanied by some vigorous elbow grease.

With a percussion lock, pay special attention to the nipple. Cock the hammer and, with a cleaning agent in the bore, push your patched cleaning rod to the base of the barrel and watch the nipple to see if the hydraulic action pushes the cleaning solution through. If it doesn't, you have a blockage in the nipple aperture and you'll need a nipple pick or similar device to clear it.

Dry everything thoroughly!

Black powder fans often lash a soft hunk of leather to the hammer area of their guns so that it can be used to seal the nipple under the presssure of the hammer. I suggest you do the same and get in the habit from the start because it is a safety feature. It cuts off the flow of air to the bore and will tend to smother smouldering remnants between shots.

You know what kind of powder you want to use and you know how much of it to employ. Get a powder dipper, or make one to hold the desired quantity *by volume*.

Place the butt of the rifle near your feet and angle the barrel out—away from your face. From your flask, powder horn or canister, take your dipper load of powder and pour it into the muzzle of the rifle. NEVER LOAD POWDER DIRECTLY FROM THE FLASK OR POWDER HORN!

Put the dipper aside and whack the side of the barrel with the palm of your hand to settle the powder at the bottom.

Next take your greatly oversized patching material (pre-lubricated) and stretch it over the muzzle. Hold it there with your left hand while placing —with the thumb and forefinger of the right hand —a round ball (sprue tip up) directly over the bore.

(If using a minie ball, dispense with the patch and simply start the minie base down in the muzzle.)

Press the ball down into the muzzle so that the topmost surface is level with the flats of the muzzle. Lift the patching material upward and, with a knife or razor, cut off the surplus patching even with the muzzle.

If working with a tight-fitting combination, you'll need a short ramrod with a rather large handle. This is called a "ball-starter." Place the starter over the ball and press down as far as you can. Remove the starter—pick up the ramrod, insert it into the muzzle and, with one smooth, steady push, press the ball down to the base of the bore. You want to seat the ball snugly against the powder charge. DON'T USE UNNECESSARY FORCE, DON'T THROW THE RAMROD DOWN AGAINST IT! All of these actions will tend to deform your projectile and accuracy goes by the boards.

The ball must be loaded gently, smoothly and it MUST BE LOADED SNUGLY AGAINST THE POWDER! If the ball is stopped short of the powder charge, so that an air space exists between the two, there is a very good possibility that you will bulge your barrel upon firing. By the same token, never attempt to shoot a stuck ball free of the bore by firing. Instead, remove the breech plug, dump the powder and hammer the ball through with your ramrod.

REMOVE THE RAMROD FROM THE BORE Your fellow shooters will howl with glee whenever you forget to extract it. But you needn't feel bad; all of us have fired a ramrod on one occasion or another.

Finally, the last step of the loading procedure: with a flintlock, open the striker hatch and fill the pan with your finest granulation of black powder (FFFG or FFFFG). With a percussion lock, place a percussion cap over the nipple and gently pinch the sides, if need be, to fasten it firmly.

Point the rifle at your target, cock the hammer with your right hand, aim carefully, and touch 'er off!

Before the smoke clears you'll be itchin' to load 'er up again. Unlike the first shot, however, the second requires MORE CAUTION! Now there's some smouldering debris down in the bore so, if you immediately throw in a new powder charge it will flash right back into your hand.

Place your leather tab over the nipple and lower

the hammer on it. (With a flintlock, close the flashpan.) By cutting off the supply of oxygen, smouldering particles should smother in the time it takes you to measure another powder charge.

AGAIN, WITH BUTT END DOWN, TIP THE MUZZLE AWAY FROM YOUR FACE Now, carefully pour the powder from your dipper into the bore and proceed as described earlier. You'll have to exercise considerably more caution though, especially when loading the ball. Never place your hand directly over the muzzle. Hold the bullet between your thumb and forefinger to start it. Hold the bullet starter and ramrod in the same manner. If you get an accidental discharge, these instruments will simply be blown out from between your fingers and the most damage you'll suffer is some scorched fingertips.

Don't fill flashpans nor prime nipples until you've finishing loading the barrel and have restored the rifle to a downrange attitude.

In a comparatively short time you'll notice that loading becomes increasingly difficult with each subsequent shot. The patched ball starts to resist your efforts to push it down the bore. Before you reach the point where you get a ball stuck midway down the barrel, stop and clean the bore thoroughly.

Hot soapy water, powder solvents, etc, are used for this purpose together with a bristle brush followed by some clean patches.

When you've had a chance to experiment, you'll find that some patch lubricants seem to encourage bore fouling. It won't take long to find the lubricant that gives you the greatest number of shots between cleanings.

Those of you who do not have the time nor inclination to cast your own balls or minies can purchase commerically-made projectiles. Some of these are swaged (formed from heavy lead wire under pressure) and are usually more accurate than cast varieties.

Some rifles are supplied with a "false muzzle"— a short piece of barrel which can be fitted to the muzzle to facilitate loading and which prevents damage to the rifling. Proper alignment is achieved by two pins in the false muzzle which are received by two holes in the face of the barrel. The bore section is tapered.

CLEANING THE MUZZLE-LOADER

One can't over-emphasize the importance of cleaning the black powder firearm *immediately* after use. Smokeless powder weapons can take a lot of abuse—black powder guns will tolerate NONE! They generate such awesome deposits of moisture-absorbing sludge and fouling that even a half day delay can leave you with a tongue-clacking rust problem.

Use commercial powder solvents, warm soapy water (in abundance) bristle brushes, patches and oil. But get every nook and cranny of that firearm clean—inside AND outside. Try to avoid having your stock contacted by cleaning agents. Plain oil and wax is best in this area.

Since the nipple passage, too, has to be cleaned and oiled, tie a soda straw to it so that cleaners will not splash over exterior surfaces. Use a soft toothbrush to work oil into corners and out of the way places. If so inclined, it's best to disassemble the rifle for cleaning purposes.

Dry all surfaces carefully after cleaning and before coating them with oil.

A word of caution—commercial solvents are just that—SOLVENTS—they have a corrosive action if handled like oil.

Solvents must be removed, and metal surfaces dried, before oiling.

If storing the muzzle-loader away for an undeter-

Just look at the smoke a black powder load generates!

Map

Blower

Phone

mined period of time, oil carefully and treat the bore, nipple, lock, etc., with a liberal coating of grease. (Be sure to clean it thoroughly before subsequent use.)

BLACK POWDER BITS & PIECES

Often, when discovering an old muzzle-loader in a forgotten corner of an attic, you'll be amazed to find that *it contains a charge* in the bore. Sometimes more than one!

After some of our famous Civil War battles, ordnance men who picked up the weapons in the field frequently found guns with four, five or six charges lodged in the bore. Apparently, in the heat of battle there were those who didn't realize that they were loading but not shooting.

With any new discovery, take the ramrod and measure the distance from the muzzle to the flash hole. Score a line on the ramrod where it abuts the muzzle and then slide it into the bore. If your scored line falls short of the muzzle, you've got a charge in that barrel and you'll have to work carefully to remove it. The best way, of course, is to simply separate the barrel from the stock, clamp the barrel in a vise and use a wrench on the breech plug. Most old breech plugs however, are damned stubborn, especially after having been faced by a rust-encouraging powder charge for any length of time.

Old timers used to employ a rod having a screw-like device on one end and a right-angle handle on the other. They would slip the screw end down the bore, press and thread it into the lead ball and then, with a mallet, tap the handle at the opposite end to pull the charge. I haven't seen one of these tools in years.

Today, I think I would prefer to treat the breech plug with some Liquid-Wrench. Let it soak for a few days with repeated applications and, with luck, that stubborn plug should loosen.

Patching materials have a very definite effect on performance, so you'll want to check yours to see if they're functioning properly. After firing a number of shots from one position, go out in front of your firing point and gather up a number of your spent patches. They should all be within fifteen feet of your former muzzle position. Examine them back at the bench.

Patches that are punctured or torn through the center are too thin or are of poor consistency. Overall blackness is also an indication of poor or thin material.

A good patch is one that has distinct black and gray lines emanating from a black (but unpunctured) center. Clean areas in the patch indicate effective gas sealing.

Shooters of the Daniel Boone era used a hollowed-out steer horn as a powder container. This hung from the neck on a rawhide strap. A small solid horn tip, strapped to the horn, served as the measuring device and dipper. When a good charge was found, the shooter simply hollowed the center of the horn measure with his knife until the cavity accepted the desired charge.

Later, copper-alloyed flasks became popular with the more affluent members of society. Replicas of these are being produced today and you should have little difficulty locating one. Write to Navy Arms Company, if you can't find a local source of supply.

Muzzle loading patch lubricants, solvents, oils, cleaners, etc., are marketed by Hodgdon, Micro-Lube, Lyman and Hoppe.

"Do-it-Yourself" rifle making kits are sold by Dixie Gun Works.

Ball and flint containers vary greatly in size, shape and description. Many prefer to make a simple buckskin bag with a leather shoulder strap.

Once you get bitten by the black powder bug, I wouldn't give a "hoot" for your chances to ignore muzzle-loading handguns and shotguns. It's a highly infectious sport—you'll enjoy it!

CHAPTER 18

Catalog Section

CENTER FIRE AUTOMATIC RIFLES

BROWNING: produces their popular automatic rifle in five grades (I through V) at prices ranging from $200.00 to $1,000.00. Standard calibers are .270, .308, .243 and 30/06. A special magnum model is also available in 7mm Rem. Magnum and .300 and .338 Win. Magnums with 3-shot capacity. (Std model is 4-shot.)

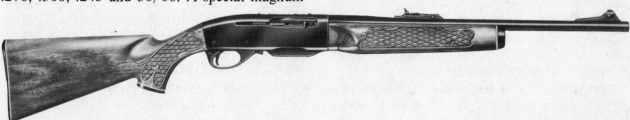

REMINGTON: the popular Model 742 is made in .243, 6mm Rem., .280 Rem., .308 Win. and 30/06. All have 4-shot magazines. "A" grade is priced at $169.95; "BDL" grade at $189.95 and "D", "F" and "Premier" grades at $595.00, $1,295.00 and $2,000.00, respectively. A special carbine model is also available, at similar prices, with an 18½" barrel in .308 and 30/06 calibers.

Note: Price fluctuations at press time made it impossible for us to report these accurately. The shooter can expect all prices to be from 10 to 25% higher than the early 1974 prices shown here!

WINCHESTER: the Model 100 Autoloading rifle is made with a one-piece stock and 22-inch barrel in calibers .243, .284 and .308. The standard grade is cataloged at $169.95, however, deluxe grades are also probably available on special order. The Model 100 is also available in a special carbine version (in .243 and .308) having a 19-inch barrel.

RUGER: produces the Model 44 autoloading carbine in .44 Magnum caliber with a 4-shot tubular magazine. Barrel measures 18½ inches and weight is 5¾ lbs. Standard model is $117.00. A deluxe grade is $122.00 and a special "sporter" version with Monte Carlo stock is $125.00.

HARRINGTON & RICHARDSON: (not illustrated) is offering their Model 360 Ultra Auto in .243 and .308 Winchester calibers at $189.00—the deluxe version at $199.95. The H & R also has a one-piece stock though theirs is made with a roll-over Monte Carlo comb. Three shot magazine capacity. Weight 7½ lbs.

PLAINFIELD MACHINE COMPANY: produces a carbine comparable to the famous M-1 caliber 30 of WW II. Plainfield's is offered in .30 Carbine caliber and in .223. Barrel measures 18 inches, weight is 5½ lbs. Prices start at $105.00.

UNIVERSAL CARBINES: also similar to the .30M1, Universal offers their 1000-series in a number of versions, including two models in .256 caliber, one with a Teflon finish with a broad choice of colors. Prices start at $116.95 and go up to $175.00.

Note: Price fluctuations at press time made it impossible for us to report these accurately. The shooter can expect all prices to be from 10 to 25% higher than the early 1974 prices shown here!

CENTER FIRE LEVER ACTION RIFLES

BROWNING: the Model BLR (photo "U") is offered in .243 and .308 calibers with a detachable 4-shot clip magazine. Weighs 7 lbs. and starts at $149.50. Has side ejection and provision for easy scope installation.

WINCHESTER: Model 94, in the standard grade, is priced at $99.95 and is made in 30/30 and .32 Special calibers. With 6-shot tubular magazine. This solid-frame, top-ejection carbine is a long popular deer favorite. Now also available in some special deluxe finishes at added cost.

Winchester also makes the Model 64 lever action rifle (very similar to the 94 but with a longer barrel) in the same calibers and priced at $124.95.

Winchester's Model 88 is a comparative newcomer, with a one-piece stock and 4-shot detachable clip magazine. Prices start at $169.95.

SAVAGE: another old favorite of deer hunters, the 99-series is made in grades: A, C, E, F and DL. Prices range from $142.95 to $169.95. Interestingly, the Model 99-A is made with a straight grip stock while the others have pistol grips. Calibers are—.250-3000, .243, .300 Savage and .308. The Model 99-C is made with a detachable 5-shot clip magazine while all of the other models boast the famous integral rotary 4-shot magazine.

MARLIN: the 336-series consists of four models (C, T, A and Octagon) priced from $115.00 to $135.00. The Model A is a rifle version while the others are carbines. Calibers .30/30 and .35 Remington.

The Marlin 1895 is a lever rifle (not illus.) in 45/70 caliber and priced at $185.00.

The Model 1894 Octagon (carbine) is made in .44 Rem. Magnum caliber at $135.00.

Marlin's 1894 Sporter is similar to the Octagon version but with a round barrel; also caliber .44 Rem. Price is $115.00.

Finally, the Model 444 Sporter, in .444 Marlin caliber, goes for $145.00 in a rifle version with 4-shot tubular magazine.

NAVY ARMS: the Model 66 Yellowboy (Deluxe Grade illustrated) is made in .38 Special and 44/40 (handgun calibers) and is available in a number of grades priced from $120.00 to $620.00.

(The $620.00 model is shown.)

A carbine, similar in appearance, bears the same model designation and is available in .22 rimfire.

CENTER FIRE BOLT ACTION RIFLES

BROWNING: makes a number of rifles on the FN-Mauser action in calibers .22/250, .222, .243, .270, .284, 30/06, .308, 7mm Magnum, .300 Win. Magnum, .308 Norma Magnum, .338, .375 and .458 Win Magnum. Safari Grade is priced from $300.00 up. The Magnum Safari Grade is slightly higher.

Browning's Medallion Grade is priced from $500.00 to $520.00. The Olympian Grade, still finer, runs over $850.00.

Note: Price fluctuations at press time made it impossible for us to report these accurately. The shooter can expect all prices to be from 10 to 25% higher than the early 1974 prices shown here!

SAVAGE: makes two popular bolt rifles—the first is their Model 340 in .222 or .30-30 caliber at about $90.00. The other is their Model 110 series which may be had in most calibers from .22-250 to .300 Win. Magnum. Prices start at about $130.00.

Savage also offers this model in a left-hand version and as a barreled action only.

WINCHESTER: the famous Model 70 is offered in a caliber and grade for every need or taste! Calibers run from .222 and .22-250 to .458 Win. Magnum. Standard grades are priced from about $175.00 to $360.00. However, special presentation grades may be had on special order with prices that can range well over $1,000.00. The Model 70 has long been a favorite of American bolt rifle enthusiasts.

Another addition to the Winchester family is their Model 770 at $140.00. Calibers start with the .222 and go up to .308. This one should prove quite popular. Also may be had in a special magnum version (in .264, 7mm Rem. Magnum and .33 Win. Magnum) at $154.95.

Another late arrival is Winchester's Model 670 in .243 and 30/06 at $129.95.

MANNLICHER–SCHOENAUER MODEL 1972: a recently announced up-dated version of their famous splitbridge design. This model will probably start at about $500.00 and go up from there. It's made in a wide selection of popular U.S. and European calibers. If they continue their former practice it will also be offered in a choice of carbine or rifle styling.

Conspicuous by its absence, is the Steyr-Mannlicher model which was announced about five years ago. While this rifle performed beautifully it had a number of unusual features that American shooters were reluctant to accept. Steyr-Mannlichers, when last offered, were priced between $264.00 and $320.00.

RUGER: comparatively new to the bolt rifle field, the Ruger Model 77 has made a name for itself in .22-250, 6mm Rem., .243, .308, .284, 6.5mm, .270, 30/06, .25-06 .350 Rem. Magnum and 7mm Rem. Magnum calibers. Prices start at $165.00.

GALEF-BSA (not illustrated) imports the BSA "Monarch" rifle in most popular U.S. calibers with prices ranging from $175.00.

COLT: (not illustrated) imports a number of German bolt action rifles bearing the famous Sauer name. These are found in 25/06, .270, 30/06, 7mm Magnum, .300 Win. Magnum and .458 Win. Magnum. Prices start at $395.00.

HARRINGTON & RICHARDSON: (not illustrated) has an extensive line of bolt rifles on a Mauser-type action. Model numbers are #300, #301, #317, #330 and #370. The Model 330 is priced at about $140.00 but the others range upward from $225.00. Available in a broad selection of varmint, deer and magnum calibers.

Note: Price fluctuations at press time made it impossible for us to report these accurately. The shooter can expect all prices to be from 10 to 25% higher than the early 1974 prices shown here!

MOSSBERG: has a series of Model 800 rifles in calibers .22-250 .243 and .308. Prices run from $125.00 to $170.00.

REMINGTON: the time-honored Model 700 is made in a broad variety of calibers and in several grades ranging in price from about $150.00 up to $1,300.00. Calibers include: .17 Rem., .222, .22-250, 6mm Rem., .243, .25-06, .270, .30/06, .308, 7mm Rem. Magnum, .264 and .300 Win. Magnum, 6.5 and .350 Rem. Magnum, .375 H&H Magnum and .458 Win. Magnum. Depending upon caliber selected, special models with heavy barrels are also available.

Remington's Model 788 is made in .222, .22-250, 6mm Rem. Magnum, .243, .30-30 and .308 calibers. At approximately $100.00, this rifle is attractively priced. The Model 788, incidentally, is also available in a left-hand version, in 6mm and .308 calibers, for about $5.00 extra.

HUSQVARNA: a Swedish-built rifle priced at $212.50 in the Model 9000 Crown Grade and $285.00 in the Model 8000 Imperial Grade. Calibers limited to 7mm, .270, 30/06 and .300 Win. Magnum.

GARCIA-SAKO RIFLES: (not illustrated) these Finnish-made bolt models start at about $210.00 and range up to $335.00. Calibers go from .22-250 to .300 Win. Magnum and .375 H&H.

SMITH & WESSON: offers a bolt action line referred to as their Models A, B, C, D & E with prices starting at $192.50. Calibers from .22-250 to .300 Win. Magnum. (not illustrated)

ITHACA: distributes the LSA-55 and LSA-65 bolt rifles in most popular calibers. Prices start at $160.00 and go up to $250.00.

CENTER FIRE SLIDE ACTION RIFLES

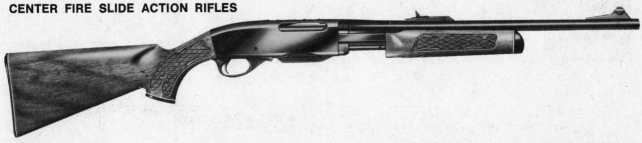

REMINGTON: the popular 760 series may be had in calibers 6mm Rem., .243, .270, .308 and 30/06. Produced in several different grades ranging in price from $149.95 to $2,000.00. Standard versions have a 22-inch barrel and detachable

4-shot clip. A carbine model is made with an 18½-inch barrel.

All models are tapped and drilled for easy scope mounting.

SAVAGE: the Model 170 (illustrated in the chapter on the "Deer Rifle") is made only in 30/30 caliber with a 3-shot magazine. It has a 22-inch

barrel, side ejection, and weighs 6¾ lbs. Price, attractively, at $99.95.

SINGLE-SHOT CENTER FIRE RIFLES

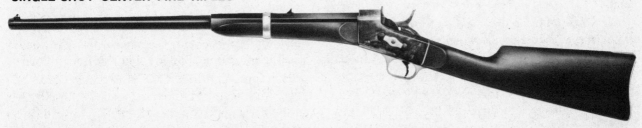

NAVY ARMS: produces a series of rolling block rifles (based on the famous Remington pattern) in .45/70 and .444 Marlin calibers. Some are equipped with octagonal barrels, others with plain

round barrels. Rifle versions have 26-inch barrels and carbines, 18-inch barrels. Prices (same for all models) is $150.00.

Note: Price fluctuations at press time made it impossible for us to report these accurately. The shooter can expect all prices to be from 10 to

25% higher than the early 1974 prices shown here!

RUGER: has created quite a stir with their broad line of "Number One" falling block rifles. Calibers include: .22-250, .243, 6mm Rem., .25-06, .270, 7mm Rem. Mag., .300 Win. Mag., .375 H&H Magnum and .458 Win. Mag. Models vary in weight according to caliber and special purpose design, but are priced similarly at $265.00. Each rifle, too, has a provision for easy scope mounting.

Ruger also makes a Model 3 single-shot Falling Block carbine in calibers .22 Hornet, 30/40 Krag and .45/70 priced at $165.00.

BROWNING: (not illustrated) produces the Model 78 single-shot falling block rifle with an exposed hammer and automatic ejector in calibers .22/250, 6mm, .25/06 and 30/06. All are priced at $229.50.

MUZZLE LOADING RIFLES

HARRINGTON & RICHARDSON: (not illustrated) offers two models—the "Huntsman" and the "Springfield Stalker." "Huntsman" is in .45 or .58 caliber, priced at $65.00, has a 28-inch barrel and weighs 7¼ to 8 lbs. Percussion lock.

The "Springfield Stalker", a cap lock, is likewise made in .45 and .58 calibers; price is $150.00; barrel measures 28 inches and weight ranges from 7¼ to 8 lbs.

HOPKINS & ALLEN (High-Standard Co.) (not illustrated) has nine muzzle-loading rifles, as follows:

MODEL	LOCK	CALIBERS	WEIGHT	BBL	PRICE
Minuteman Rifle	Flint or Perc.	.36 or .45	9–9½ lbs.	39″	$179.95
Minuteman Brush Rifle	Flint or Perc.	.45 or .50	8 lbs.	24″	169.00
Heritage Model	Underhammer Perc.	.36 or .45	8–8¼ lbs.	32″	99.95
Offhand Deluxe	Underhammer Perc.	.36 or .45	8–8¼ lbs.	32″	87.95
Pennsylvania Half-Stock	Percussion	.45 or .50	10 lbs.	32″	174.00
Swivel Breech Rifle	Percussion	.45	8½ lbs.	28″	139.95
Buggy Deluxe Carbine	Underhammer Perc.	.36 or .45	6 lbs.	20″	84.95
.45 Target	Underhammer Perc.	.45	12 lbs.	32″	84.95
Deer Stalker	Underhammer Perc.	.58	9½ lbs.	32″	87.95

INTERCONTINENTAL: (not illustrated) offers a "Kentuckian" rifle in a choice of percussion or flintlock. In .44 caliber only, priced at $135.00.

NAVY ARMS CO: makes a broad assortment of muzzle-loading rifles in both flintlock and percussion patterns. Many are illustrated here. Prices and specifications follow:

MODEL	LOCK	CALIBERS	WEIGHT	BBL	PRICE
Hawken #2073	Percussion	.45, .50 or .58	8 lbs.	24″	$175.00
Brown Bess #1778	Flintlock	.70	10½ lbs.	42″	185.00
Brown Bess #1776	Flintlock	.75	10½ lbs.	42″	275.00
Zouave Rifle	Percussion	.58	9½ lbs.	32½″	110.00
Mississippi Rifle #1841	Percussion	.58	9½ lbs.	32½″	125.00
Buffalo Hunter #1855	Percussion	.58	8 lbs.	25½″	125.00
Harper's Ferry #1801	Flintlock	.58	9½ lbs.	32½″	150.00
Enfield Musket (Smoothbore)	Percussion	.68	8½ lbs.	36″	75.00
Kentucky Rifle #1799	Flint or Perc.	.44	8 lbs.	35″	130.00

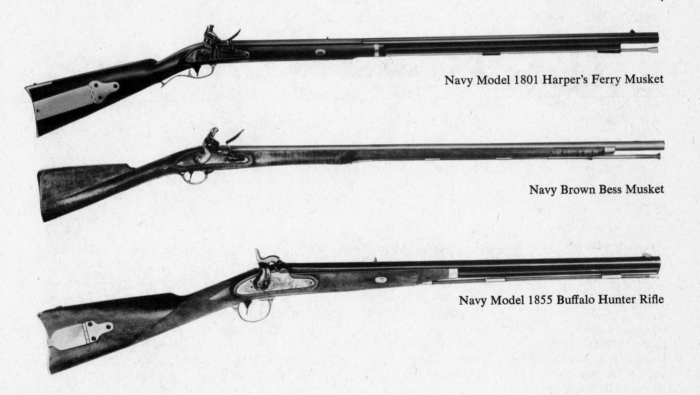

Navy Model 1801 Harper's Ferry Musket

Navy Brown Bess Musket

Navy Model 1855 Buffalo Hunter Rifle

Note: Price fluctuations at press time made it impossible for us to report these accurately. The shooter can expect all prices to be from 10 to 25% higher than the early 1974 prices shown here!

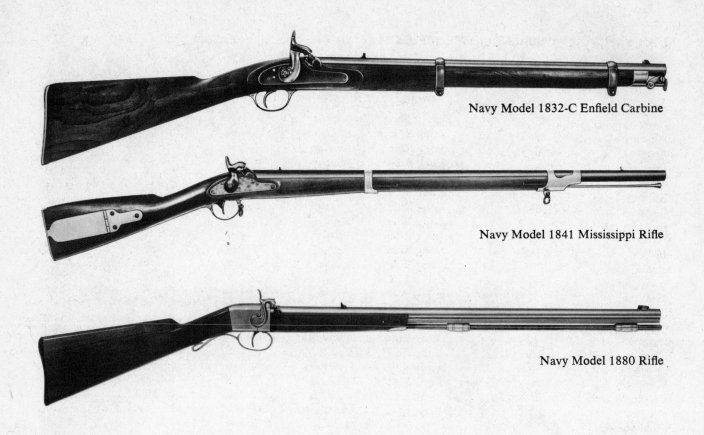

Navy Model 1832-C Enfield Carbine

Navy Model 1841 Mississippi Rifle

Navy Model 1880 Rifle

DIXIE GUN WORKS: (not illustrated) imports a number of fine muzzle-loaders, as follows:

MODEL	LOCK	CALIBERS	WEIGHT	BBL	PRICE
Squirrel Rifle	Percussion	.45	10 lbs.	40″	$139.50
Squirrel Rifle	Flintlock	.45	10 lbs.	40″	149.50
Kentucky Rifle	Percussion	.45	10 lbs.	40″	149.50
Kentucky Rifle	Flintlock	.45	10 lbs.	40″	159.50
Deluxe Pennsylvania Rifle	Percussion	.45	10 lbs.	40″	174.50
Deluxe Pennsylvania Rifle	Flintlock	.45	10 lbs.	40″	179.50
1st Model Brown Bess	Flintlock	.75	10 lbs.	46″	275.00

Note: Price fluctuations at press time made it impossible for us to report these accurately. The shooter can expect all prices to be from 10 to 25% higher than the early 1974 prices shown here!

AUTOLOADING .22 CALIBER RIMFIRE RIFLES

MAKE	MODEL	.22 Rimfire caliber (TYPE)	MAGAZINE SYSTEM	MAGAZINE CAPACITY	WEIGHT	PRICE
Browning	Grade I	L.R. or Short	tubular	11–L.R.	4 lbs. 12 ozs.	$124.50
Browning	Grade II	Long Rifle	tubular	11–L.R.	4 lbs. 12 ozs.	194.50
Browning	Grade III	Long Rifle	tubular	11–L.R.	4 lbs. 12 ozs.	347.50
Colt	Colteer	Long Rifle	tubular	11–L.R.	4¾ lbs.	57.95
Armalite	AR-7	Long Rifle	clip	8–L.R.	2¾ lbs.	65.00
High-Standard	Sport-King	Long Rifle	tubular	15–L.R.	5½ lbs.	59.95
Marlin	49 DL	Long Rifle	tubular	18–L.R.	5½ lbs.	69.95
Marlin	99 C	Long Rifle	tubular	18–L.R.	5½ lbs.	64.95
Marlin	99 MI	Long Rifle	tubular	9–L.R.	4½ lbs.	57.95
Marlin	989 M2	Long Rifle	clip	7–L.R.	4½ lbs.	57.95
Mossberg	353	Long Rifle	clip	7–L.R.	5 lbs.	58.95
Remington	552–A	S, L & L.R.	tubular	15–L.R.	5½ lbs.	74.95
Remington	552 Deluxe	S, L & L.R.	tubular	15–L.R.	5½ lbs.	84.95
Remington	552–C	S, L & L.R.	tubular	15–L.R.	5 lbs.	74.95
Remington	Nylon–66	Long Rifle	tubular	14–L.R.	4 lbs.	59.95
Ruger	10/22 Carbine	Long Rifle	rot. clip	10–L.R.	5 lbs.	57.50
Ruger	Deluxe 10/22	Long Rifle	rot. clip	10–L.R.	5 lbs.	74.50
Savage-Stevens	88	Long Rifle	tubular	16–L.R.	5½ lbs.	49.95
Weatherby	Mark XXII	Long Rifle	clip	5–10 L.R.	6 lbs.	129.50
Weatherby	Mark XXII	Long Rifle	tubular	15–L.R.	6 lbs.	129.50
Winchester	190	Long Rifle	tubular	15–L.R.	5 lbs.	54.95
Winchester	290	Long Rifle	tubular	15–L.R.	5 lbs.	66.95

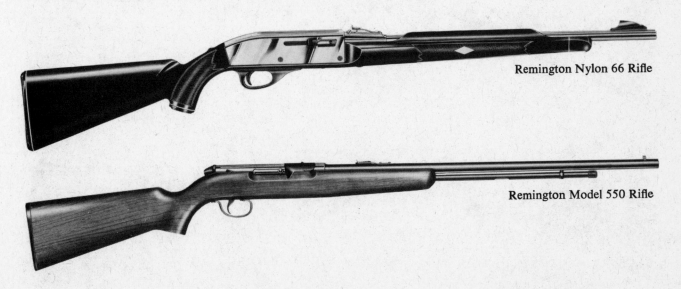

Remington Nylon 66 Rifle

Remington Model 550 Rifle

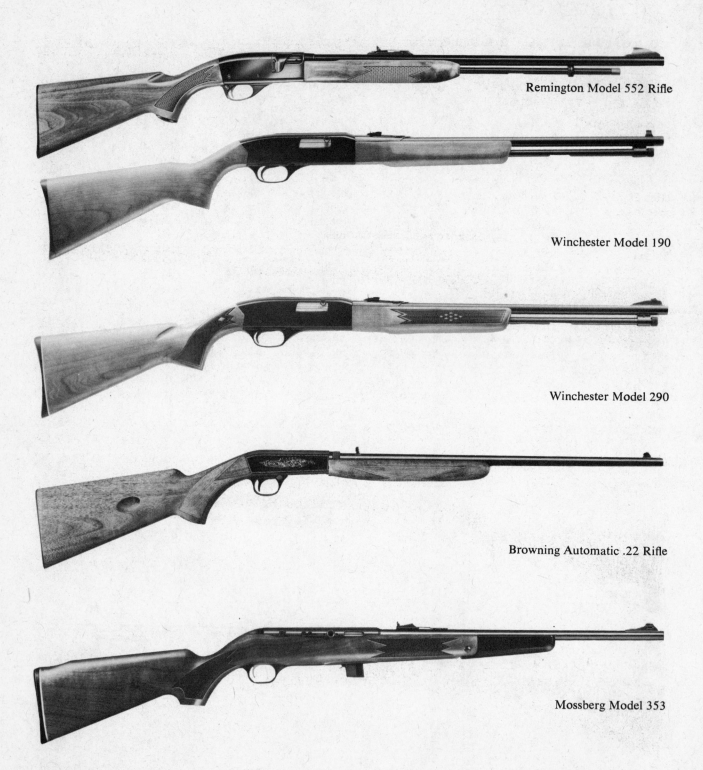

Remington Model 552 Rifle

Winchester Model 190

Winchester Model 290

Browning Automatic .22 Rifle

Mossberg Model 353

Savage-Stevens Model 88

Marlin Model 99C

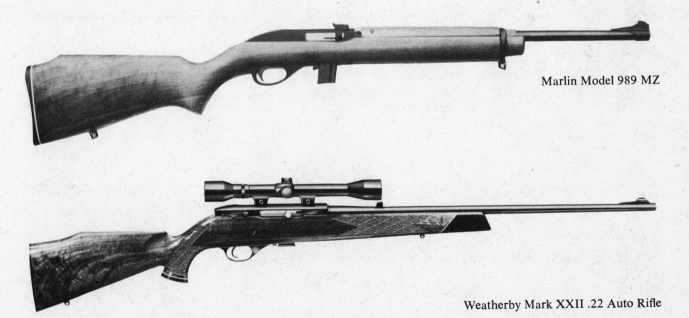

Marlin Model 989 MZ

Weatherby Mark XXII .22 Auto Rifle

BROWNING: the Model BL-22 lever rifle is made in grades I and II priced at $96.50. and $116.50, respectively. Designed with a 20-inch barrel, overall length of 36¾ inches, tubular magazine will handle Shorts, Longs and Long rifles interchangeably. Capacity is fifteen long rifle cartridges. Weight—5 lbs.

Grade II, the deluxe version, is decorated with an engraved receiver and checkered stock.

ITHACA: (not illustrated) produces their Model 72 Saddlegun to sell for $79.95. Chambered for .22 long rifle cartridges, it has a tubular magazine with a capacity for fifteen shells.

MARLIN: the Golden 39-A was one of the first lever action .22's. Today it is priced at $109.95 (without scope). Weight is 6 lbs. Overall length 36″. Will handle Short, Long and Long rifle cartridges. Tubular magazine has a capacity for fifteen long rifle shells.

Note: Price fluctuations at press time made it impossible for us to report these accurately. The shooter can expect all prices to be from 10 to 25% higher than the early 1974 prices shown here!

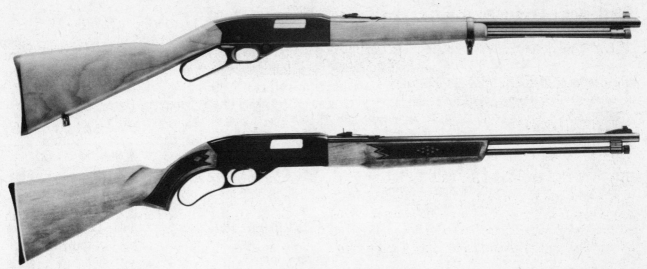

WINCHESTER: puts out two popular lever rifles in .22 caliber—the Model 150, tubular fed with a capacity for fifteen long rifle cartridges; weight of 5 lbs., overall length of 39 inches and price of $62.95.

The Model 250 is very similar but offered with a deluxe stock and without swivels for $69.95.

PUMP ACTION .22 CALIBER RIMFIRE RIFLES

MAKE	MODEL	RIMFIRE TYPE	MAGAZINE SYSTEM	MAGAZINE CAPACITY	WEIGHT	PRICE
Winchester	270	S, L–L.R.	tubular	15–L.R.	5 lbs.	$72.95
Remington	572A	S, L–L.R.	tubular	14–L.R.	5½ lbs.	74.95
Remington	572BDL	S, L–L.R.	tubular	14–L.R.	5½ lbs.	84.95
High-Standard	Sport-King	S, L–L.R.	tubular	17–L.R.	5½ lbs.	69.95

Winchester Model 270

Remington Model 572 BDL

LIGHT .22 CALIBER TARGET RIFLES

There are a number of light rimfire target rifles intended for the youthful beginner and the feminine shooter. (Some of these are illustrated in the chapter "The Youngster's First Rifle.")

MOSSBERG: The Model 340B is reasonably priced at $55.40 and is equipped with a 7-shot clip magazine that will handle all three sizes of rimfire cartridge. (This model can double as a hunting rifle.) Barrel measures 24 inches. Equipped with adjustable receiver sight. Bolt-action. Weight is 6 lbs.

A bit heavier (8 lbs.) and probably better suited for the youthful target enthusiast, is Mossberg's Model 144. A bolt-action priced at $73.75 and made with a seven-shot clip magazine. Barrel measures 26 inches. Equipped with globe (target) front sight and adjustable receiver sight. Medium weight target stock is equipped with hand stop and swivels.

WINCHESTER: Model 310 single-shot light-weight rifle for the very young target enthusiast. Bolt action, with provision for receiver sight mounting. Price $49.95. Weight 5 lbs. 10 ozs.

REMINGTON: Model 540-X, a heavier bolt-action single-shot target rifle probably best classified as an "intermediate weight." Boasts a number of superior target features: heavier stock, target trigger, sophisticated sighting equipment, hand stop, etc. Price is $124.95, with sights. Weight is 8½ lbs. Ideal for the competition-bound teenage shooter.

INTERMEDIATE AND HEAVY TARGET RIFLES

There are three lines of intermediate and heavy target rifles popular in the U.S.; these are—the Remington 40 series, Winchester 52 series and the Savage-Anschutz line (which is made in Germany).

The Savage-Anschutz line starts with the Model 64 (photo "A") which is an intermediate weight rifle in .22 rimfire caliber, selling for about $110.00. Three better, and heavier, grades are also available ranging up to about $450.00 in price. The top of the line is their Model 1413 Super Match 54 Free Rifle which has been used extensively in Olympic and International competitions and is illustrated elsewhere in this volume.

The Remington Model 40 series replaced their former Model 37, some years back. The new Model 40 may be had in rimfire or center fire calibers and with standard weight or heavy weight barrels. Price range from about $200.00, for a rifle without sights; up to something over $400.00 for an International Free Rifle with palm rest and hook (illus. "D"). The Remington 40XB "Rangemaster" .22 caliber rifle is shown in photo "B". While .22 caliber versions are made single-shot, center fire versions may be had as clip-fed repeaters. Bench rest model also available.

Winchester differentiates between rimfire and center fire target models: rimfires are found in the Model 52 and center fires, in the Model 70. (Model 52 International rifle is illustrated in figure "C.") The model 52D .22 Target rifle ranges in price from approximately $200.00 up to $450.00. Model 70 is priced from $255.00 to $400.00.

Many features of competition rifles, such as these, are optional. The shooter would do well to study manufacturers' catalogs before making a selection.

Other target rifles, encountered at international matches are: the Swiss Hammerli and the English BSA-Martini. The Russians, too, make a number of heavyweight models for rimfire and center fire calibers.

Another British maker, Parker-Hale, puts out a Model 1200TX Target rifle in 7.62mm (.308 caliber). Schultz and Larsen (of Denmark) makes a .22 rimfire international style Free rifle that sells for approximately $600.00. Walther, a German maker, has a .22 Free rifle that goes for $320.00.

Savage-Anschutz Model 64 Rifle

Remington Model 40XB Target Rifle

Winchester Model 52
International Free Rifle

Remington Model 40X
International Free Rifle

Note: Price fluctuations at press time made it impossible for us to report these accurately. The shooter can expect all prices to be from 10 to 25% higher than the early 1974 prices shown here!

BOLT ACTION .22 RIMFIRE REPEATING RIFLES

MAKE	MODEL	RIMFIRE CALIBER TYPE	MAGAZINE SYSTEM	MAGAZINE CAPACITY	WEIGHT	PRICE
Winchester	320	S, L–L.R.	clip	5 L.R.	6 lbs.	$ 59.95
Savage-Anschutz	164	Long Rifle	clip	6 L.R.	6 lbs.	119.95
Savage-Anschutz	164	.22 Magnum	clip	6 L.R.	6 lbs.	129.95
Savage-Anschutz	54-Sporter	Long Rifle	clip	6 L.R.	6¾ lbs.	199.95
Savage-Anschutz	54-M	.22 Magnum	clip	6 L.R.	6¾ lbs.	209.95
Savage-Anschutz	184	Long Rifle	clip	6 L.R.	4½ lbs.	99.95
Savage-Stevens	46	Long Rifle	tubular	16 L.R.	5¾ lbs.	47.95
Savage-Stevens	34	Long Rifle	clip	6 L.R.	5½ lbs.	42.95
Savage-Stevens	34-M	.22 Magnum	clip	6 L.R.	5½ lbs.	46.95
Savage-Stevens	65	Long Rifle	clip	6 L.R.	5½ lbs.	49.95
Savage-Stevens	65-M	.22 Magnum	clip	6 L.R.	5½ lbs.	53.95
Remington	541-S	Long Rifle	clip	5–10 L.R.	6 lbs.	134.95
Remington	591	5mm Rem. Mag.	clip	5 L.R.	5 lbs.	74.95
Remington	592	5mm Rem. Mag.	tubular	10 L.R.	5½ lbs.	79.95
Remington	581	S, L–L.R.	clip	5 L.R.	5¼ lbs.	57.95
Remington	582	S, L–L.R.	tubular	14 L.R.	5¼ lbs.	64.95
Mossberg	640K	.22 Magnum	clip	5 L.R.	6 lbs.	58.95
Mossberg	341	S, L–L.R.	clip	7 L.R.	6½ lbs.	51.90
Marlin	780	S, L–L.R.	clip	7 L.R.	5½ lbs.	53.95
Marlin	781	S, L–L.R.	tubular	17 L.R.	6 lbs.	55.95
Marlin	782	.22 Win.Mag.	clip	7 L.R.	6 lbs.	58.95
Marlin	783	.22 Win.Mag.	tubular	12 L.R.	6 lbs.	59.95
Harrington & Richardson	865	S, L–L.R.	clip	5 L.R.	5 lbs.	44.95
Harrington & Richardson	866	S, L–L.R.	clip	5 L.R.	5½ lbs.	44.95
Browning	T-Bolt	Long Rifle	clip	5 L.R.	6 lbs.	107.50

Note: Price fluctuations at press time made it impossible for us to report these accurately. The shooter can expect all prices to be from 10 to 25% higher than the early 1974 prices shown here!

Browning T-Bolt Rifle

Mossberg Model 640 K

Stevens Model 34

Savage-Anschutz Model 54 Sporter

Savage Model 65

Remington Model 582

Remington Model 591

Appendix

AMERICAN RELOADERS ASSOCIATION
Box 4007
Covina, California 91722

AMERICAN SOCIETY OF ARMS COLLECTORS
6550 Baywood Lane
Cincinnati, Ohio 45224

BOONE & CROCKETT CLUB
4400 Forbes Avenue
Pittsburgh, Pennsylvania 15213

NATIONAL BENCHREST SHOOTERS ASSOC.
607 W. Line Street
Minerva, Ohio 44657

NATIONAL MUZZLE-LOADING RIFLE ASSOC.
Box 67
Friendship, Indiana 47021

NATIONAL RIFLE ASSOCIATION
1600 Rhode Island Avenue
Washington, D.C. 20036

NATIONAL SHOOTING SPORTS FOUNDATION
1075 Post Road
Riverside, Connecticut 06878

NORTH-SOUTH SKIRMISH ASSOCIATION
P.O. Box 114
McLean, Virginia 22101

DIRECTORY OF MANUFACTURERS

A

Abercrombie & Fitch, 45th & Madison Ave.,
   New York, N.Y. 10017
P. O. Ackley, P.O. Box 17347, Salt Lake City, Utah 84117
Alcan Company Inc., 3640 Seminary Road,
   Alton, Illinois 62002
American Optical Corp., Mechanic St.,
   Southbridge, Mass. 01550

B

Bausch & Lomb Co., 635 St. Paul St.,
   Rochester, N.Y. 14602
Benjamin Air Rifle Co., 1525 So. 8th St.,
   St. Louis, Mo. 63104
Jim Brobst Pedestals, 229 Poplar, Hamburg, Pa. 19526
Bob Brownell's, Main & Third, Montezuma, Iowa 50171
Browning Arms Co., Box 624-B, Arnold, Missouri 63010
Maynard P. Buehler Inc., 17 Orinda Hwy.,
   Orinda, Calif. 94563

C

Canadian Ind. Ltd., (C.I.L.) Box 10, Montreal, Que., Canada
M. H. Canjar, 500 E. 45th, Denver, Colorado 80216
W. R. Case Knives, 20 Russell Blvd., Bradford, Pa. 16701
Colts Patent Firearms Co., Hartford, Conn. 06102
Craft Industries, 719 No. East Street, Anaheim, Calif. 92800
Crosman Gun Co., Inc., Fairport, New York 14450

D

Daisy Mfg. Co., Rogers, Arkansas 72756
Dayton-Traister Co., P.O. Box 93, Oak Harbor, Wash. 98277
Dem-Bart Co., 3333 N. Grove Street, Tacoma, Wash. 98407
Division Lead Co., 7742 W. 61 Place, Summit, Illinois 60502
Dixie Gun Works Inc., Hwy. 51 So., Union City, Tenn. 38261
Dremel Mfg. Co., P.O. Box 518, Racine, Wisc. 53401
DuPont Explosives Div., Wilmington, Delaware 19898

E

Eder Instru. Co. Borescope, 2293 N. Clybourn,
   Chicago, Ill. 60614

F

Forster Appelt Mfg. Co., 82 E. Lanark Ave.,
   Lanark, Ill. 61046
Freeland's Scope Stands, 3737 14th Ave.,
   Rock Island, Ill. 61201

G

Garcia Sporting Arms Corp., 329 Alfred Ave.,
   Teaneck, N.J. 07666
Grace Metal Prod., Box 67, Elk Rapids, Mich. 49629
Gopher Shooter's Supply, Box 246, Faribault, Minn. 55021
H. F. Grieden, Box 487, Knoxville, Ill. 61448
Griffin & Howe, 589 8th Avenue, New York, N.Y. 10017

H

Harrington & Richardson Arms Co., 320 Park Ave.,
   Worchester, Mass. 01610
Hercules Powder Co., 910 Market St., Wilmington, Del. 19899
B. E. Hodgdon, 7710 W. 50th Hwy.,
   Shawnee Mission, Kansas 66202
Frank C. Hoppe Co., P.O. Box 97, Parkesburg, Pa. 19365
Hornady Mfg. Co., Box 1848, Grand Island, Nebr. 68801

I

Interarms Ltd., 10 Prince St., Alexandria, Va. 22313
Ithaca Gun Company, Ithaca, New York 14850

J

Paul Jaeger Inc., 211 Leedom St., Jenkintown, Pa. 19046
Phil Judd Swivels, 83 E. Park St., Butte, Montana 59701

L

Geo. Lawrence Co., 306 S.W. First Avenue,
   Portland, Ore. 97204
Liquid Wrench, Box 10628, Charlotte, N.C. 28201
Lyman Gun Sight Co., Middlefield, Conn. 06455

M

Markell Inc., 4115 Judah St., San Francisco, Calif. 94112
Merit Gunsight Co., P.O. Box 995, Sequin, Wash. 98382
Michaels of Oregon Co., P.O. Box 13010, Portland, Ore. 97213
Micro Sight Co., 242 Harbor Blvd., Belmont, Calif. 94002
Miller Single Trigger Co., Box 69, Millersburg, Pa. 17061
O. F. Mossberg & Sons Inc., 7 Grasso St.,
   No. Haven, Conn. 06473

N

Navy Arms Co., 689 Bergen Blvd., Ridgefield, N.J. 07657
Norma-Precision Co., South Lansing, New York 14882
Nosler Bullets, P.O. Box 688, Beaverton, Oregon 97005

O

John Olson Co., (Arms Books), P.O. Box 767,
Paramus, N.J. 07652

Omark–CCI Inc., Box 856, Lewiston, Idaho 83501

Outers Laboratories, Box 37, Onalaska, Wisc. 54650

P

Pachmayr Gun Works, 1220 S. Grand Ave.,
Los Angeles, Calif. 90015

Penguin Assoc. Inc., Box 97, Parkesburg, Pa. 19365

Plainfield Machine Co. Inc., Box 447, Dunellen, N.J. 08812

R

Realist Inc., 16288 Megal Dr., Menomonee Falls, Wisc. 53051

Remington Arms Co., Barnum Avenue,
Bridgeport, Conn. 06602

Replica Arms Co., Box 640, Marietta, Ohio 45750

Rig Products Co., Box 279, Oregon, Illnois 61061

S

San Francisco Gun Exchange, 75 Fourth St.,
San Francisco, Calif. 94118

Savage Arms Corp., Westfield, Mass. 01085

Service Armament, 689 Bergen Blvd., Ridgefield, N.J. 07657

Shiloh Inc., 173 Washington Place,
Hasbrouck Hgts., N.J. 07604

Sierra Bullets Inc. 10532 So. Painter Ave.,
Santa Fe Springs, Ca. 90670

Sigma Eng. Co., 11320 Burbank Blvd.,
N. Hollywood, Calif. 91601

Simmons Gun Spec., 700 Rogers Rd., Olathe, Kansas 66061

Smith & Wesson Co., Springfield, Mass. 01101

Speer, Box 896, Lewiston, Idaho 83501

Sturm-Ruger Co., Southport, Conn. 06490

Swaine Machine Co., 195 O'Connell,
Providence, R.I. 02905

T

10–X Mfg. Co., 100 S.W. 3rd St., Des Moines, Iowa 50309

Timney Mfg. Co., 5625 Imperial Hwy., So. Gate, Calif. 90280

Thompson-Center Arms, Box 2405, Rochester, N.H. 03867

Tradewinds Inc., P.O. Box 1191, Tacoma, Wash. 98401

W

WD–40 Co., 5390 Napa St., San Diego, Calif. 92110

Weatherby's, 2781 E. Firestone Blvd., So. Gate, Calif. 90280

H. P. White Laboratories, Box 331, Bel Air, Md. 21014

Williams Gun Sight Co., 7389 Lapeer Rd.,
Davison, Mich. 48423

Winchester Repeating Arms Co., New Haven, Conn. 06510

Index

hammer rifling, 11–12
hammering process, 11–12
Handbook for Shooters and Reloaders, 16, 171
handicapped hunter, 61
Handloader's Digest, 171
handloaders, accuracy of, 166
handloading, 149–165
   annealing cases, 154
   powder, 159
   primer-seating, 158
   savings through, 149–150
   sizing method, 155–156
   tools needed for, 150
Harquebus, *See* Arquebus
Harrington & Richardson single shot rifle, 25;
    varmint caliber, 67
hats, 89
headspace: in cartridges, 22–23; gauges, 23
hole, pilot; cutting of, 10–11, 14
Holland & Holland, 28, 69; magnum .300, 72–73;
    .375, 74
hook rifling, 10
Hornet cartridges, 63
Hunter-Safety Program, 117
hunting: bullet types for, 161; choice of rifle for, 13
hunting rifle, German, 28
Huntington, Fred, 66

I

identification, personal, for travel, 174
igniting, gunpowder, 7. *See also* firing systems
inletting, 201–205; tools for, 202
iron sights, 128
Ithaca lever action rifle, 30

J

jackets, hunting, 89
Jaeger trigger, 31
Jeffrey shells, magnum, 69

K

Kiefuss, firing system, 8
kneeling position, 92, 93, 94, 100–101, 107

Kodiak Brown bear, magnum rifle for shooting, 72,
   74
Kollner, gunsmith, 7

L

law, regulating firearms, 118
lead, in bullets, 214
LeFaucheux, 8
left-eye dominance, 87
left-handed bolt action rifle, 60–61
lens
   cap, 132
   coating, 129
   eyepiece, 126, 129
   objective, 127, 129
lenses, fogged, 131–132
let-off, 31, 39. *See also* trigger, double-stage
lever action rifle, 30, 33
light gathering power, 127, 129
loading
   powder, 159–160
   procedures, 7–8
   rimfire and centerfire rifles, 36
   through magazine, 35
long-range shooting, zeroing, 141
Luger, Navy Model, 20
Lyman Ideal Handbook, 153
Lyman Reloading Handbook, 171

M

machine gun, 8, 11
magazine rifle, loading of, 35
magazine systems, 28, 34–36
magnification, 59–60, 66–67, 127–128, 129
magnum cartridges, belted, 23
magnum rifle, 27, 68–76
mahogany, in gun stocks, 43
mandrel, 11
Mannlicher rifles: bolt action, 28, 30; double set
    trigger, 33
Marlin rifle, 30, 40, 51, 57, 75, 336
marksmanship, 89–107
"match," for igniting gunpowder, 7–8